A MARVEL COMICS EVENT

CIVIL WAR

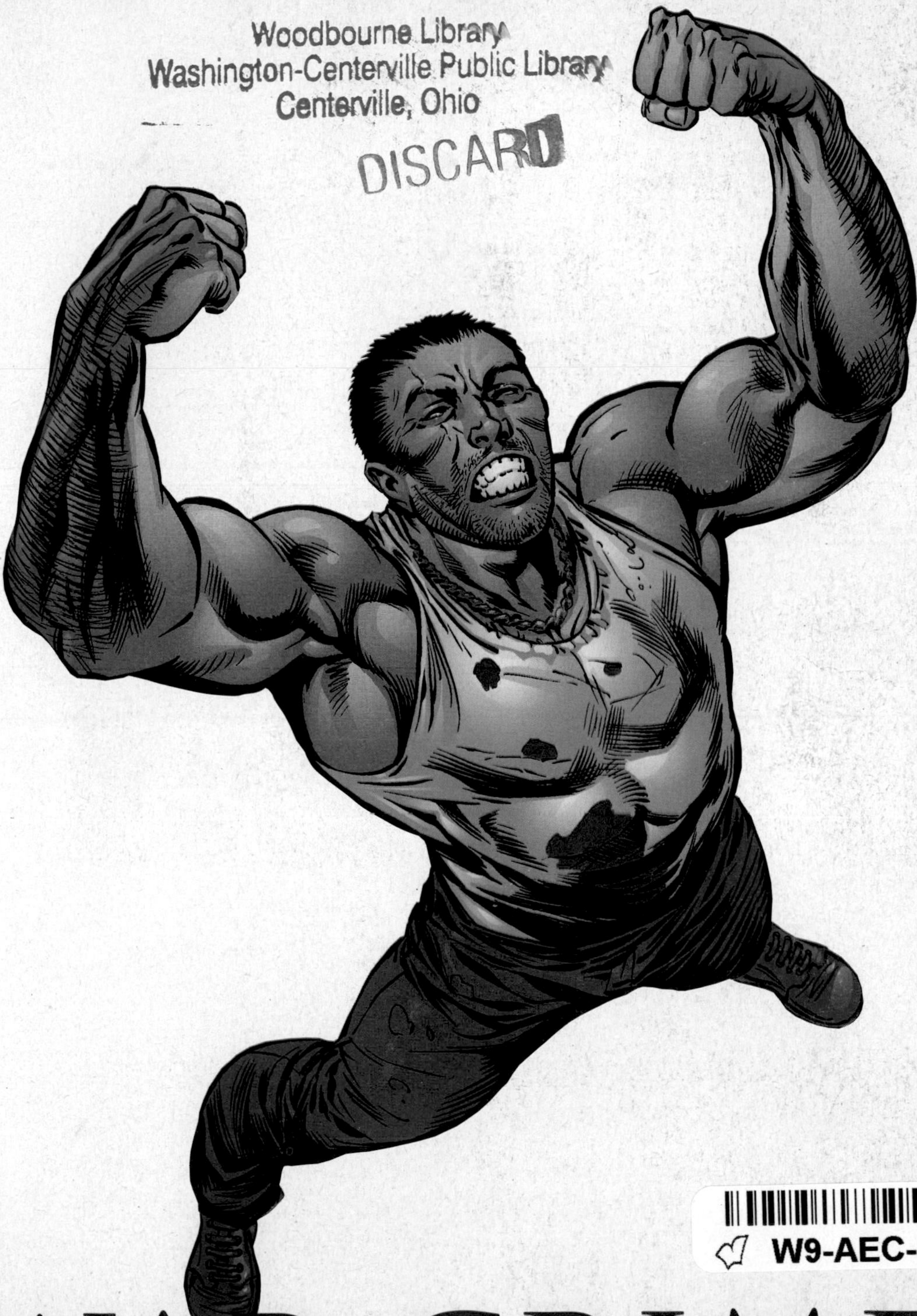

WAR CRIMES

A
MARVEL COMICS
PRESENTATION

CIVIL WAR
WAR CRIME

WRITER
FRANK TIERI

PENCILER
STAZ JOHNSON

INKERS
TOM PALMER &
ROBIN RIGGS
(CIVIL WAR: WAR CRIMES)

COLORIST
IAN HANNIN

LETTERER
VIRTUAL CALLIGRAPHY'S
JOE CARAMAGNA

ASSISTANT EDITORS
MICHAEL O'CONNOR,
AUBREY SITTERSON &
MOLLY LAZER

EDITORS
AXEL ALONSO &
TOM BREVOORT

COLLECTION EDITOR
JENNIFER GRÜNWALD

ASSISTANT EDITORS
MICHAEL SHORT &
CORY LEVINE

ASSOCIATE EDITOR
MARK D. BEAZLEY

SENIOR EDITOR,
SPECIAL PROJECTS
JEFF YOUNGQUIST

SENIOR VICE PRESIDENT
OF SALES
DAVID GABRIEL

PRODUCTION
JERRY KALINOWSKI

BOOK DESIGNER
DAYLE CHESLER

VICE PRESIDENT OF CREATIVE
TOM MARVELLI

EDITOR IN CHIEF
JOE QUESADA

PUBLISHER
DAN BUCKLEY

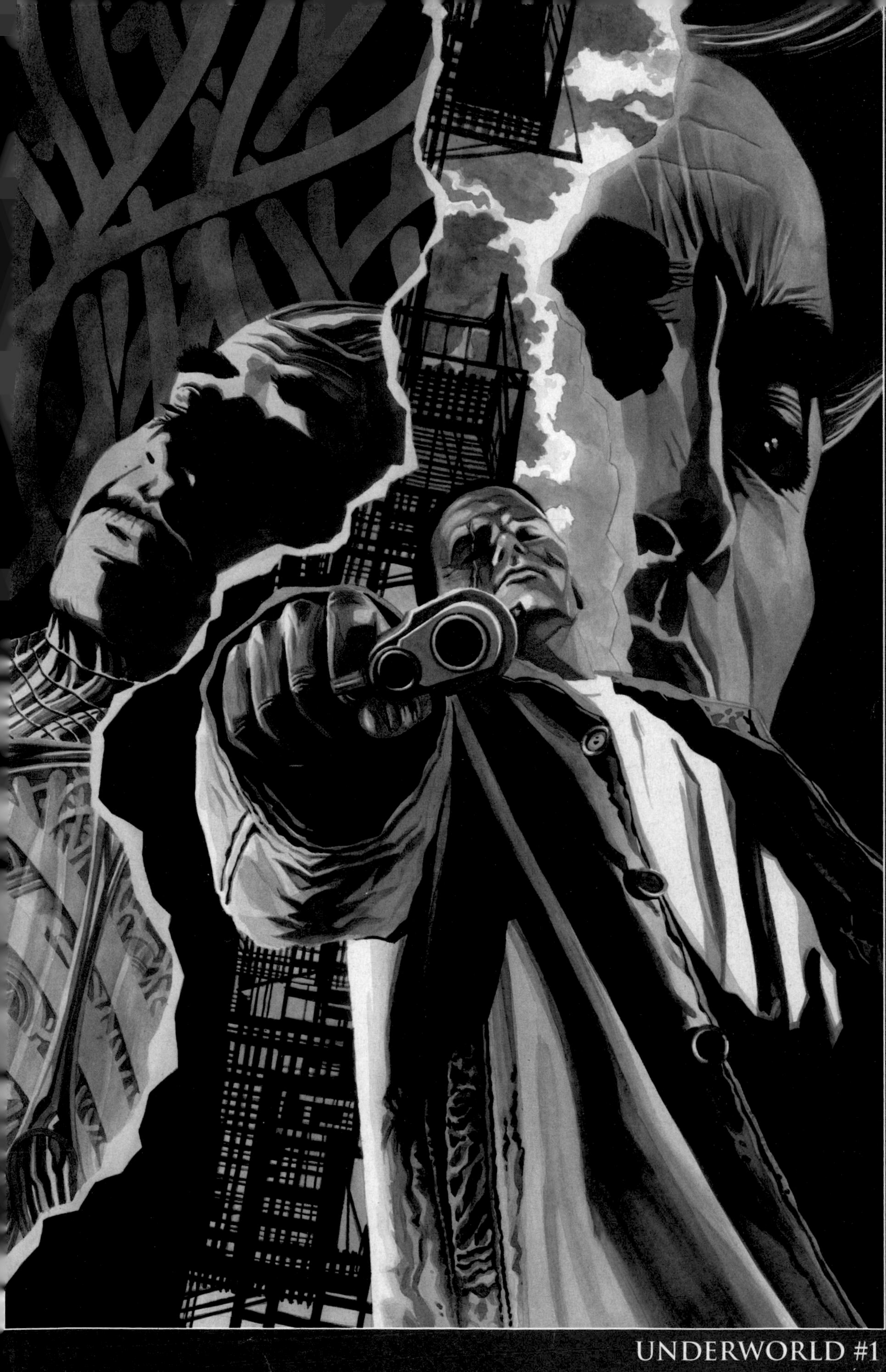

UNDERWORLD #1

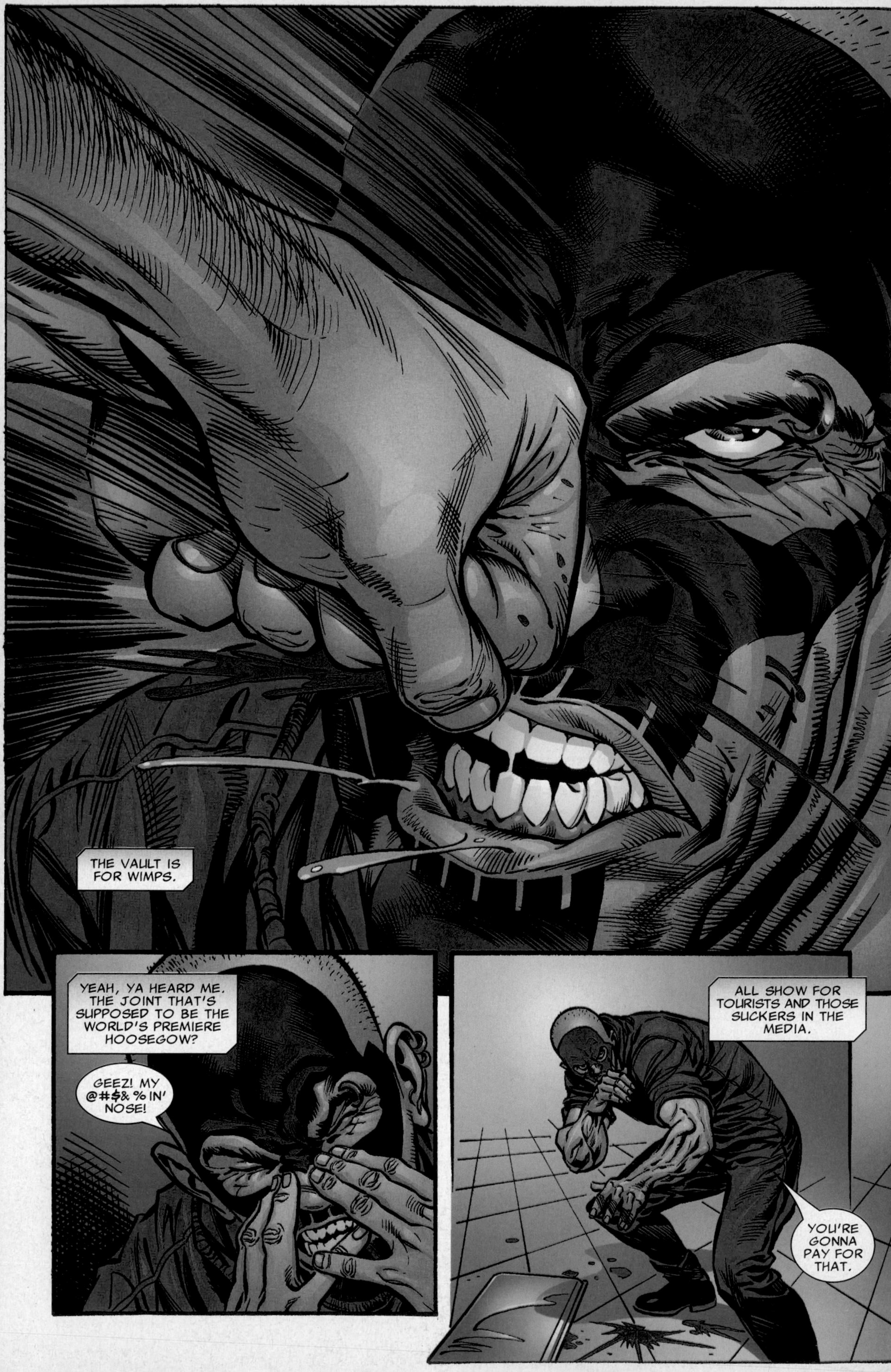
THE VAULT IS FOR WIMPS.
YEAH, YA HEARD ME. THE JOINT THAT'S SUPPOSED TO BE THE WORLD'S PREMIERE HOOSEGOW?
GEEZ! MY @#$&%IN' NOSE!
ALL SHOW FOR TOURISTS AND THOSE SUCKERS IN THE MEDIA.
YOU'RE GONNA PAY FOR THAT.

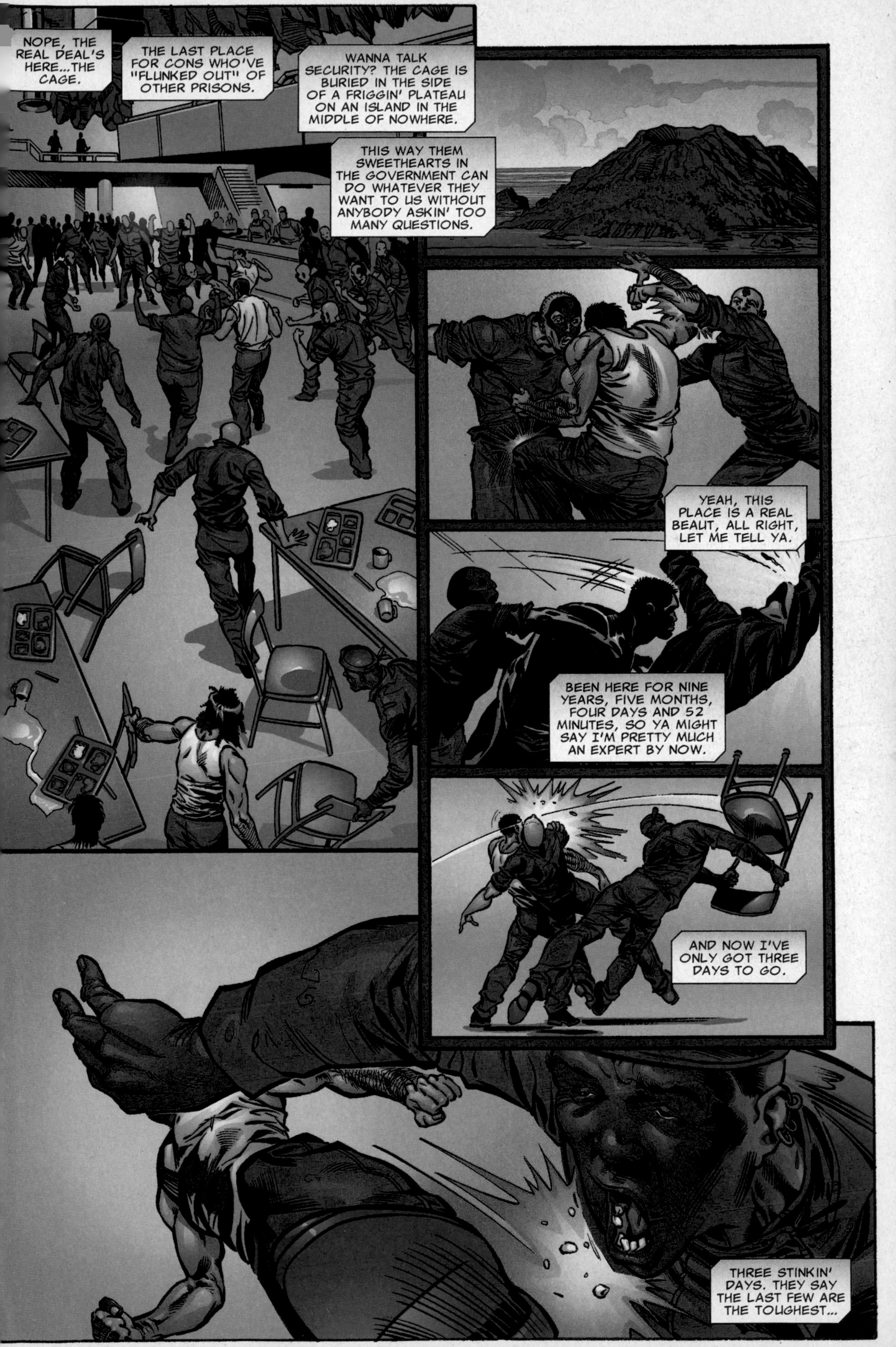

NOPE, THE REAL DEAL'S HERE...THE CAGE.
THE LAST PLACE FOR CONS WHO'VE "FLUNKED OUT" OF OTHER PRISONS.
WANNA TALK SECURITY? THE CAGE IS BURIED IN THE SIDE OF A FRIGGIN' PLATEAU ON AN ISLAND IN THE MIDDLE OF NOWHERE.
THIS WAY THEM SWEETHEARTS IN THE GOVERNMENT CAN DO WHATEVER THEY WANT TO US WITHOUT ANYBODY ASKIN' TOO MANY QUESTIONS.
YEAH, THIS PLACE IS A REAL BEAUT, ALL RIGHT, LET ME TELL YA.
BEEN HERE FOR NINE YEARS, FIVE MONTHS, FOUR DAYS AND 52 MINUTES, SO YA MIGHT SAY I'M PRETTY MUCH AN EXPERT BY NOW.
AND NOW I'VE ONLY GOT THREE DAYS TO GO.
THREE STINKIN' DAYS. THEY SAY THE LAST FEW ARE THE TOUGHEST...

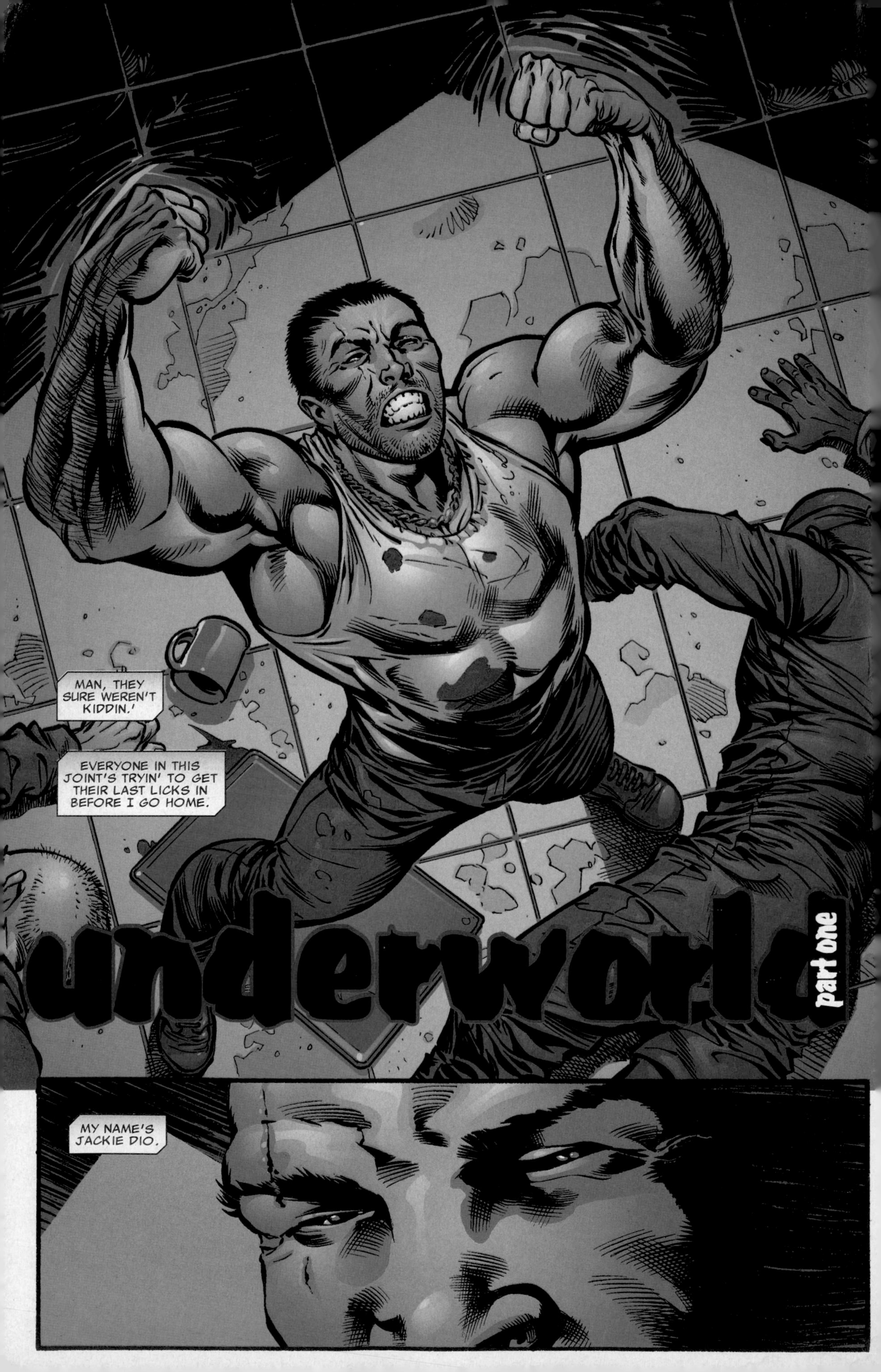
MAN, THEY SURE WEREN'T KIDDIN.'
EVERYONE IN THIS JOINT'S TRYIN' TO GET THEIR LAST LICKS IN BEFORE I GO HOME.
underworld
part one
MY NAME'S JACKIE DIO.

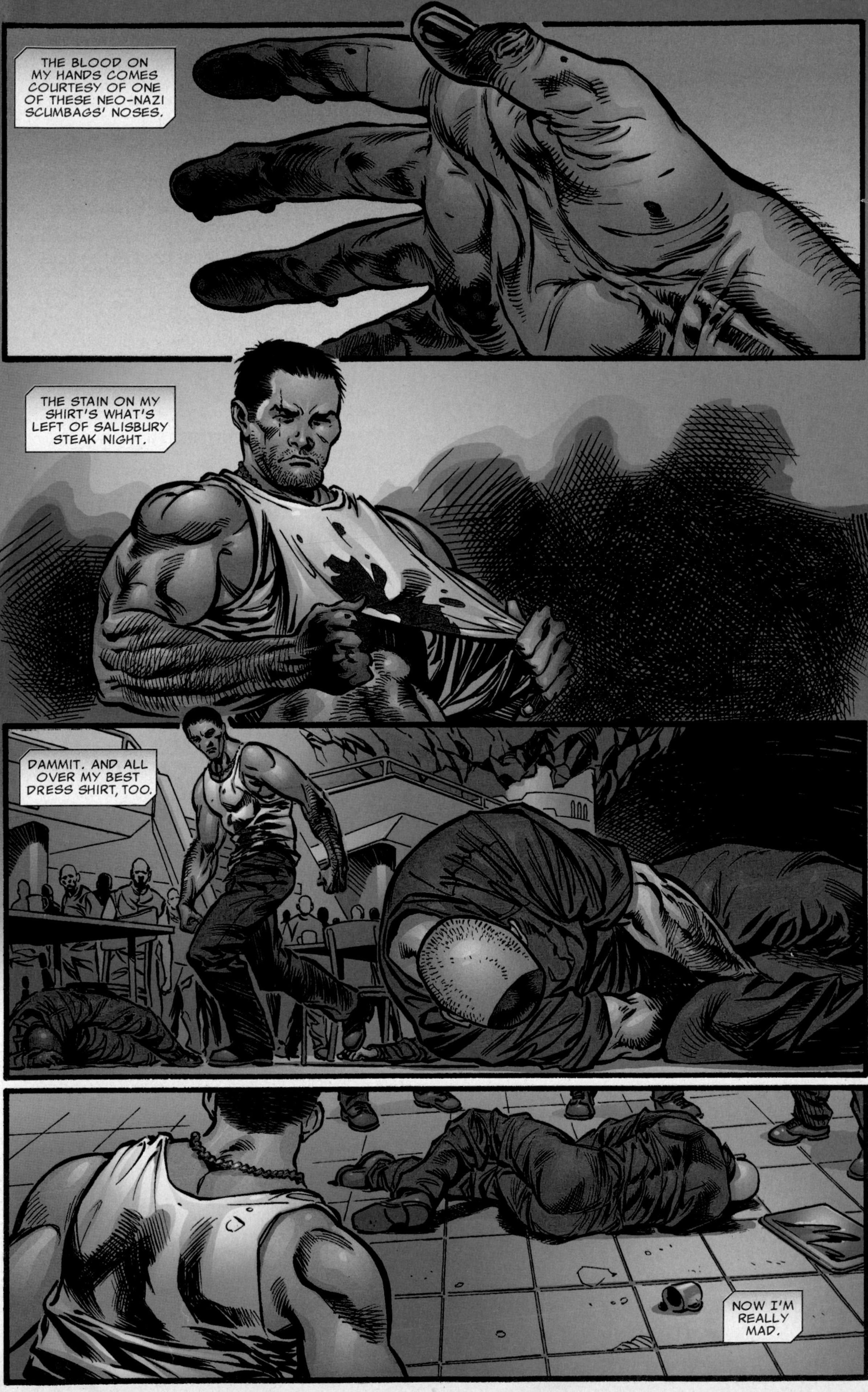
THE BLOOD ON MY HANDS COMES COURTESY OF ONE OF THESE NEO-NAZI SCUMBAGS' NOSES.
THE STAIN ON MY SHIRT'S WHAT'S LEFT OF SALISBURY STEAK NIGHT.
DAMMIT. AND ALL OVER MY BEST DRESS SHIRT, TOO.
NOW I'M REALLY MAD.

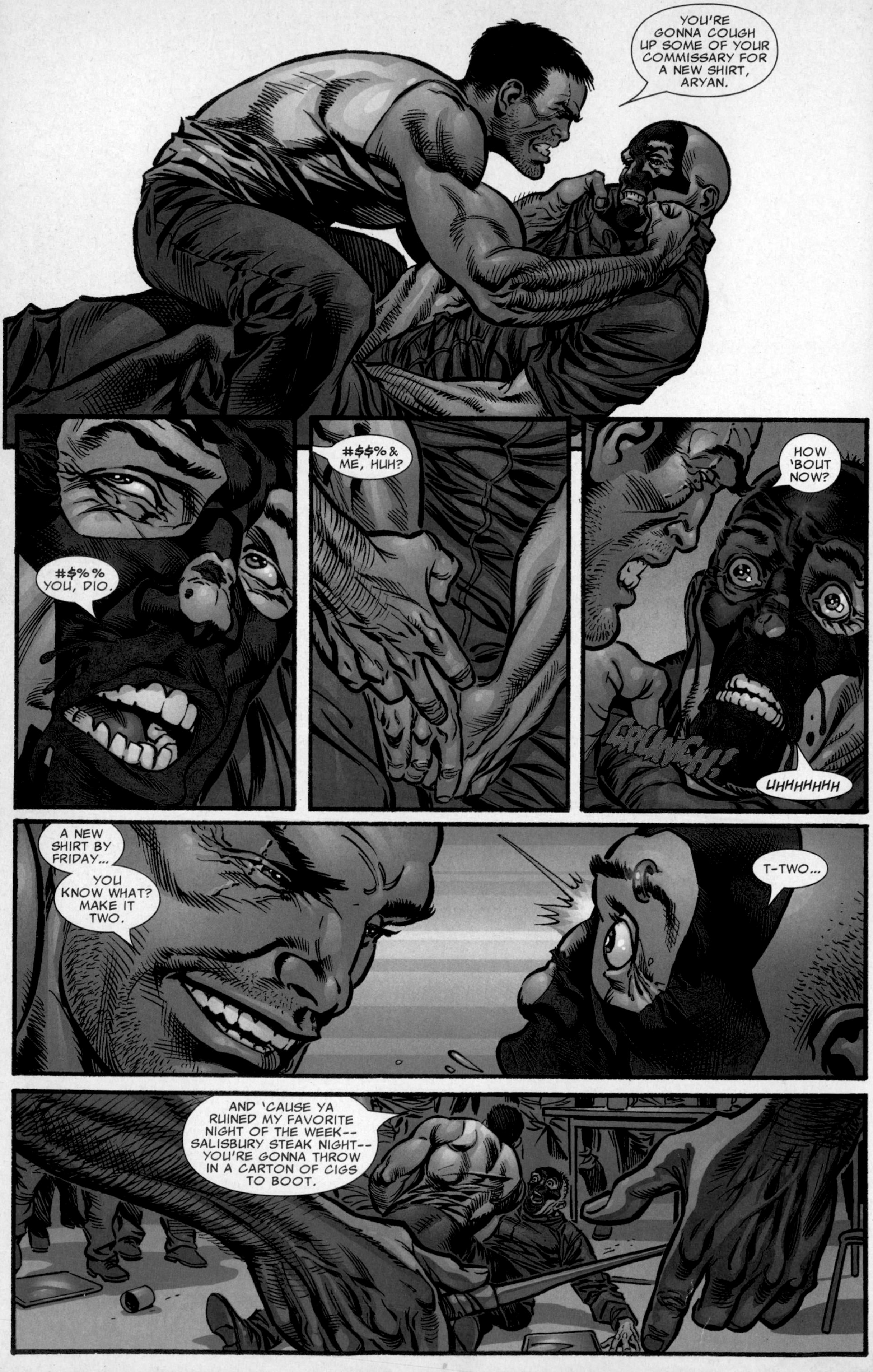
YOU'RE GONNA COUGH UP SOME OF YOUR COMMISSARY FOR A NEW SHIRT, ARYAN.
#$%% YOU, DIO.
#$$% & ME, HUH?
HOW 'BOUT NOW?
CRUNCH!
UHHHHHHH
A NEW SHIRT BY FRIDAY...
YOU KNOW WHAT? MAKE IT TWO.
T-TWO...
AND 'CAUSE YA RUINED MY FAVORITE NIGHT OF THE WEEK-- SALISBURY STEAK NIGHT-- YOU'RE GONNA THROW IN A CARTON OF CIGS TO BOOT.

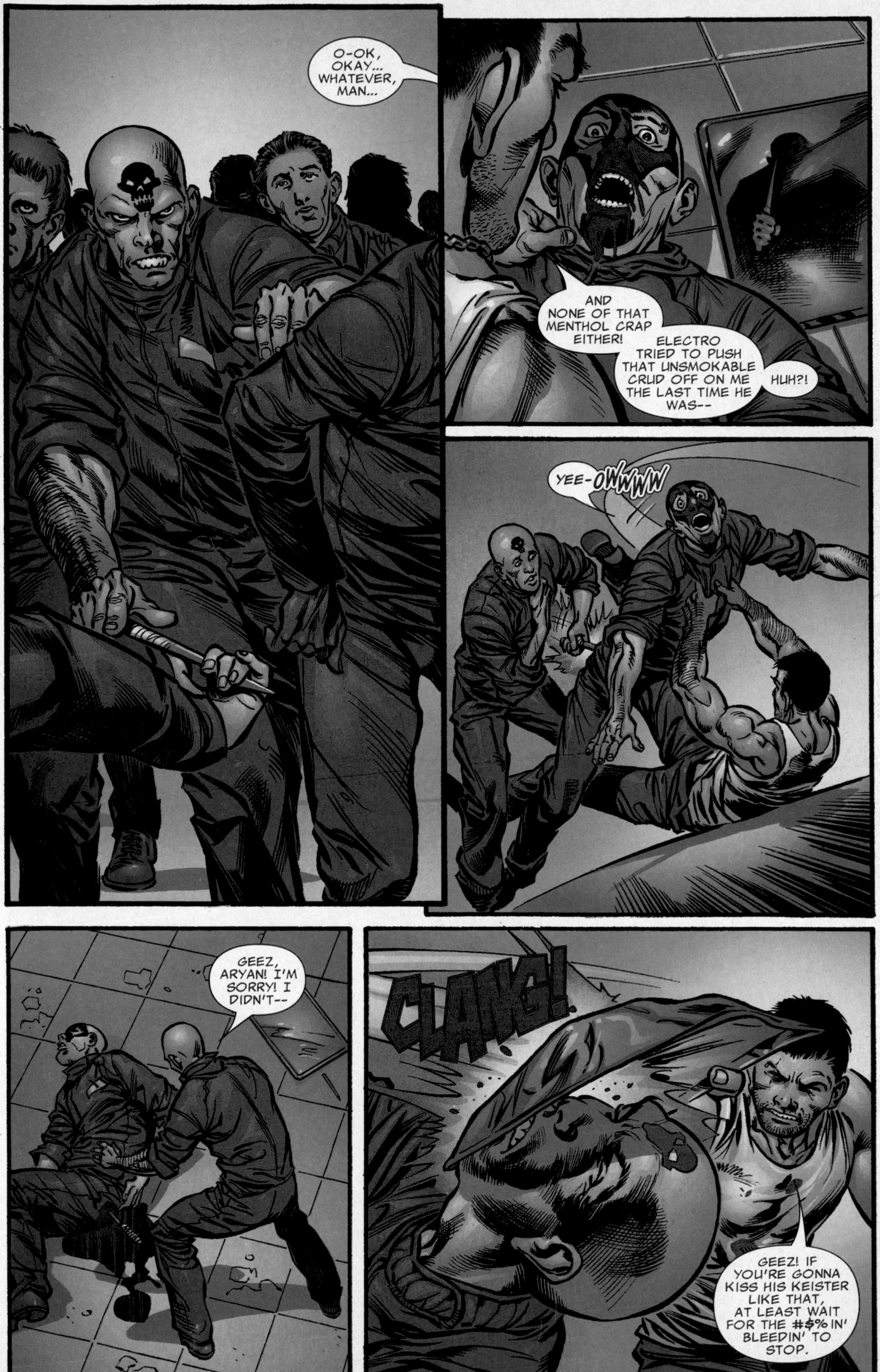
O-OK, OKAY... WHATEVER, MAN...
AND NONE OF THAT MENTHOL CRAP EITHER!
ELECTRO TRIED TO PUSH THAT UNSMOKABLE CRUD OFF ON ME THE LAST TIME HE WAS--
HUH?!
YEE-OWWWW
GEEZ, ARYAN! I'M SORRY! I DIDN'T--
CLANG!
GEEZ! IF YOU'RE GONNA KISS HIS KEISTER LIKE THAT, AT LEAST WAIT FOR THE #$%IN' BLEEDIN' TO STOP.

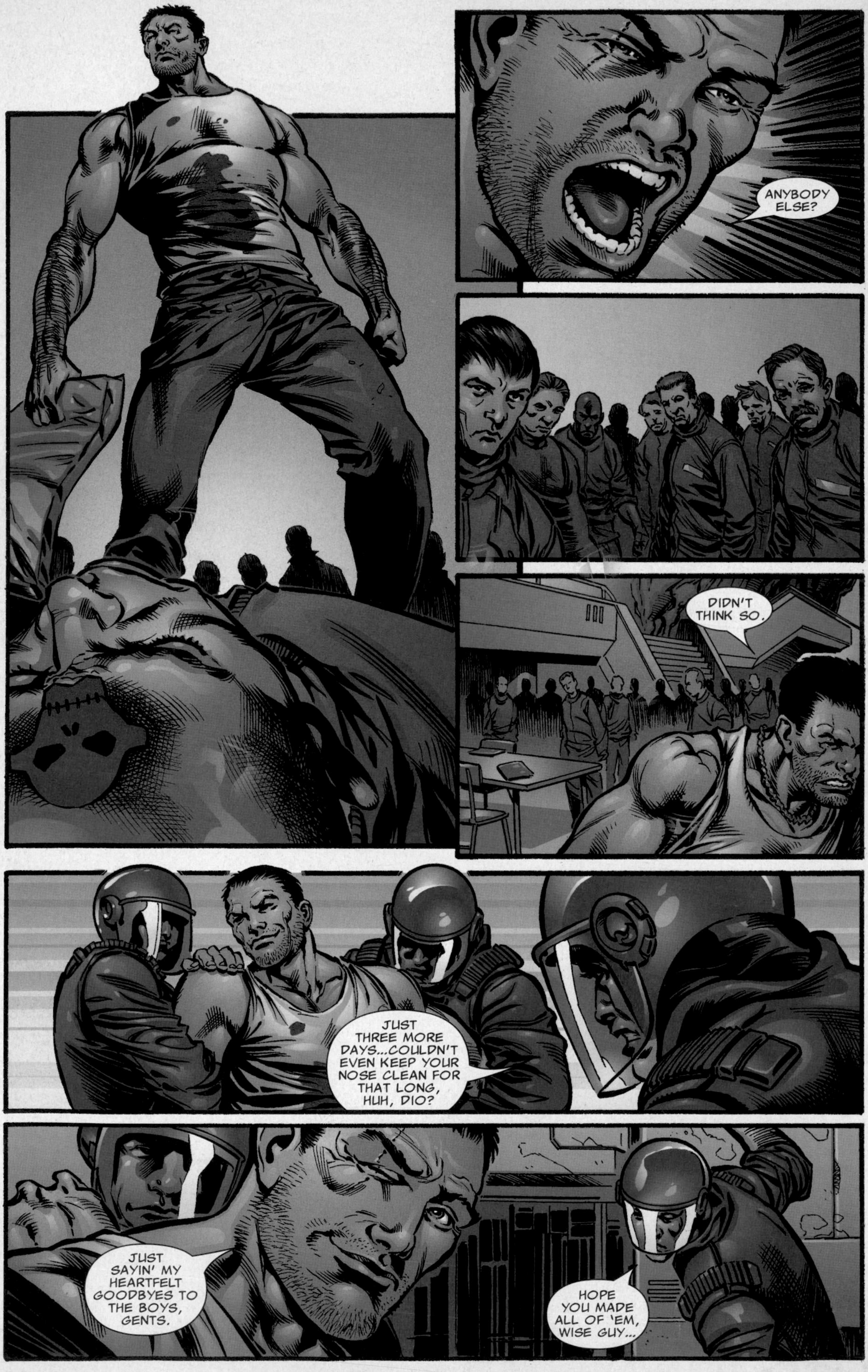
ANYBODY ELSE?
DIDN'T THINK SO.
JUST THREE MORE DAYS...COULDN'T EVEN KEEP YOUR NOSE CLEAN FOR THAT LONG, HUH, DIO?
JUST SAYIN' MY HEARTFELT GOODBYES TO THE BOYS, GENTS.
HOPE YOU MADE ALL OF 'EM, WISE GUY...

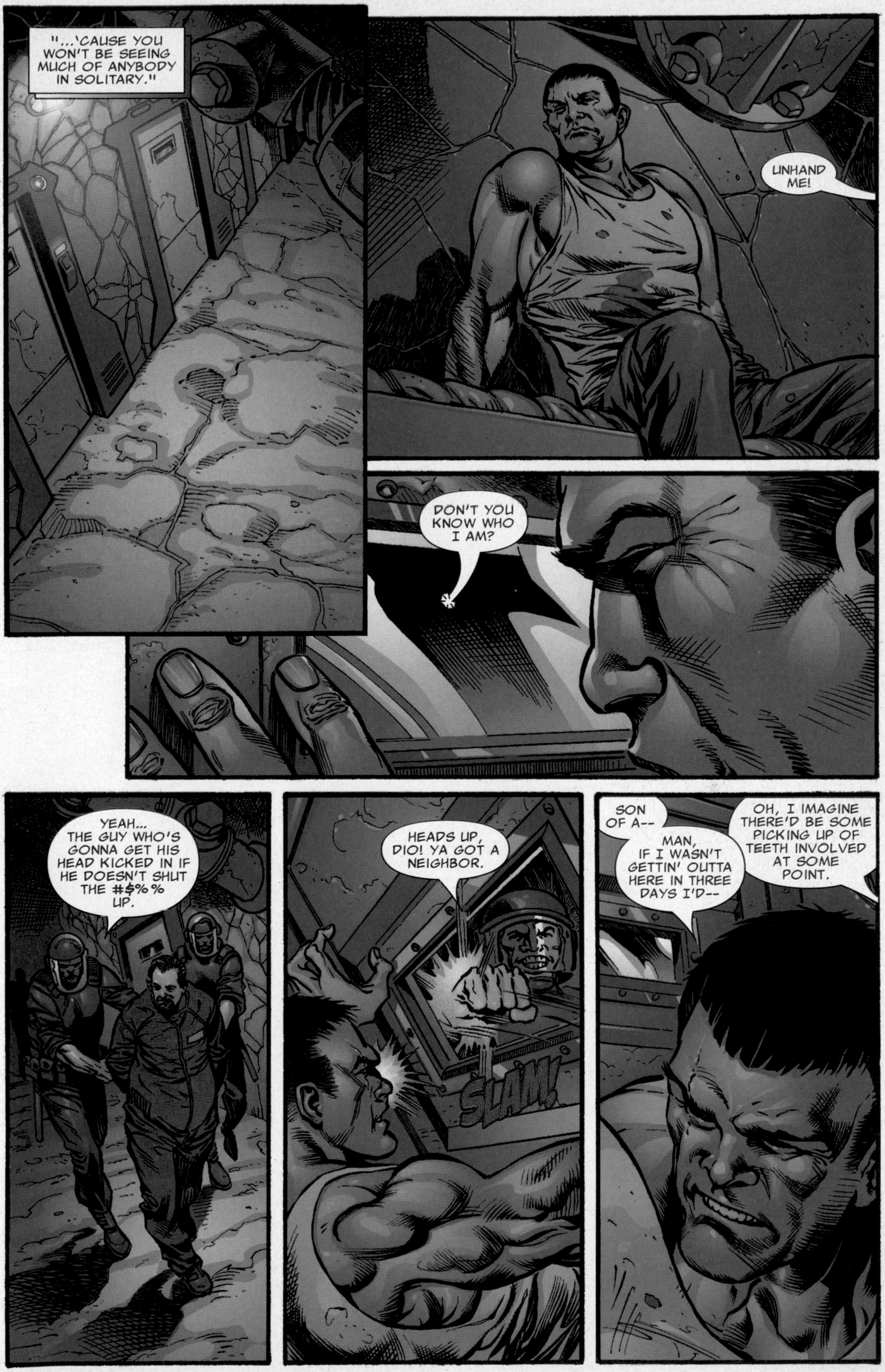
"...'CAUSE YOU WON'T BE SEEING MUCH OF ANYBODY IN SOLITARY."
UNHAND ME!
DON'T YOU KNOW WHO I AM?
YEAH... THE GUY WHO'S GONNA GET HIS HEAD KICKED IN IF HE DOESN'T SHUT THE #$%% UP.
HEADS UP, DIO! YA GOT A NEIGHBOR.
SLAM!
SON OF A--
MAN, IF I WASN'T GETTIN' OUTTA HERE IN THREE DAYS I'D--
OH, I IMAGINE THERE'D BE SOME PICKING UP OF TEETH INVOLVED AT SOME POINT.

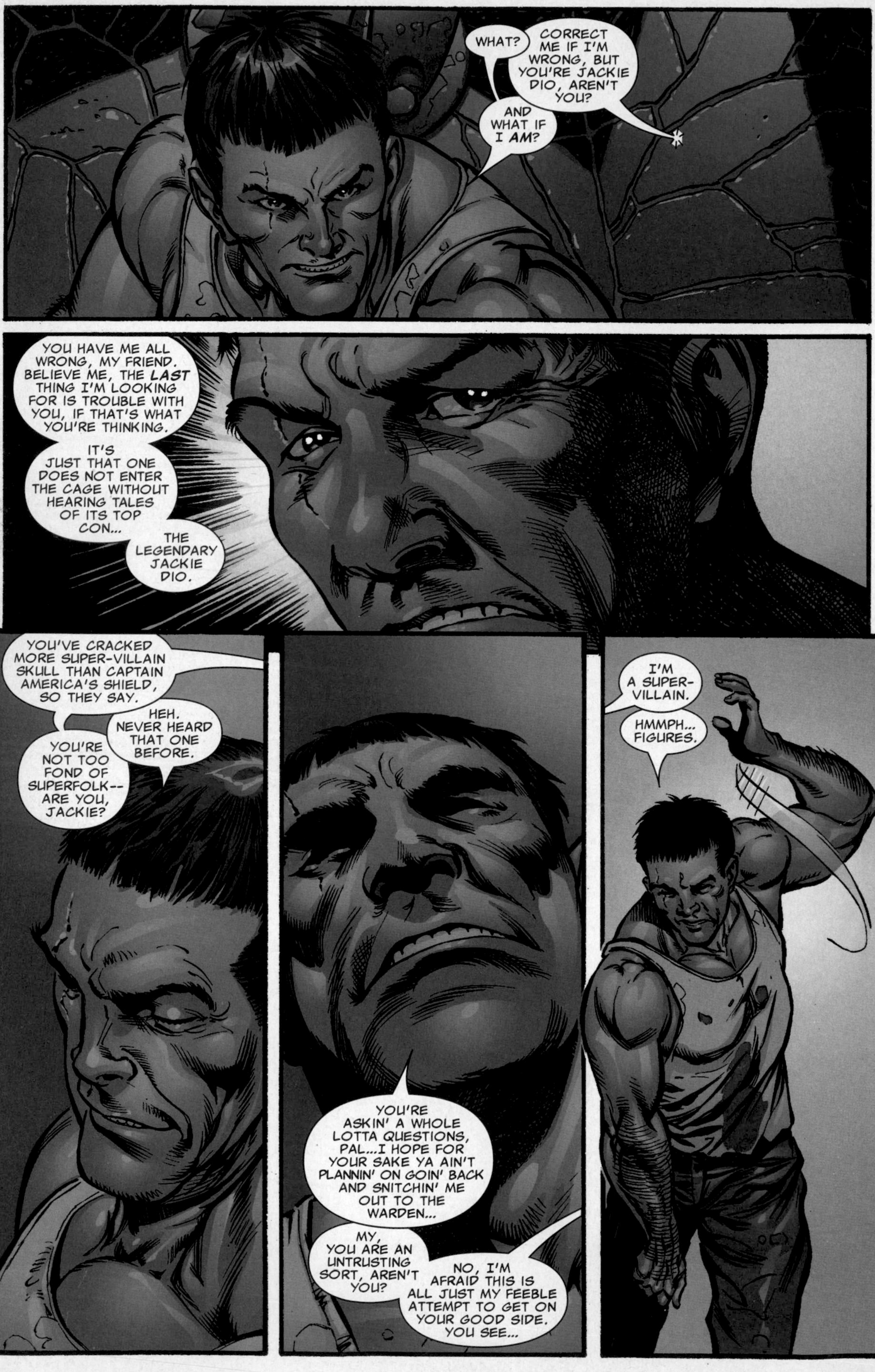
CORRECT ME IF I'M WRONG, BUT YOU'RE JACKIE DIO, AREN'T YOU?
WHAT?
AND WHAT IF I AM?
YOU HAVE ME ALL WRONG, MY FRIEND. BELIEVE ME, THE LAST THING I'M LOOKING FOR IS TROUBLE WITH YOU, IF THAT'S WHAT YOU'RE THINKING.
IT'S JUST THAT ONE DOES NOT ENTER THE CAGE WITHOUT HEARING TALES OF ITS TOP CON...
THE LEGENDARY JACKIE DIO.
YOU'VE CRACKED MORE SUPER-VILLAIN SKULL THAN CAPTAIN AMERICA'S SHIELD, SO THEY SAY.
HEH. NEVER HEARD THAT ONE BEFORE.
YOU'RE NOT TOO FOND OF SUPERFOLK-- ARE YOU, JACKIE?
YOU'RE ASKIN' A WHOLE LOTTA QUESTIONS, PAL...I HOPE FOR YOUR SAKE YA AIN'T PLANNIN' ON GOIN' BACK AND SNITCHIN' ME OUT TO THE WARDEN...
MY, YOU ARE AN UNTRUSTING SORT, AREN'T YOU?
NO, I'M AFRAID THIS IS ALL JUST MY FEEBLE ATTEMPT TO GET ON YOUR GOOD SIDE. YOU SEE...
I'M A SUPER-VILLAIN.
HMMPH... FIGURES.

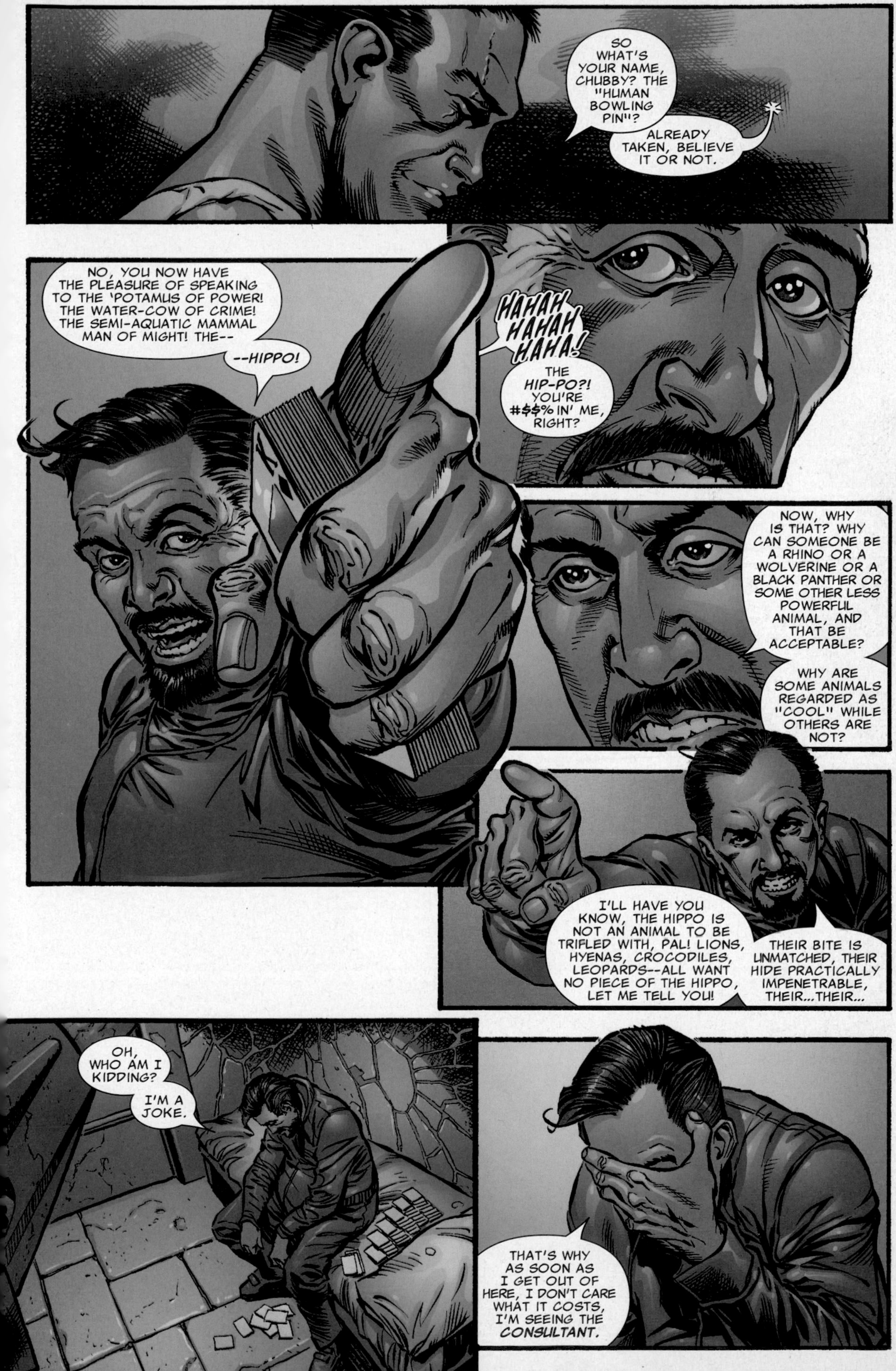
SO WHAT'S YOUR NAME, CHUBBY? THE "HUMAN BOWLING PIN"?
ALREADY TAKEN, BELIEVE IT OR NOT.
NO, YOU NOW HAVE THE PLEASURE OF SPEAKING TO THE 'POTAMUS OF POWER! THE WATER-COW OF CRIME! THE SEMI-AQUATIC MAMMAL MAN OF MIGHT! THE--
--HIPPO!
HAHAH HAHAH HAHA!
THE HIP-PO?! YOU'RE #$$% IN' ME, RIGHT?
NOW, WHY IS THAT? WHY CAN SOMEONE BE A RHINO OR A WOLVERINE OR A BLACK PANTHER OR SOME OTHER LESS POWERFUL ANIMAL, AND THAT BE ACCEPTABLE?
WHY ARE SOME ANIMALS REGARDED AS "COOL" WHILE OTHERS ARE NOT?
I'LL HAVE YOU KNOW, THE HIPPO IS NOT AN ANIMAL TO BE TRIFLED WITH, PAL! LIONS, HYENAS, CROCODILES, LEOPARDS--ALL WANT NO PIECE OF THE HIPPO, LET ME TELL YOU!
THEIR BITE IS UNMATCHED, THEIR HIDE PRACTICALLY IMPENETRABLE, THEIR...THEIR...
OH, WHO AM I KIDDING?
I'M A JOKE.
THAT'S WHY AS SOON AS I GET OUT OF HERE, I DON'T CARE WHAT IT COSTS, I'M SEEING THE CONSULTANT.

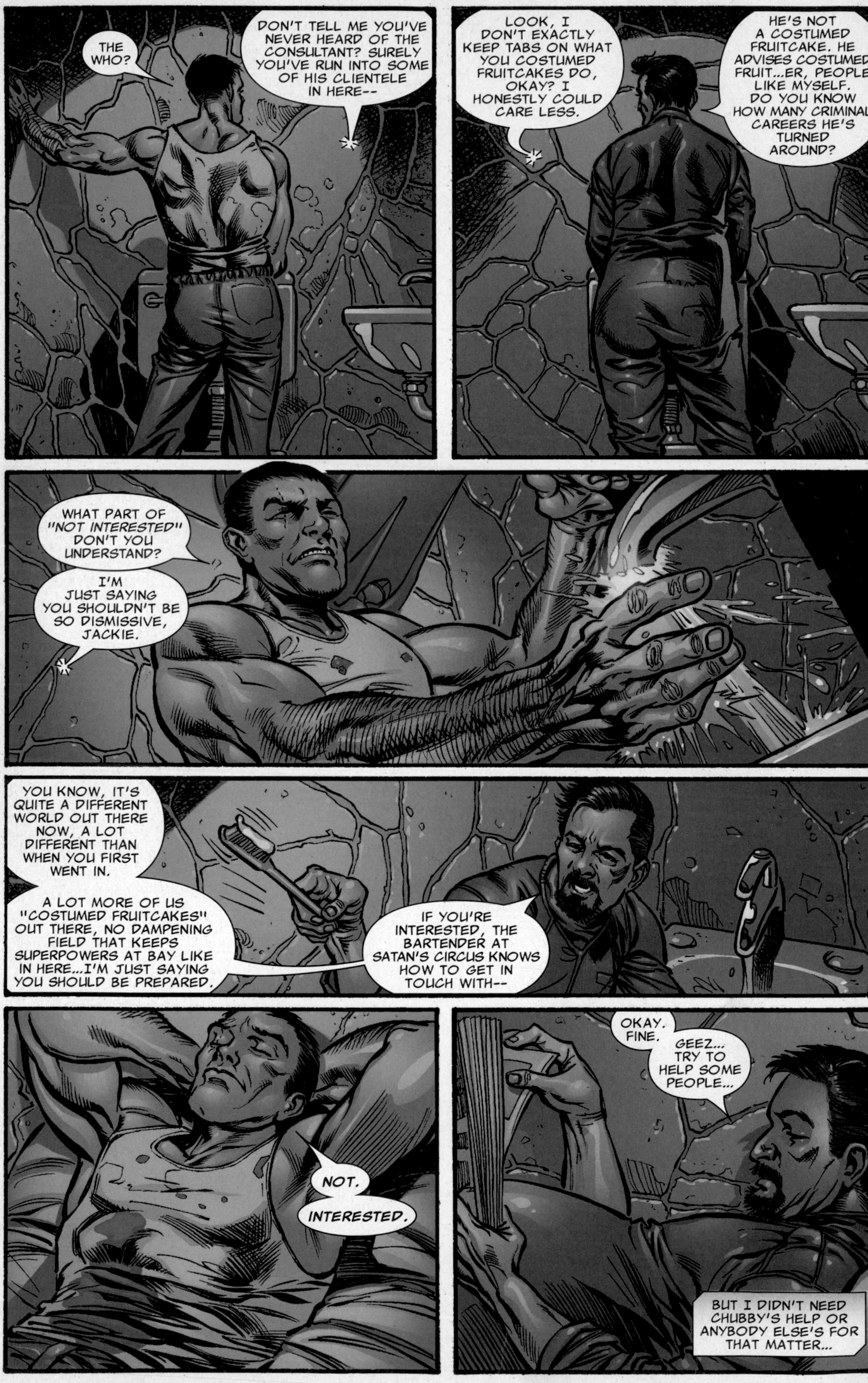
THE WHO?
DON'T TELL ME YOU'VE NEVER HEARD OF THE CONSULTANT? SURELY YOU'VE RUN INTO SOME OF HIS CLIENTELE IN HERE--
LOOK, I DON'T EXACTLY KEEP TABS ON WHAT YOU COSTUMED FRUITCAKES DO, OKAY? I HONESTLY COULD CARE LESS.
HE'S NOT A COSTUMED FRUITCAKE. HE ADVISES COSTUMED FRUIT...ER, PEOPLE LIKE MYSELF. DO YOU KNOW HOW MANY CRIMINAL CAREERS HE'S TURNED AROUND?
WHAT PART OF *"NOT INTERESTED"* DON'T YOU UNDERSTAND?
I'M JUST SAYING YOU SHOULDN'T BE SO DISMISSIVE, JACKIE.
YOU KNOW, IT'S QUITE A DIFFERENT WORLD OUT THERE NOW, A LOT DIFFERENT THAN WHEN YOU FIRST WENT IN.
A LOT MORE OF US "COSTUMED FRUITCAKES" OUT THERE, NO DAMPENING FIELD THAT KEEPS SUPERPOWERS AT BAY LIKE IN HERE...I'M JUST SAYING YOU SHOULD BE PREPARED.
IF YOU'RE INTERESTED, THE BARTENDER AT SATAN'S CIRCUS KNOWS HOW TO GET IN TOUCH WITH--
NOT.
INTERESTED.
OKAY. FINE.
GEEZ... TRY TO HELP SOME PEOPLE...
BUT I DIDN'T NEED CHUBBY'S HELP OR ANYBODY ELSE'S FOR THAT MATTER...

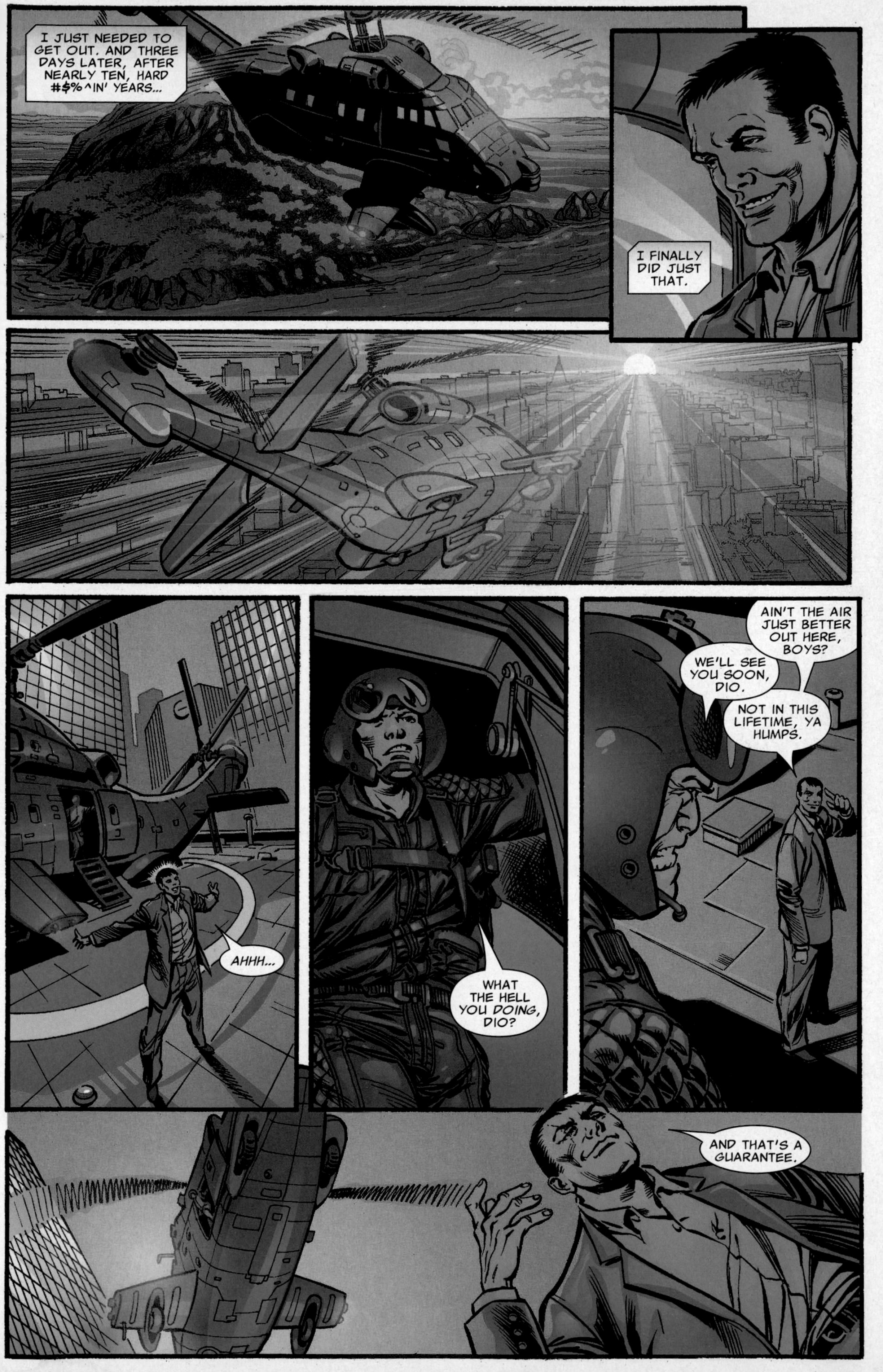
I JUST NEEDED TO GET OUT. AND THREE DAYS LATER, AFTER NEARLY TEN, HARD #$%^IN' YEARS...
I FINALLY DID JUST THAT.
AHHH...
WHAT THE HELL YOU DOING, DIO?
AIN'T THE AIR JUST BETTER OUT HERE, BOYS?
WE'LL SEE YOU SOON, DIO.
NOT IN THIS LIFETIME, YA HUMPS.
AND THAT'S A GUARANTEE.

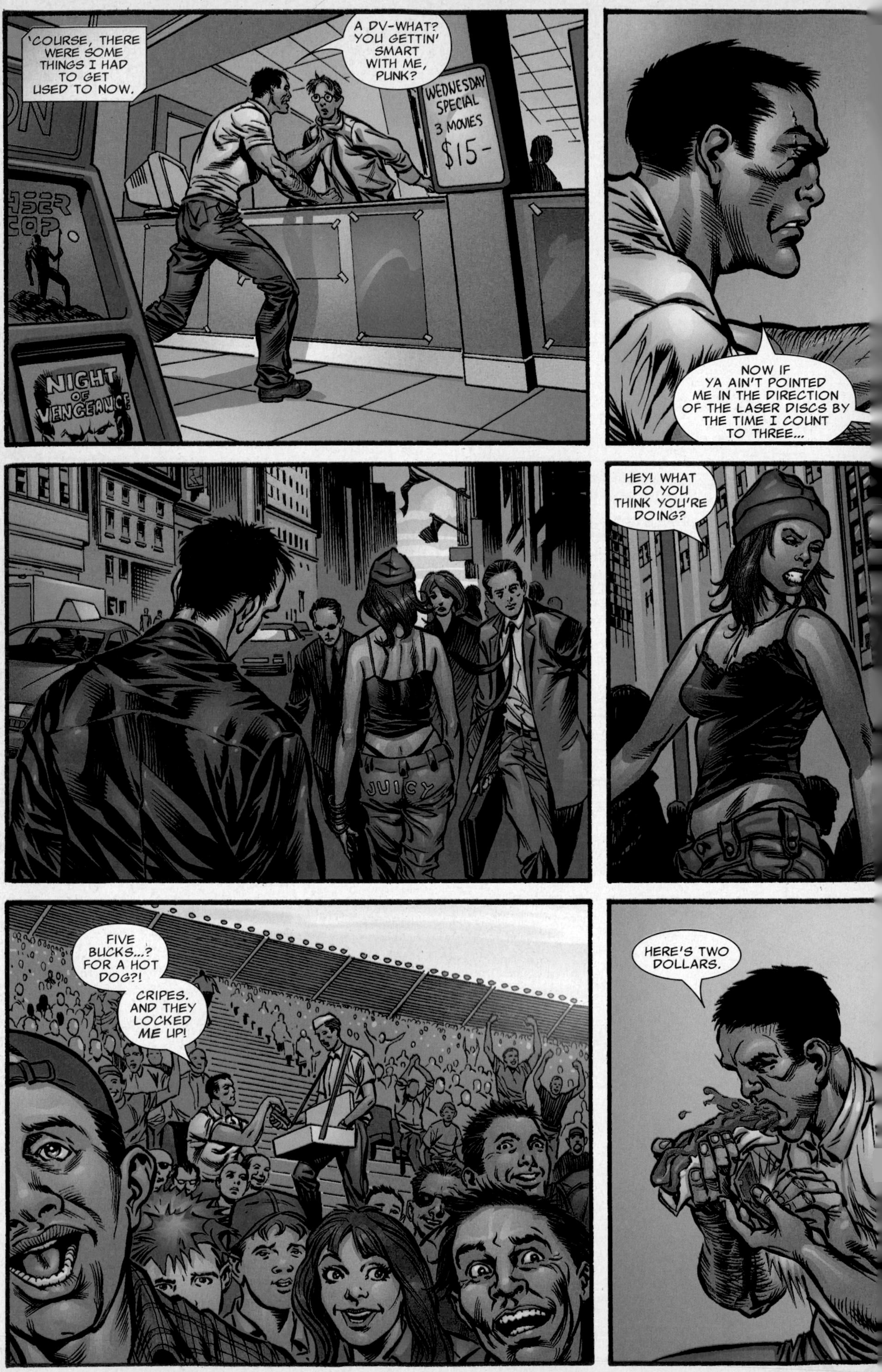
'COURSE, THERE WERE SOME THINGS I HAD TO GET USED TO NOW.
A DV-WHAT? YOU GETTIN' SMART WITH ME, PUNK?
WEDNESDAY SPECIAL 3 MOVIES $15-
NIGHT OF VENGEANCE
NOW IF YA AIN'T POINTED ME IN THE DIRECTION OF THE LASER DISCS BY THE TIME I COUNT TO THREE...
JUICY
HEY! WHAT DO YOU THINK YOU'RE DOING?
FIVE BUCKS...? FOR A HOT DOG?!
CRIPES. AND THEY LOCKED ME UP!
HERE'S TWO DOLLARS.

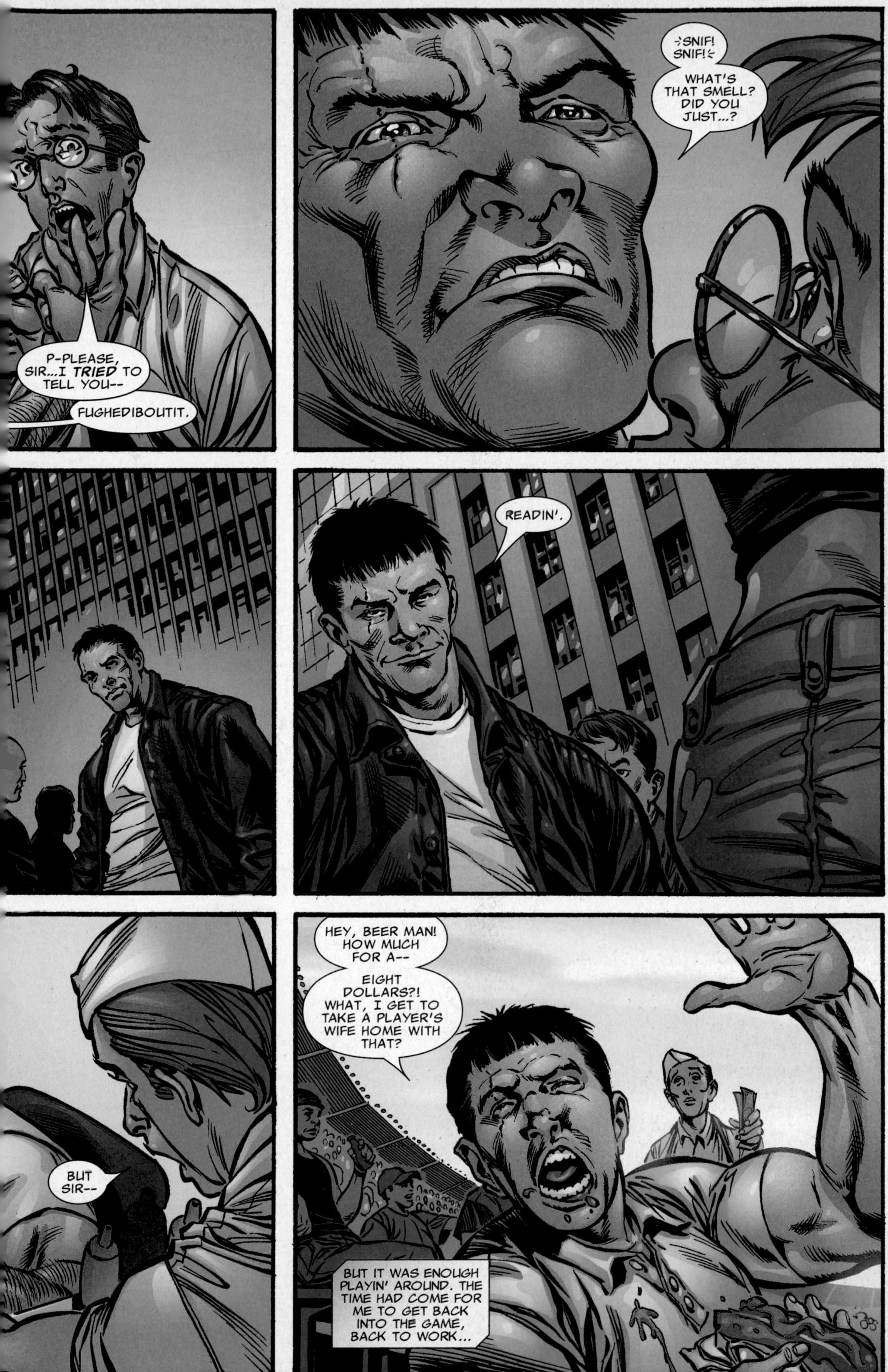
P-PLEASE, SIR...I TRIED TO TELL YOU--
FUGHEDIBOUTIT.
SNIF! SNIF!
WHAT'S THAT SMELL? DID YOU JUST...?
READIN'.
BUT SIR--
HEY, BEER MAN! HOW MUCH FOR A--
EIGHT DOLLARS?! WHAT, I GET TO TAKE A PLAYER'S WIFE HOME WITH THAT?
BUT IT WAS ENOUGH PLAYIN' AROUND. THE TIME HAD COME FOR ME TO GET BACK INTO THE GAME, BACK TO WORK...

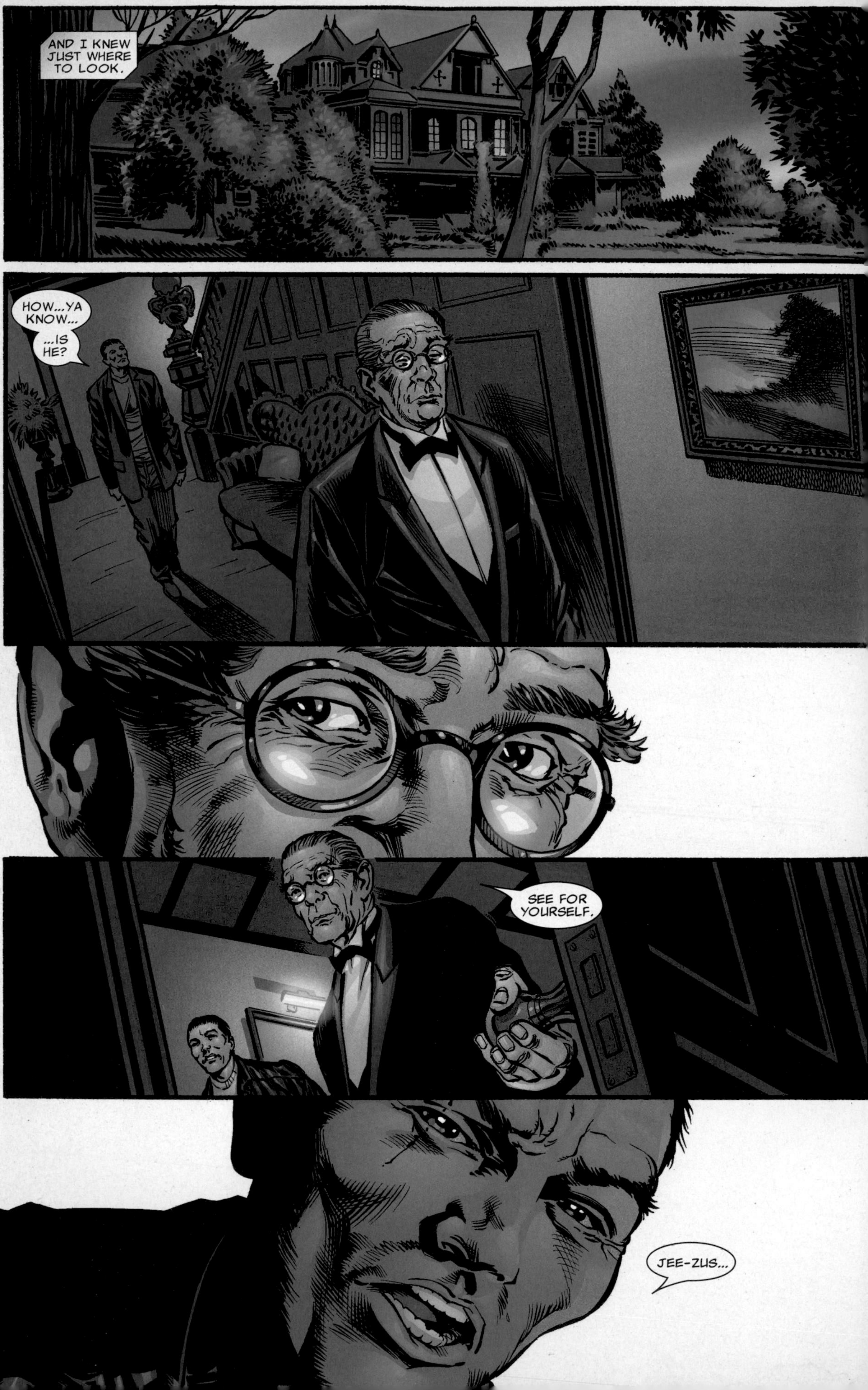
AND I KNEW JUST WHERE TO LOOK.
HOW...YA KNOW...
...IS HE?
SEE FOR YOURSELF.
JEE-ZUS...

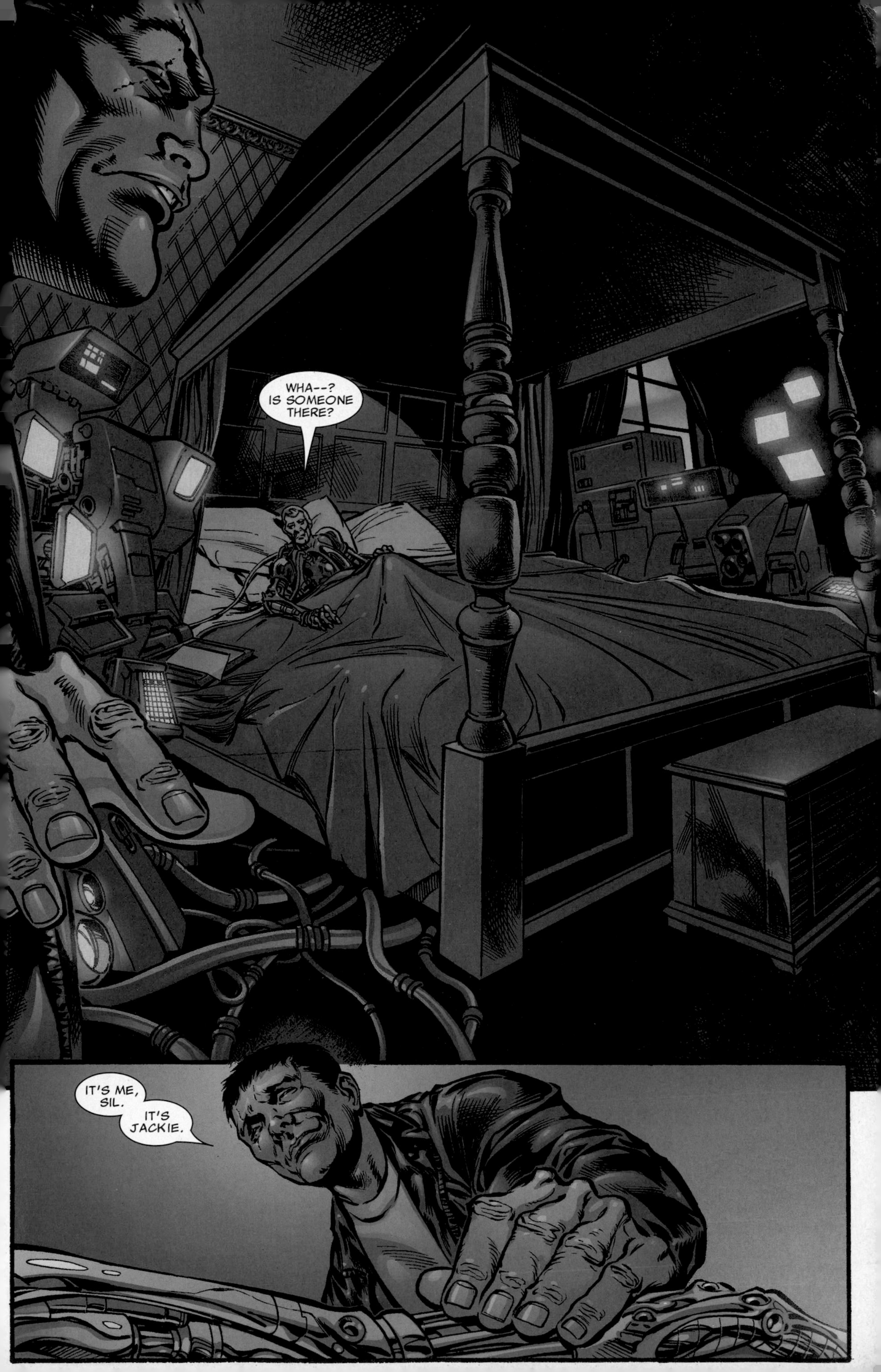
WHA--? IS SOMEONE THERE?
IT'S ME, SIL.
IT'S JACKIE.

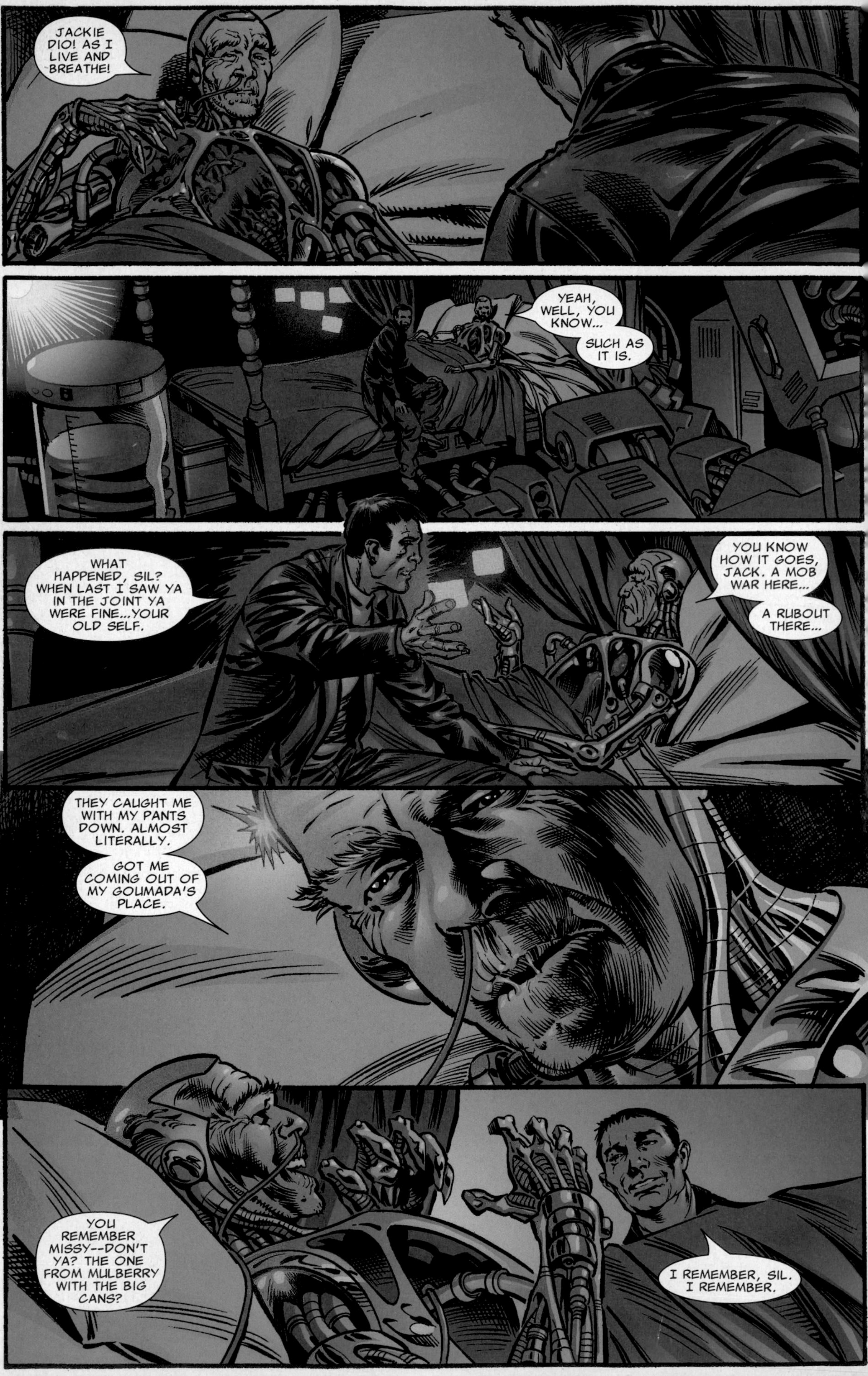
JACKIE DIO! AS I LIVE AND BREATHE!
YEAH, WELL, YOU KNOW...
SUCH AS IT IS.
WHAT HAPPENED, SIL? WHEN LAST I SAW YA IN THE JOINT YA WERE FINE...YOUR OLD SELF.
YOU KNOW HOW IT GOES, JACK. A MOB WAR HERE...
A RUBOUT THERE...
THEY CAUGHT ME WITH MY PANTS DOWN. ALMOST LITERALLY.
GOT ME COMING OUT OF MY GOUMADA'S PLACE.
YOU REMEMBER MISSY--DON'T YA? THE ONE FROM MULBERRY WITH THE BIG CANS?
I REMEMBER, SIL. I REMEMBER.

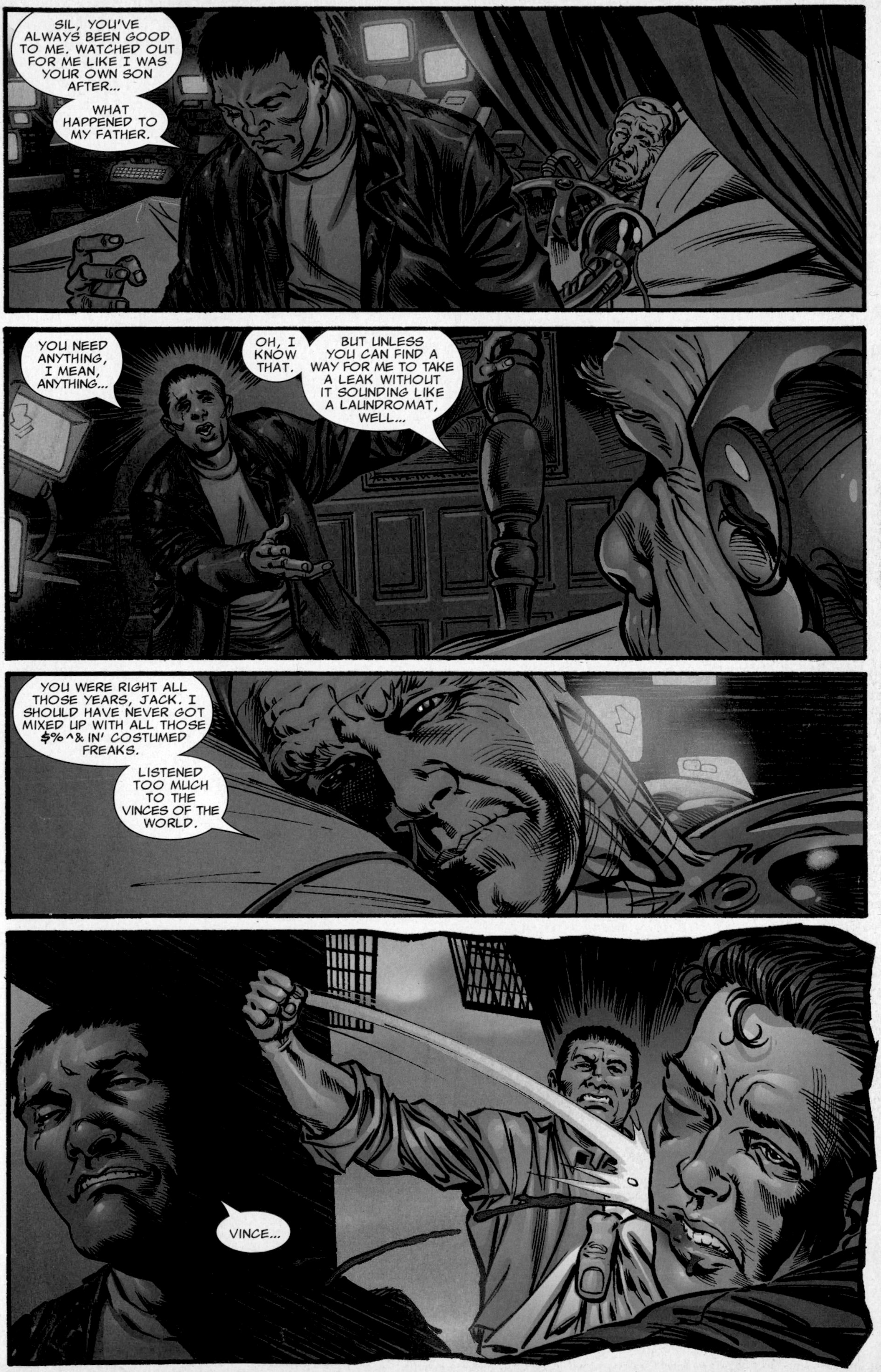
SIL, YOU'VE ALWAYS BEEN GOOD TO ME. WATCHED OUT FOR ME LIKE I WAS YOUR OWN SON AFTER...
WHAT HAPPENED TO MY FATHER.
YOU NEED ANYTHING, I MEAN, ANYTHING...
OH, I KNOW THAT.
BUT UNLESS YOU CAN FIND A WAY FOR ME TO TAKE A LEAK WITHOUT IT SOUNDING LIKE A LAUNDROMAT, WELL...
YOU WERE RIGHT ALL THOSE YEARS, JACK. I SHOULD HAVE NEVER GOT MIXED UP WITH ALL THOSE $%^& IN' COSTUMED FREAKS.
LISTENED TOO MUCH TO THE VINCES OF THE WORLD.
VINCE...

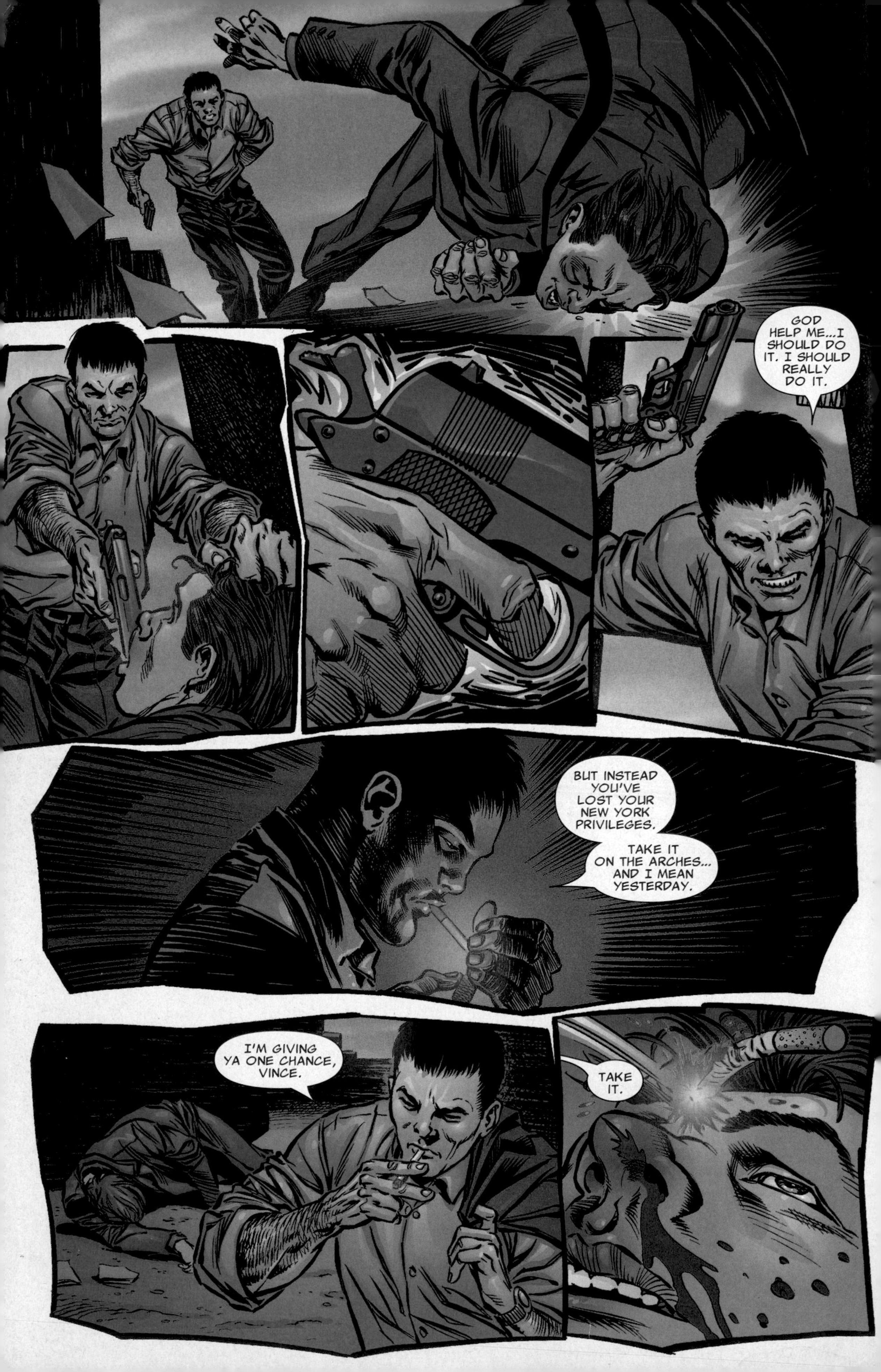
GOD HELP ME...I SHOULD DO IT. I SHOULD REALLY DO IT.
BUT INSTEAD YOU'VE LOST YOUR NEW YORK PRIVILEGES.
TAKE IT ON THE ARCHES... AND I MEAN YESTERDAY.
I'M GIVING YA ONE CHANCE, VINCE.
TAKE IT.

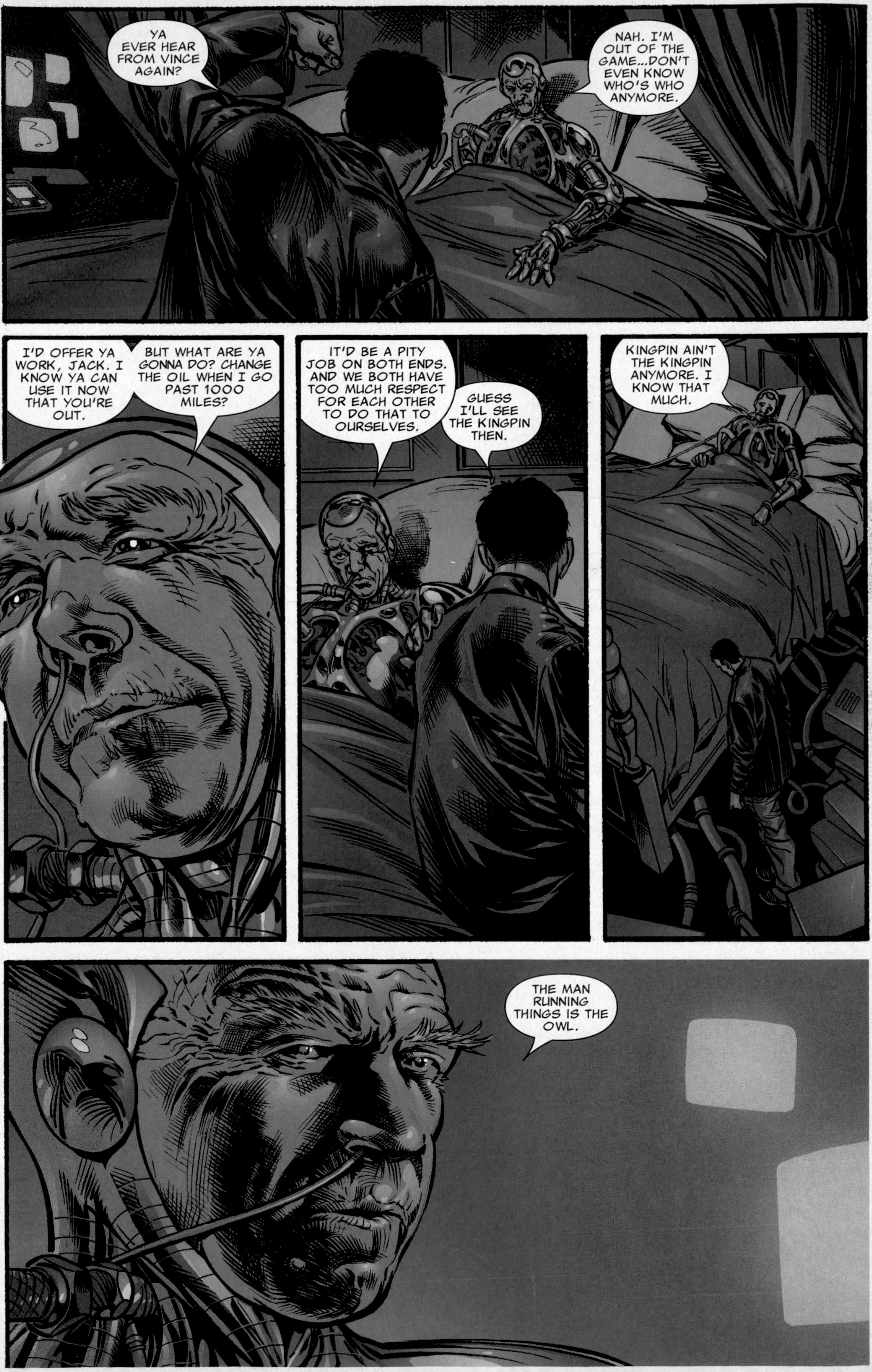
YA EVER HEAR FROM VINCE AGAIN?
NAH. I'M OUT OF THE GAME...DON'T EVEN KNOW WHO'S WHO ANYMORE.
I'D OFFER YA WORK, JACK. I KNOW YA CAN USE IT NOW THAT YOU'RE OUT.
BUT WHAT ARE YA GONNA DO? CHANGE THE OIL WHEN I GO PAST 1000 MILES?
IT'D BE A PITY JOB ON BOTH ENDS. AND WE BOTH HAVE TOO MUCH RESPECT FOR EACH OTHER TO DO THAT TO OURSELVES.
GUESS I'LL SEE THE KINGPIN THEN.
KINGPIN AIN'T THE KINGPIN ANYMORE. I KNOW THAT MUCH.
THE MAN RUNNING THINGS IS THE OWL.

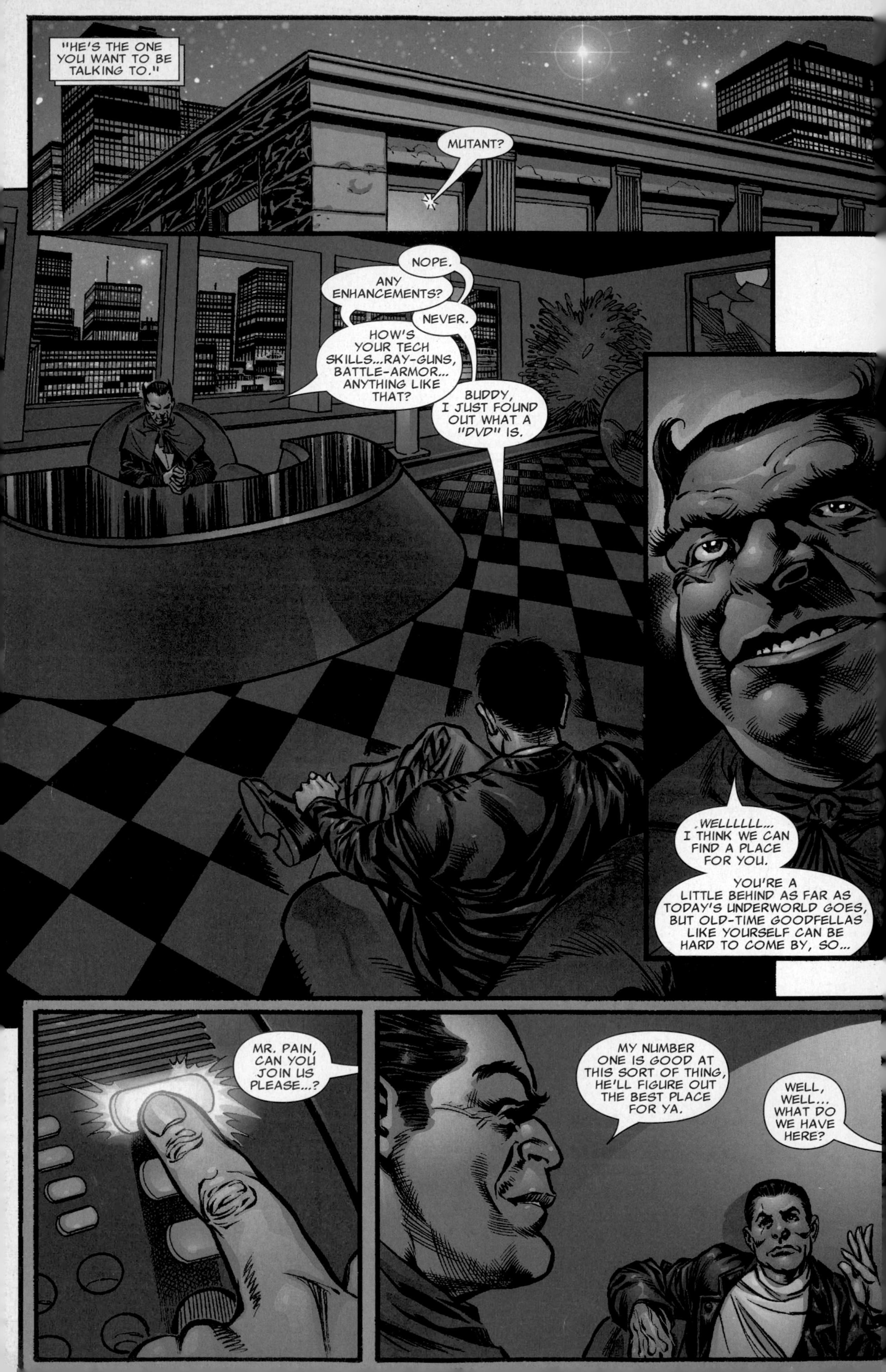
"HE'S THE ONE YOU WANT TO BE TALKING TO."
MUTANT?
NOPE.
ANY ENHANCEMENTS?
NEVER.
HOW'S YOUR TECH SKILLS...RAY-GUNS, BATTLE-ARMOR... ANYTHING LIKE THAT?
BUDDY, I JUST FOUND OUT WHAT A "DVD" IS.
WELLLLLLL... I THINK WE CAN FIND A PLACE FOR YOU.
YOU'RE A LITTLE BEHIND AS FAR AS TODAY'S UNDERWORLD GOES, BUT OLD-TIME GOODFELLAS LIKE YOURSELF CAN BE HARD TO COME BY, SO...
MR. PAIN, CAN YOU JOIN US PLEASE...?
MY NUMBER ONE IS GOOD AT THIS SORT OF THING, HE'LL FIGURE OUT THE BEST PLACE FOR YA.
WELL, WELL... WHAT DO WE HAVE HERE?

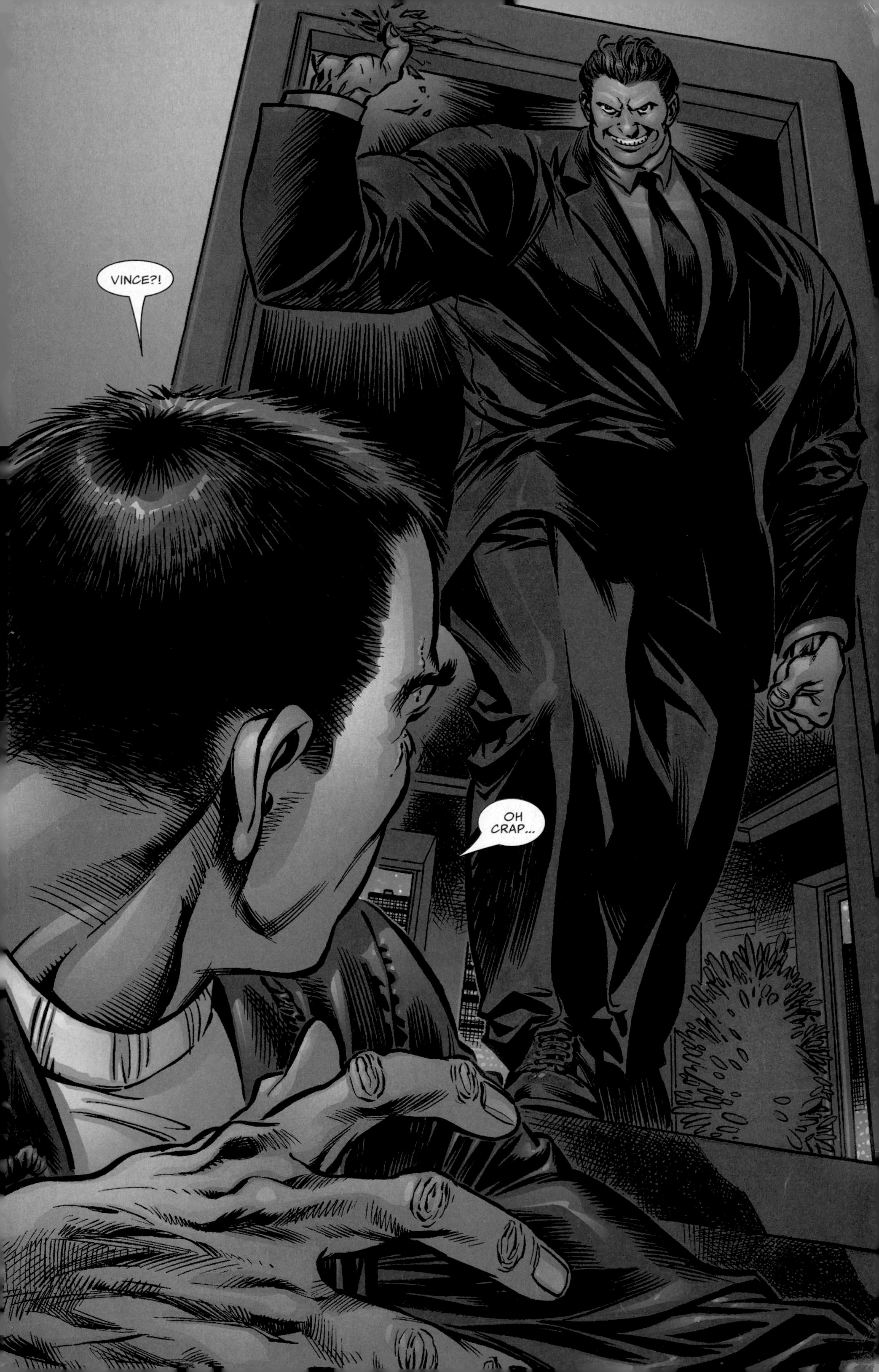
VINCE?!
OH CRAP...

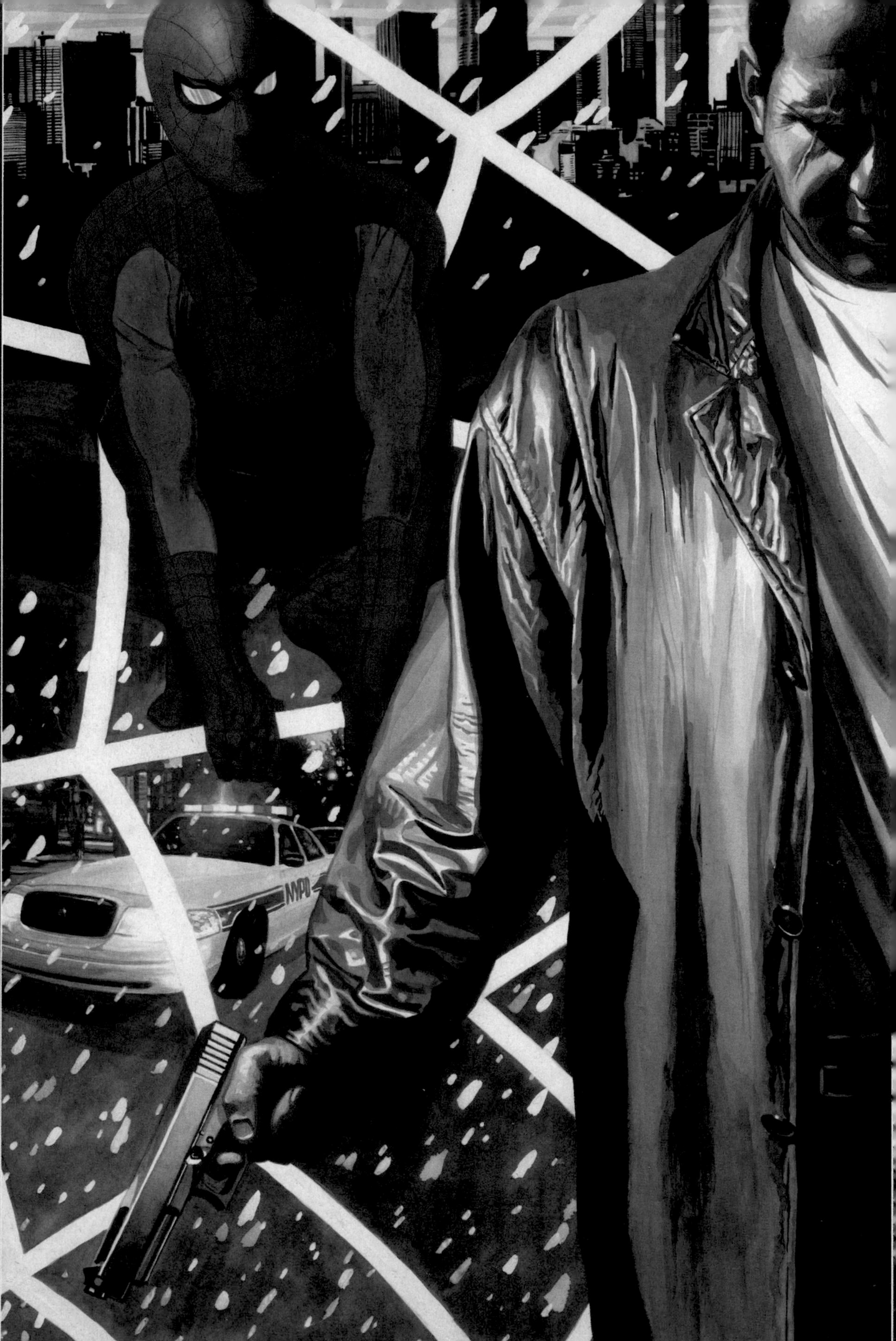
NYPD

UNDERWORLD #2

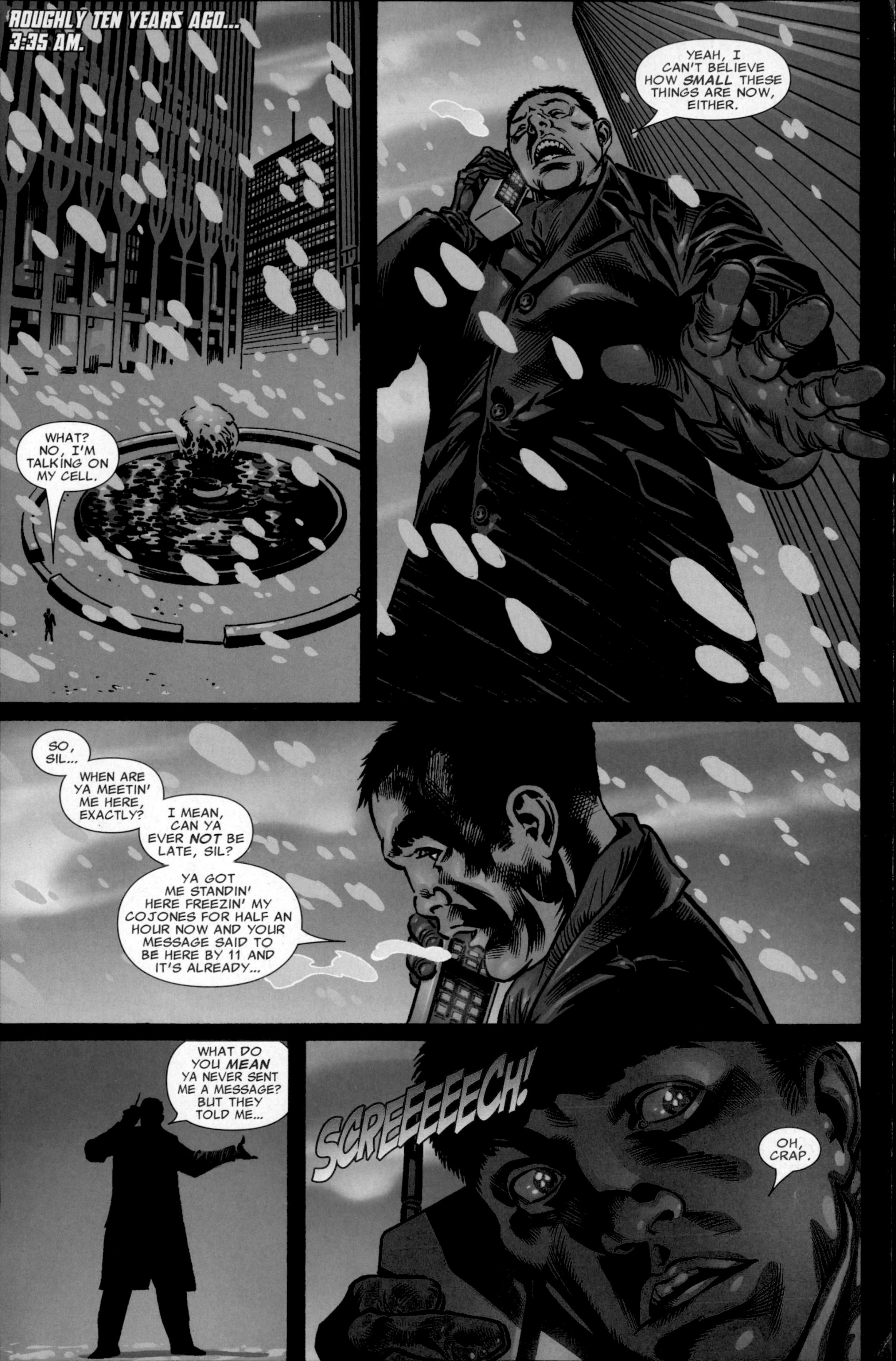
ROUGHLY TEN YEARS AGO...
3:35 AM.
WHAT? NO, I'M TALKING ON MY CELL.
YEAH, I CAN'T BELIEVE HOW SMALL THESE THINGS ARE NOW, EITHER.
SO, SIL...
WHEN ARE YA MEETIN' ME HERE, EXACTLY?
I MEAN, CAN YA EVER NOT BE LATE, SIL?
YA GOT ME STANDIN' HERE FREEZIN' MY COJONES FOR HALF AN HOUR NOW AND YOUR MESSAGE SAID TO BE HERE BY 11 AND IT'S ALREADY...
WHAT DO YOU MEAN YA NEVER SENT ME A MESSAGE? BUT THEY TOLD ME...
SCREEEEEECH!
OH, CRAP.

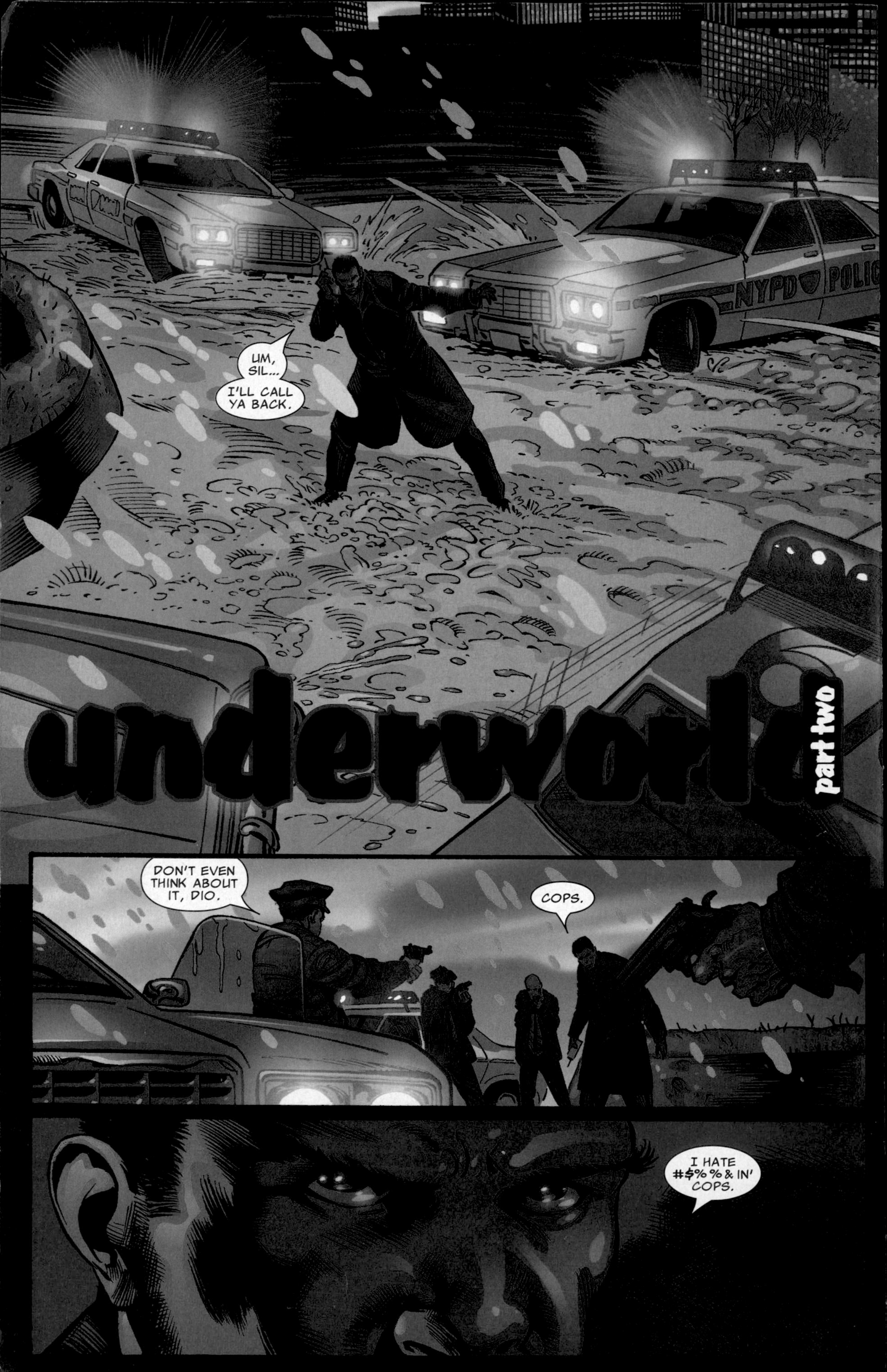
UM, SIL... I'LL CALL YA BACK.
NYPD POLICE
underworld part two
DON'T EVEN THINK ABOUT IT, DIO.
COPS.
I HATE #$%%& IN' COPS.

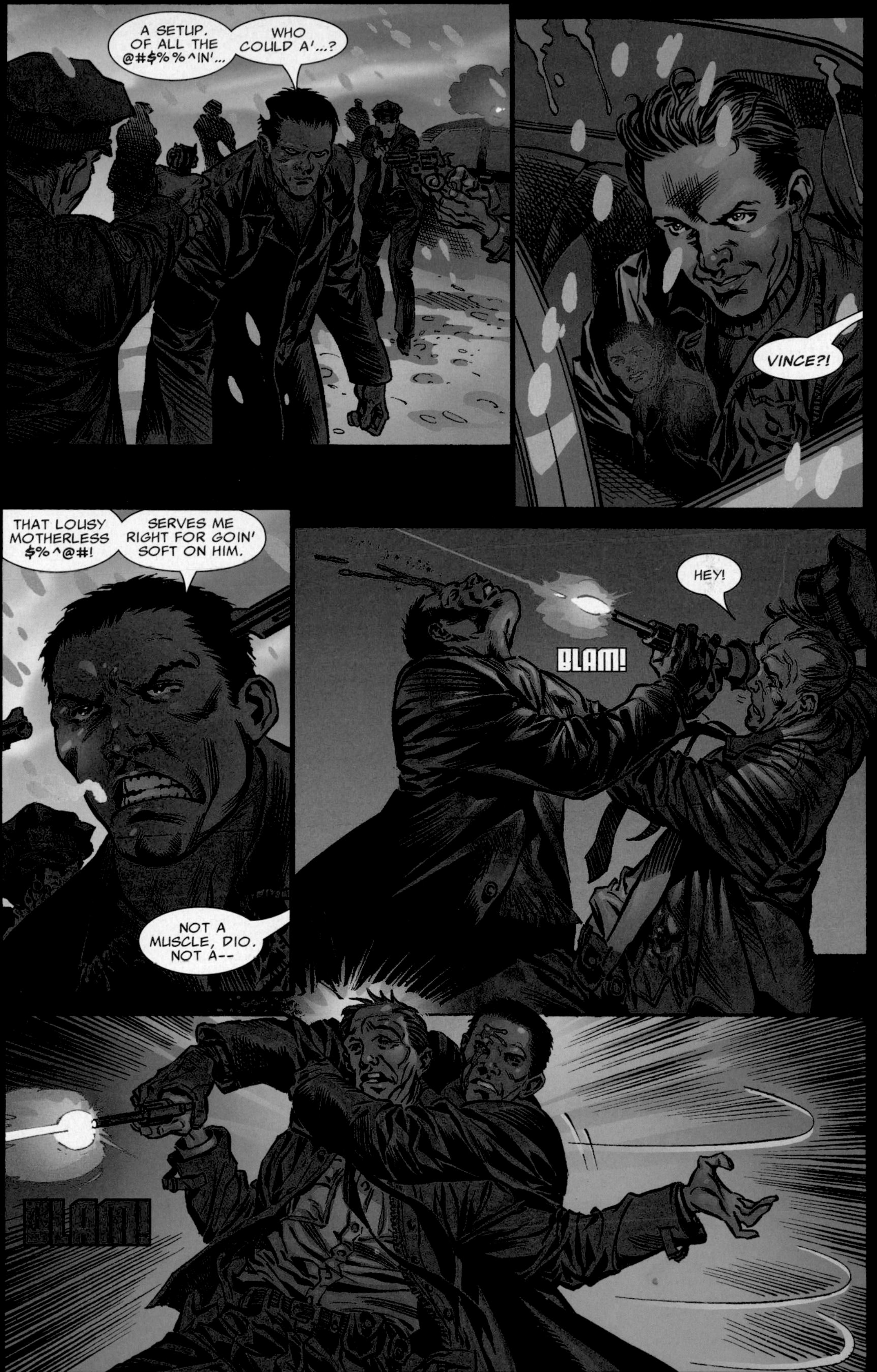

A SETUP. OF ALL THE @#$%%^IN'...
WHO COULD A'...?
VINCE?!
THAT LOUSY MOTHERLESS $%^@#!
SERVES ME RIGHT FOR GOIN' SOFT ON HIM.
NOT A MUSCLE, DIO. NOT A--
HEY!
BLAM!
BLAM!

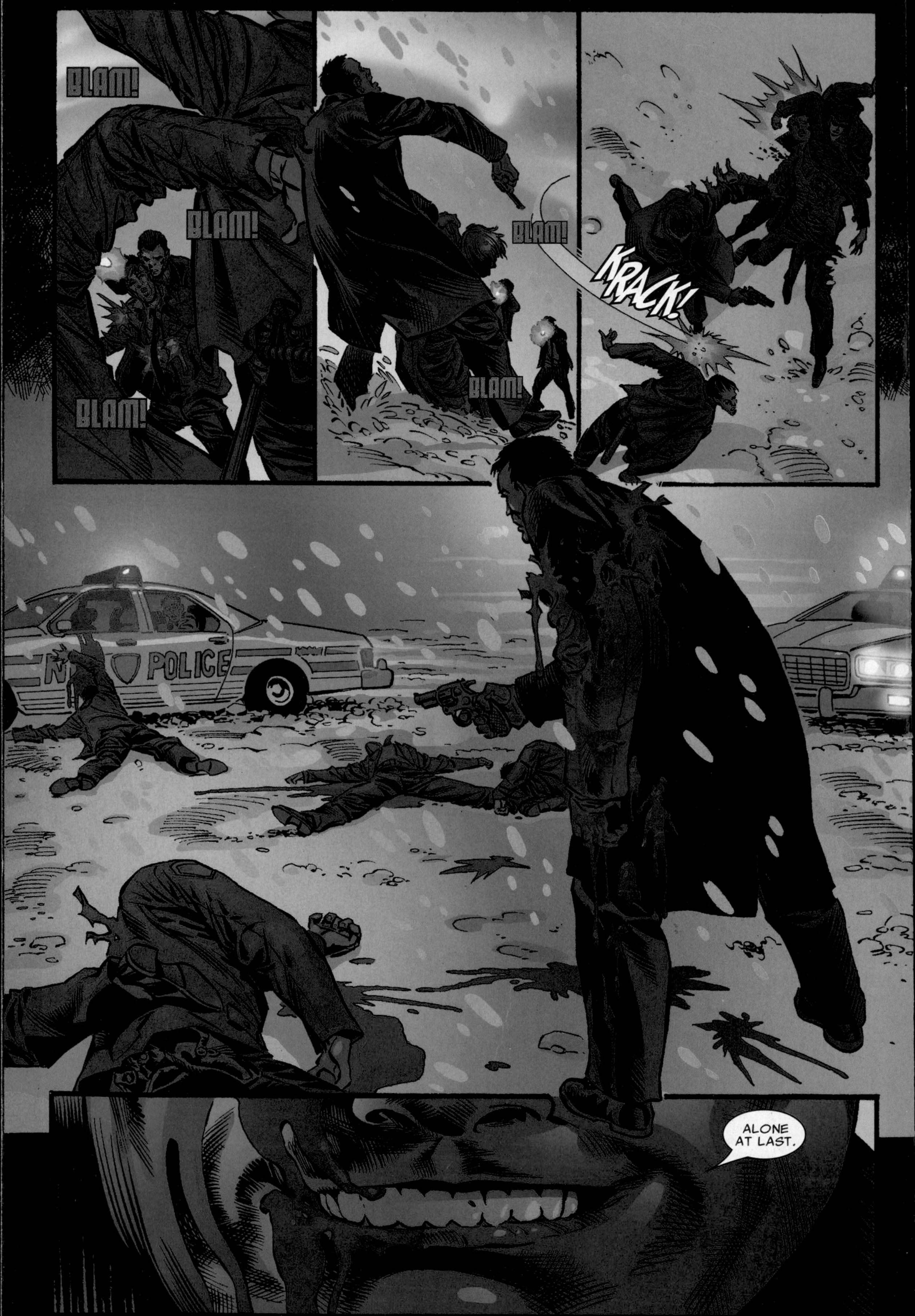
BLAM!
BLAM!
BLAM!
BLAM!
BLAM!
KRACK!
POLICE
ALONE AT LAST.

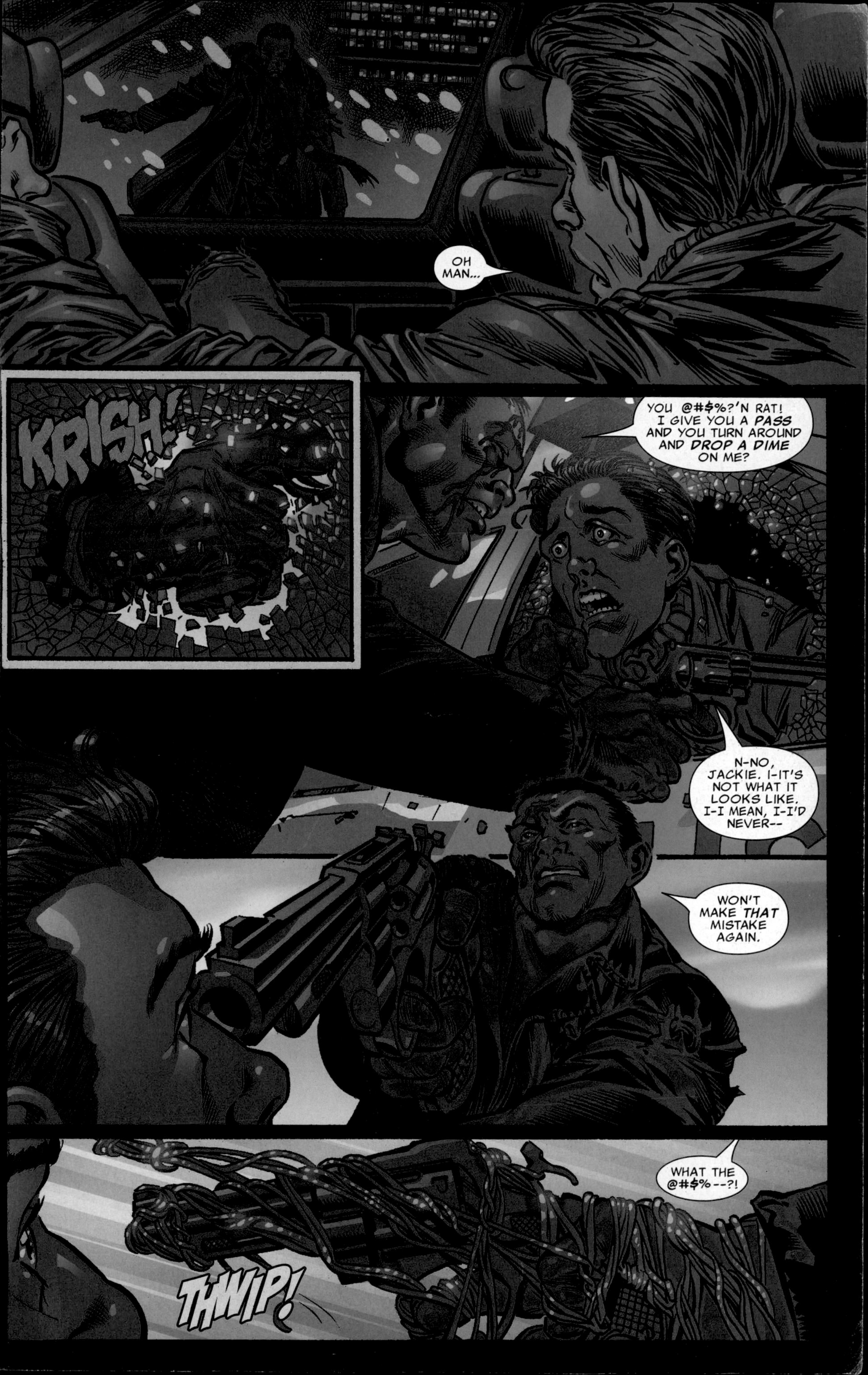
OH MAN...
KRISH!
YOU @#$%?'N RAT! I GIVE YOU A PASS AND YOU TURN AROUND AND DROP A DIME ON ME?
N-NO, JACKIE. I-IT'S NOT WHAT IT LOOKS LIKE. I-I MEAN, I-I'D NEVER--
WON'T MAKE THAT MISTAKE AGAIN.
WHAT THE @#$%--?!
THWIP!

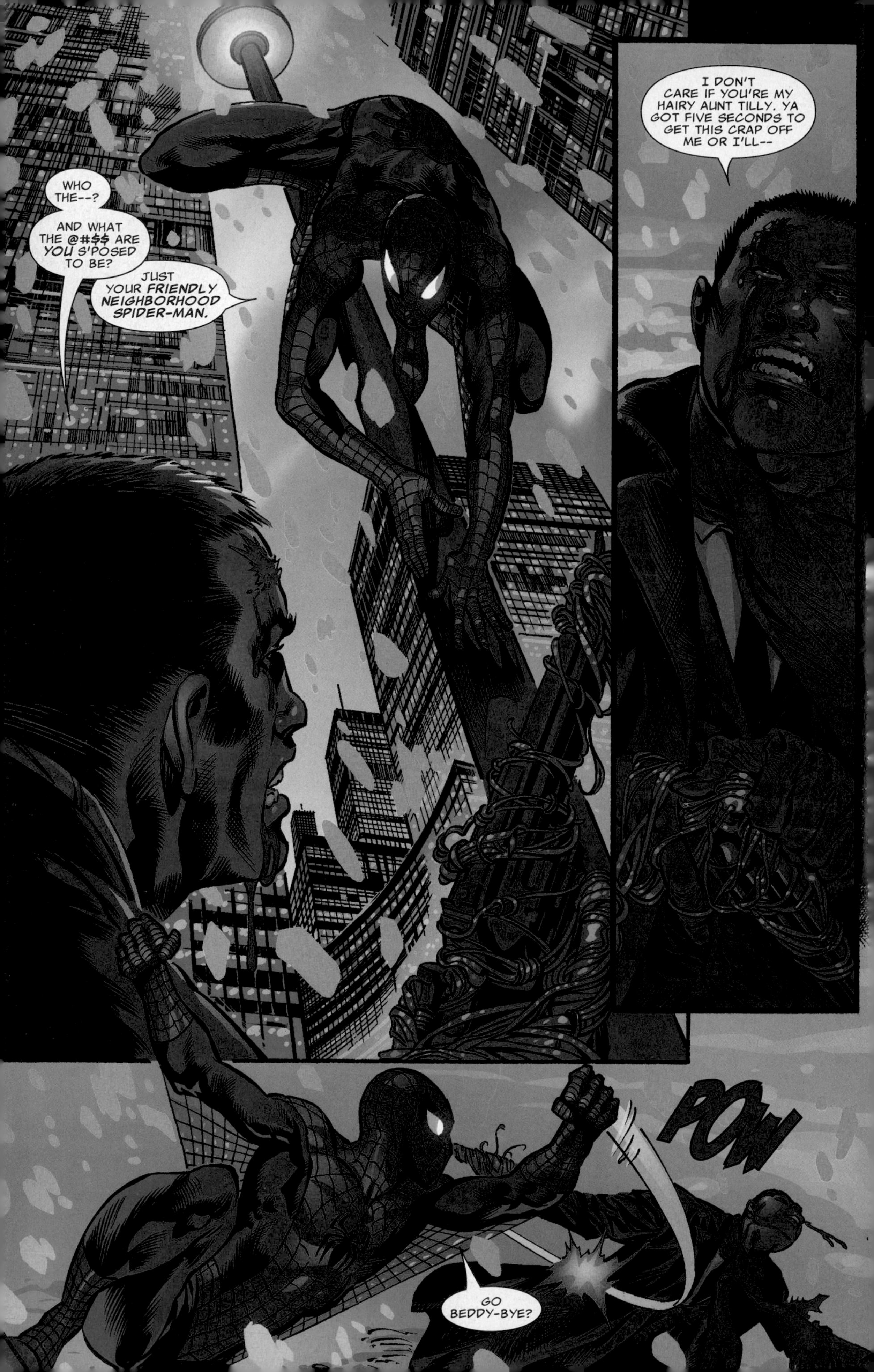
WHO THE--?
AND WHAT THE @#$$ ARE YOU S'POSED TO BE?
JUST YOUR FRIENDLY NEIGHBORHOOD SPIDER-MAN.
I DON'T CARE IF YOU'RE MY HAIRY AUNT TILLY. YA GOT FIVE SECONDS TO GET THIS CRAP OFF ME OR I'LL--
POW
GO BEDDY-BYE?

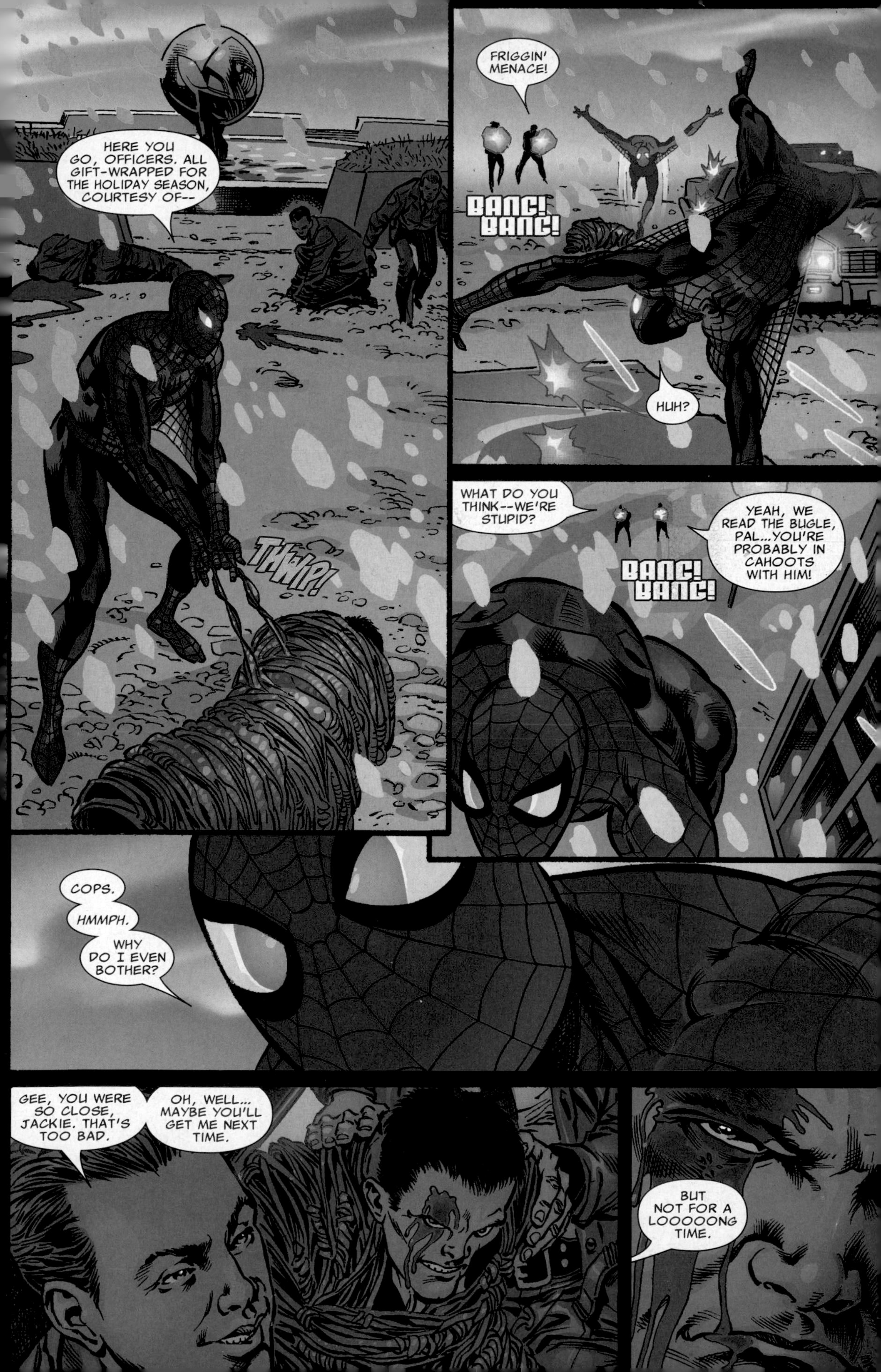
HERE YOU GO, OFFICERS. ALL GIFT-WRAPPED FOR THE HOLIDAY SEASON, COURTESY OF--
THWIP!
FRIGGIN' MENACE!
BANG! BANG!
HUH?
WHAT DO YOU THINK--WE'RE STUPID?
YEAH, WE READ THE BUGLE, PAL...YOU'RE PROBABLY IN CAHOOTS WITH HIM!
BANG! BANG!
COPS.
HMMPH.
WHY DO I EVEN BOTHER?
GEE, YOU WERE SO CLOSE, JACKIE. THAT'S TOO BAD.
OH, WELL... MAYBE YOU'LL GET ME NEXT TIME.
BUT NOT FOR A LOOOOONG TIME.

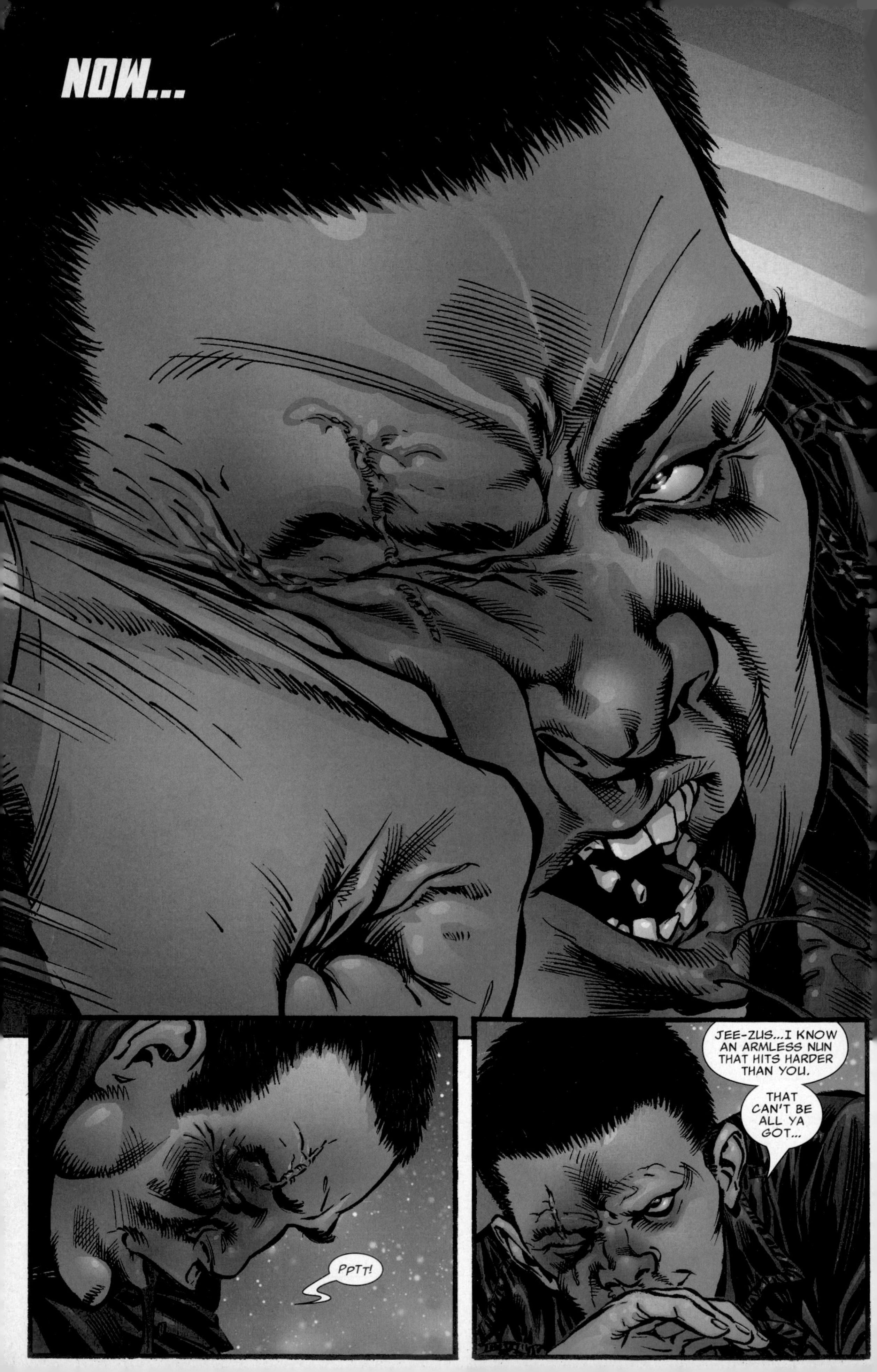
NOW...
PPTT!
JEE-ZUS...I KNOW AN ARMLESS NUN THAT HITS HARDER THAN YOU.
THAT CAN'T BE ALL YA GOT...

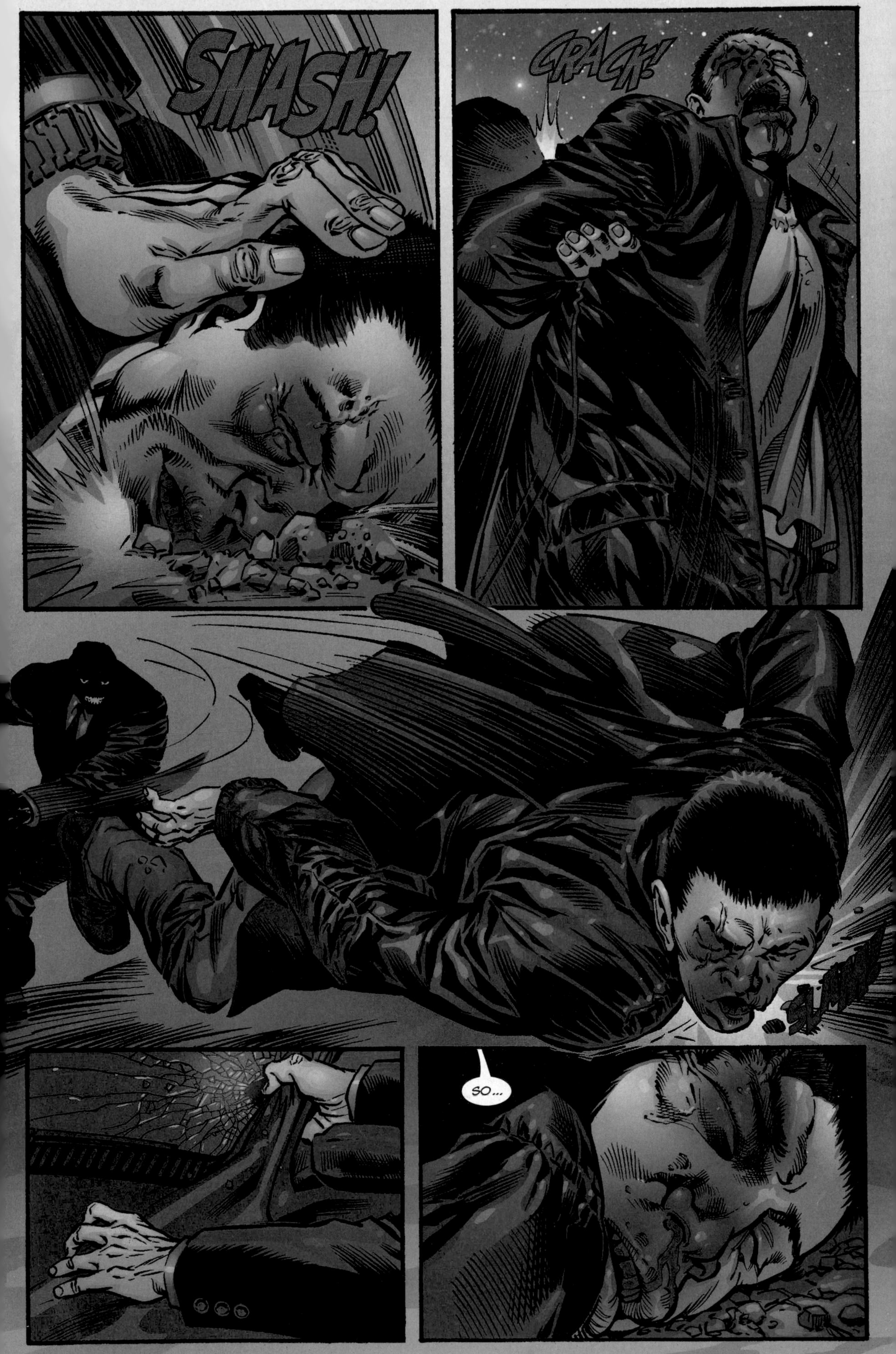
SMASH!
CRACK!
SO...

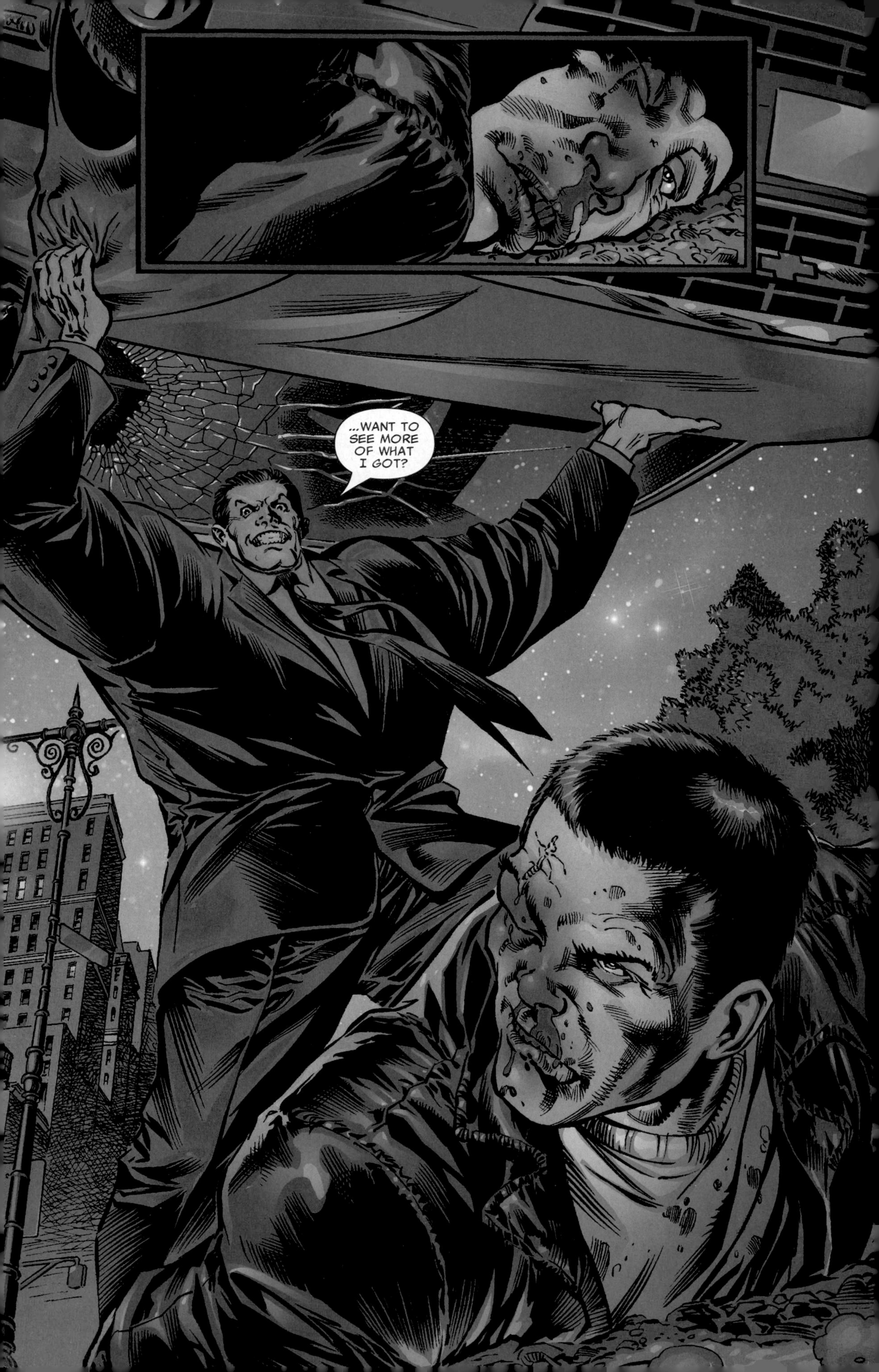
...WANT TO SEE MORE OF WHAT I GOT?

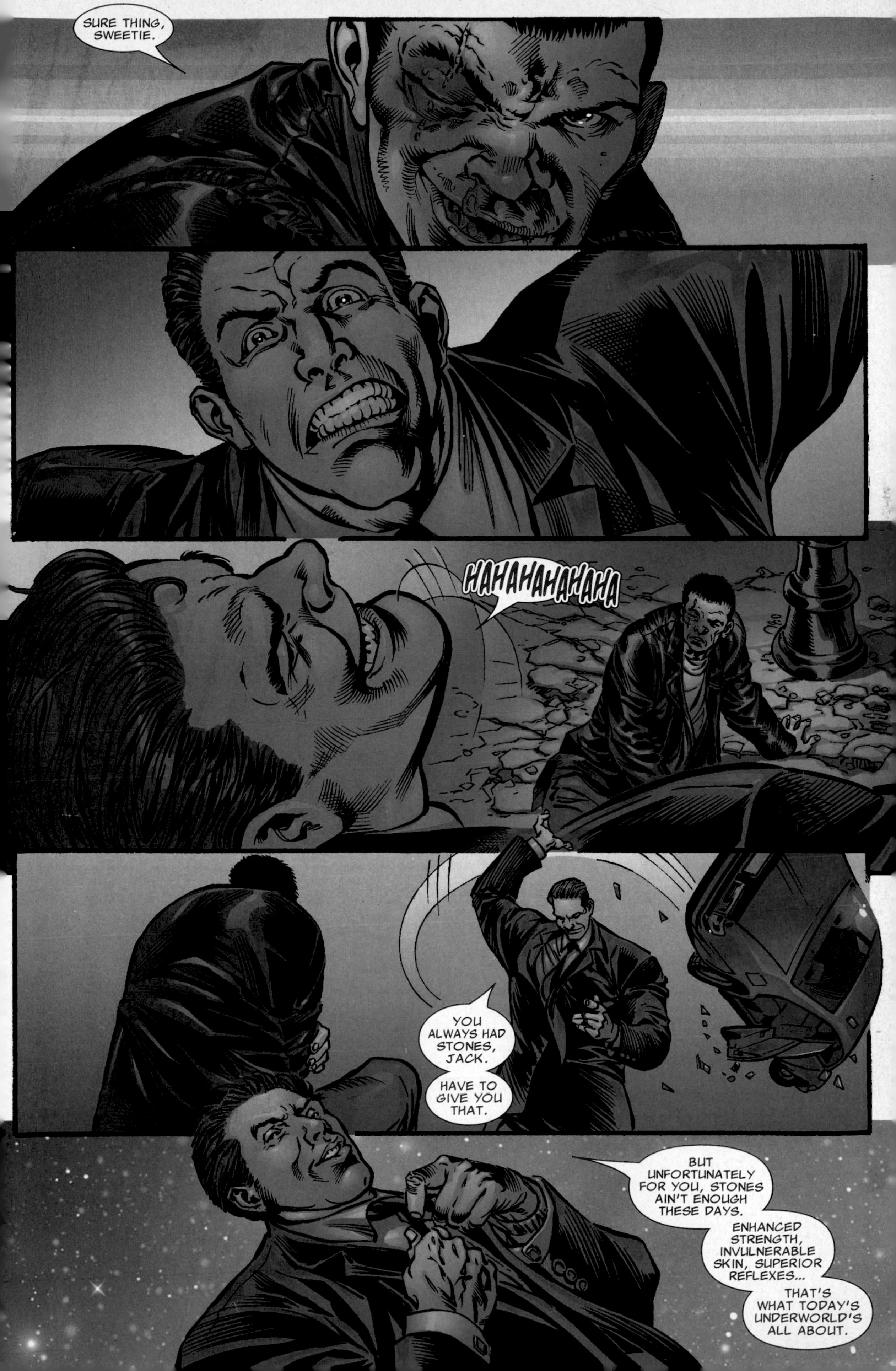
SURE THING, SWEETIE.
HAHAHAHAHAHA
YOU ALWAYS HAD STONES, JACK.
HAVE TO GIVE YOU THAT.
BUT UNFORTUNATELY FOR YOU, STONES AIN'T ENOUGH THESE DAYS.
ENHANCED STRENGTH, INVULNERABLE SKIN, SUPERIOR REFLEXES...
THAT'S WHAT TODAY'S UNDERWORLD'S ALL ABOUT.

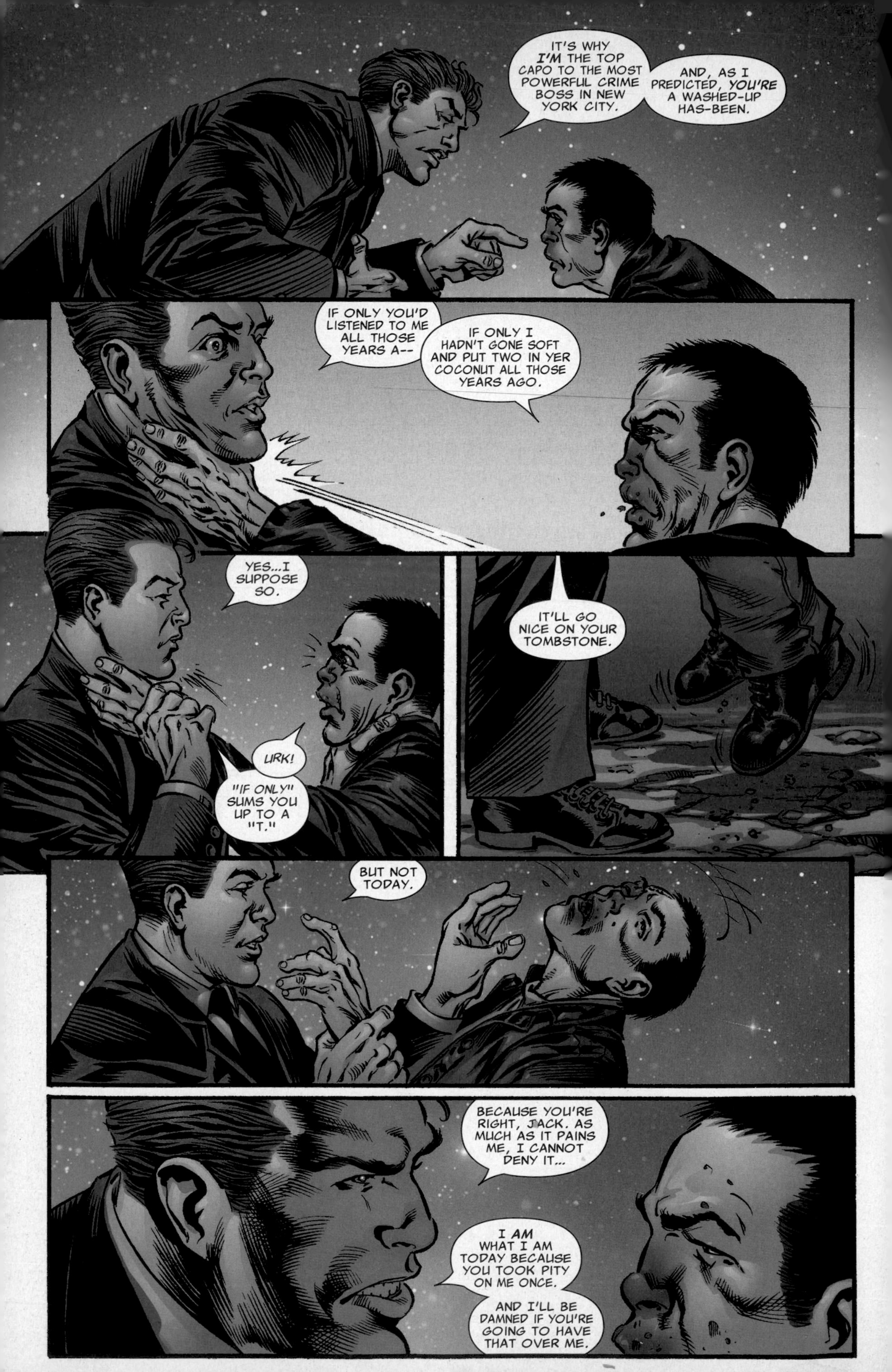
IT'S WHY I'M THE TOP CAPO TO THE MOST POWERFUL CRIME BOSS IN NEW YORK CITY.
AND, AS I PREDICTED, YOU'RE A WASHED-UP HAS-BEEN.
IF ONLY YOU'D LISTENED TO ME ALL THOSE YEARS A--
IF ONLY I HADN'T GONE SOFT AND PUT TWO IN YER COCONUT ALL THOSE YEARS AGO.
YES...I SUPPOSE SO.
URK!
"IF ONLY" SUMS YOU UP TO A "T."
IT'LL GO NICE ON YOUR TOMBSTONE.
BUT NOT TODAY.
BECAUSE YOU'RE RIGHT, JACK. AS MUCH AS IT PAINS ME, I CANNOT DENY IT...
I AM WHAT I AM TODAY BECAUSE YOU TOOK PITY ON ME ONCE.
AND I'LL BE DAMNED IF YOU'RE GOING TO HAVE THAT OVER ME.

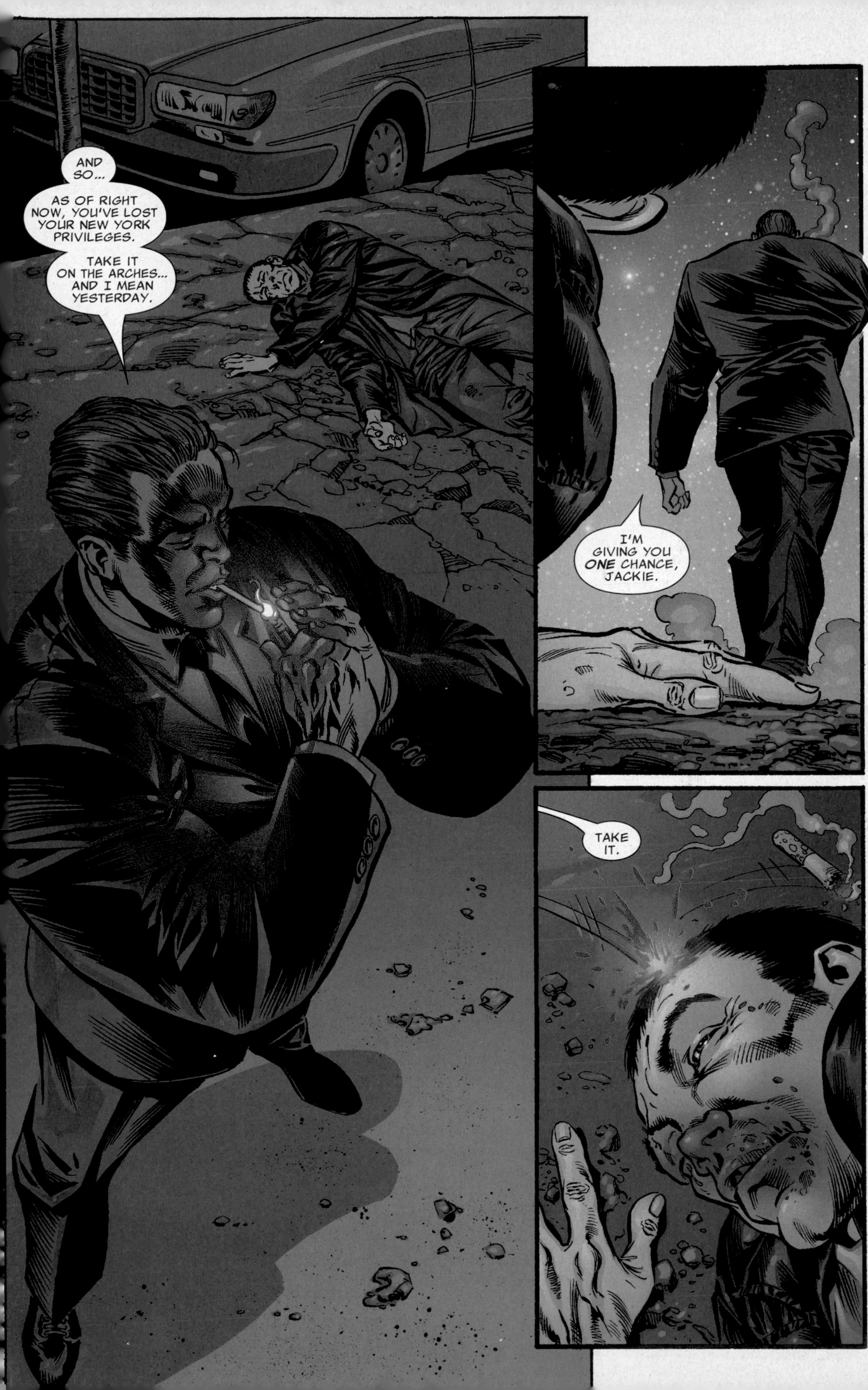
AND SO...
AS OF RIGHT NOW, YOU'VE LOST YOUR NEW YORK PRIVILEGES.
TAKE IT ON THE ARCHES... AND I MEAN YESTERDAY.
I'M GIVING YOU ONE CHANCE, JACKIE.
TAKE IT.

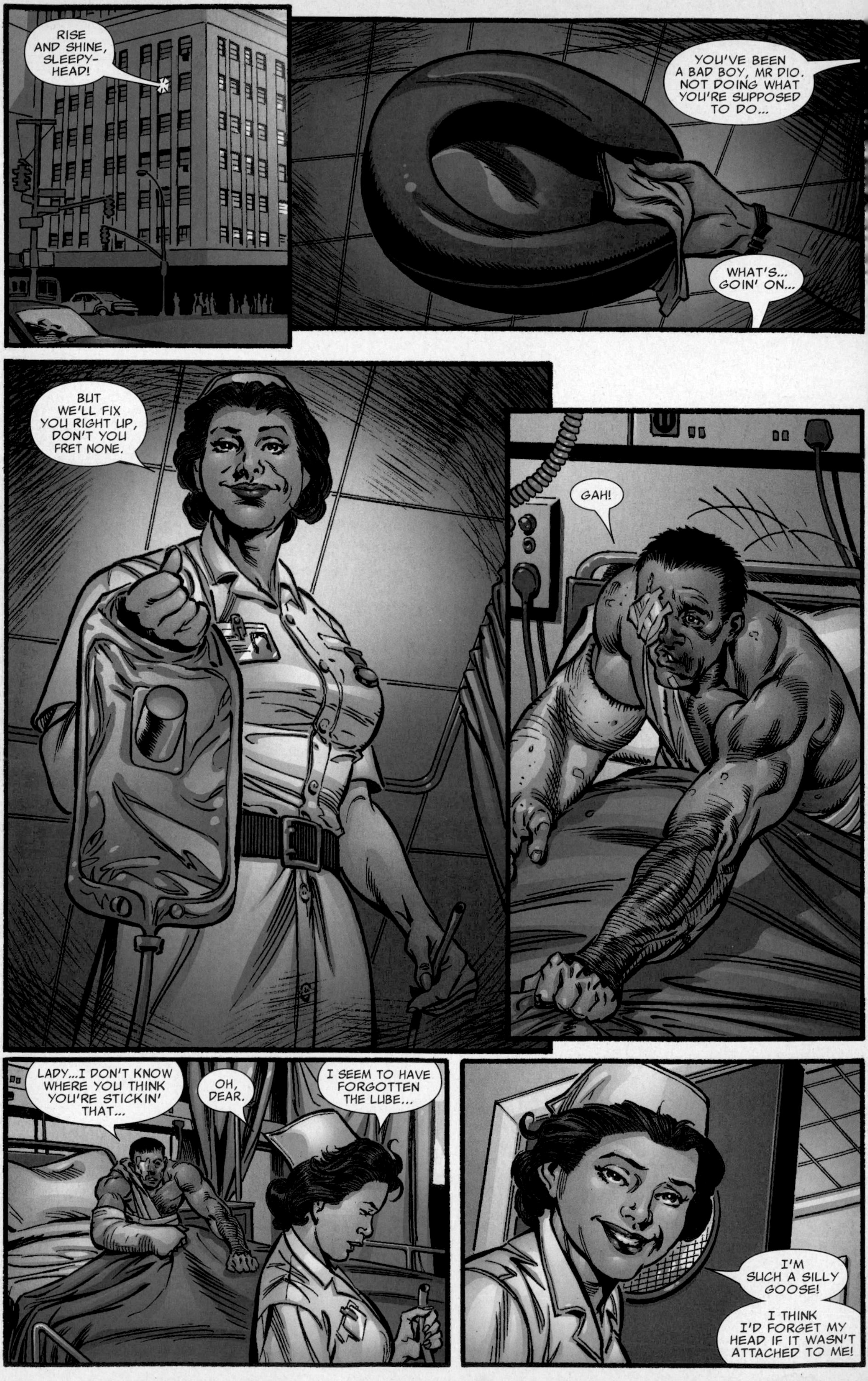
RISE AND SHINE, SLEEPY-HEAD!
YOU'VE BEEN A BAD BOY, MR DIO. NOT DOING WHAT YOU'RE SUPPOSED TO DO...
WHAT'S... GOIN' ON...
BUT WE'LL FIX YOU RIGHT UP, DON'T YOU FRET NONE.
GAH!
LADY...I DON'T KNOW WHERE YOU THINK YOU'RE STICKIN' THAT...
OH, DEAR.
I SEEM TO HAVE FORGOTTEN THE LUBE...
I'M SUCH A SILLY GOOSE!
I THINK I'D FORGET MY HEAD IF IT WASN'T ATTACHED TO ME!

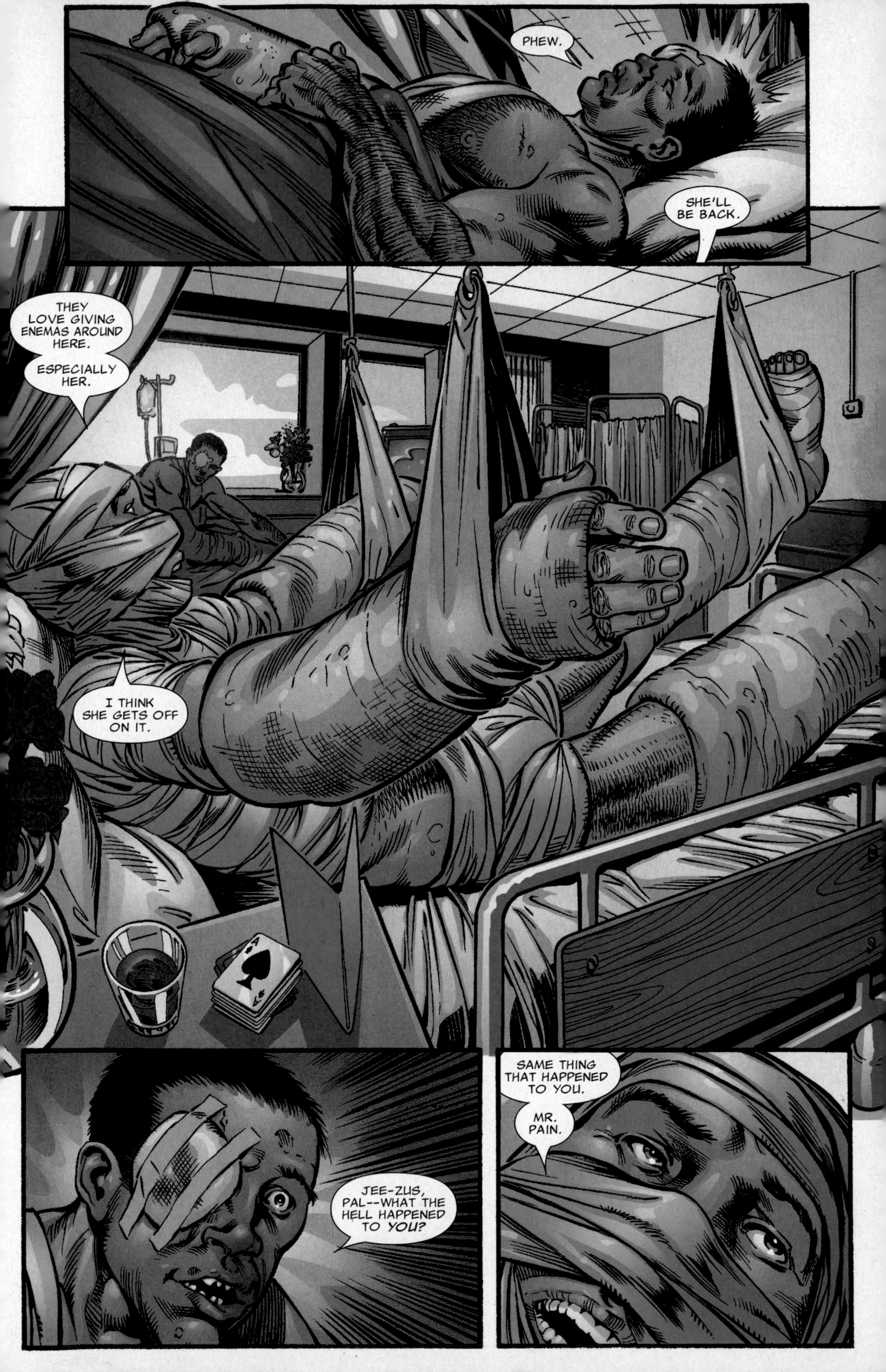
PHEW.
SHE'LL BE BACK.
THEY LOVE GIVING ENEMAS AROUND HERE.
ESPECIALLY HER.
I THINK SHE GETS OFF ON IT.
JEE-ZUS, PAL--WHAT THE HELL HAPPENED TO YOU?
SAME THING THAT HAPPENED TO YOU.
MR. PAIN.

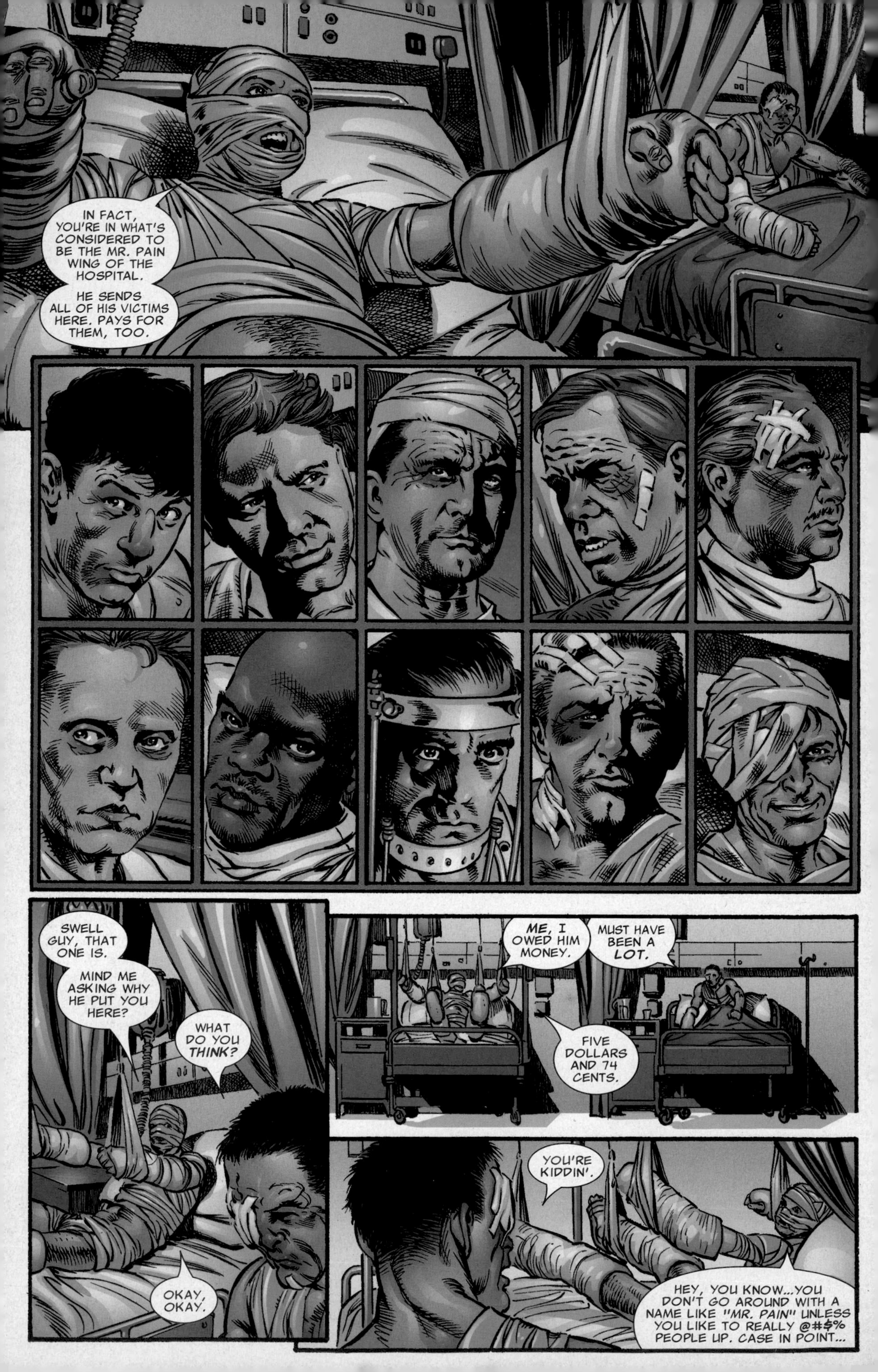
IN FACT, YOU'RE IN WHAT'S CONSIDERED TO BE THE MR. PAIN WING OF THE HOSPITAL.
HE SENDS ALL OF HIS VICTIMS HERE. PAYS FOR THEM, TOO.
SWELL GUY, THAT ONE IS.
MIND ME ASKING WHY HE PUT YOU HERE?
WHAT DO YOU *THINK?*
OKAY, OKAY.
ME, I OWED HIM MONEY.
MUST HAVE BEEN A *LOT.*
FIVE DOLLARS AND 74 CENTS.
YOU'RE KIDDIN'.
HEY, YOU KNOW...YOU DON'T GO AROUND WITH A NAME LIKE "*MR. PAIN*" UNLESS YOU LIKE TO REALLY @#$% PEOPLE UP. CASE IN POINT...

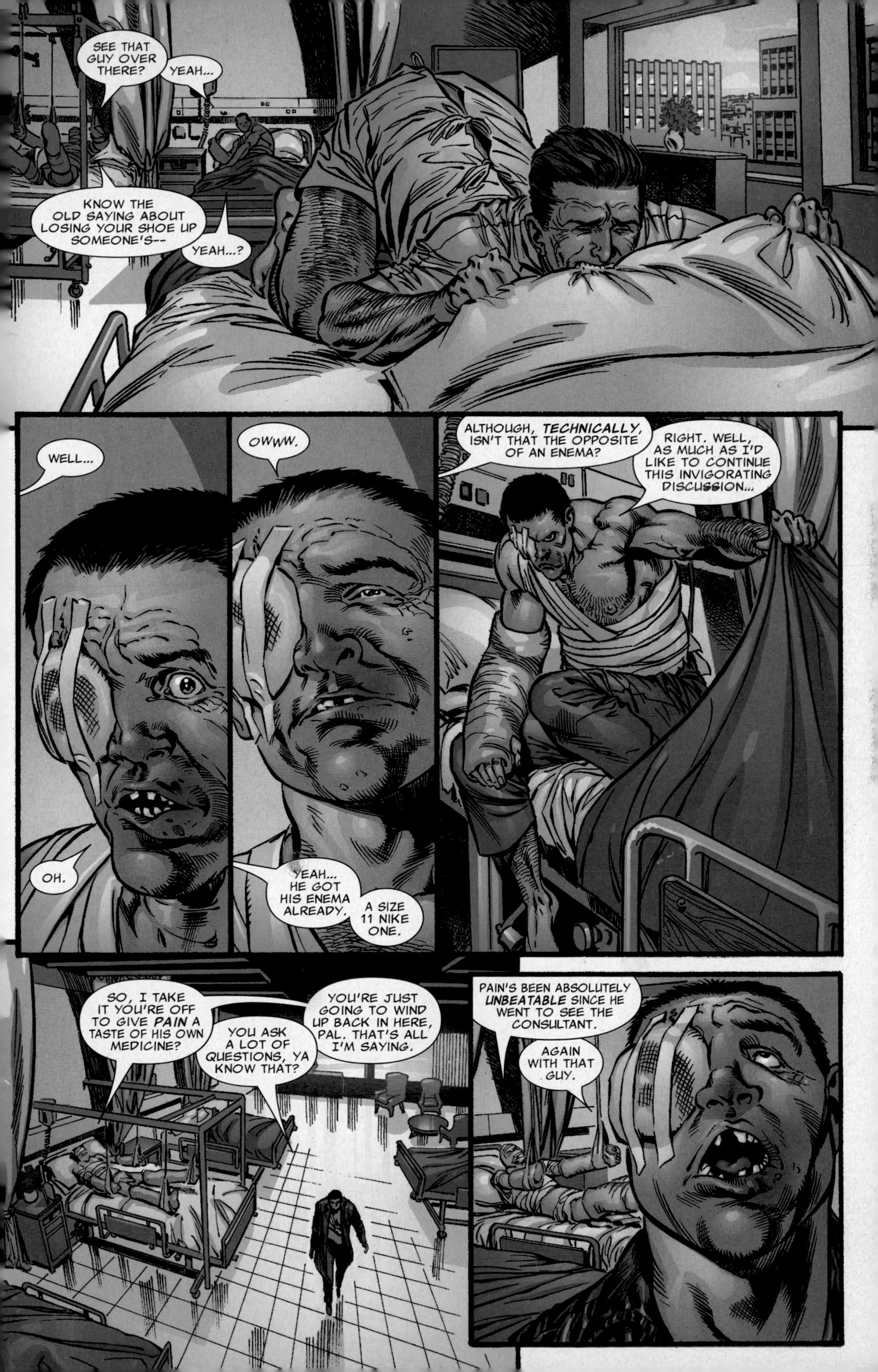

SEE THAT GUY OVER THERE?
YEAH...
KNOW THE OLD SAYING ABOUT LOSING YOUR SHOE UP SOMEONE'S--
YEAH...?
WELL...
OH.
OWWW.
YEAH... HE GOT HIS ENEMA ALREADY.
A SIZE 11 NIKE ONE.
ALTHOUGH, *TECHNICALLY*, ISN'T THAT THE OPPOSITE OF AN ENEMA?
RIGHT. WELL, AS MUCH AS I'D LIKE TO CONTINUE THIS INVIGORATING DISCUSSION...
SO, I TAKE IT YOU'RE OFF TO GIVE *PAIN* A TASTE OF HIS OWN MEDICINE?
YOU ASK A LOT OF QUESTIONS, YA KNOW THAT?
YOU'RE JUST GOING TO WIND UP BACK IN HERE, PAL. THAT'S ALL I'M SAYING.
PAIN'S BEEN ABSOLUTELY *UNBEATABLE* SINCE HE WENT TO SEE THE CONSULTANT.
AGAIN WITH THAT GUY.

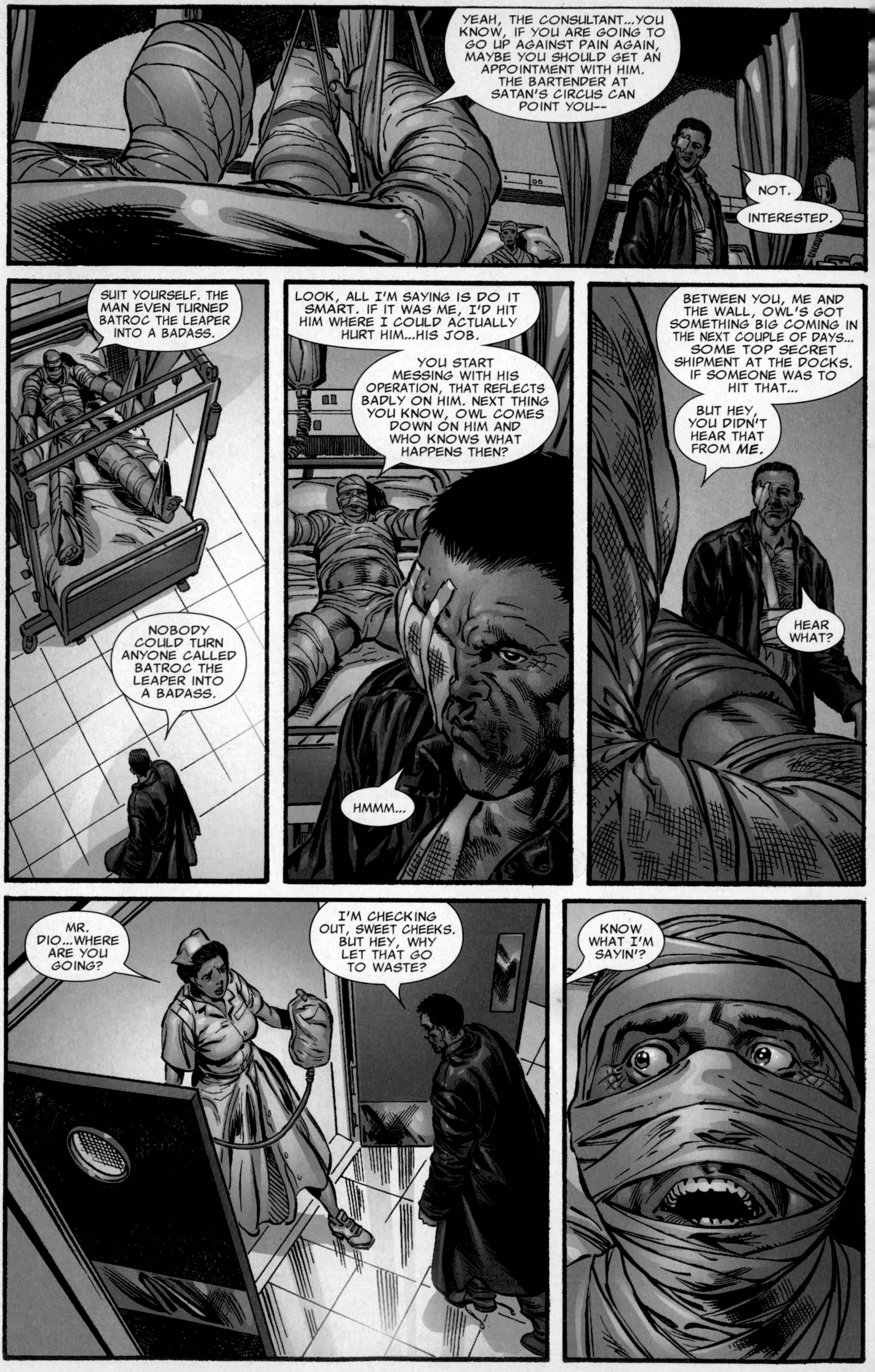

YEAH, THE CONSULTANT...YOU KNOW, IF YOU ARE GOING TO GO UP AGAINST PAIN AGAIN, MAYBE YOU SHOULD GET AN APPOINTMENT WITH HIM. THE BARTENDER AT SATAN'S CIRCUS CAN POINT YOU--
NOT.
INTERESTED.
SUIT YOURSELF. THE MAN EVEN TURNED BATROC THE LEAPER INTO A BADASS.
NOBODY COULD TURN ANYONE CALLED BATROC THE LEAPER INTO A BADASS.
LOOK, ALL I'M SAYING IS DO IT SMART. IF IT WAS ME, I'D HIT HIM WHERE I COULD ACTUALLY HURT HIM...HIS JOB.
YOU START MESSING WITH HIS OPERATION, THAT REFLECTS BADLY ON HIM. NEXT THING YOU KNOW, OWL COMES DOWN ON HIM AND WHO KNOWS WHAT HAPPENS THEN?
HMMM...
BETWEEN YOU, ME AND THE WALL, OWL'S GOT SOMETHING BIG COMING IN THE NEXT COUPLE OF DAYS... SOME TOP SECRET SHIPMENT AT THE DOCKS. IF SOMEONE WAS TO HIT THAT...
BUT HEY, YOU DIDN'T HEAR THAT FROM ME.
HEAR WHAT?
MR. DIO...WHERE ARE YOU GOING?
I'M CHECKING OUT, SWEET CHEEKS. BUT HEY, WHY LET THAT GO TO WASTE?
KNOW WHAT I'M SAYIN'?

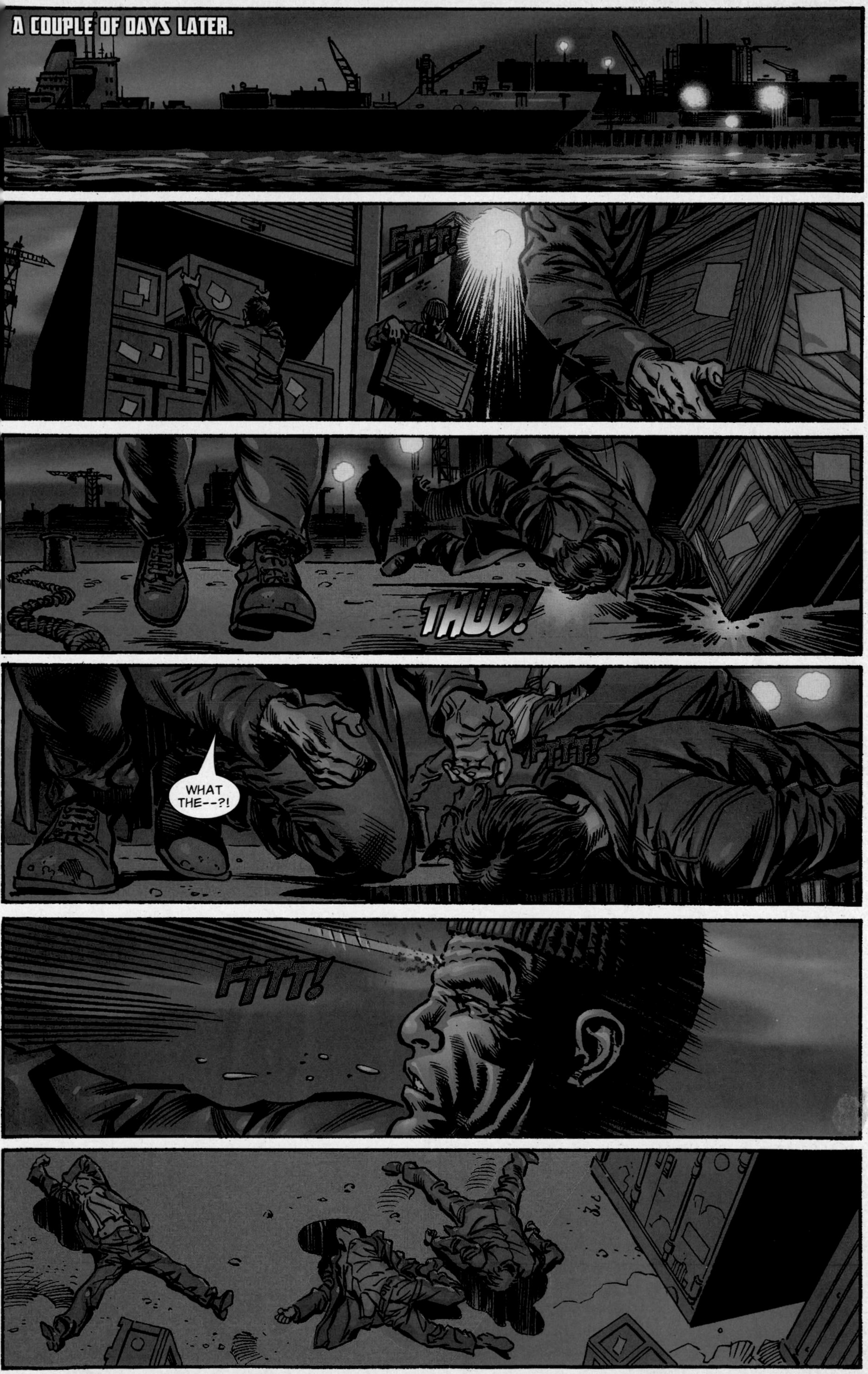

A COUPLE OF DAYS LATER.
FTTTT!
THUD!
WHAT THE--?!
FTTTT!
FTTTT!

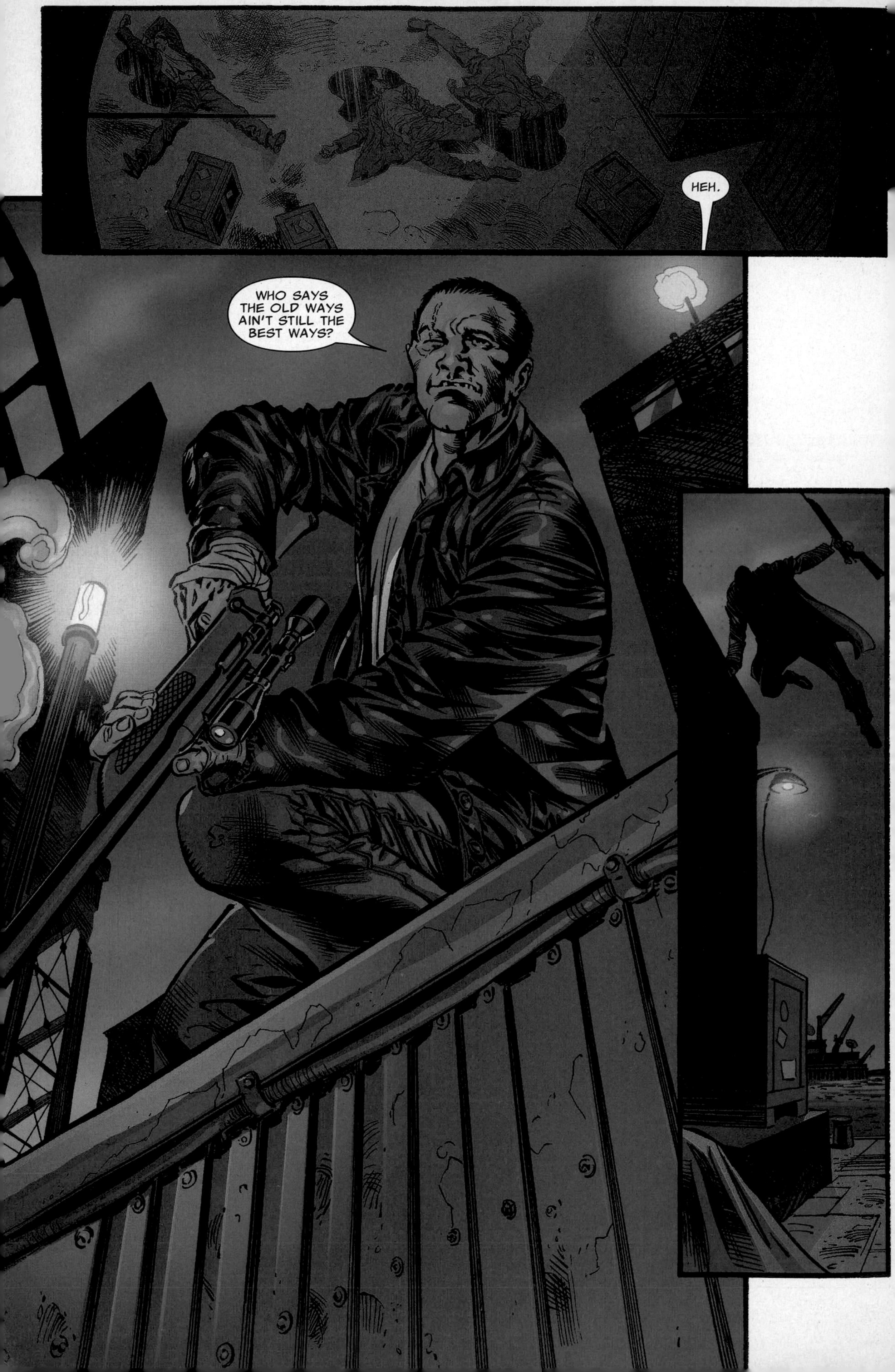
HEH.
WHO SAYS THE OLD WAYS AIN'T STILL THE BEST WAYS?

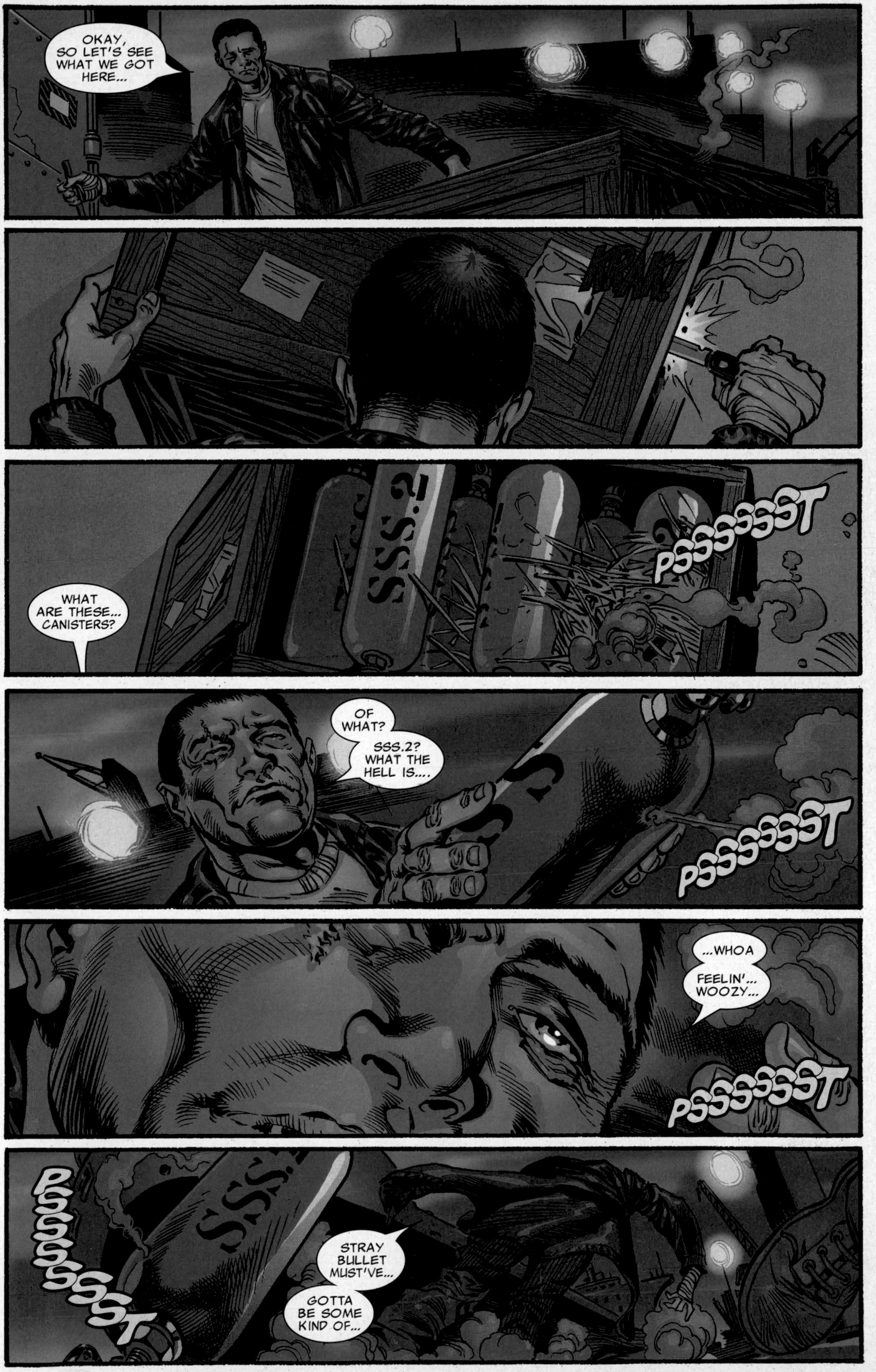

OKAY, SO LET'S SEE WHAT WE GOT HERE...
WHAT ARE THESE... CANISTERS?
PSSSSSST
OF WHAT?
SSS.2? WHAT THE HELL IS....
PSSSSSST
...WHOA
FEELIN'... WOOZY...
PSSSSSST
PSSSSSST
STRAY BULLET MUST'VE...
GOTTA BE SOME KIND OF...

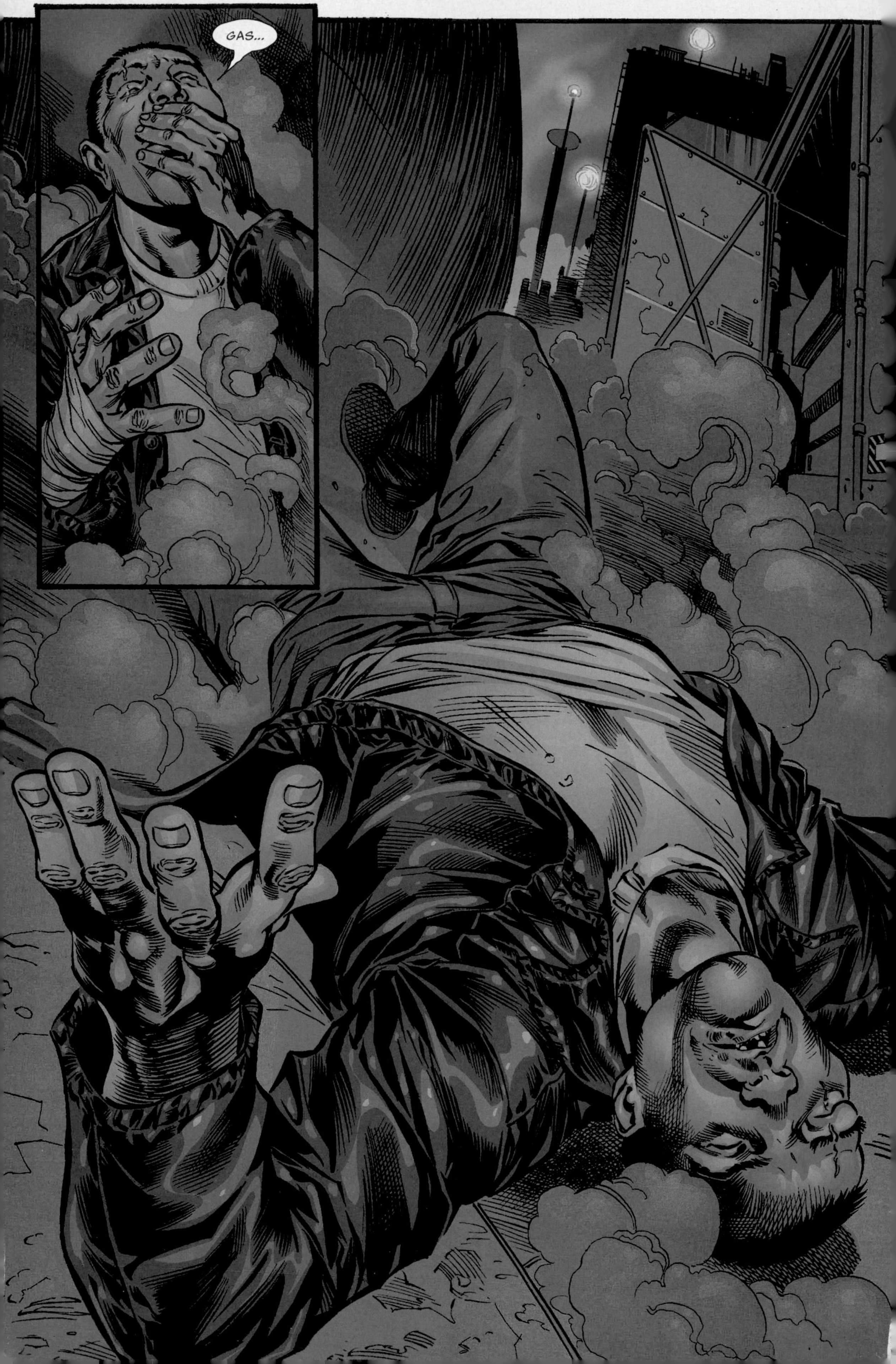
GAS...

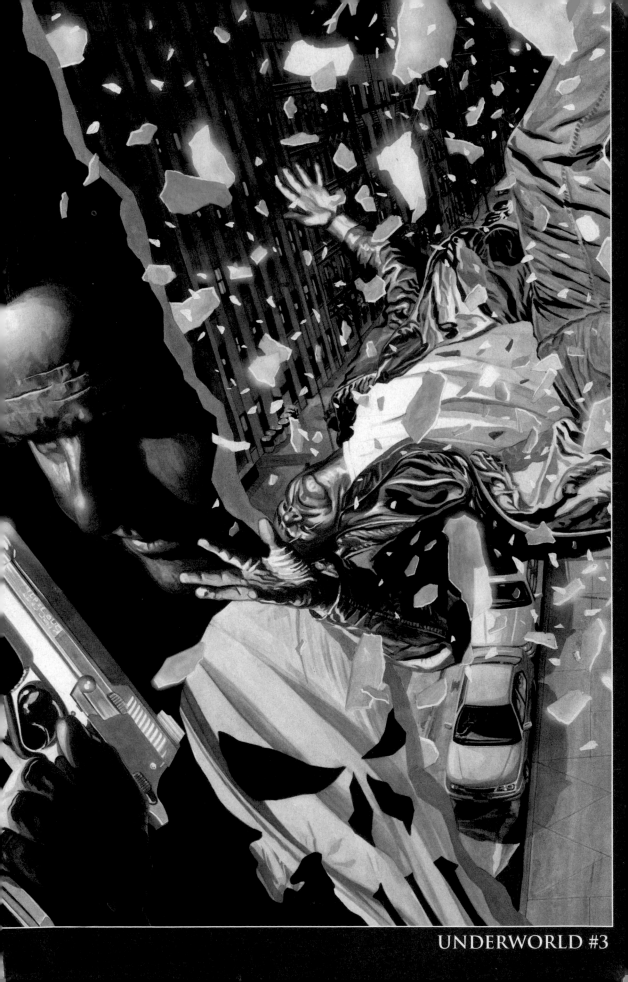

UNDERWORLD #3

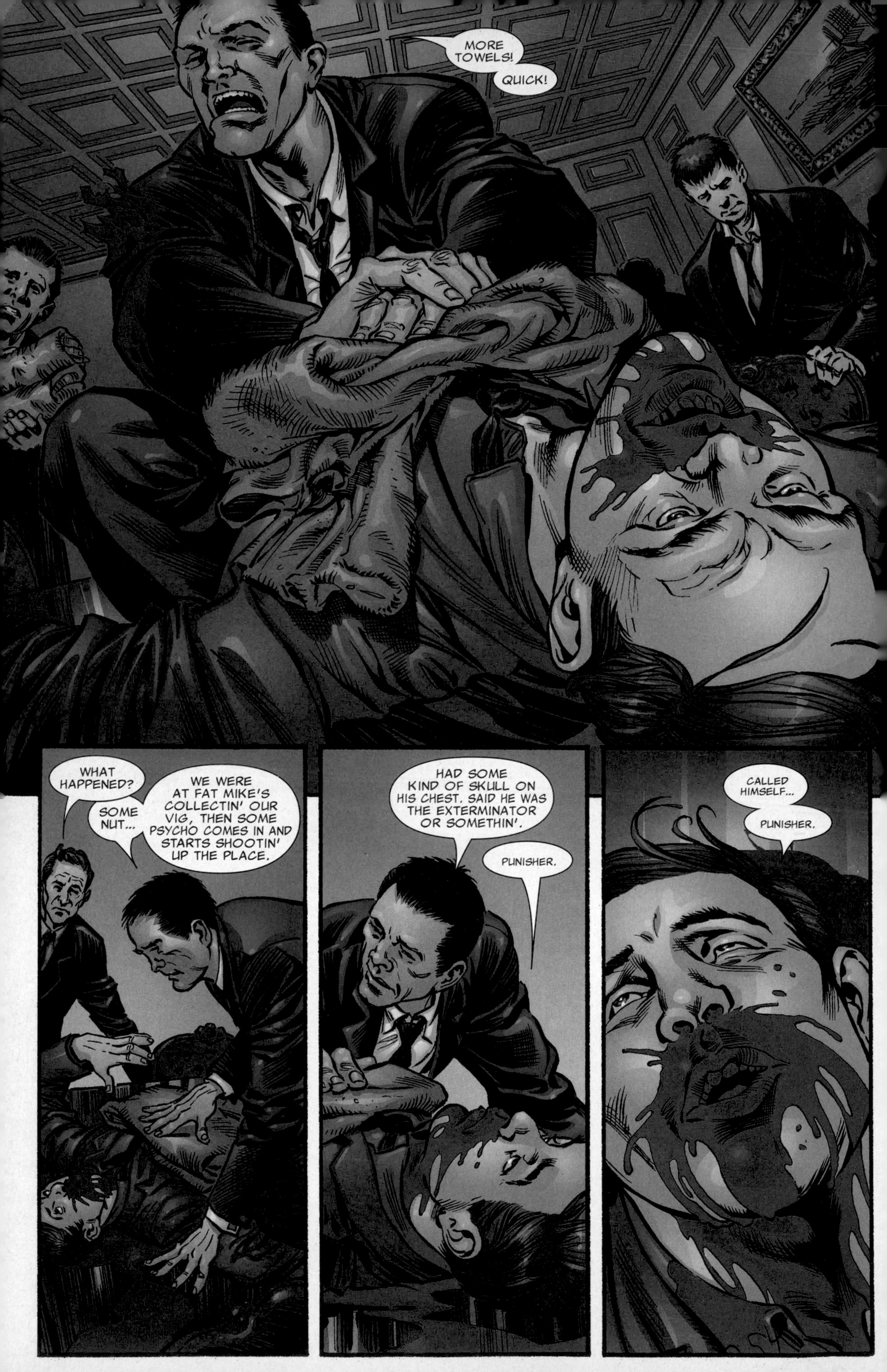

MORE TOWELS!
QUICK!
WHAT HAPPENED?
SOME NUT...
WE WERE AT FAT MIKE'S COLLECTIN' OUR VIG, THEN SOME PSYCHO COMES IN AND STARTS SHOOTIN' UP THE PLACE.
HAD SOME KIND OF SKULL ON HIS CHEST. SAID HE WAS THE EXTERMINATOR OR SOMETHIN'.
PUNISHER.
CALLED HIMSELF...
PUNISHER.

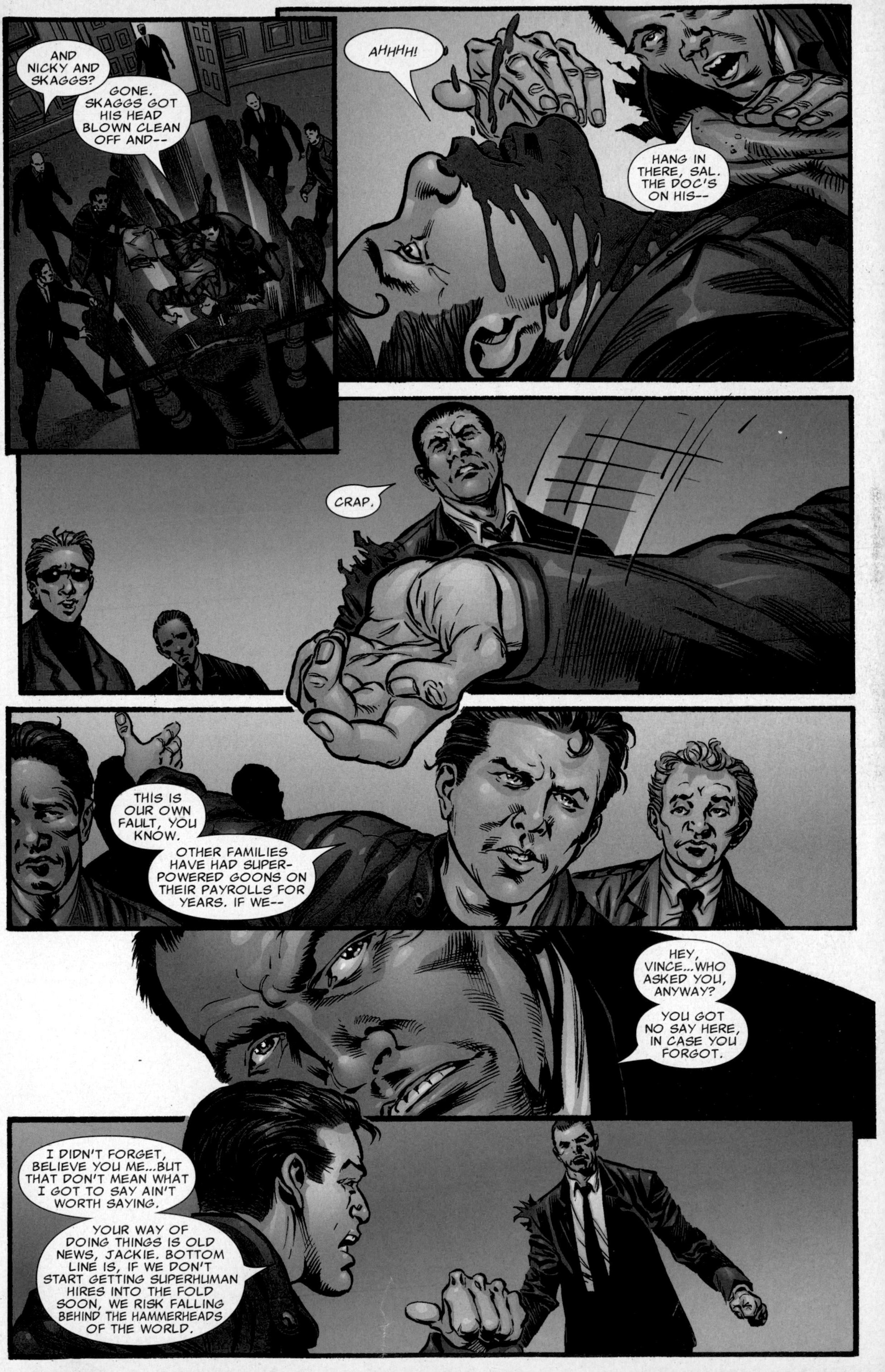
AND NICKY AND SKAGGS?
GONE. SKAGGS GOT HIS HEAD BLOWN CLEAN OFF AND--
AHHHH!
HANG IN THERE, SAL. THE DOC'S ON HIS--
CRAP.
THIS IS OUR OWN FAULT, YOU KNOW.
OTHER FAMILIES HAVE HAD SUPER-POWERED GOONS ON THEIR PAYROLLS FOR YEARS. IF WE--
HEY, VINCE...WHO ASKED YOU, ANYWAY?
YOU GOT NO SAY HERE, IN CASE YOU FORGOT.
I DIDN'T FORGET, BELIEVE YOU ME...BUT THAT DON'T MEAN WHAT I GOT TO SAY AIN'T WORTH SAYING.
YOUR WAY OF DOING THINGS IS OLD NEWS, JACKIE. BOTTOM LINE IS, IF WE DON'T START GETTING SUPERHUMAN HIRES INTO THE FOLD SOON, WE RISK FALLING BEHIND THE HAMMERHEADS OF THE WORLD.

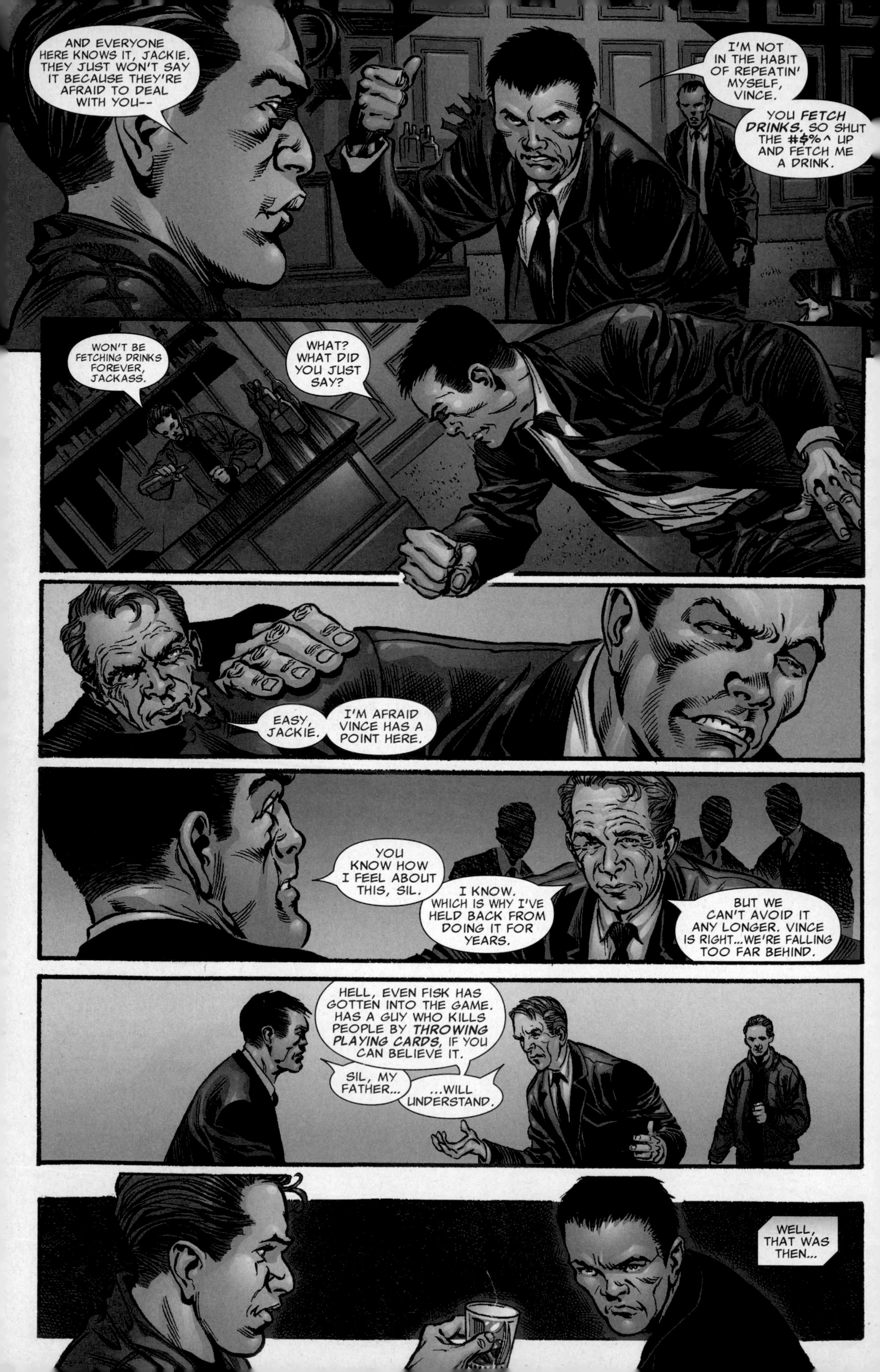
AND EVERYONE HERE KNOWS IT, JACKIE. THEY JUST WON'T SAY IT BECAUSE THEY'RE AFRAID TO DEAL WITH YOU--
I'M NOT IN THE HABIT OF REPEATIN' MYSELF, VINCE.
YOU FETCH DRINKS. SO SHUT THE #$%^ UP AND FETCH ME A DRINK.
WON'T BE FETCHING DRINKS FOREVER, JACKASS.
WHAT? WHAT DID YOU JUST SAY?
EASY, JACKIE.
I'M AFRAID VINCE HAS A POINT HERE.
YOU KNOW HOW I FEEL ABOUT THIS, SIL.
I KNOW. WHICH IS WHY I'VE HELD BACK FROM DOING IT FOR YEARS.
BUT WE CAN'T AVOID IT ANY LONGER. VINCE IS RIGHT...WE'RE FALLING TOO FAR BEHIND.
HELL, EVEN FISK HAS GOTTEN INTO THE GAME. HAS A GUY WHO KILLS PEOPLE BY THROWING PLAYING CARDS, IF YOU CAN BELIEVE IT.
SIL, MY FATHER...
...WILL UNDERSTAND.
WELL, THAT WAS THEN...

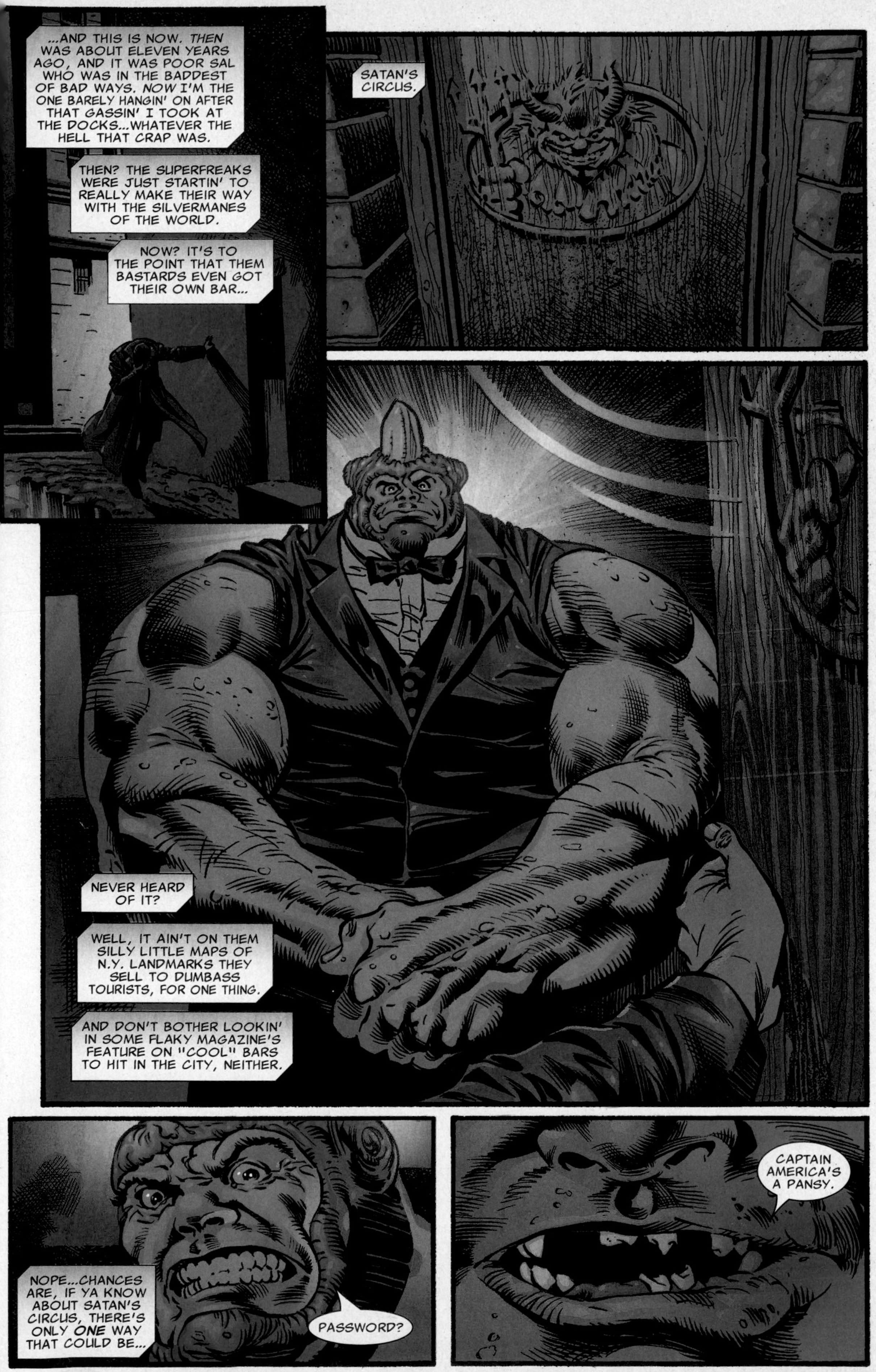
...AND THIS IS NOW. THEN WAS ABOUT ELEVEN YEARS AGO, AND IT WAS POOR SAL WHO WAS IN THE BADDEST OF BAD WAYS. NOW I'M THE ONE BARELY HANGIN' ON AFTER THAT GASSIN' I TOOK AT THE DOCKS...WHATEVER THE HELL THAT CRAP WAS.
THEN? THE SUPERFREAKS WERE JUST STARTIN' TO REALLY MAKE THEIR WAY WITH THE SILVERMANES OF THE WORLD.
NOW? IT'S TO THE POINT THAT THEM BASTARDS EVEN GOT THEIR OWN BAR...
SATAN'S CIRCUS.
NEVER HEARD OF IT?
WELL, IT AIN'T ON THEM SILLY LITTLE MAPS OF N.Y. LANDMARKS THEY SELL TO DUMBASS TOURISTS, FOR ONE THING.
AND DON'T BOTHER LOOKIN' IN SOME FLAKY MAGAZINE'S FEATURE ON "COOL" BARS TO HIT IN THE CITY, NEITHER.
NOPE...CHANCES ARE, IF YA KNOW ABOUT SATAN'S CIRCUS, THERE'S ONLY ONE WAY THAT COULD BE...
PASSWORD?
CAPTAIN AMERICA'S A PANSY.

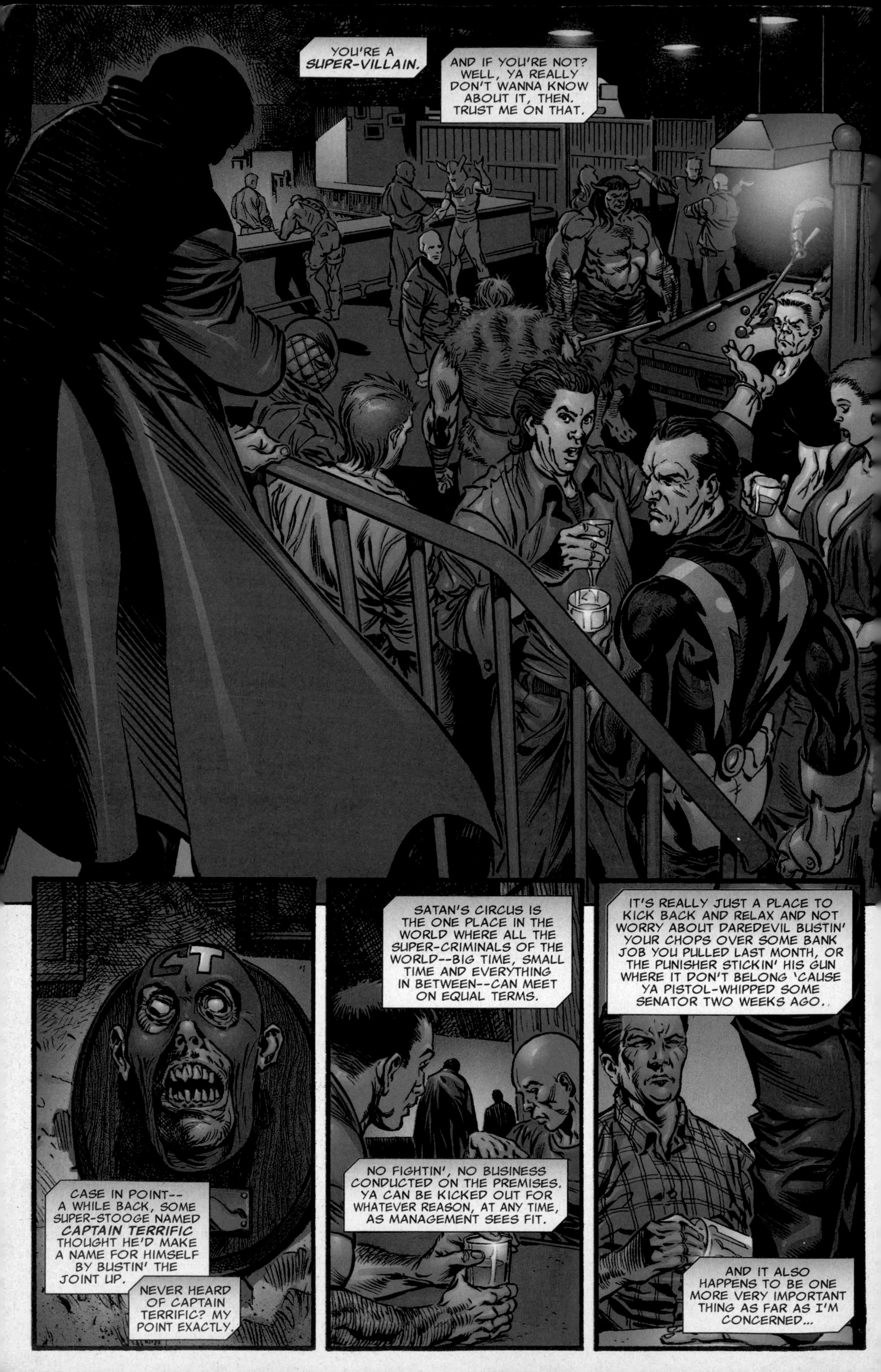
YOU'RE A SUPER-VILLAIN.
AND IF YOU'RE NOT? WELL, YA REALLY DON'T WANNA KNOW ABOUT IT, THEN. TRUST ME ON THAT.
CASE IN POINT-- A WHILE BACK, SOME SUPER-STOOGE NAMED CAPTAIN TERRIFIC THOUGHT HE'D MAKE A NAME FOR HIMSELF BY BUSTIN' THE JOINT UP.
NEVER HEARD OF CAPTAIN TERRIFIC? MY POINT EXACTLY.
SATAN'S CIRCUS IS THE ONE PLACE IN THE WORLD WHERE ALL THE SUPER-CRIMINALS OF THE WORLD--BIG TIME, SMALL TIME AND EVERYTHING IN BETWEEN--CAN MEET ON EQUAL TERMS.
NO FIGHTIN', NO BUSINESS CONDUCTED ON THE PREMISES. YA CAN BE KICKED OUT FOR WHATEVER REASON, AT ANY TIME, AS MANAGEMENT SEES FIT.
IT'S REALLY JUST A PLACE TO KICK BACK AND RELAX AND NOT WORRY ABOUT DAREDEVIL BUSTIN' YOUR CHOPS OVER SOME BANK JOB YOU PULLED LAST MONTH, OR THE PUNISHER STICKIN' HIS GUN WHERE IT DON'T BELONG 'CAUSE YA PISTOL-WHIPPED SOME SENATOR TWO WEEKS AGO.
AND IT ALSO HAPPENS TO BE ONE MORE VERY IMPORTANT THING AS FAR AS I'M CONCERNED...

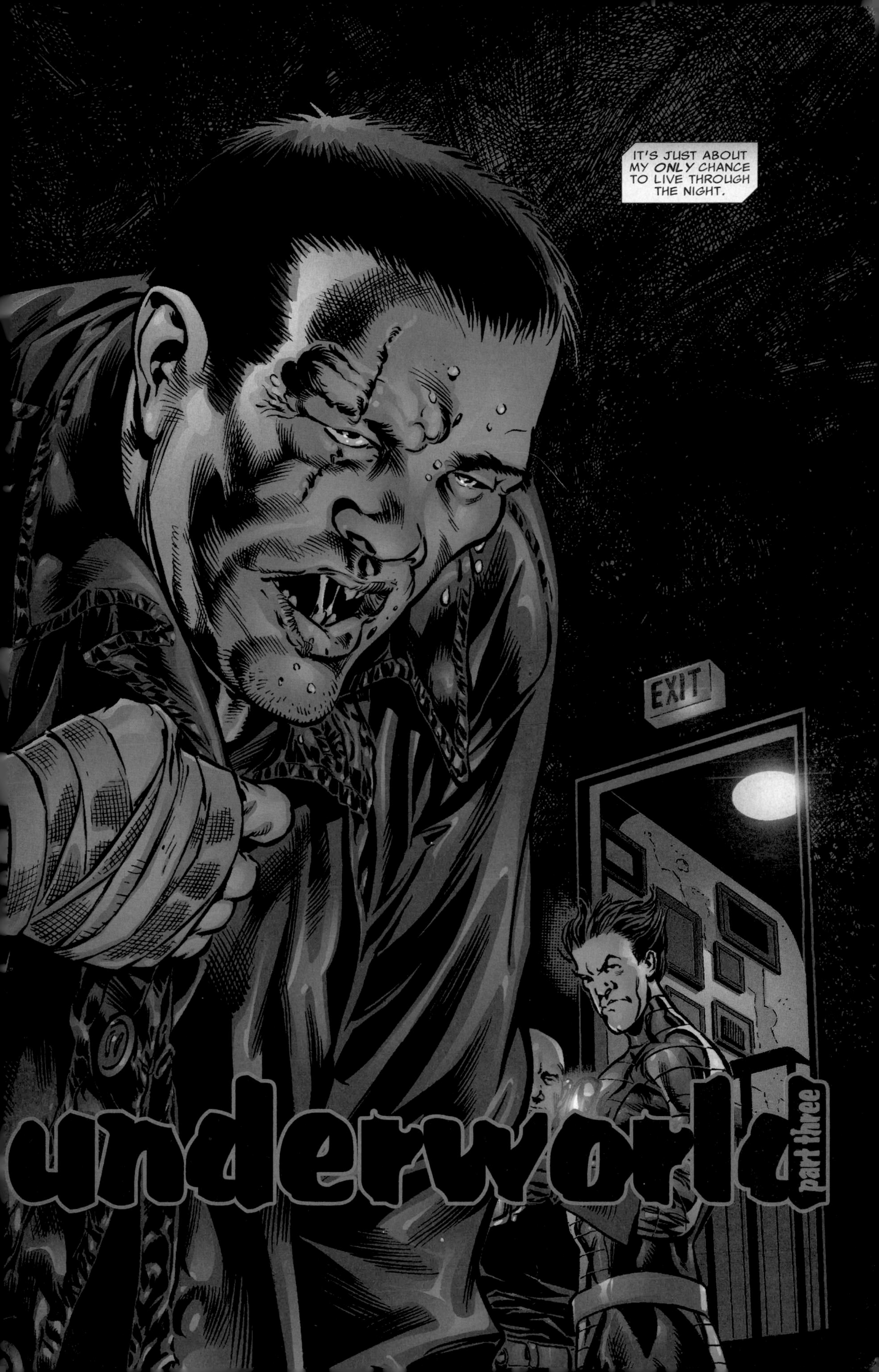
IT'S JUST ABOUT MY ONLY CHANCE TO LIVE THROUGH THE NIGHT.
EXIT
underworld
part three

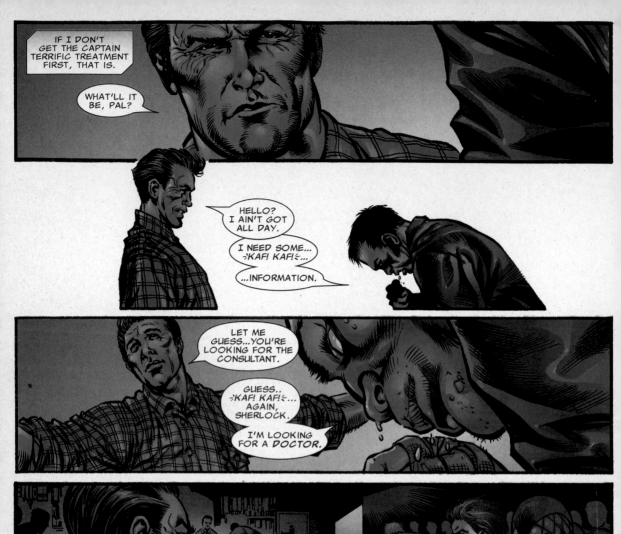

IF I DON'T GET THE CAPTAIN TERRIFIC TREATMENT FIRST, THAT IS.

WHAT'LL IT BE, PAL?

HELLO? I AIN'T GOT ALL DAY.

I NEED SOME... ⸖KAF! KAF!⸕...

...INFORMATION.

LET ME GUESS...YOU'RE LOOKING FOR THE CONSULTANT.

GUESS.. ⸖KAF! KAF!⸕... AGAIN, SHERLOCK.

I'M LOOKING FOR A DOCTOR.

I FIGURE IF YOU'RE SUPPOSEDLY ABLE TO POINT ME IN THE DIRECTION OF THIS CONSULTANT CLOWN, YOU CAN ALSO TIP ME OFF TO A DOC WHO AIN'T GONNA ASK TOO MANY QUESTIONS.

EXCUSE ME A SEC, PAL.

WHAT THE !#✳&^ ARE YOU ALL LOOKIN' AT?

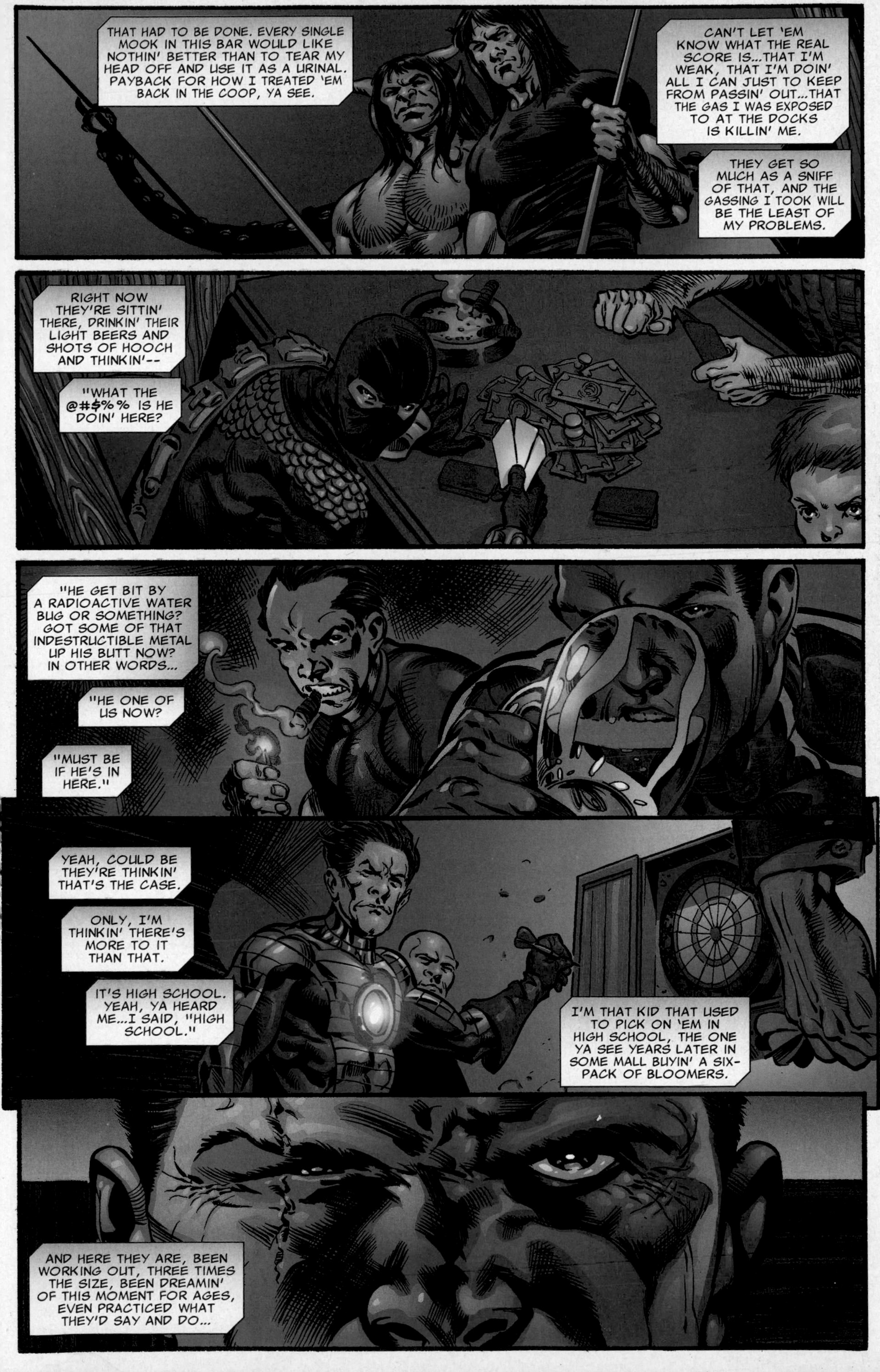
THAT HAD TO BE DONE. EVERY SINGLE MOOK IN THIS BAR WOULD LIKE NOTHIN' BETTER THAN TO TEAR MY HEAD OFF AND USE IT AS A URINAL. PAYBACK FOR HOW I TREATED 'EM BACK IN THE COOP, YA SEE.
CAN'T LET 'EM KNOW WHAT THE REAL SCORE IS...THAT I'M WEAK, THAT I'M DOIN' ALL I CAN JUST TO KEEP FROM PASSIN' OUT...THAT THE GAS I WAS EXPOSED TO AT THE DOCKS IS KILLIN' ME.
THEY GET SO MUCH AS A SNIFF OF THAT, AND THE GASSING I TOOK WILL BE THE LEAST OF MY PROBLEMS.
RIGHT NOW THEY'RE SITTIN' THERE, DRINKIN' THEIR LIGHT BEERS AND SHOTS OF HOOCH AND THINKIN'--
"WHAT THE @#$%% IS HE DOIN' HERE?
"HE GET BIT BY A RADIOACTIVE WATER BUG OR SOMETHING? GOT SOME OF THAT INDESTRUCTIBLE METAL UP HIS BUTT NOW? IN OTHER WORDS...
"HE ONE OF US NOW?
"MUST BE IF HE'S IN HERE."
YEAH, COULD BE THEY'RE THINKIN' THAT'S THE CASE.
ONLY, I'M THINKIN' THERE'S MORE TO IT THAN THAT.
IT'S HIGH SCHOOL. YEAH, YA HEARD ME...I SAID, "HIGH SCHOOL."
I'M THAT KID THAT USED TO PICK ON 'EM IN HIGH SCHOOL, THE ONE YA SEE YEARS LATER IN SOME MALL BUYIN' A SIX-PACK OF BLOOMERS.
AND HERE THEY ARE, BEEN WORKING OUT, THREE TIMES THE SIZE, BEEN DREAMIN' OF THIS MOMENT FOR AGES, EVEN PRACTICED WHAT THEY'D SAY AND DO...

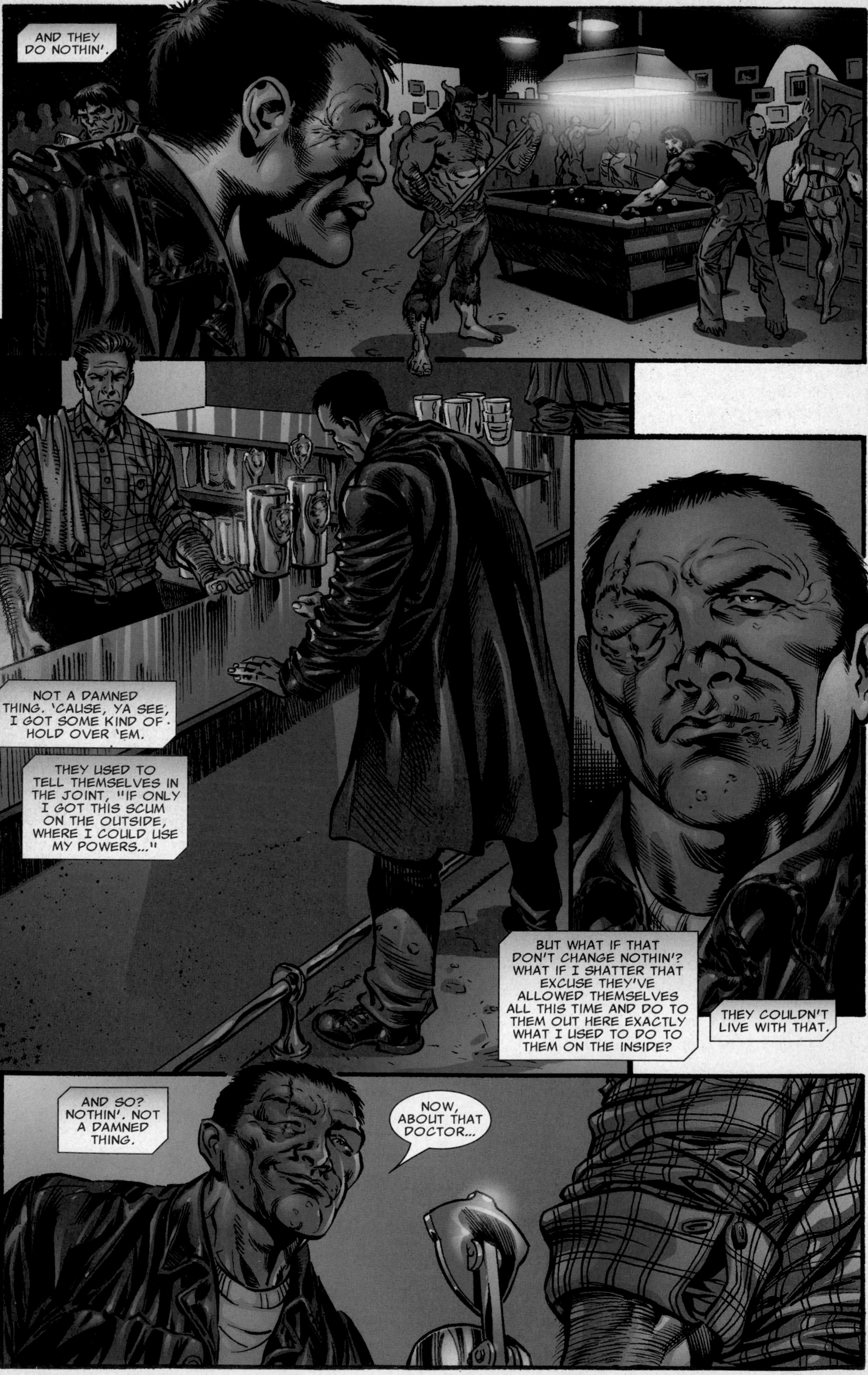
AND THEY DO NOTHIN'.
NOT A DAMNED THING. 'CAUSE, YA SEE, I GOT SOME KIND OF HOLD OVER 'EM.
THEY USED TO TELL THEMSELVES IN THE JOINT, "IF ONLY I GOT THIS SCUM ON THE OUTSIDE, WHERE I COULD USE MY POWERS..."
BUT WHAT IF THAT DON'T CHANGE NOTHIN'? WHAT IF I SHATTER THAT EXCUSE THEY'VE ALLOWED THEMSELVES ALL THIS TIME AND DO TO THEM OUT HERE EXACTLY WHAT I USED TO DO TO THEM ON THE INSIDE?
THEY COULDN'T LIVE WITH THAT.
AND SO? NOTHIN'. NOT A DAMNED THING.
NOW, ABOUT THAT DOCTOR...

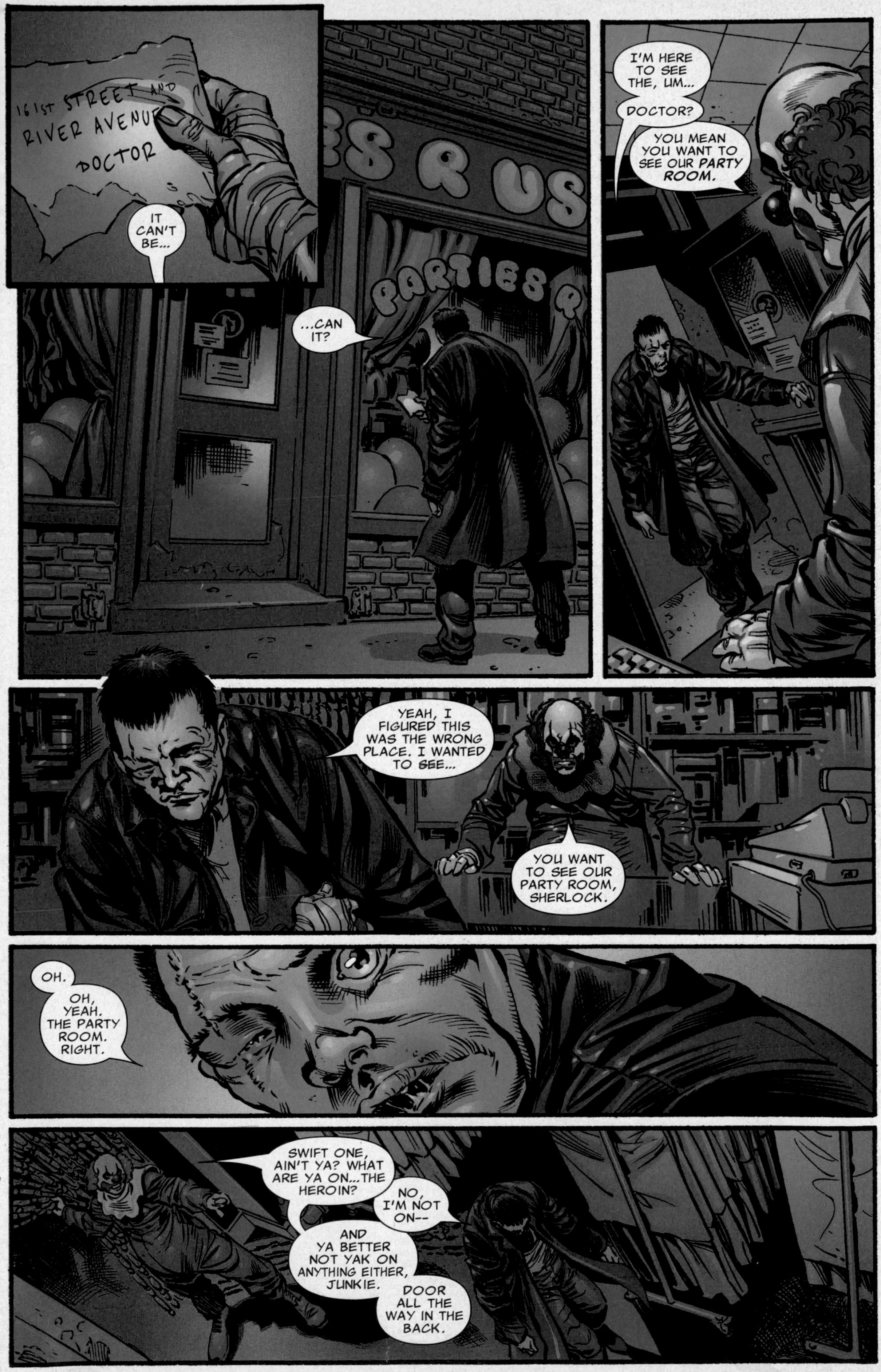
161st STREET AND
RIVER AVENUE
DOCTOR
IT CAN'T BE...
...CAN IT?
I'M HERE TO SEE THE, UM...
DOCTOR?
YOU MEAN YOU WANT TO SEE OUR PARTY ROOM.
YEAH, I FIGURED THIS WAS THE WRONG PLACE. I WANTED TO SEE...
YOU WANT TO SEE OUR PARTY ROOM, SHERLOCK.
OH.
OH, YEAH. THE PARTY ROOM. RIGHT.
SWIFT ONE, AIN'T YA? WHAT ARE YA ON...THE HEROIN?
NO, I'M NOT ON--
AND YA BETTER NOT YAK ON ANYTHING EITHER, JUNKIE.
DOOR ALL THE WAY IN THE BACK.

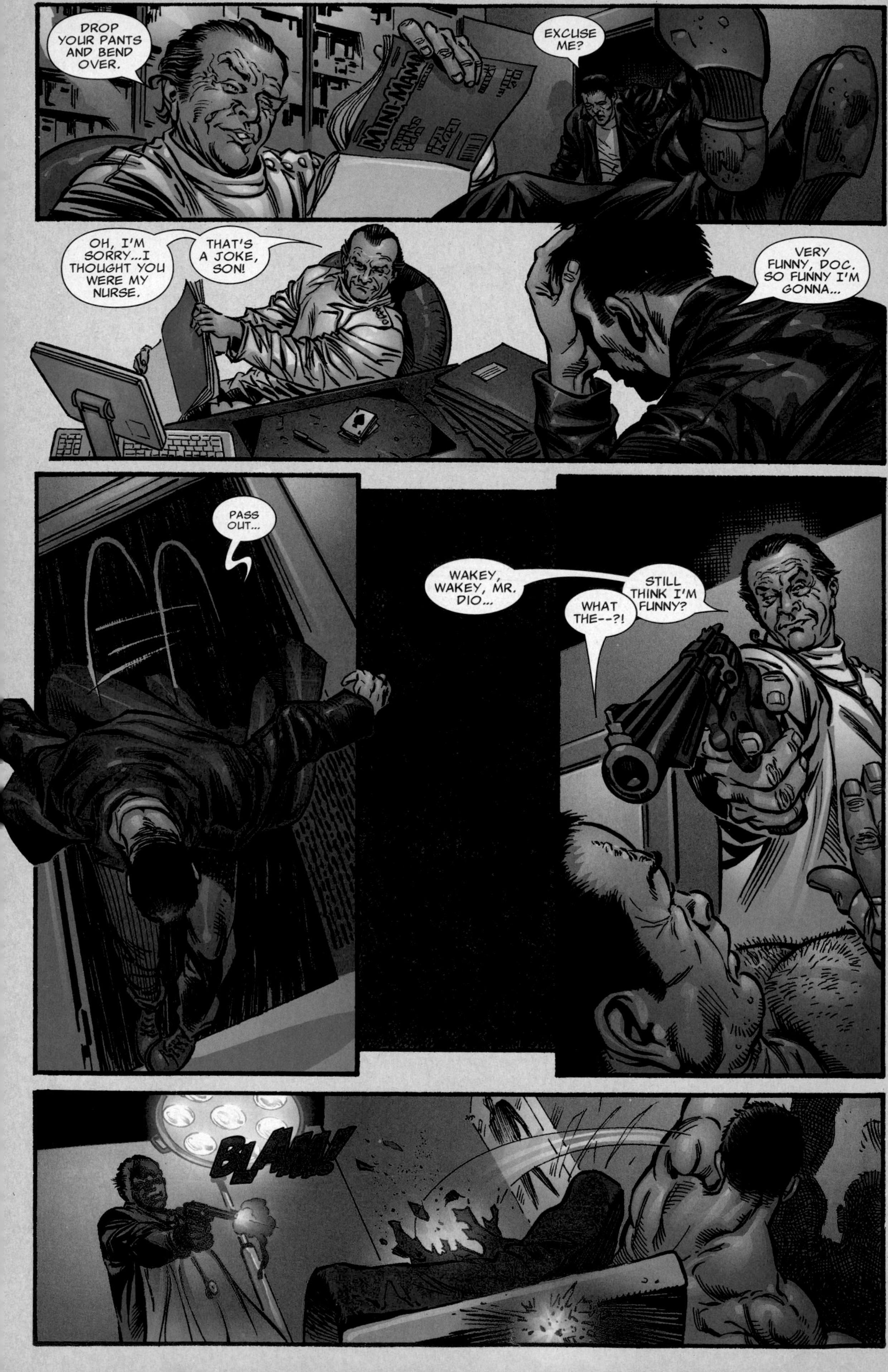
DROP YOUR PANTS AND BEND OVER.
EXCUSE ME?
MINI-MAM
OH, I'M SORRY...I THOUGHT YOU WERE MY NURSE.
THAT'S A JOKE, SON!
VERY FUNNY, DOC. SO FUNNY I'M GONNA...
PASS OUT...
WAKEY, WAKEY, MR. DIO...
STILL THINK I'M FUNNY?
WHAT THE--?!
BLAM!

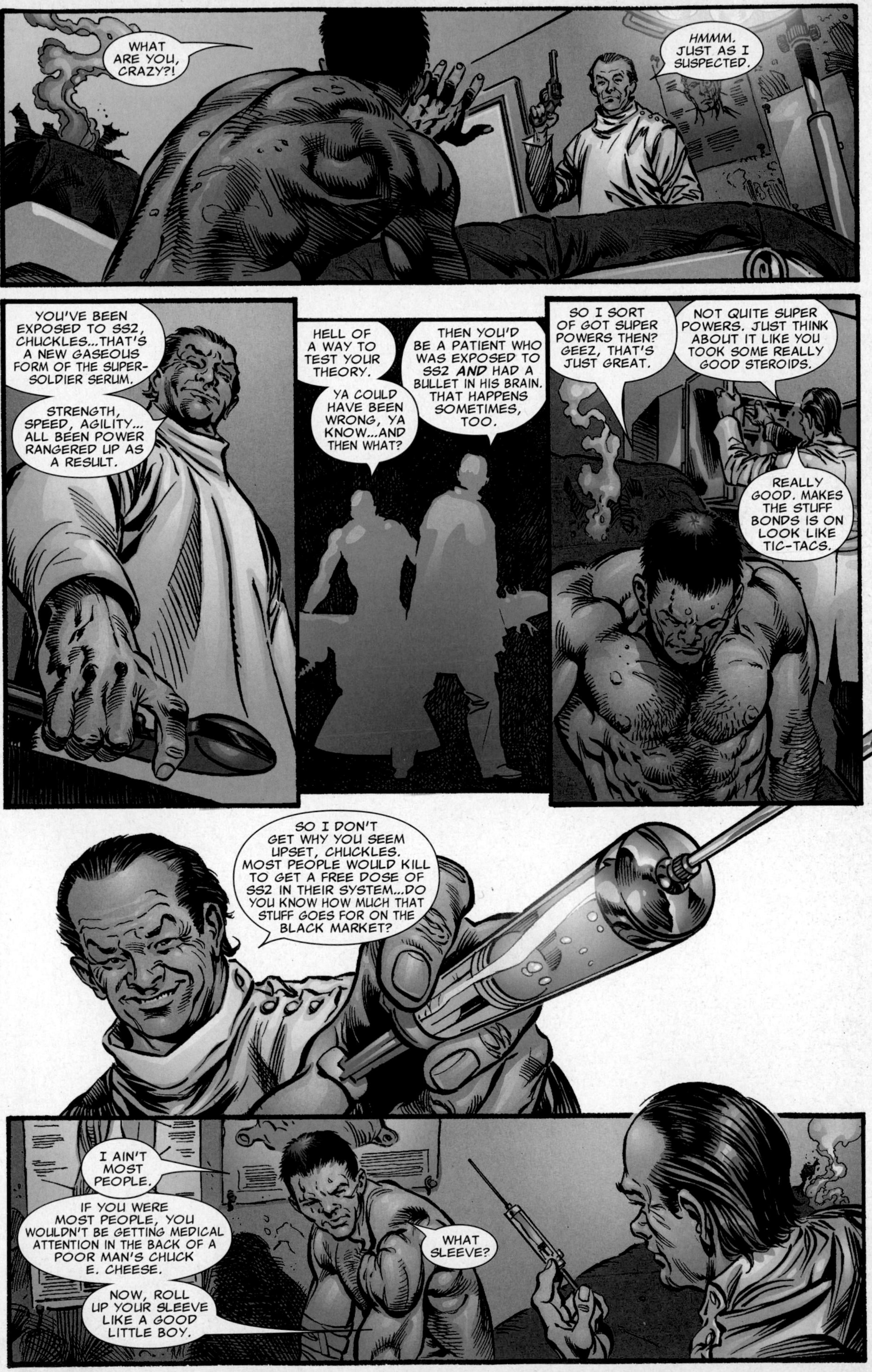
WHAT ARE YOU, CRAZY?!
HMMM. JUST AS I SUSPECTED.
YOU'VE BEEN EXPOSED TO SS2, CHUCKLES...THAT'S A NEW GASEOUS FORM OF THE SUPER-SOLDIER SERUM.
STRENGTH, SPEED, AGILITY... ALL BEEN POWER RANGERED UP AS A RESULT.
HELL OF A WAY TO TEST YOUR THEORY.
YA COULD HAVE BEEN WRONG, YA KNOW...AND THEN WHAT?
THEN YOU'D BE A PATIENT WHO WAS EXPOSED TO SS2 AND HAD A BULLET IN HIS BRAIN. THAT HAPPENS SOMETIMES, TOO.
SO I SORT OF GOT SUPER POWERS THEN? GEEZ, THAT'S JUST GREAT.
NOT QUITE SUPER POWERS. JUST THINK ABOUT IT LIKE YOU TOOK SOME REALLY GOOD STEROIDS.
REALLY GOOD. MAKES THE STUFF BONDS IS ON LOOK LIKE TIC-TACS.
SO I DON'T GET WHY YOU SEEM UPSET, CHUCKLES. MOST PEOPLE WOULD KILL TO GET A FREE DOSE OF SS2 IN THEIR SYSTEM...DO YOU KNOW HOW MUCH THAT STUFF GOES FOR ON THE BLACK MARKET?
I AIN'T MOST PEOPLE.
IF YOU WERE MOST PEOPLE, YOU WOULDN'T BE GETTING MEDICAL ATTENTION IN THE BACK OF A POOR MAN'S CHUCK E. CHEESE.
NOW, ROLL UP YOUR SLEEVE LIKE A GOOD LITTLE BOY.
WHAT SLEEVE?

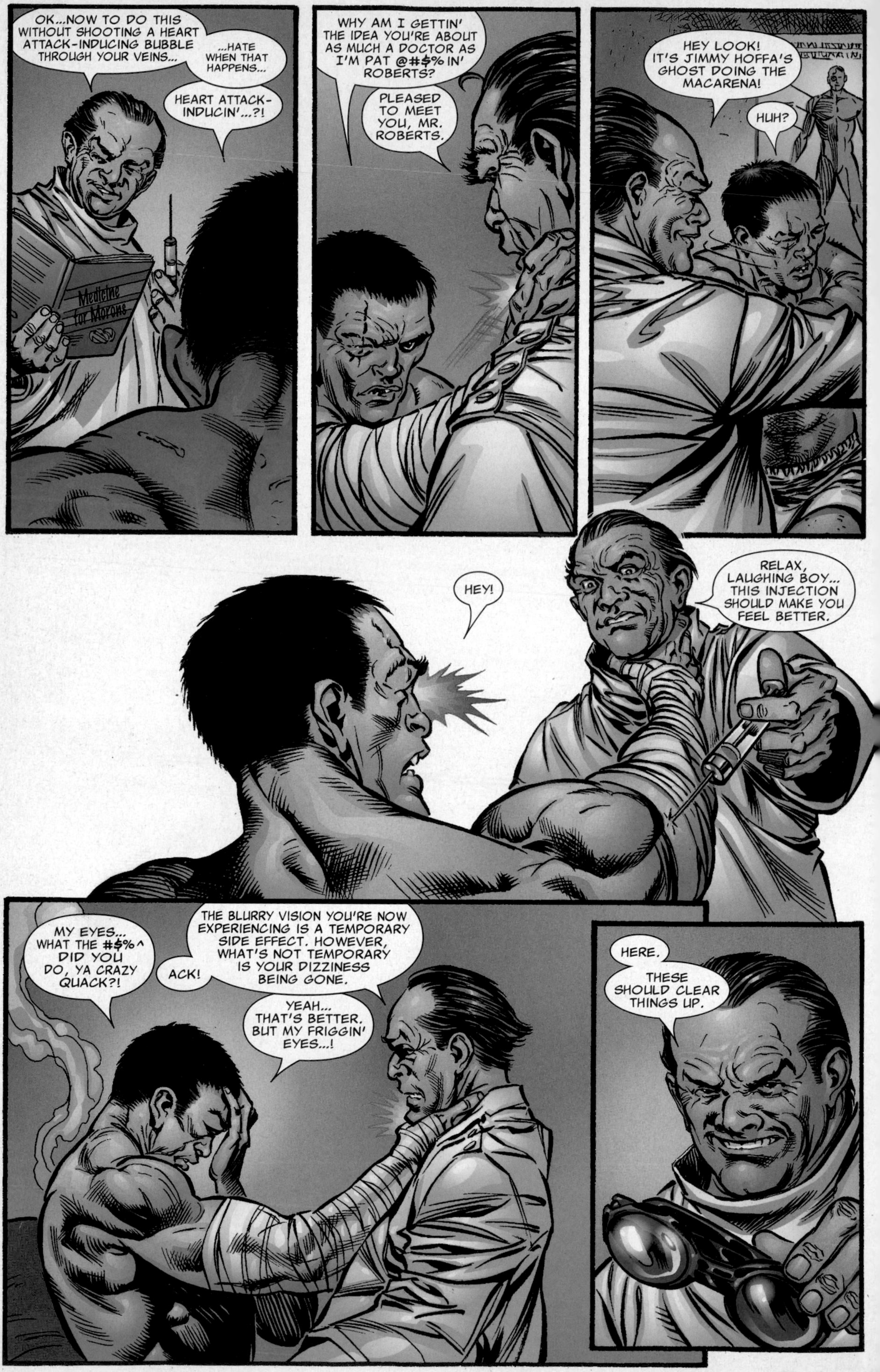
OK...NOW TO DO THIS WITHOUT SHOOTING A HEART ATTACK-INDUCING BUBBLE THROUGH YOUR VEINS...
...HATE WHEN THAT HAPPENS...
HEART ATTACK-INDUCIN'...?!
Medicine for Morons
WHY AM I GETTIN' THE IDEA YOU'RE ABOUT AS MUCH A DOCTOR AS I'M PAT @#$% IN' ROBERTS?
PLEASED TO MEET YOU, MR. ROBERTS.
HEY LOOK! IT'S JIMMY HOFFA'S GHOST DOING THE MACARENA!
HUH?
HEY!
RELAX, LAUGHING BOY... THIS INJECTION SHOULD MAKE YOU FEEL BETTER.
MY EYES... WHAT THE #$%^ DID YOU DO, YA CRAZY QUACK?!
ACK!
THE BLURRY VISION YOU'RE NOW EXPERIENCING IS A TEMPORARY SIDE EFFECT. HOWEVER, WHAT'S NOT TEMPORARY IS YOUR DIZZINESS BEING GONE.
YEAH... THAT'S BETTER. BUT MY FRIGGIN' EYES...!
HERE.
THESE SHOULD CLEAR THINGS UP.

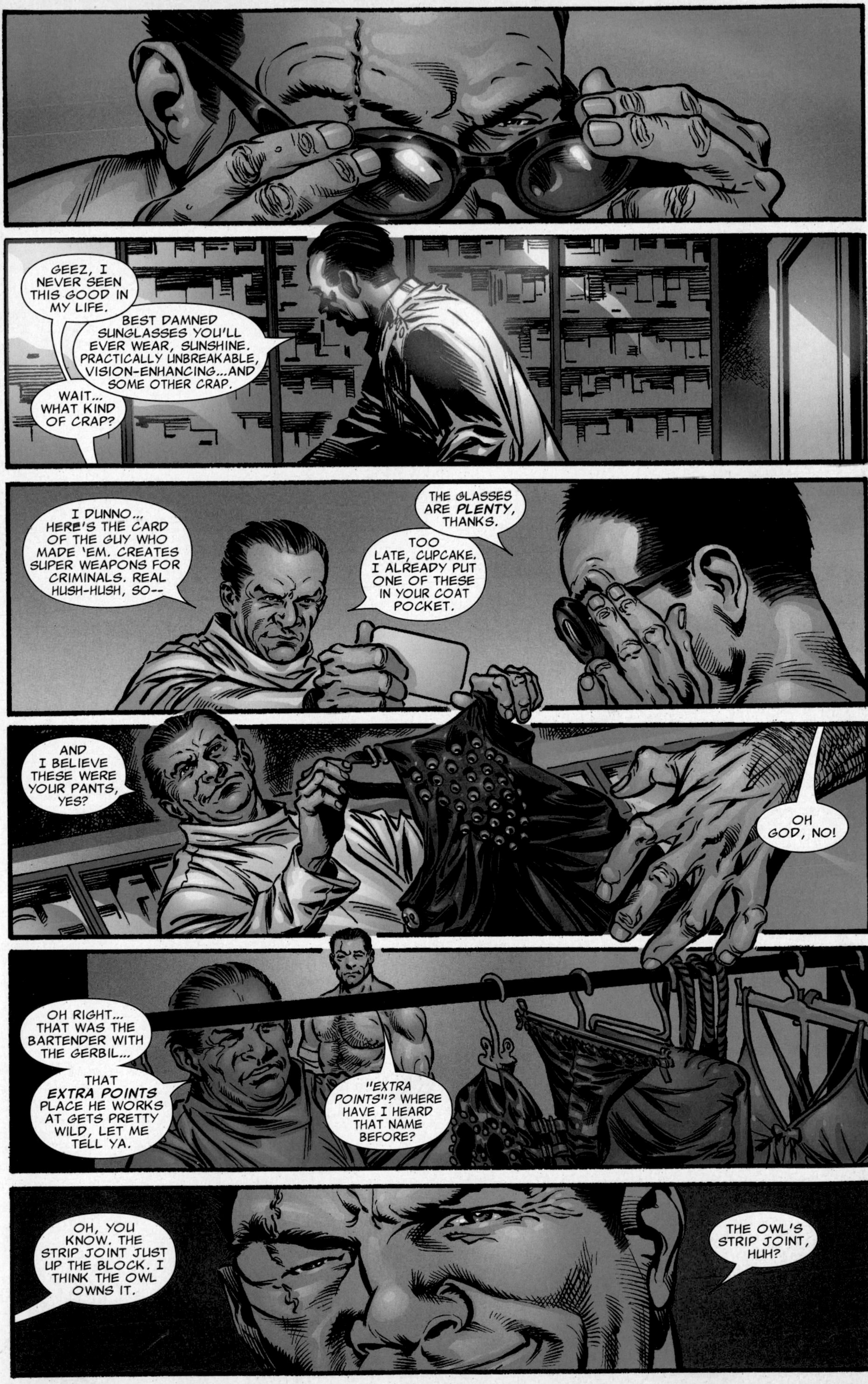
GEEZ, I NEVER SEEN THIS GOOD IN MY LIFE.
BEST DAMNED SUNGLASSES YOU'LL EVER WEAR, SUNSHINE. PRACTICALLY UNBREAKABLE, VISION-ENHANCING...AND SOME OTHER CRAP.
WAIT... WHAT KIND OF CRAP?
I DUNNO... HERE'S THE CARD OF THE GUY WHO MADE 'EM. CREATES SUPER WEAPONS FOR CRIMINALS. REAL HUSH-HUSH, SO--
THE GLASSES ARE PLENTY, THANKS.
TOO LATE, CUPCAKE. I ALREADY PUT ONE OF THESE IN YOUR COAT POCKET.
AND I BELIEVE THESE WERE YOUR PANTS, YES?
OH GOD, NO!
OH RIGHT... THAT WAS THE BARTENDER WITH THE GERBIL...
THAT EXTRA POINTS PLACE HE WORKS AT GETS PRETTY WILD, LET ME TELL YA.
"EXTRA POINTS"? WHERE HAVE I HEARD THAT NAME BEFORE?
OH, YOU KNOW. THE STRIP JOINT JUST UP THE BLOCK. I THINK THE OWL OWNS IT.
THE OWL'S STRIP JOINT, HUH?

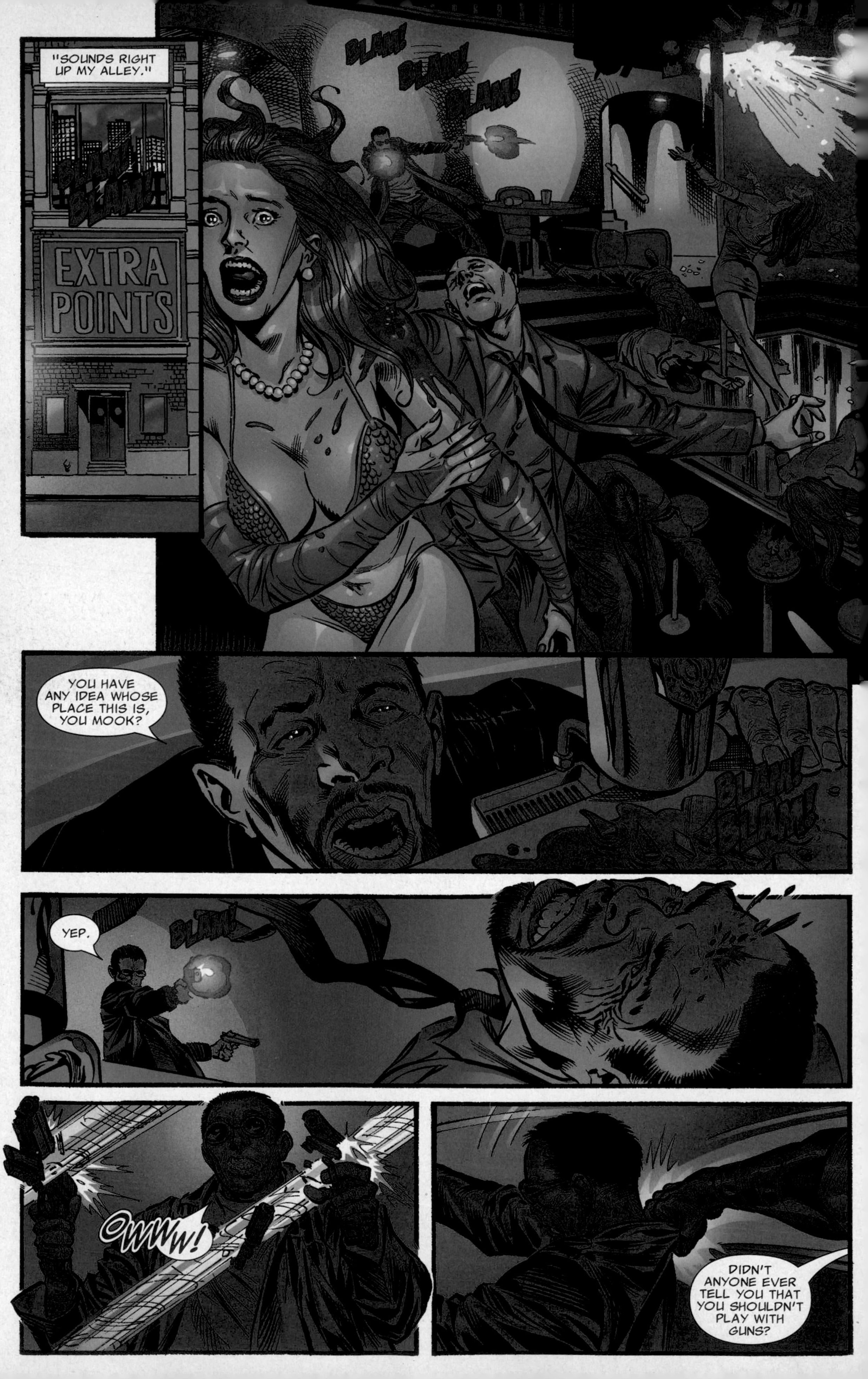
"SOUNDS RIGHT UP MY ALLEY."
BLAM! BLAM!
EXTRA POINTS
BLAM! BLAM! BLAM!
YOU HAVE ANY IDEA WHOSE PLACE THIS IS, YOU MOOK?
BLAM! BLAM!
YEP.
BLAM!
OWWW!
DIDN'T ANYONE EVER TELL YOU THAT YOU SHOULDN'T PLAY WITH GUNS?

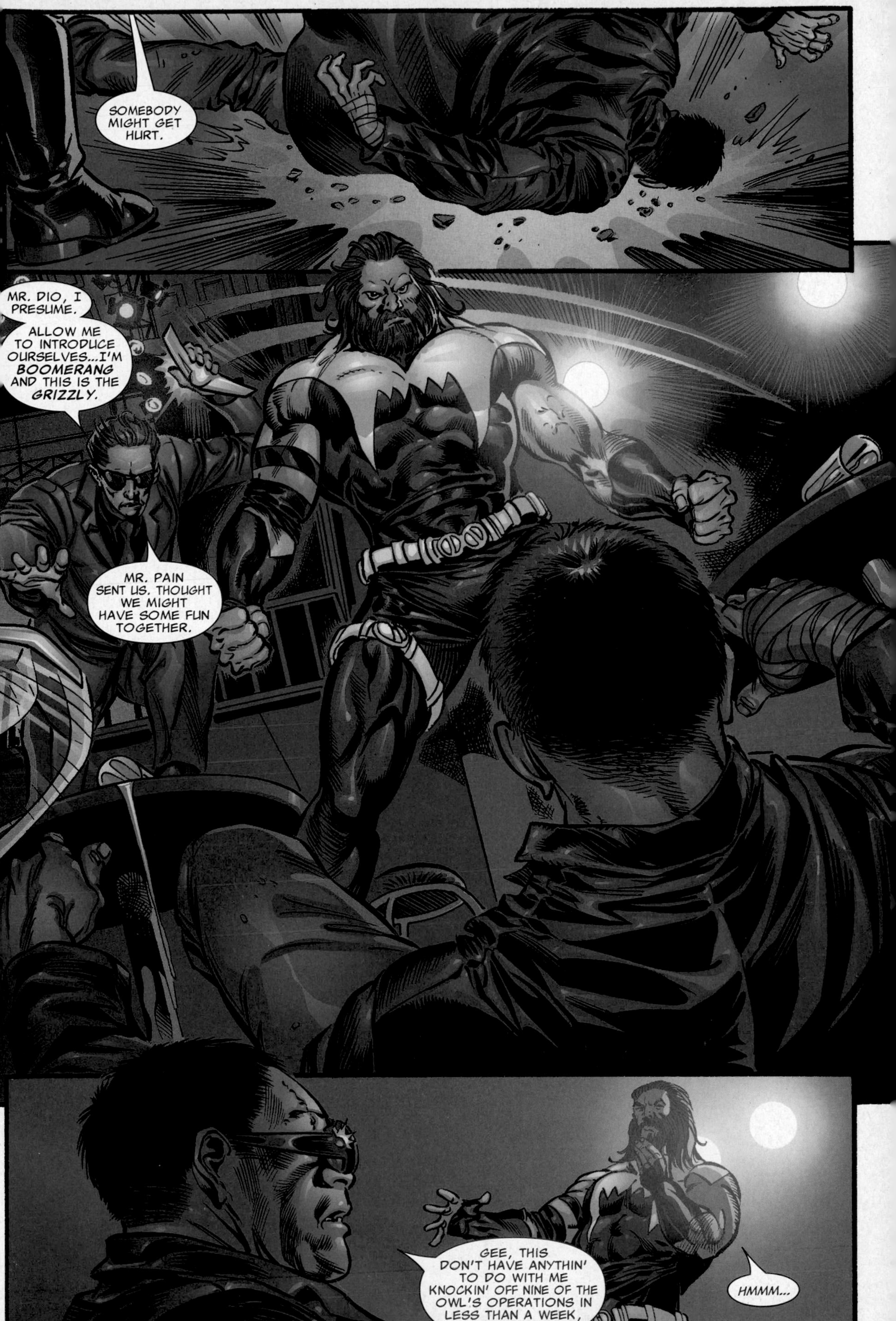
SOMEBODY MIGHT GET HURT.
MR. DIO, I PRESUME.
ALLOW ME TO INTRODUCE OURSELVES...I'M *BOOMERANG* AND THIS IS THE *GRIZZLY*.
MR. PAIN SENT US. THOUGHT WE MIGHT HAVE SOME FUN TOGETHER.
GEE, THIS DON'T HAVE ANYTHIN' TO DO WITH ME KNOCKIN' OFF NINE OF THE OWL'S OPERATIONS IN LESS THAN A WEEK, DOES IT?
HMMM...

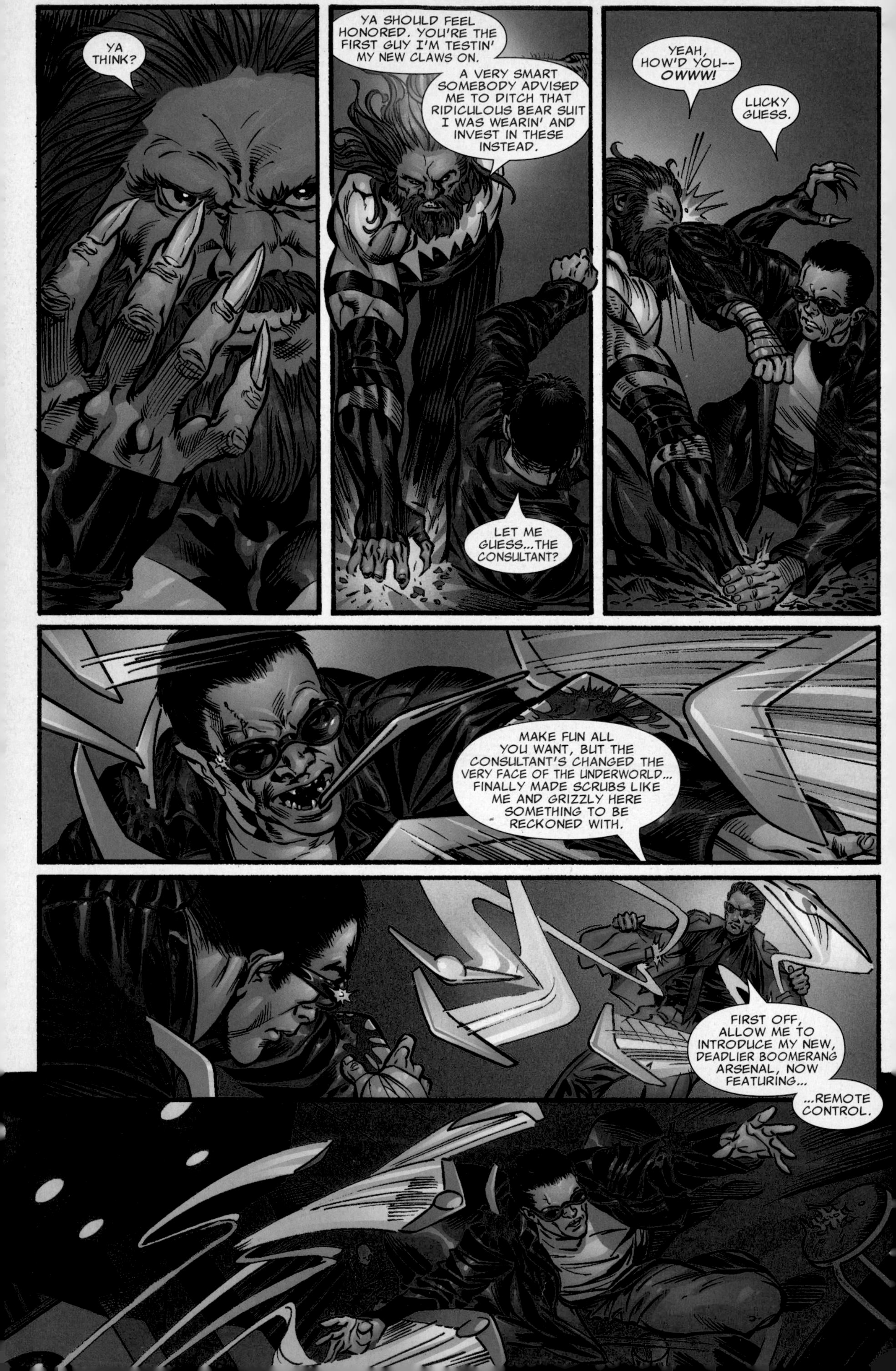

YA THINK?
YA SHOULD FEEL HONORED. YOU'RE THE FIRST GUY I'M TESTIN' MY NEW CLAWS ON.
A VERY SMART SOMEBODY ADVISED ME TO DITCH THAT RIDICULOUS BEAR SUIT I WAS WEARIN' AND INVEST IN THESE INSTEAD.
LET ME GUESS...THE CONSULTANT?
YEAH, HOW'D YOU-- OWWW!
LUCKY GUESS.
MAKE FUN ALL YOU WANT, BUT THE CONSULTANT'S CHANGED THE VERY FACE OF THE UNDERWORLD... FINALLY MADE SCRUBS LIKE ME AND GRIZZLY HERE SOMETHING TO BE RECKONED WITH.
FIRST OFF, ALLOW ME TO INTRODUCE MY NEW, DEADLIER BOOMERANG ARSENAL, NOW FEATURING...
...REMOTE CONTROL.

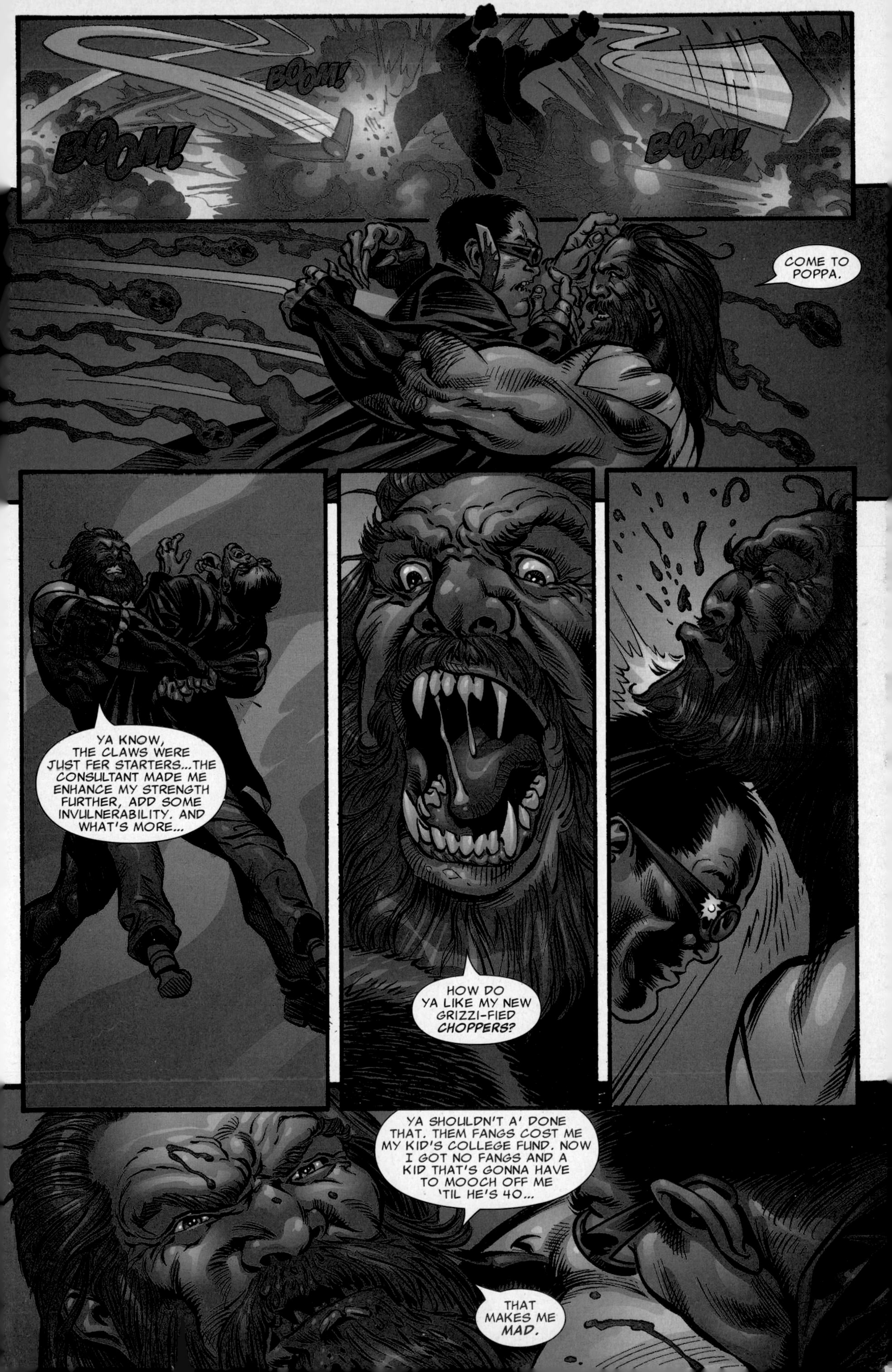
BOOM!
BOOM!
BOOM!
COME TO POPPA.
YA KNOW, THE CLAWS WERE JUST FER STARTERS...THE CONSULTANT MADE ME ENHANCE MY STRENGTH FURTHER, ADD SOME INVULNERABILITY. AND WHAT'S MORE...
HOW DO YA LIKE MY NEW GRIZZI-FIED CHOPPERS?
YA SHOULDN'T A' DONE THAT. THEM FANGS COST ME MY KID'S COLLEGE FUND. NOW I GOT NO FANGS AND A KID THAT'S GONNA HAVE TO MOOCH OFF ME 'TIL HE'S 40...
THAT MAKES ME MAD.

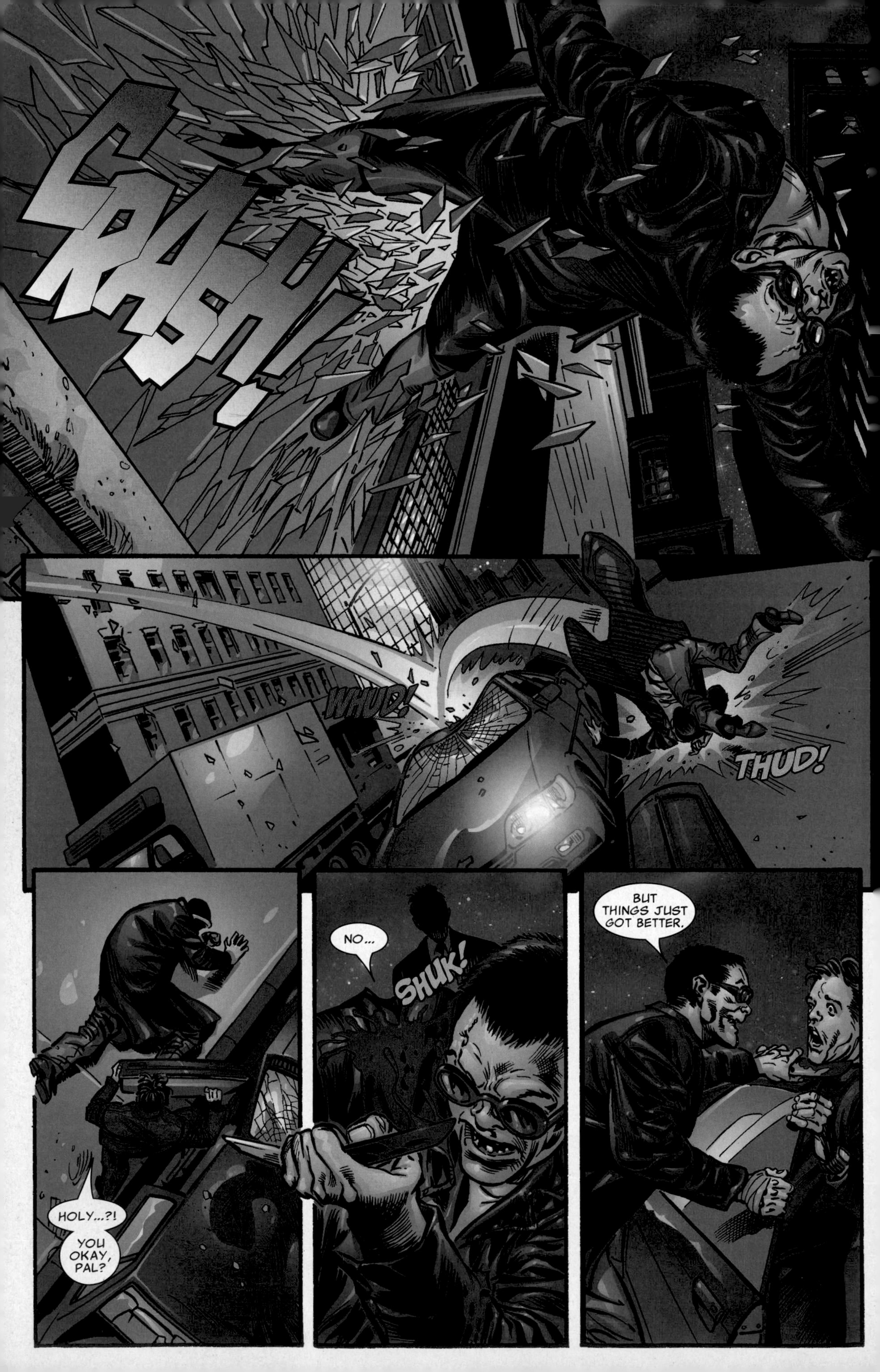
CRASH!
WHUD!
THUD!
HOLY...?!
YOU OKAY, PAL?
NO...
SHUK!
BUT THINGS JUST GOT BETTER.

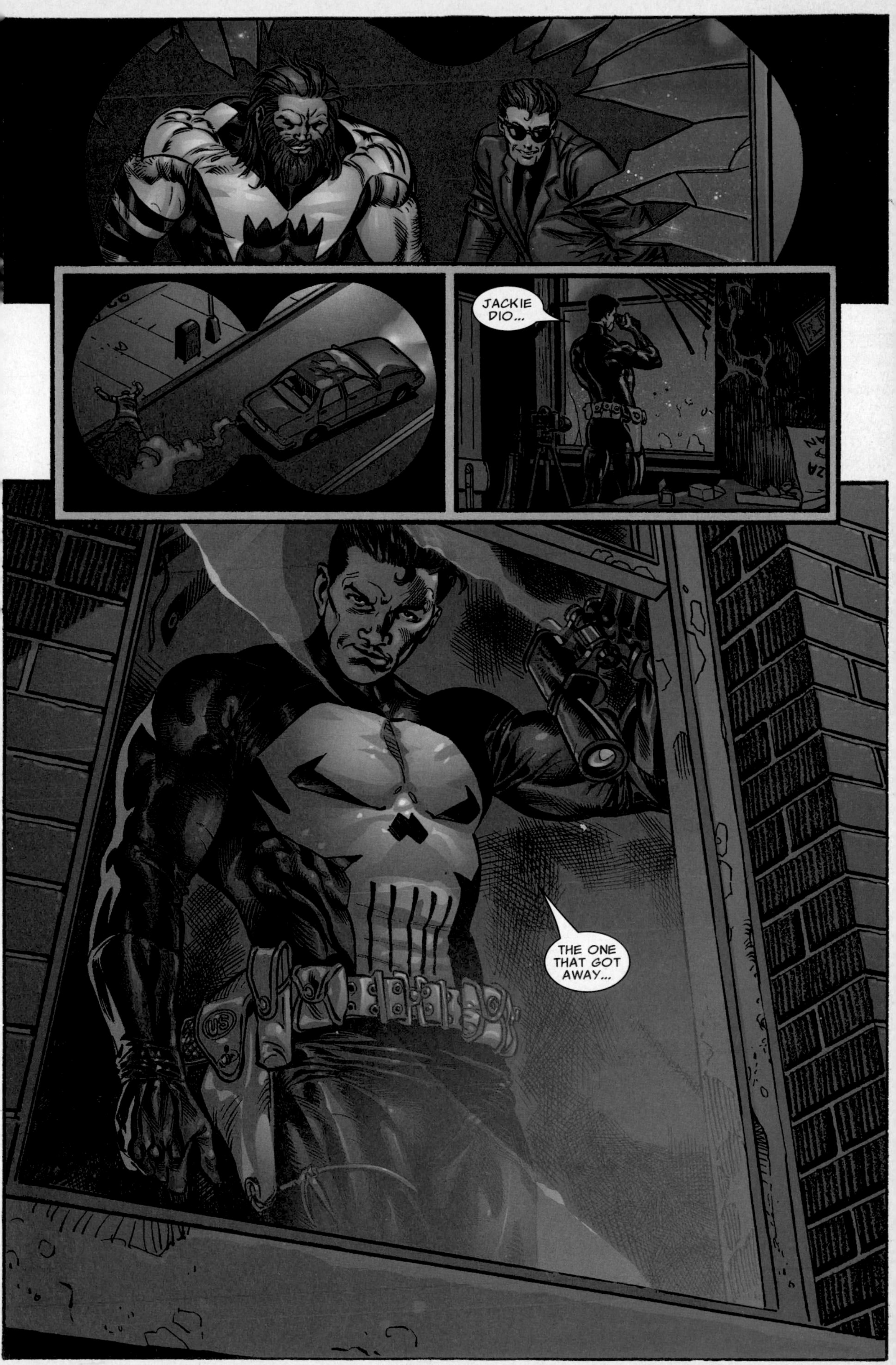
JACKIE DIO...
THE ONE THAT GOT AWAY...

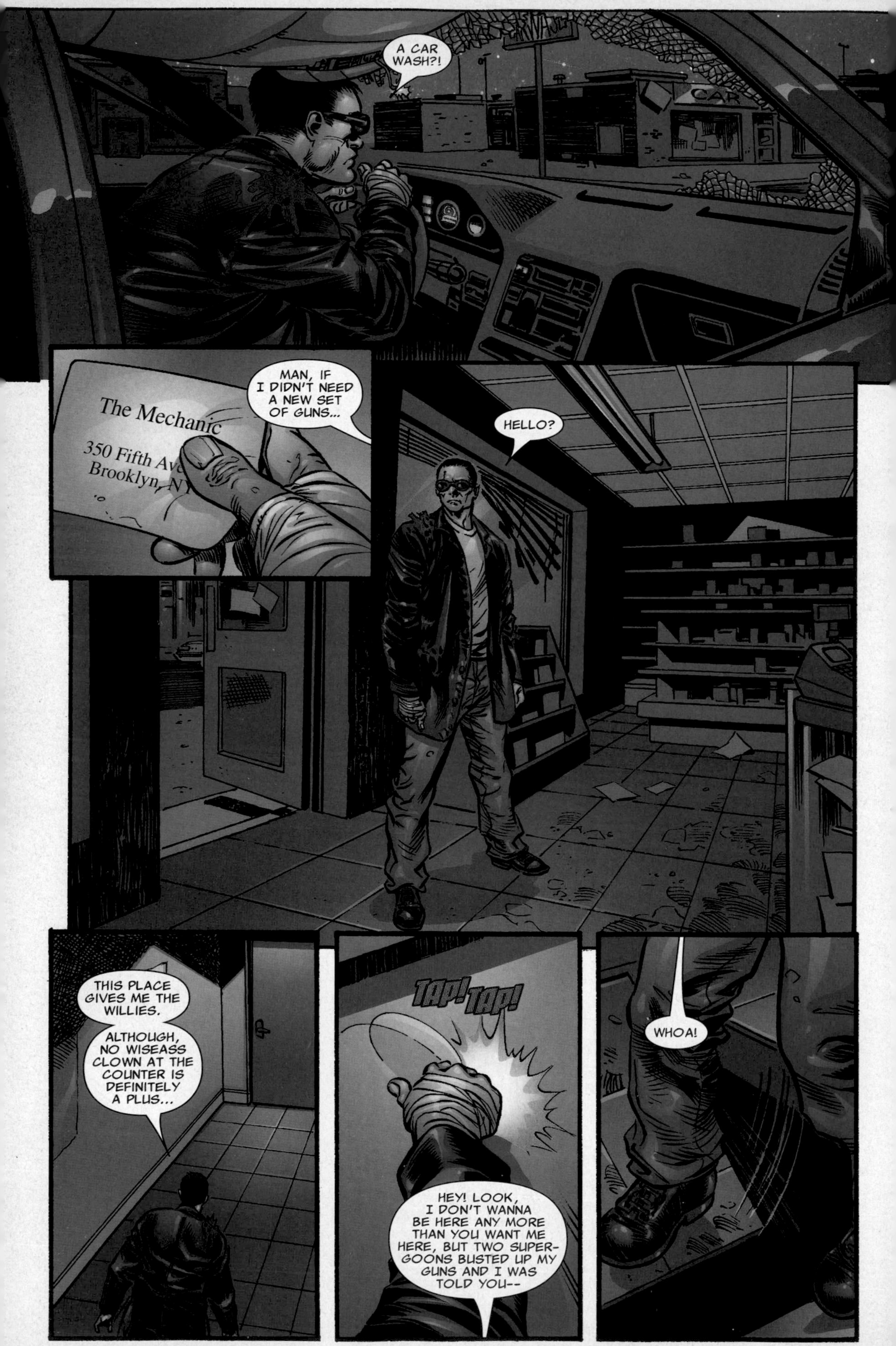
A CAR WASH?!
CAR
The Mechanic
350 Fifth Ave
Brooklyn, NY
MAN, IF I DIDN'T NEED A NEW SET OF GUNS...
HELLO?
THIS PLACE GIVES ME THE WILLIES.
ALTHOUGH, NO WISEASS CLOWN AT THE COUNTER IS DEFINITELY A PLUS...
TAP! TAP!
HEY! LOOK, I DON'T WANNA BE HERE ANY MORE THAN YOU WANT ME HERE, BUT TWO SUPER-GOONS BUSTED UP MY GUNS AND I WAS TOLD YOU--
WHOA!

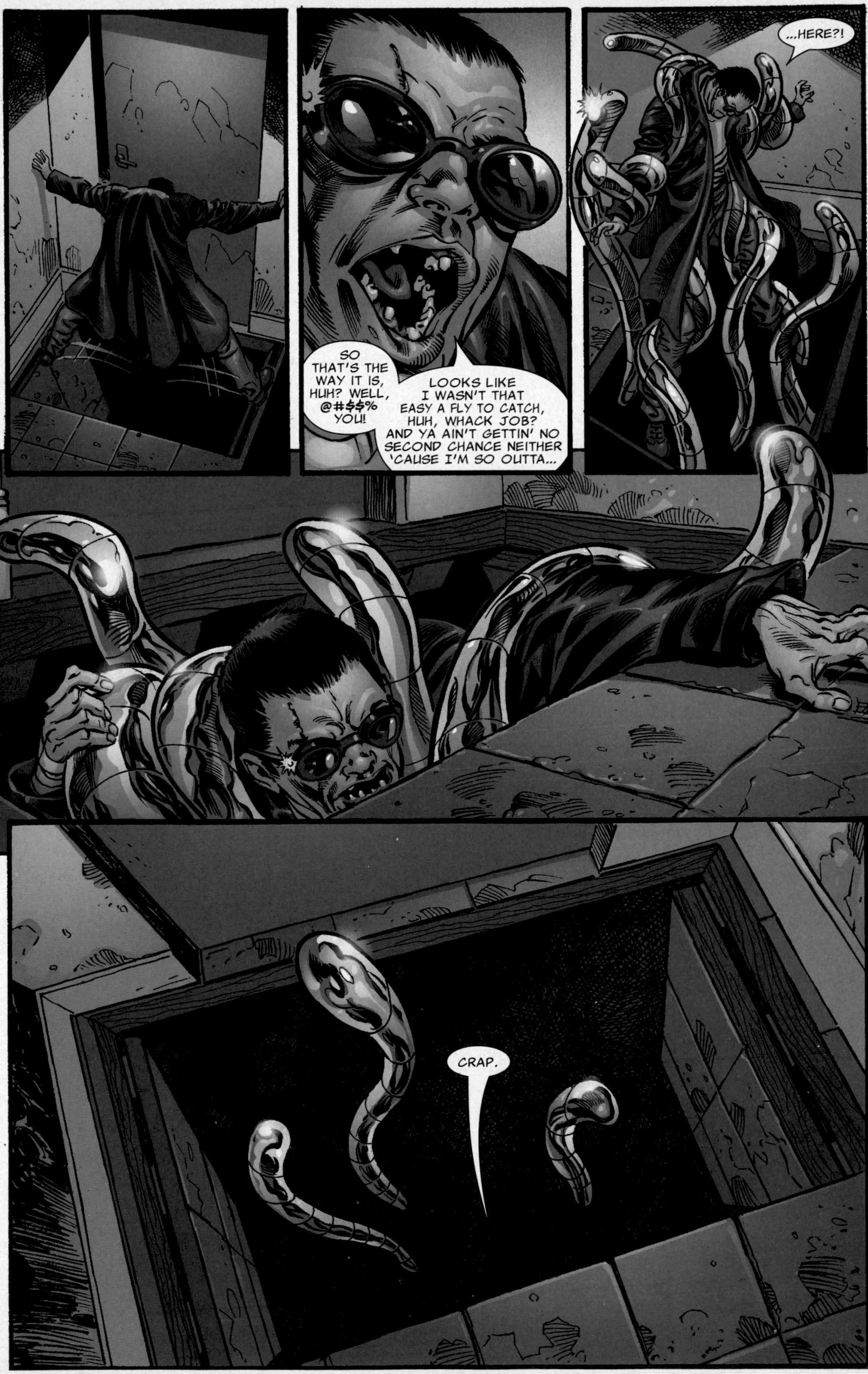

SO THAT'S THE WAY IT IS, HUH? WELL, @#$$% YOU!
LOOKS LIKE I WASN'T THAT EASY A FLY TO CATCH, HUH, WHACK JOB? AND YA AIN'T GETTIN' NO SECOND CHANCE NEITHER 'CAUSE I'M SO OUTTA...
...HERE?!
CRAP.

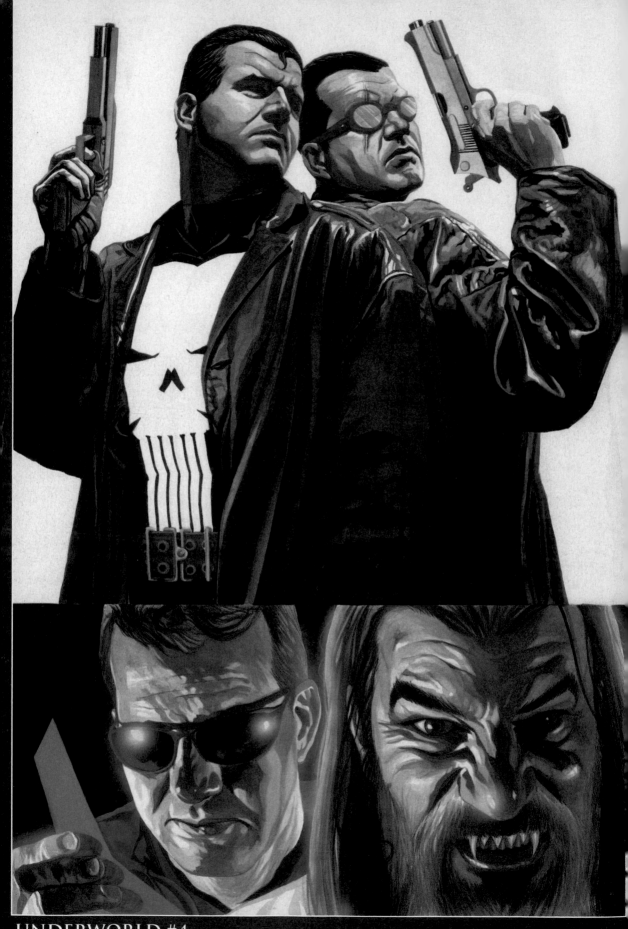

UNDERWORLD #4

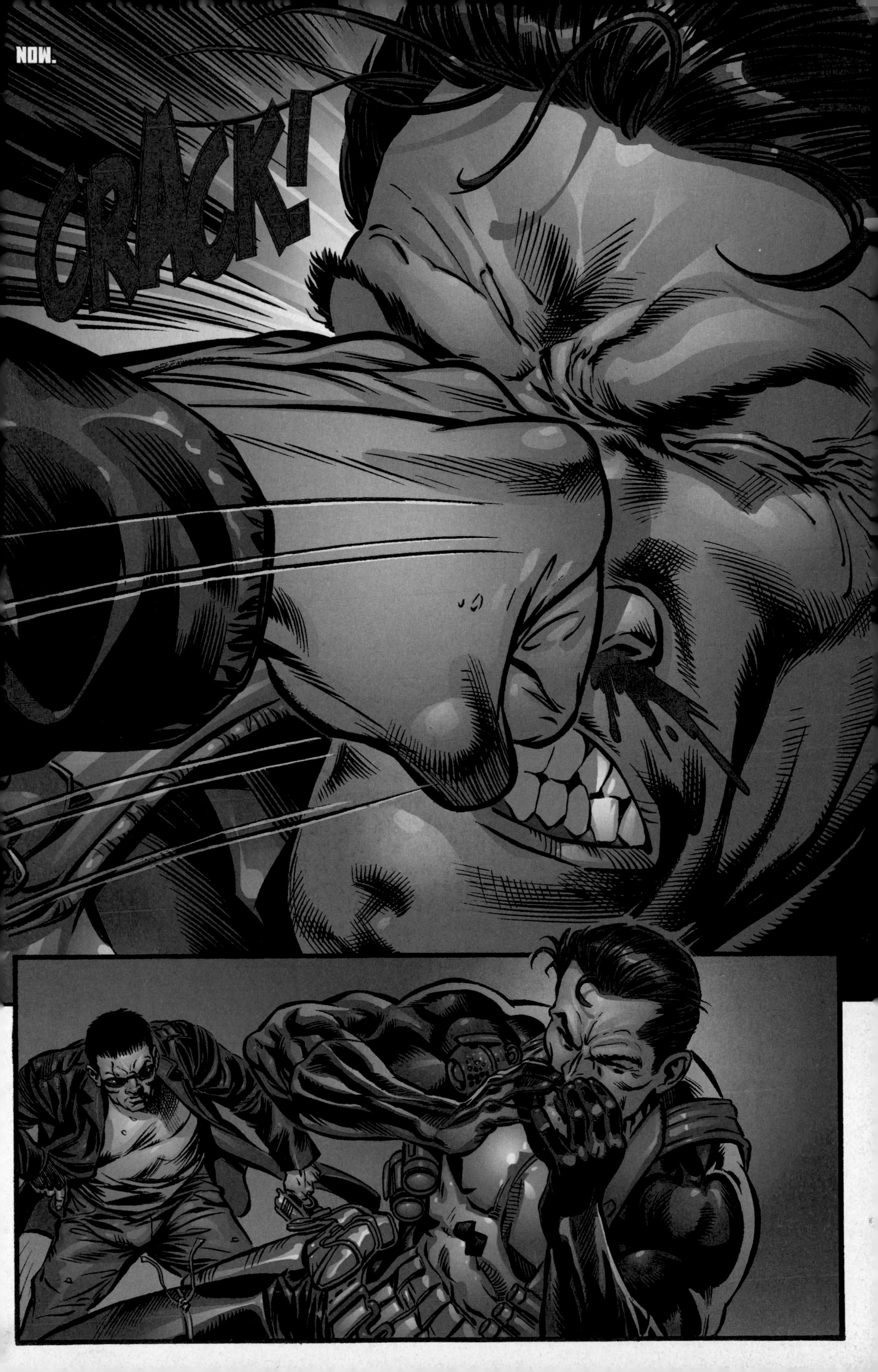
NOW.
CRACK!

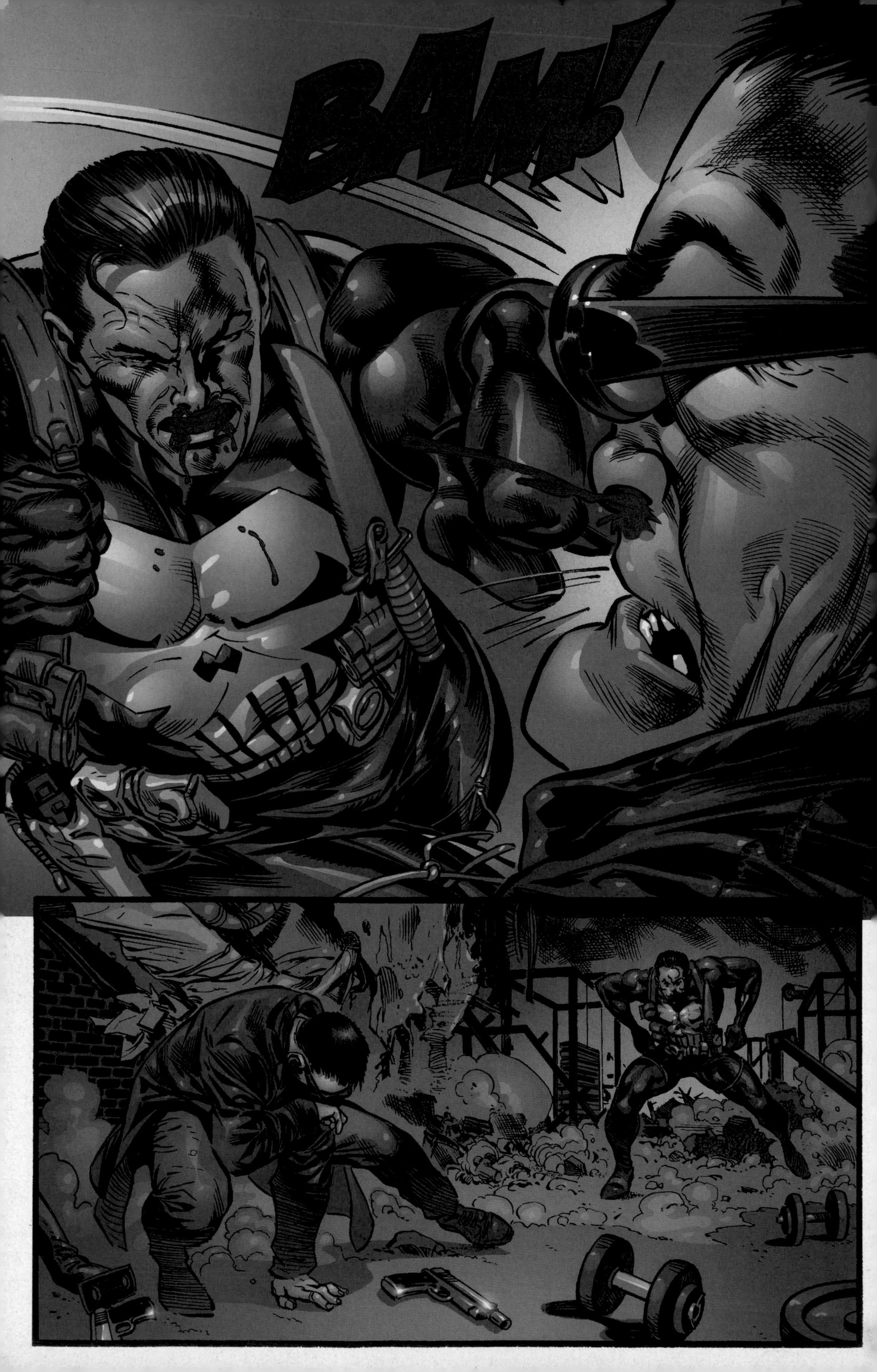
BAM!

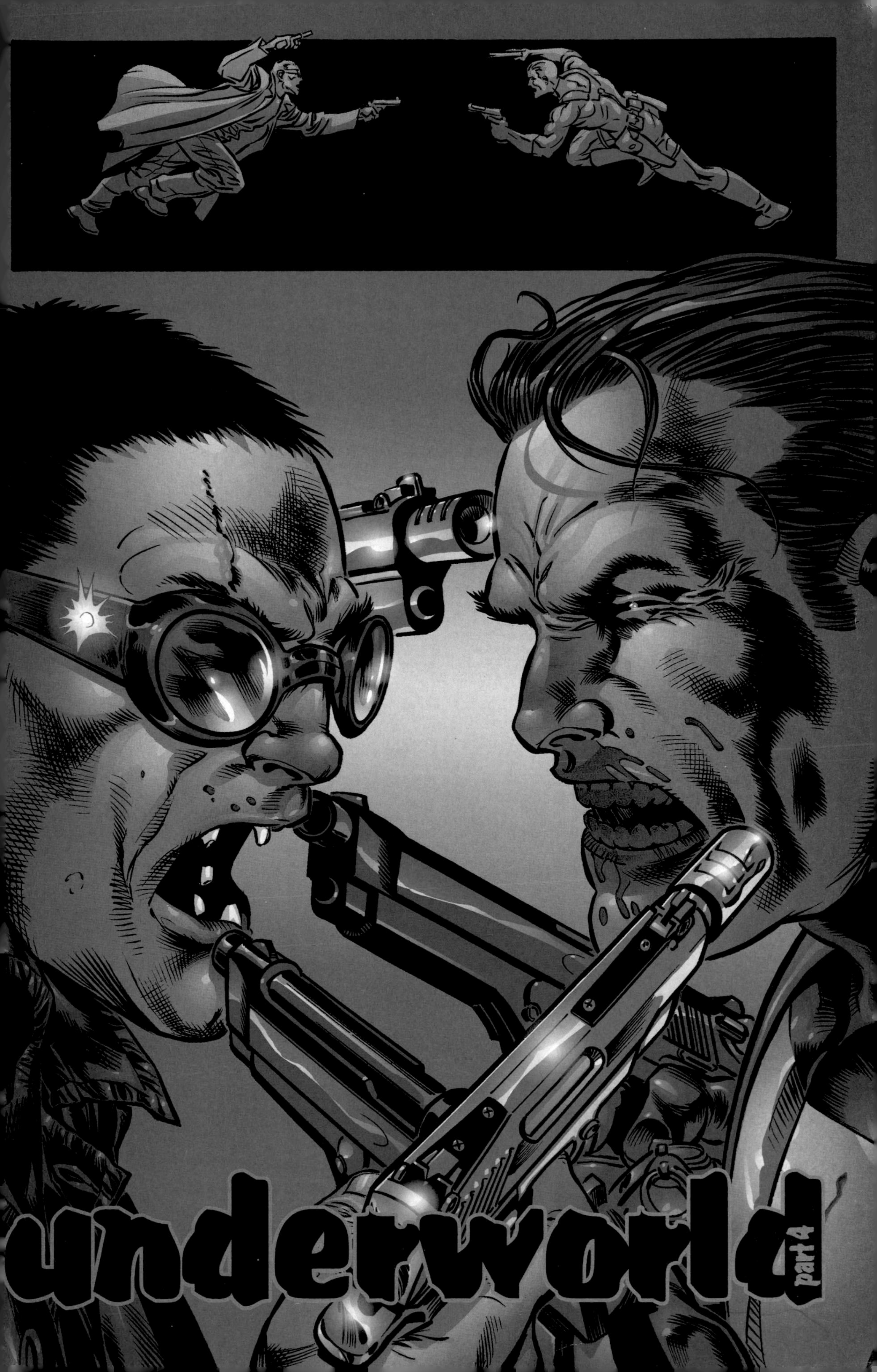
underworld
part 4

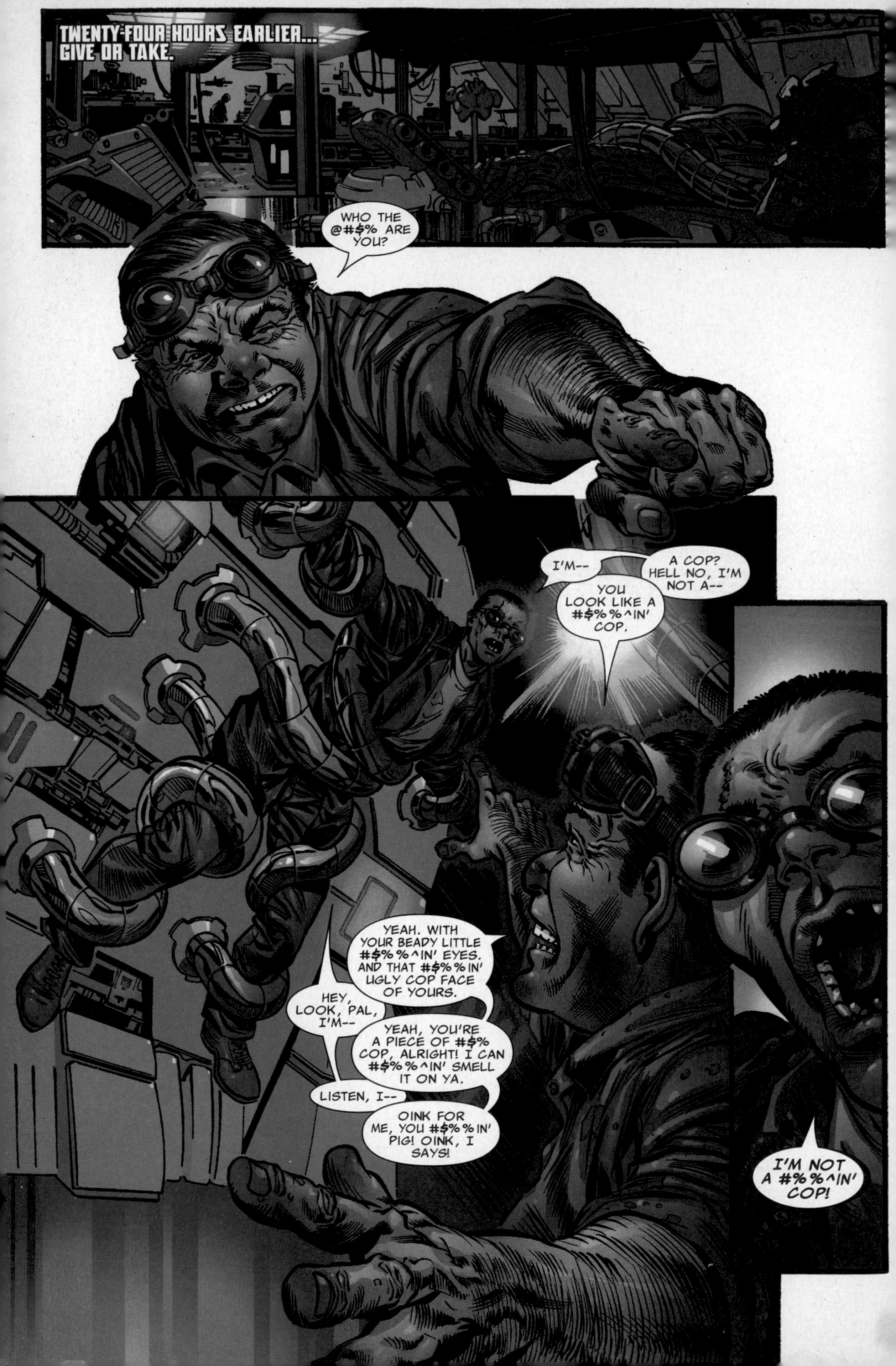
TWENTY-FOUR HOURS EARLIER... GIVE OR TAKE.
WHO THE @#$% ARE YOU?
I'M--
A COP? HELL NO, I'M NOT A--
YOU LOOK LIKE A #$%%^IN' COP.
YEAH. WITH YOUR BEADY LITTLE #$%%^IN' EYES. AND THAT #$%%IN' UGLY COP FACE OF YOURS.
HEY, LOOK, PAL, I'M--
YEAH, YOU'RE A PIECE OF #$% COP, ALRIGHT! I CAN #$%%^IN' SMELL IT ON YA.
LISTEN, I--
OINK FOR ME, YOU #$%%IN' PIG! OINK, I SAYS!
I'M NOT A #%%^IN' COP!

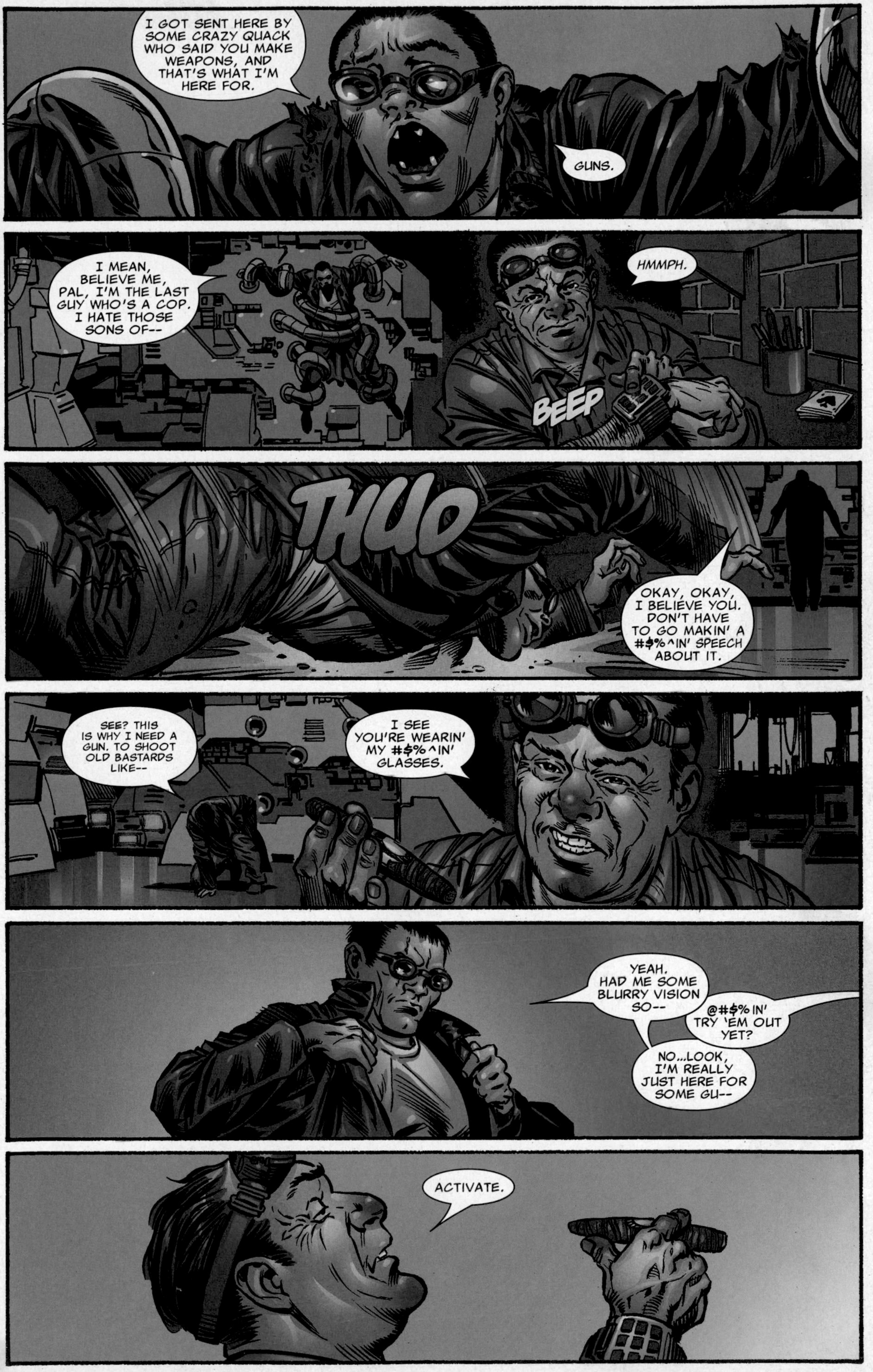
I GOT SENT HERE BY SOME CRAZY QUACK WHO SAID YOU MAKE WEAPONS, AND THAT'S WHAT I'M HERE FOR.
GUNS.
I MEAN, BELIEVE ME, PAL, I'M THE LAST GUY WHO'S A COP. I HATE THOSE SONS OF--
HMMPH.
BEEP
THUD
OKAY, OKAY, I BELIEVE YOU. DON'T HAVE TO GO MAKIN' A #$%^IN' SPEECH ABOUT IT.
SEE? THIS IS WHY I NEED A GUN. TO SHOOT OLD BASTARDS LIKE--
I SEE YOU'RE WEARIN' MY #$%^IN' GLASSES.
YEAH. HAD ME SOME BLURRY VISION SO--
@#$%IN' TRY 'EM OUT YET?
NO...LOOK, I'M REALLY JUST HERE FOR SOME GU--
ACTIVATE.

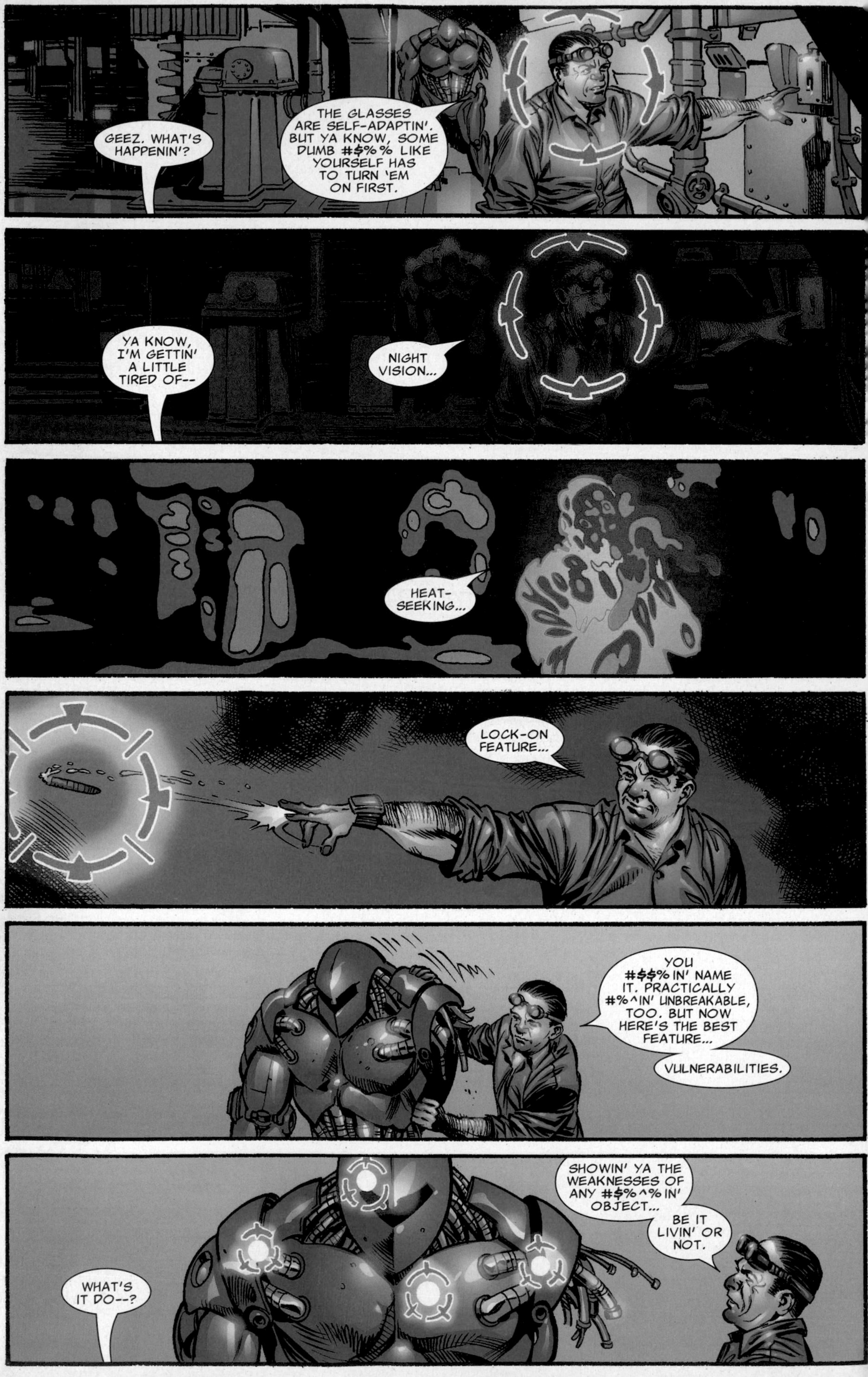
GEEZ. WHAT'S HAPPENIN'?
THE GLASSES ARE SELF-ADAPTIN'. BUT YA KNOW, SOME DUMB #$%% LIKE YOURSELF HAS TO TURN 'EM ON FIRST.
YA KNOW, I'M GETTIN' A LITTLE TIRED OF--
NIGHT VISION...
HEAT-SEEKING...
LOCK-ON FEATURE...
YOU #$$%IN' NAME IT. PRACTICALLY #%^IN' UNBREAKABLE, TOO. BUT NOW HERE'S THE BEST FEATURE...
VULNERABILITIES.
SHOWIN' YA THE WEAKNESSES OF ANY #$%^%IN' OBJECT...
BE IT LIVIN' OR NOT.
WHAT'S IT DO--?

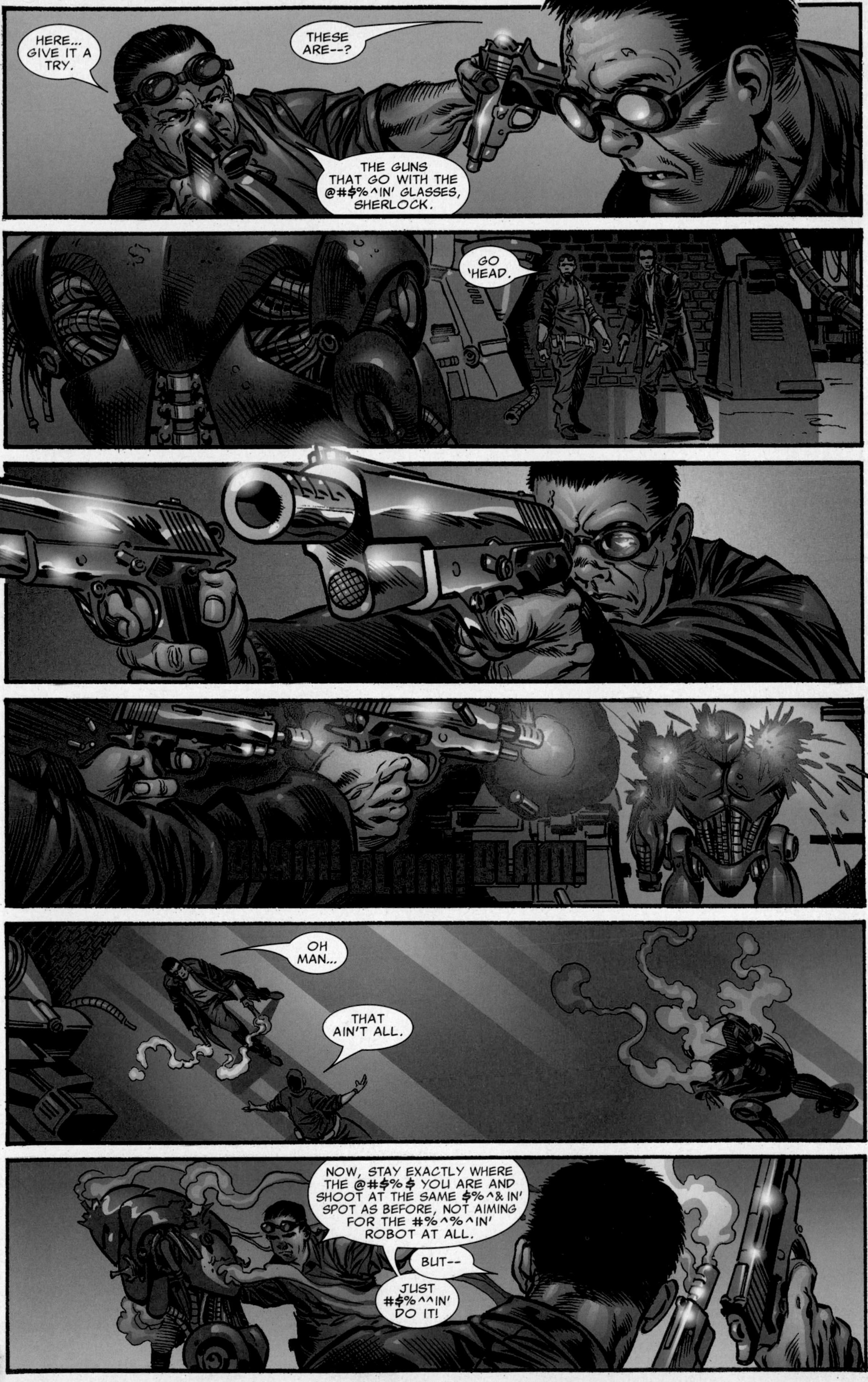
HERE... GIVE IT A TRY.
THESE ARE--?
THE GUNS THAT GO WITH THE @#$%^IN' GLASSES, SHERLOCK.
GO 'HEAD.
BLAM! BLAM! BLAM!
OH MAN...
THAT AIN'T ALL.
NOW, STAY EXACTLY WHERE THE @#$%$ YOU ARE AND SHOOT AT THE SAME $%^& IN' SPOT AS BEFORE, NOT AIMING FOR THE #%^%^IN' ROBOT AT ALL.
BUT--
JUST #$%^^IN' DO IT!

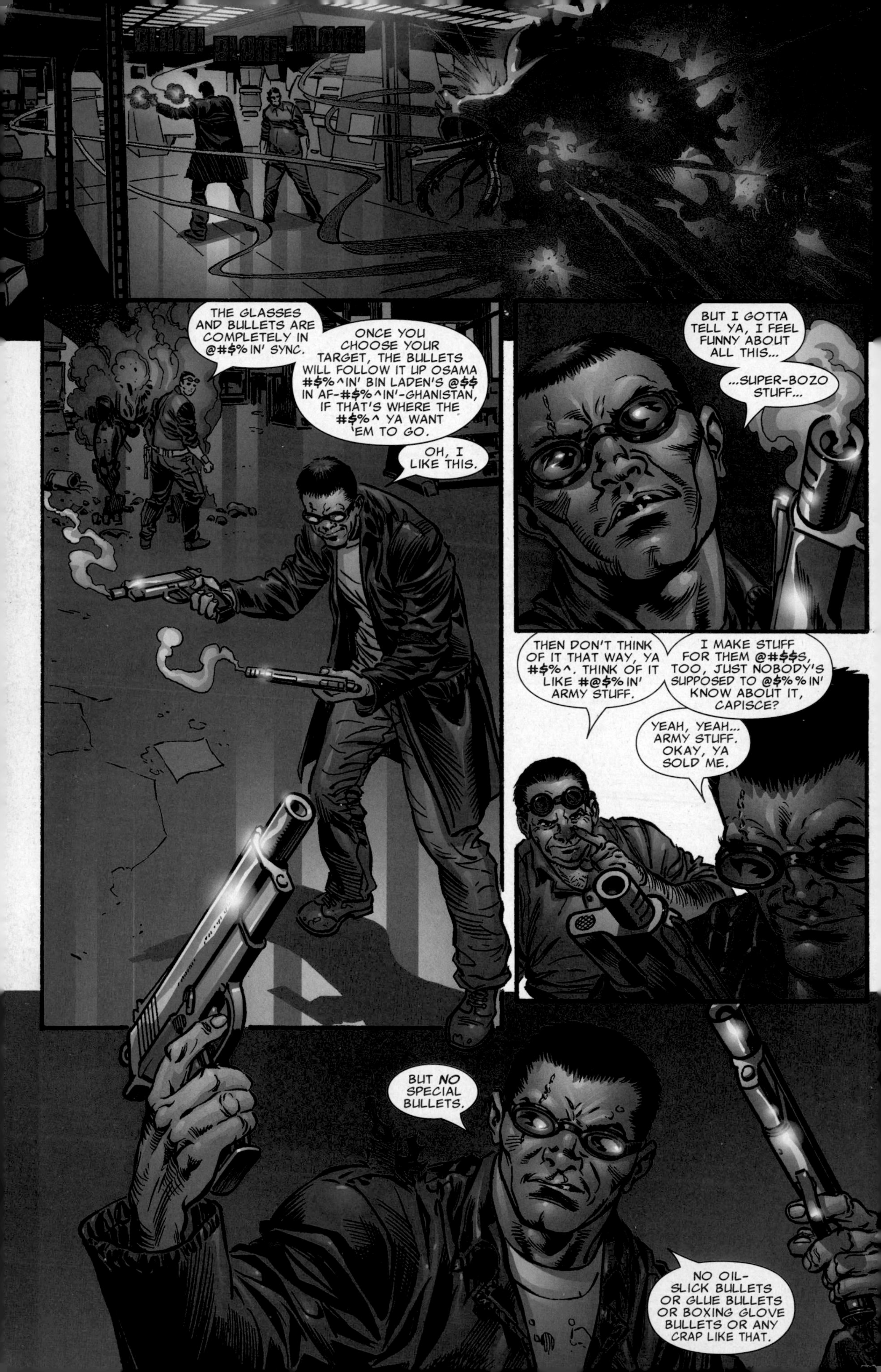
THE GLASSES AND BULLETS ARE COMPLETELY IN @#$%IN' SYNC.
ONCE YOU CHOOSE YOUR TARGET, THE BULLETS WILL FOLLOW IT UP OSAMA #$%^IN' BIN LADEN'S @$$ IN AF-#$%^IN'-GHANISTAN, IF THAT'S WHERE THE #$%^ YA WANT 'EM TO GO.
OH, I LIKE THIS.
BUT I GOTTA TELL YA, I FEEL FUNNY ABOUT ALL THIS...
...SUPER-BOZO STUFF...
THEN DON'T THINK OF IT THAT WAY, YA #$%^. THINK OF IT LIKE #@$%IN' ARMY STUFF.
I MAKE STUFF FOR THEM @#$$S, TOO, JUST NOBODY'S SUPPOSED TO @$%%IN' KNOW ABOUT IT, CAPISCE?
YEAH, YEAH... ARMY STUFF. OKAY, YA SOLD ME.
BUT NO SPECIAL BULLETS.
NO OIL-SLICK BULLETS OR GLUE BULLETS OR BOXING GLOVE BULLETS OR ANY CRAP LIKE THAT.

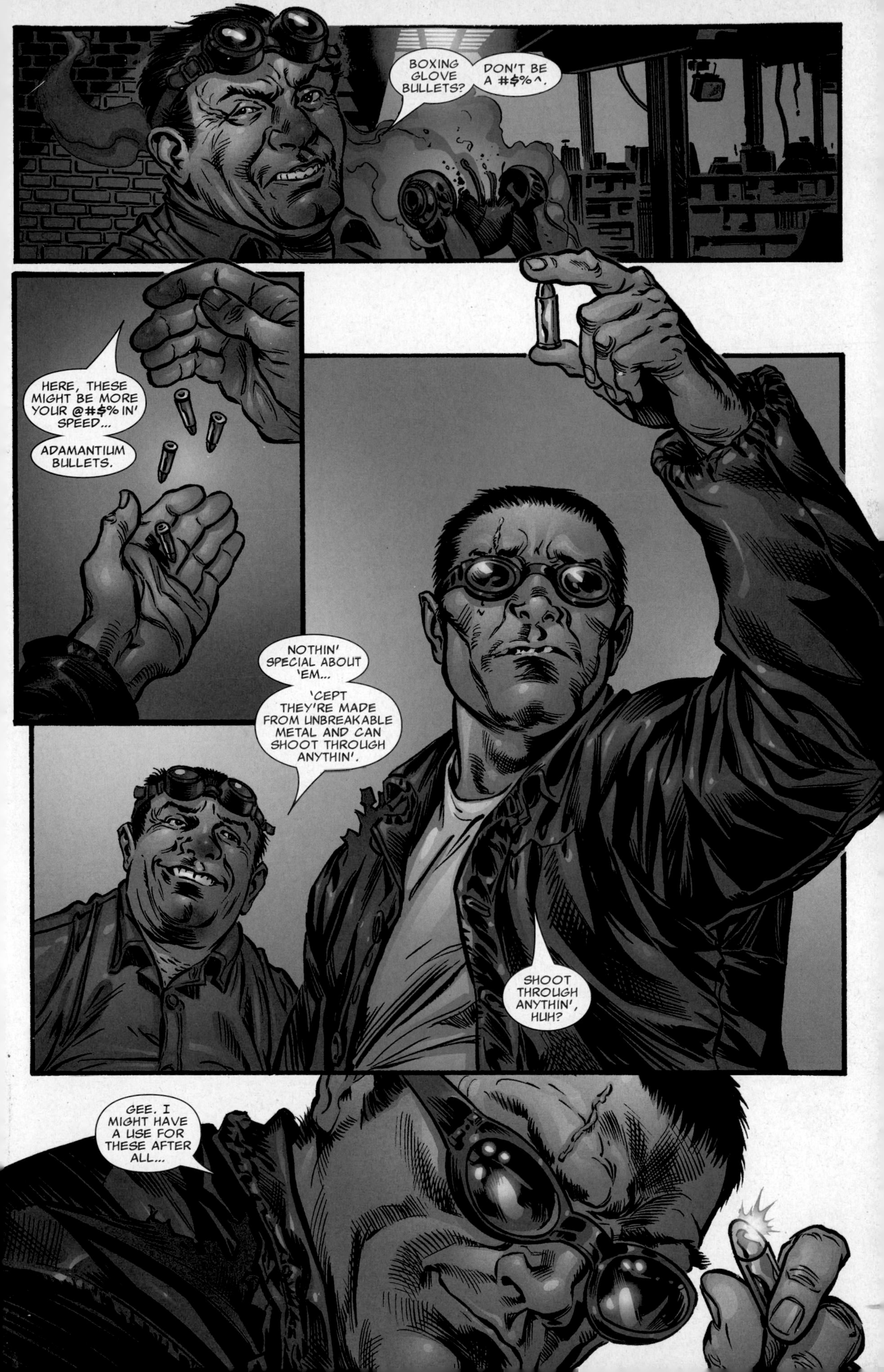
BOXING GLOVE BULLETS?
DON'T BE A #$%^.
HERE, THESE MIGHT BE MORE YOUR @#$% IN' SPEED...
ADAMANTIUM BULLETS.
NOTHIN' SPECIAL ABOUT 'EM...
'CEPT THEY'RE MADE FROM UNBREAKABLE METAL AND CAN SHOOT THROUGH ANYTHIN'.
SHOOT THROUGH ANYTHIN', HUH?
GEE. I MIGHT HAVE A USE FOR THESE AFTER ALL...

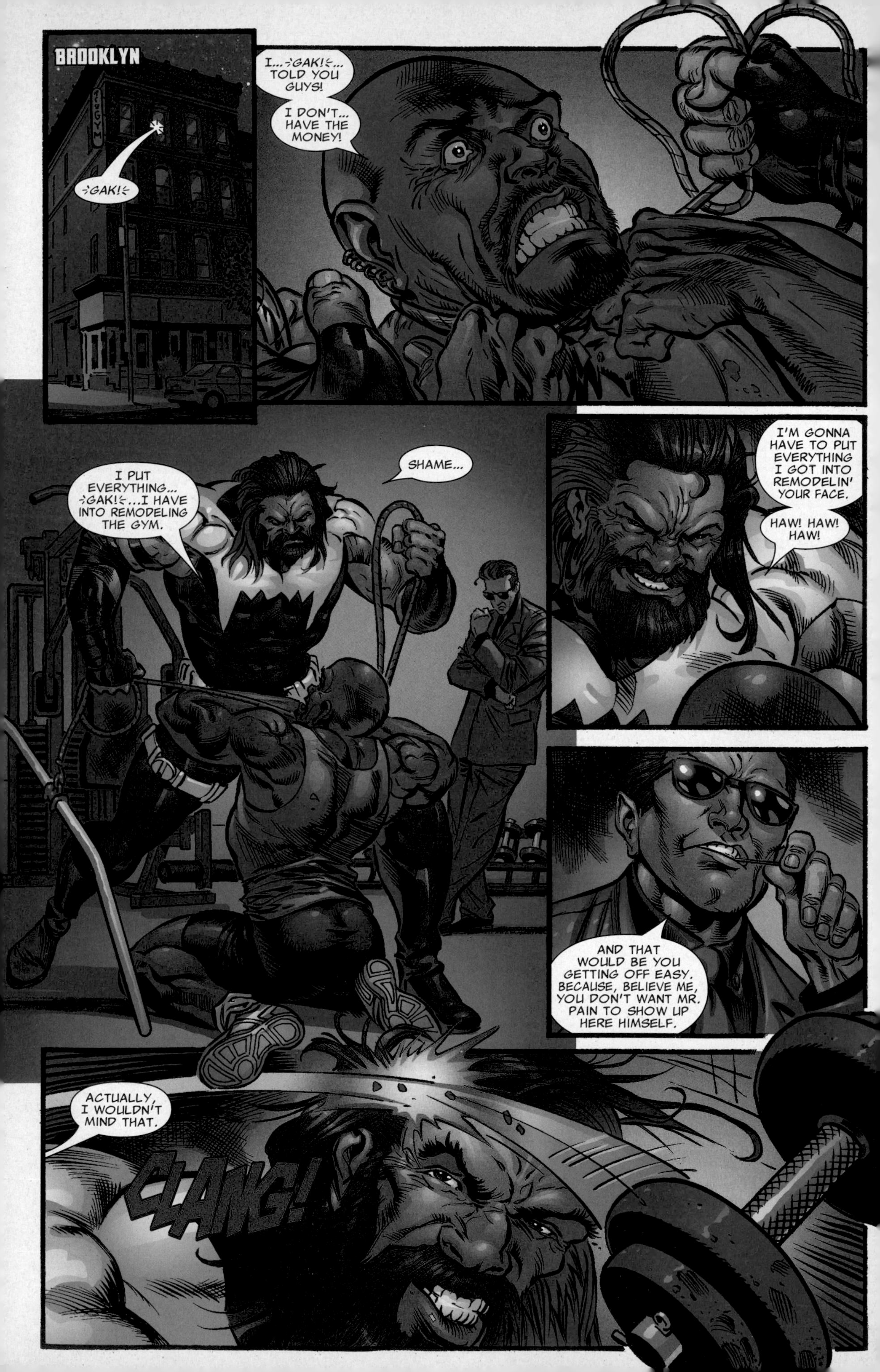
BROOKLYN
GYM
GAK!
I... GAK! ... TOLD YOU GUYS!
I DON'T... HAVE THE MONEY!
I PUT EVERYTHING... GAK! ...I HAVE INTO REMODELING THE GYM.
SHAME...
I'M GONNA HAVE TO PUT EVERYTHING I GOT INTO REMODELIN' YOUR FACE.
HAW! HAW! HAW!
AND THAT WOULD BE YOU GETTING OFF EASY. BECAUSE, BELIEVE ME, YOU DON'T WANT MR. PAIN TO SHOW UP HERE HIMSELF.
ACTUALLY, I WOULDN'T MIND THAT.
CLANG!

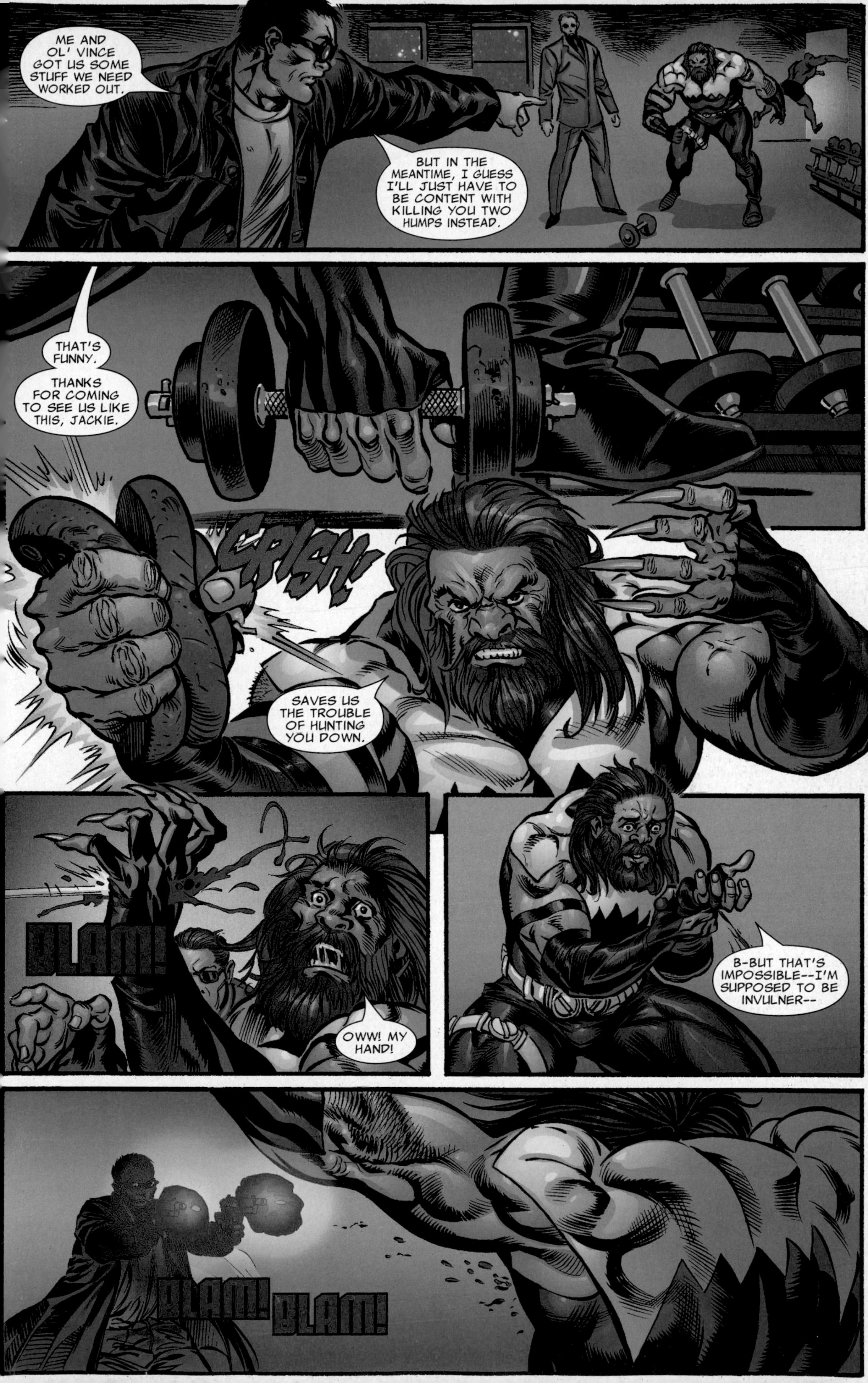
ME AND OL' VINCE GOT US SOME STUFF WE NEED WORKED OUT.
BUT IN THE MEANTIME, I GUESS I'LL JUST HAVE TO BE CONTENT WITH KILLING YOU TWO HUMPS INSTEAD.
THAT'S FUNNY.
THANKS FOR COMING TO SEE US LIKE THIS, JACKIE.
CRISH!
SAVES US THE TROUBLE OF HUNTING YOU DOWN.
BLAM!
OWW! MY HAND!
B-BUT THAT'S IMPOSSIBLE--I'M SUPPOSED TO BE INVULNER--
BLAM! BLAM!

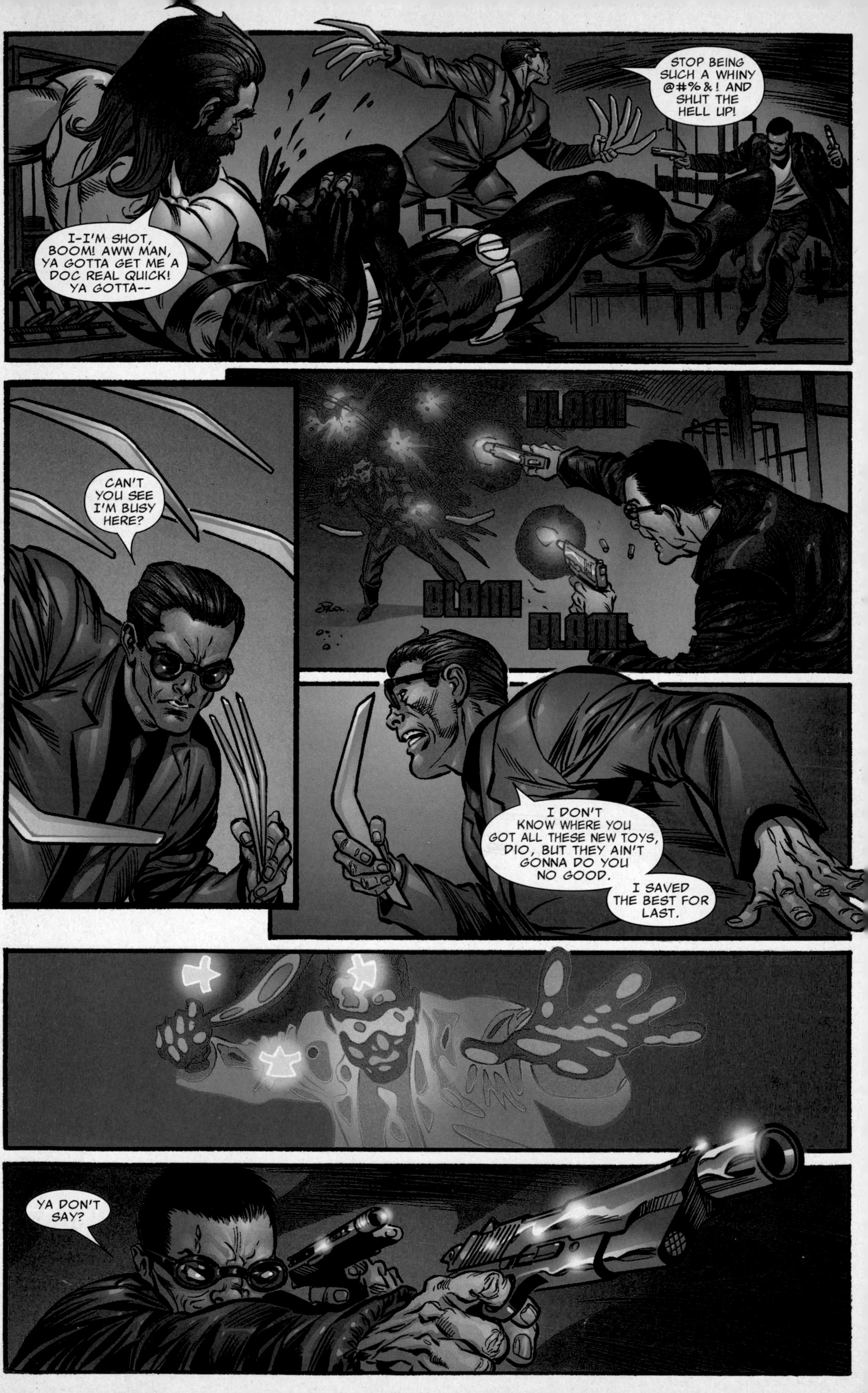

I-I'M SHOT, BOOM! AWW MAN, YA GOTTA GET ME A DOC REAL QUICK! YA GOTTA--
STOP BEING SUCH A WHINY @#%&! AND SHUT THE HELL UP!
CAN'T YOU SEE I'M BUSY HERE?
BLAM!
BLAM!
BLAM!
I DON'T KNOW WHERE YOU GOT ALL THESE NEW TOYS, DIO, BUT THEY AIN'T GONNA DO YOU NO GOOD.
I SAVED THE BEST FOR LAST.
YA DON'T SAY?

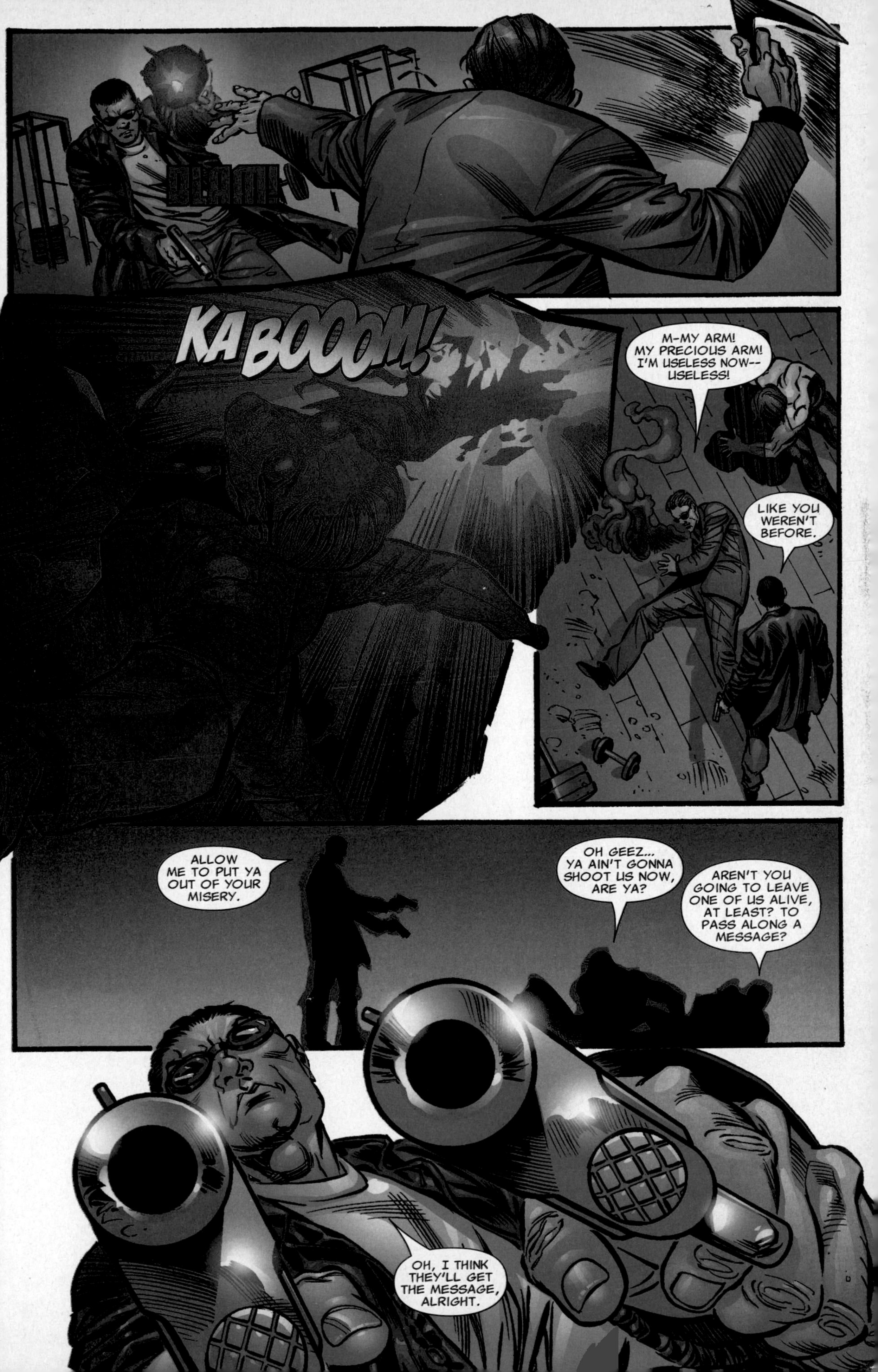
KA BOOOM!
M-MY ARM! MY PRECIOUS ARM! I'M USELESS NOW-- USELESS!
LIKE YOU WEREN'T BEFORE.
ALLOW ME TO PUT YA OUT OF YOUR MISERY.
OH GEEZ... YA AIN'T GONNA SHOOT US NOW, ARE YA?
AREN'T YOU GOING TO LEAVE ONE OF US ALIVE, AT LEAST? TO PASS ALONG A MESSAGE?
OH, I THINK THEY'LL GET THE MESSAGE, ALRIGHT.

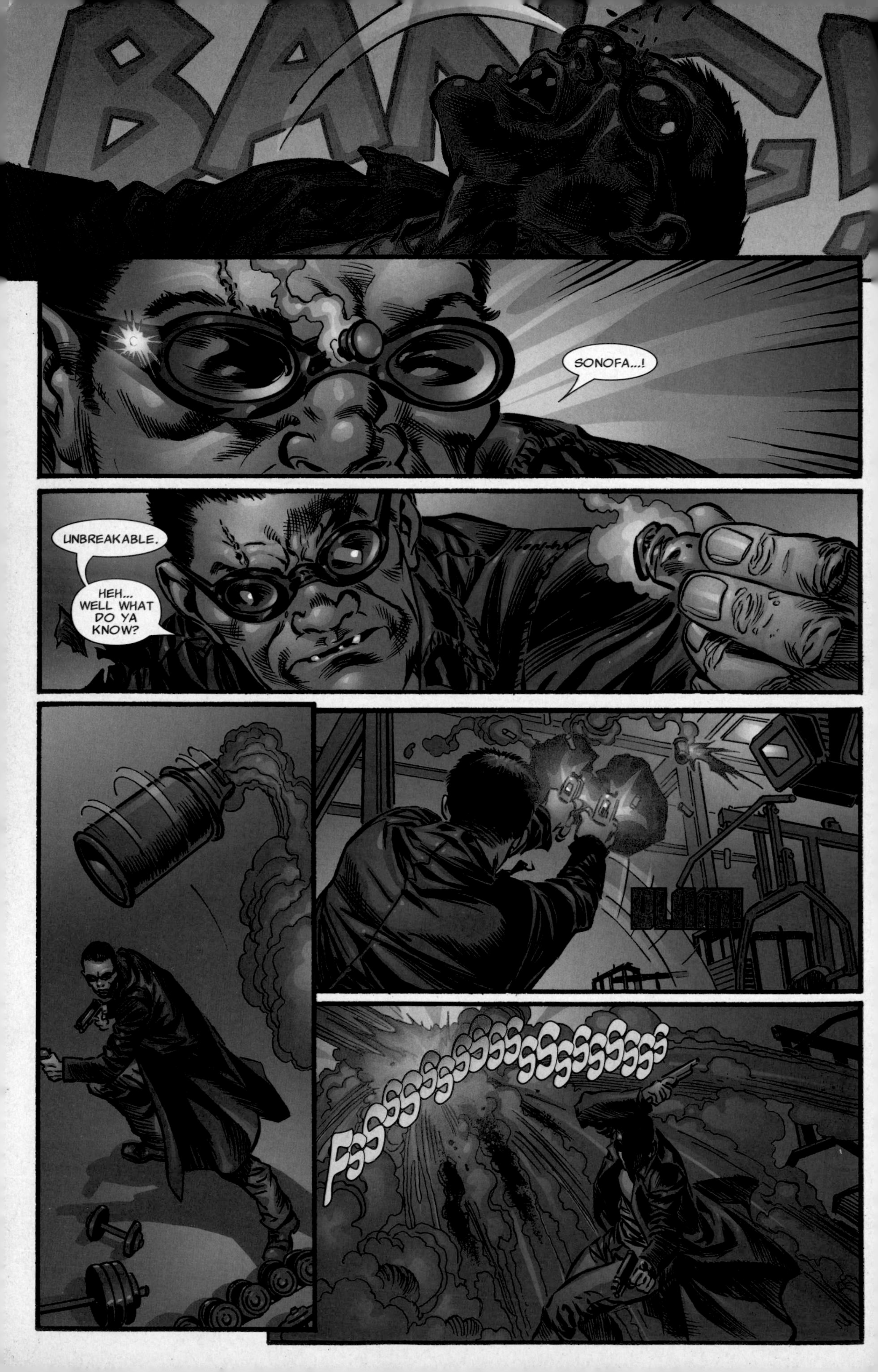
SONOFA...!
UNBREAKABLE.
HEH... WELL WHAT DO YA KNOW?

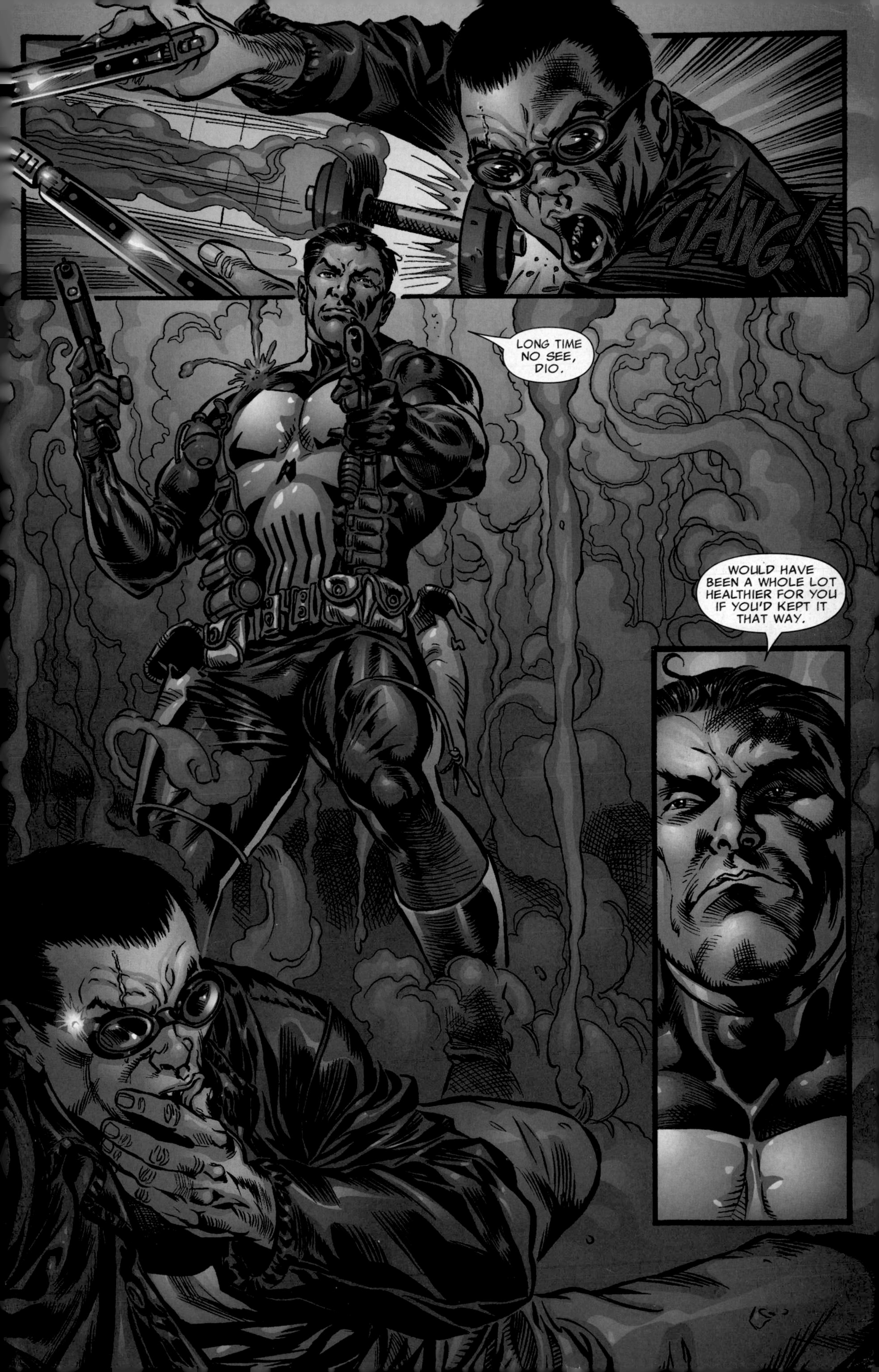
CLANG!
LONG TIME NO SEE, DIO.
WOULD HAVE BEEN A WHOLE LOT HEALTHIER FOR YOU IF YOU'D KEPT IT THAT WAY.

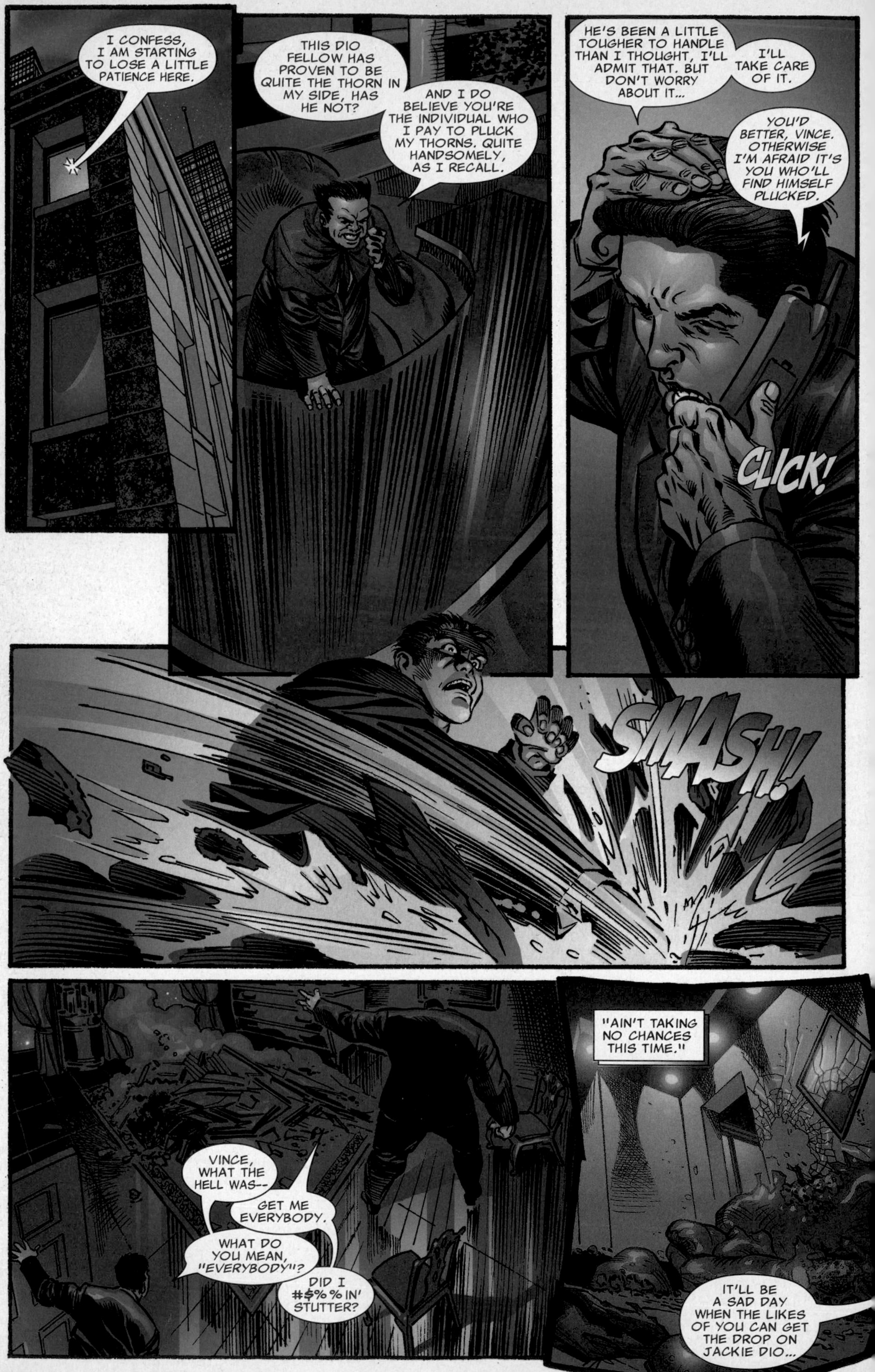

I CONFESS, I AM STARTING TO LOSE A LITTLE PATIENCE HERE.
THIS DIO FELLOW HAS PROVEN TO BE QUITE THE THORN IN MY SIDE, HAS HE NOT?
AND I DO BELIEVE YOU'RE THE INDIVIDUAL WHO I PAY TO PLUCK MY THORNS. QUITE HANDSOMELY, AS I RECALL.
HE'S BEEN A LITTLE TOUGHER TO HANDLE THAN I THOUGHT, I'LL ADMIT THAT. BUT DON'T WORRY ABOUT IT...
I'LL TAKE CARE OF IT.
YOU'D BETTER, VINCE. OTHERWISE I'M AFRAID IT'S YOU WHO'LL FIND HIMSELF PLUCKED.
CLICK!
SMASH!
VINCE, WHAT THE HELL WAS--
GET ME EVERYBODY.
WHAT DO YOU MEAN, "EVERYBODY"?
DID I #$%%IN' STUTTER?
"AIN'T TAKING NO CHANCES THIS TIME."
IT'LL BE A SAD DAY WHEN THE LIKES OF YOU CAN GET THE DROP ON JACKIE DIO...

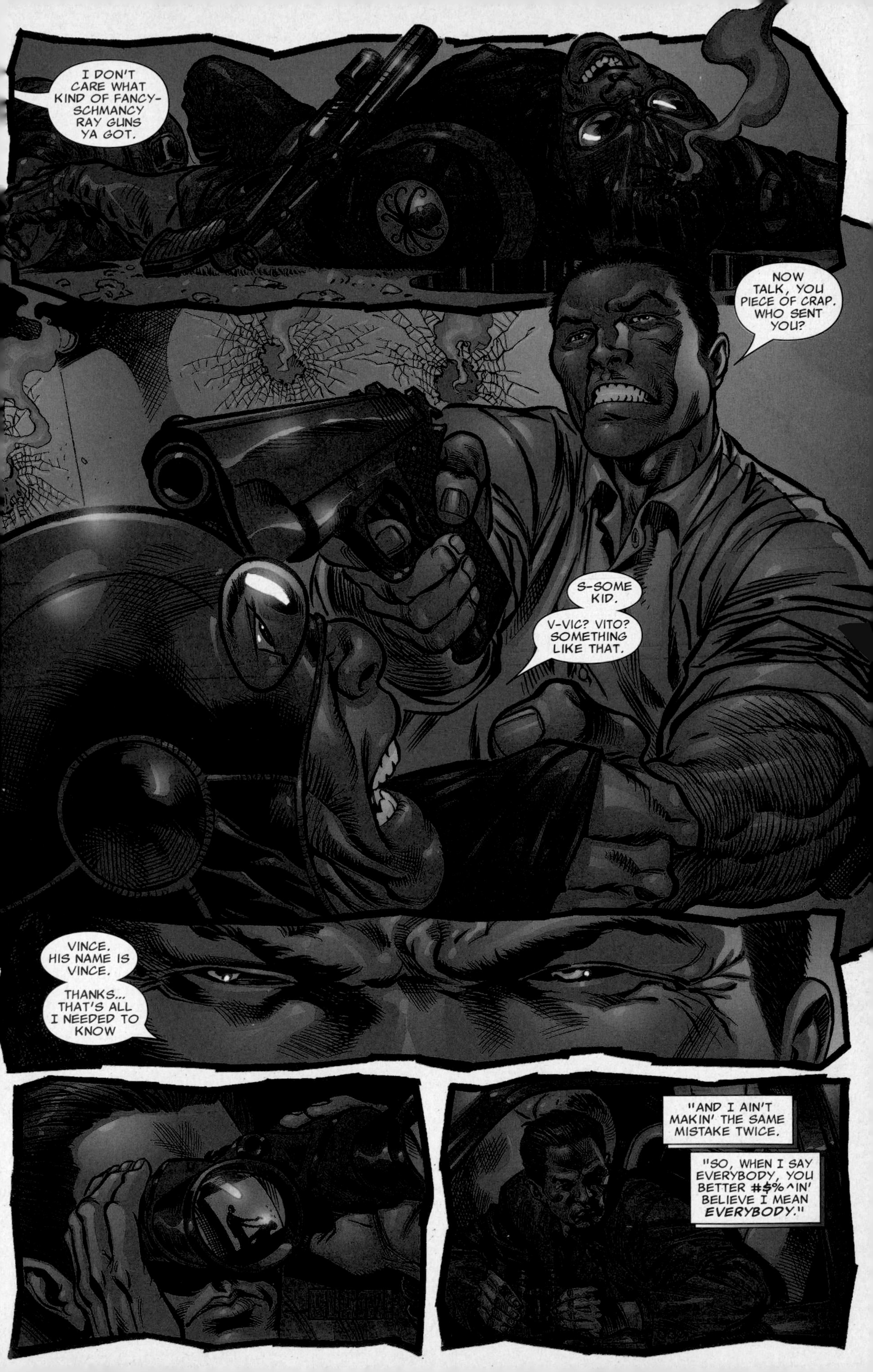
I DON'T CARE WHAT KIND OF FANCY-SCHMANCY RAY GUNS YA GOT.
NOW TALK, YOU PIECE OF CRAP. WHO SENT YOU?
S-SOME KID.
V-VIC? VITO? SOMETHING LIKE THAT.
VINCE. HIS NAME IS VINCE.
THANKS... THAT'S ALL I NEEDED TO KNOW
"AND I AIN'T MAKIN' THE SAME MISTAKE TWICE.
"SO, WHEN I SAY EVERYBODY, YOU BETTER #$%^IN' BELIEVE I MEAN *EVERYBODY*."

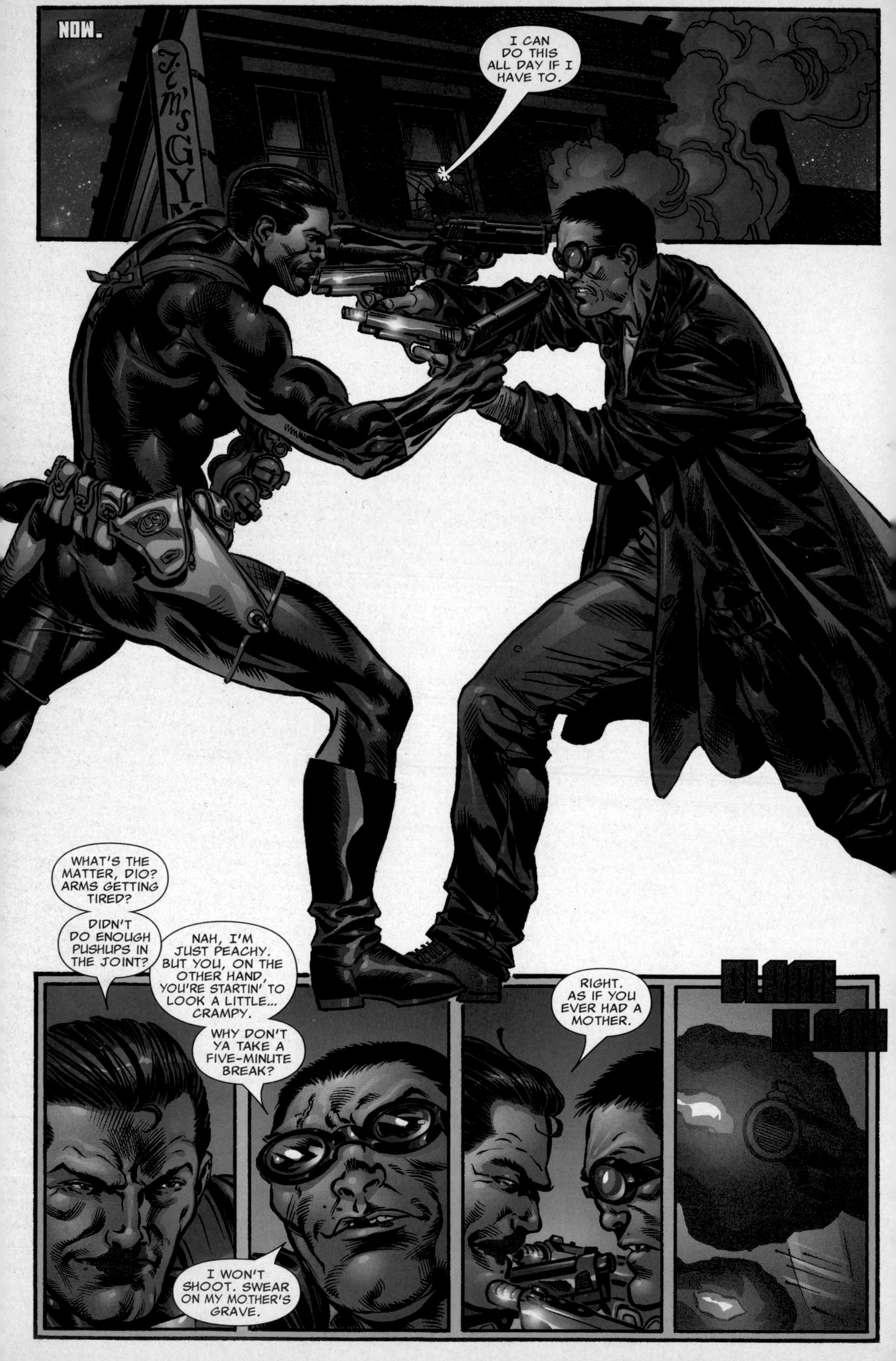
NOW.
I CAN DO THIS ALL DAY IF I HAVE TO.
WHAT'S THE MATTER, DIO? ARMS GETTING TIRED?
DIDN'T DO ENOUGH PUSHUPS IN THE JOINT?
NAH, I'M JUST PEACHY. BUT YOU, ON THE OTHER HAND, YOU'RE STARTIN' TO LOOK A LITTLE... CRAMPY.
WHY DON'T YA TAKE A FIVE-MINUTE BREAK?
I WON'T SHOOT. SWEAR ON MY MOTHER'S GRAVE.
RIGHT. AS IF YOU EVER HAD A MOTHER.

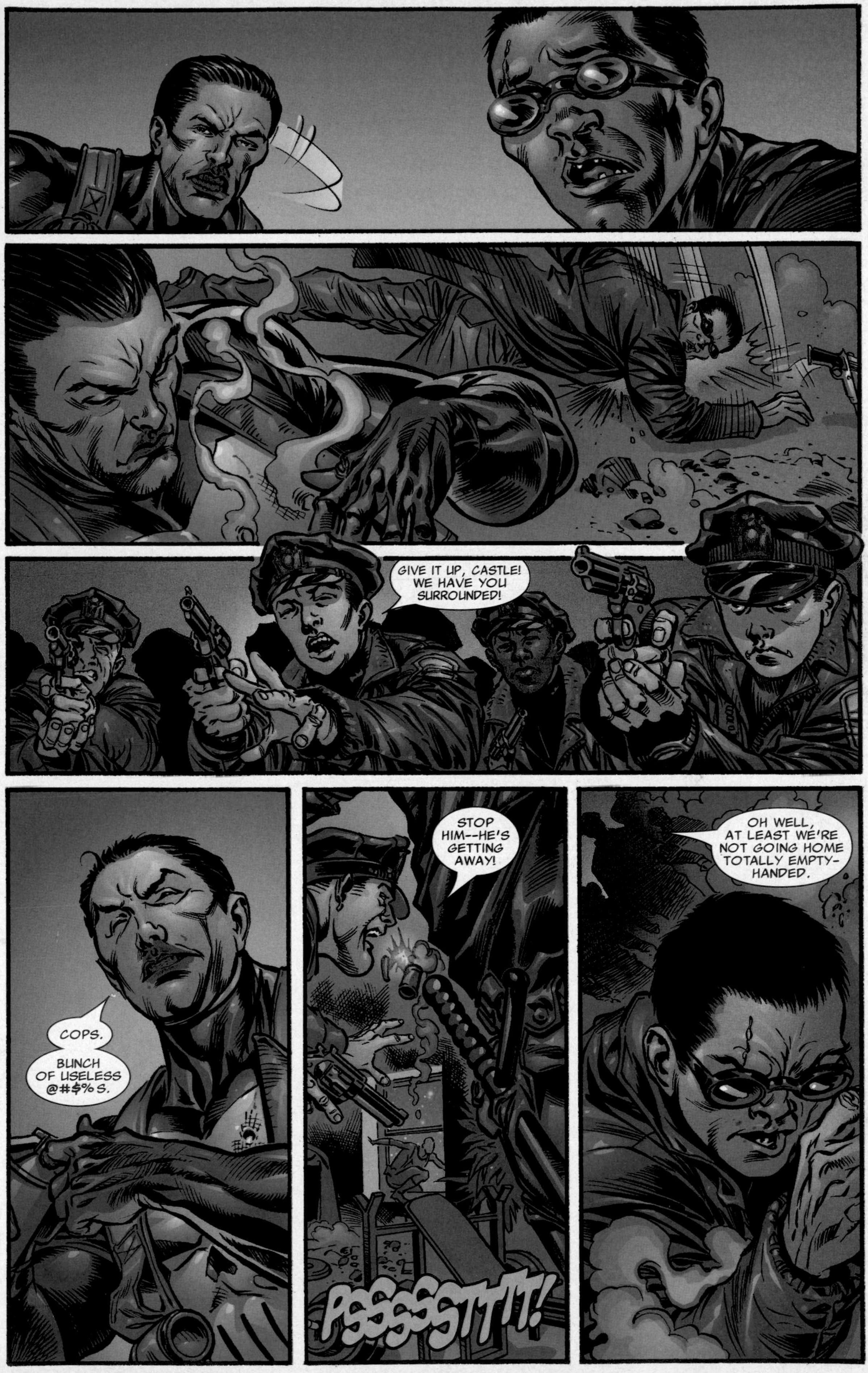
GIVE IT UP, CASTLE! WE HAVE YOU SURROUNDED!
COPS.
BUNCH OF USELESS @#$% S.
STOP HIM--HE'S GETTING AWAY!
PSSSSSTTTT!
OH WELL, AT LEAST WE'RE NOT GOING HOME TOTALLY EMPTY-HANDED.

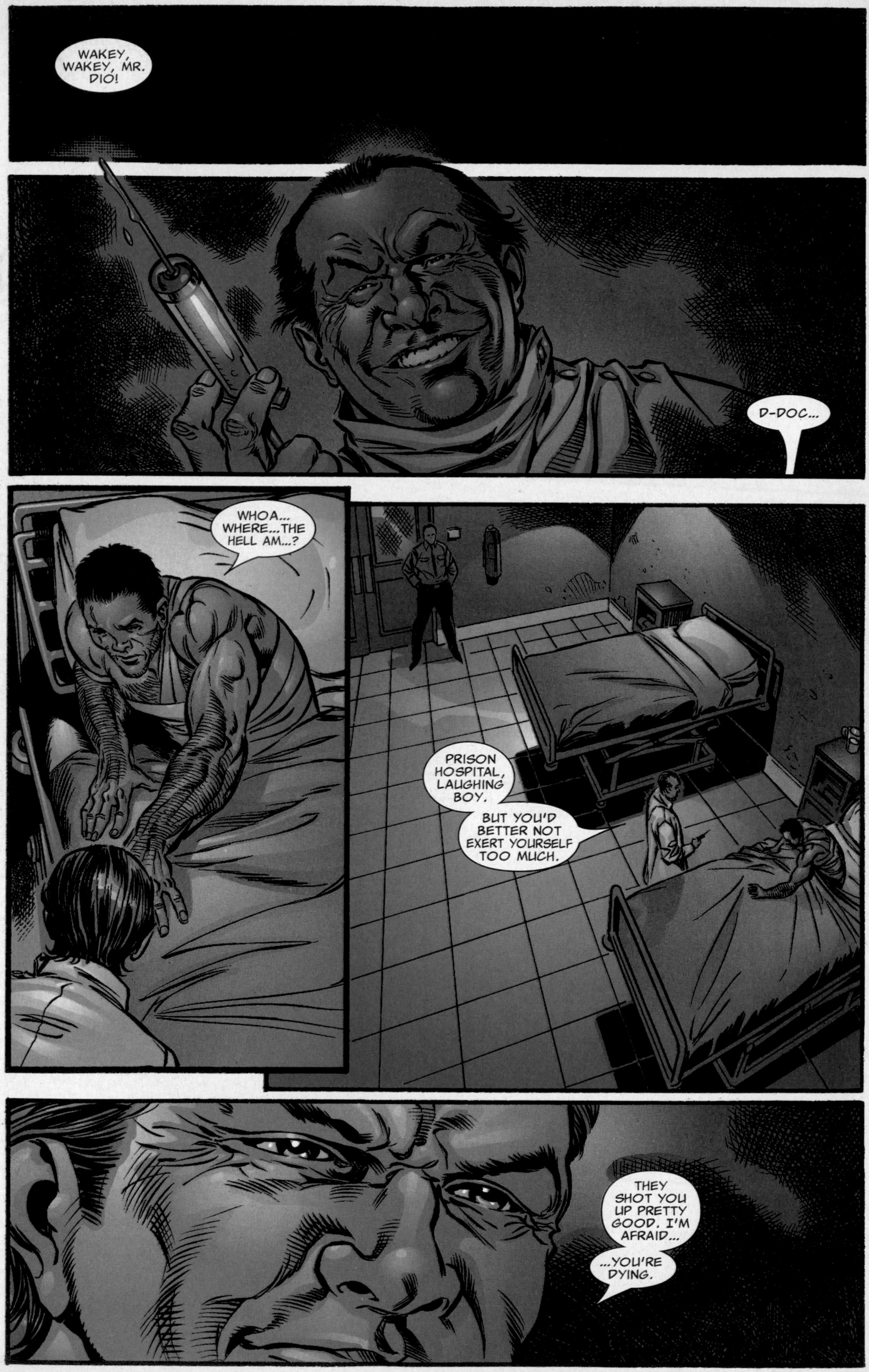
WAKEY, WAKEY, MR. DIO!
D-DOC...
WHOA... WHERE...THE HELL AM...?
PRISON HOSPITAL, LAUGHING BOY.
BUT YOU'D BETTER NOT EXERT YOURSELF TOO MUCH.
THEY SHOT YOU UP PRETTY GOOD. I'M AFRAID...
...YOU'RE DYING.

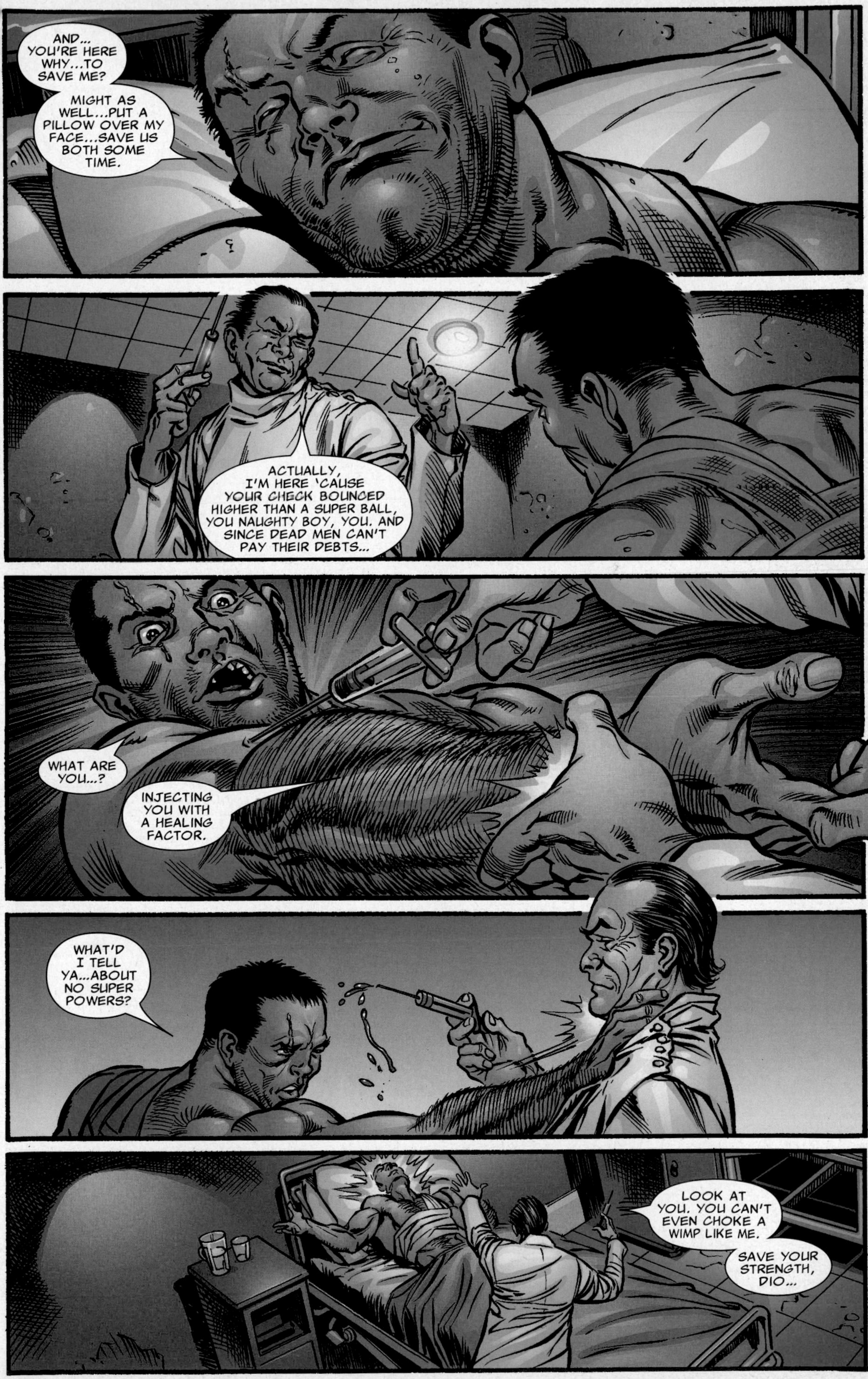
AND... YOU'RE HERE WHY...TO SAVE ME?
MIGHT AS WELL...PUT A PILLOW OVER MY FACE...SAVE US BOTH SOME TIME.
ACTUALLY, I'M HERE 'CAUSE YOUR CHECK BOUNCED HIGHER THAN A SUPER BALL, YOU NAUGHTY BOY, YOU. AND SINCE DEAD MEN CAN'T PAY THEIR DEBTS...
WHAT ARE YOU...?
INJECTING YOU WITH A HEALING FACTOR.
WHAT'D I TELL YA...ABOUT NO SUPER POWERS?
LOOK AT YOU. YOU CAN'T EVEN CHOKE A WIMP LIKE ME.
SAVE YOUR STRENGTH, DIO...

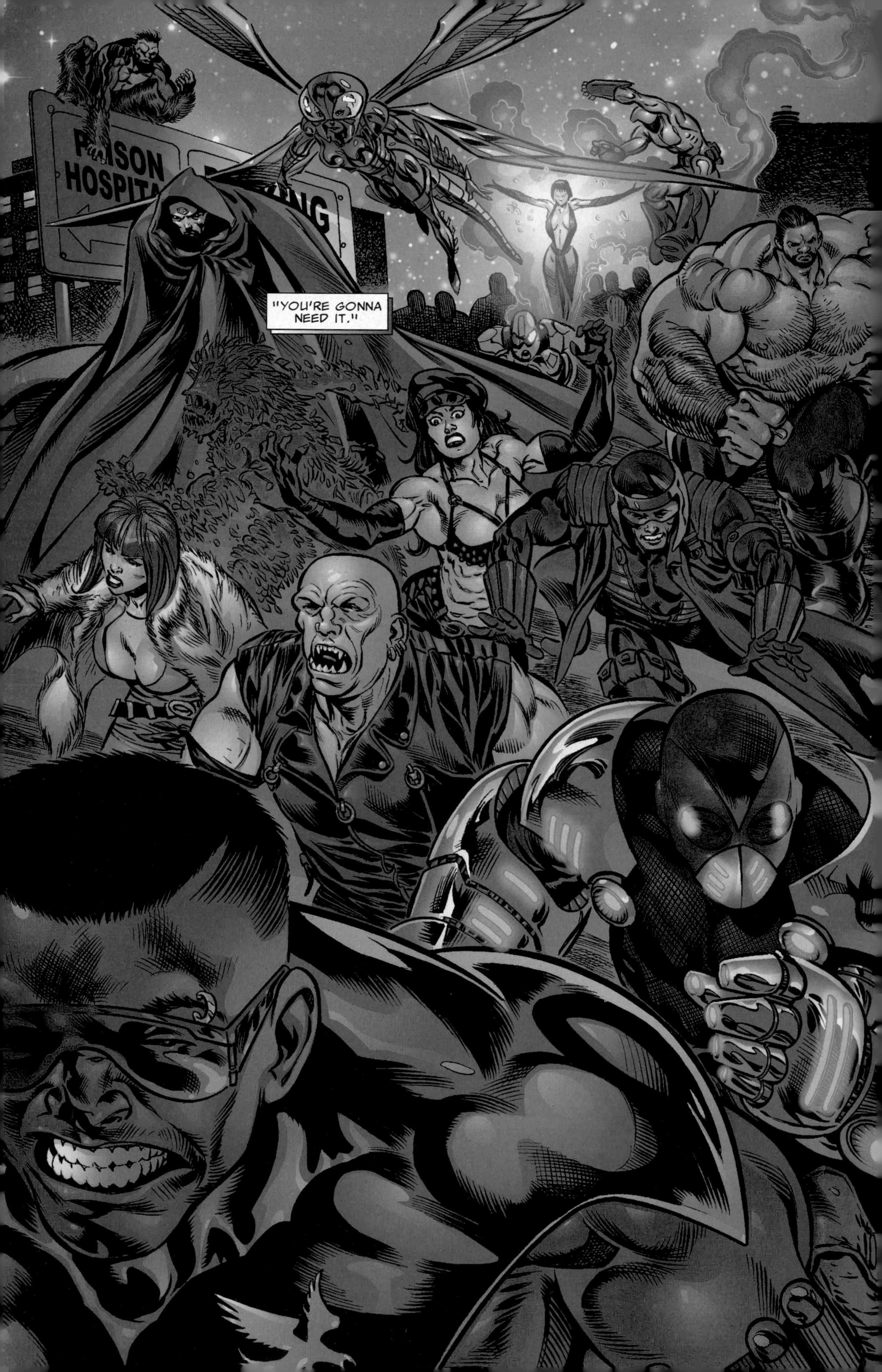

PRISON
HOSPITAL
"YOU'RE GONNA NEED IT."

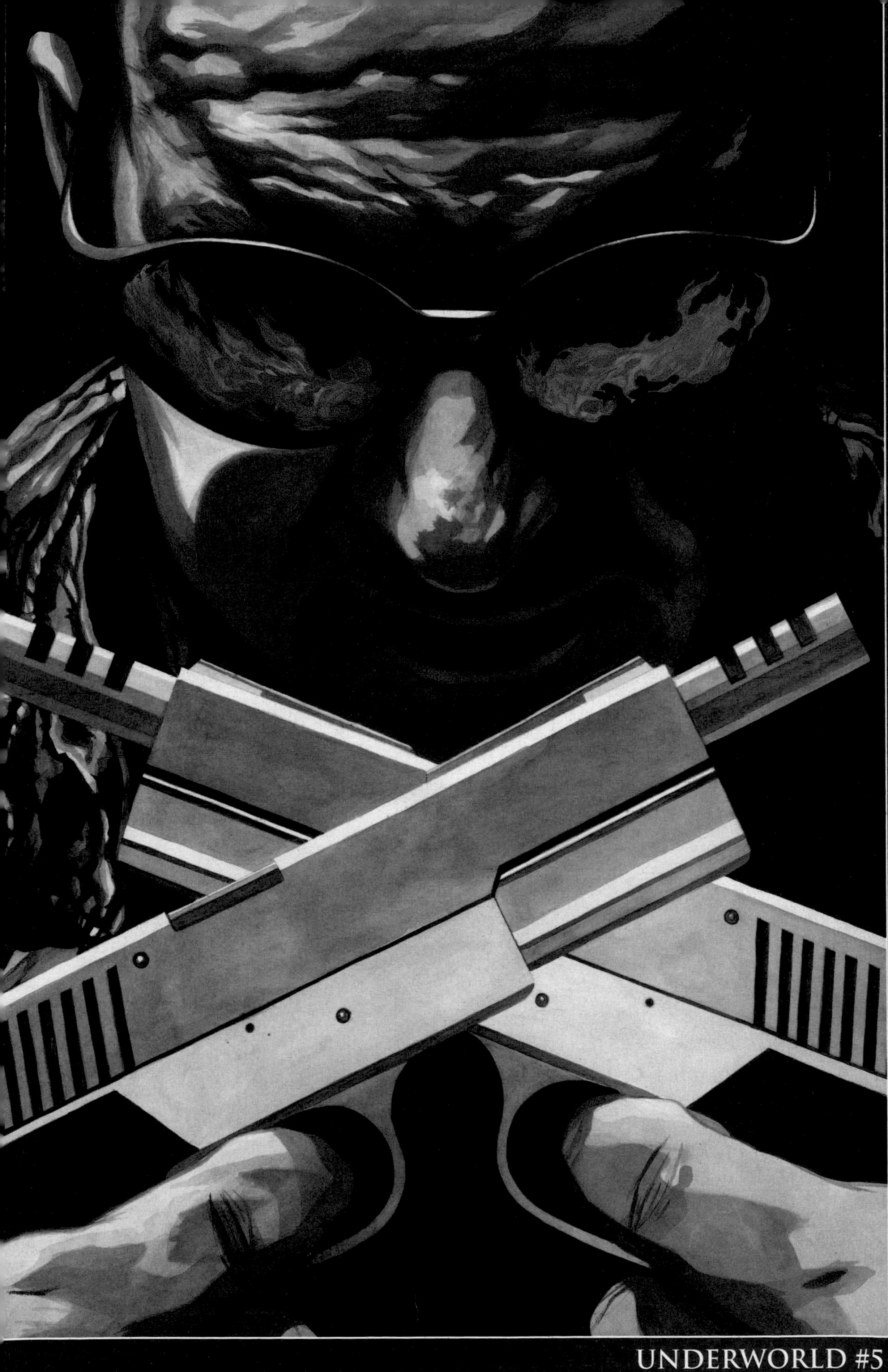

UNDERWORLD #5

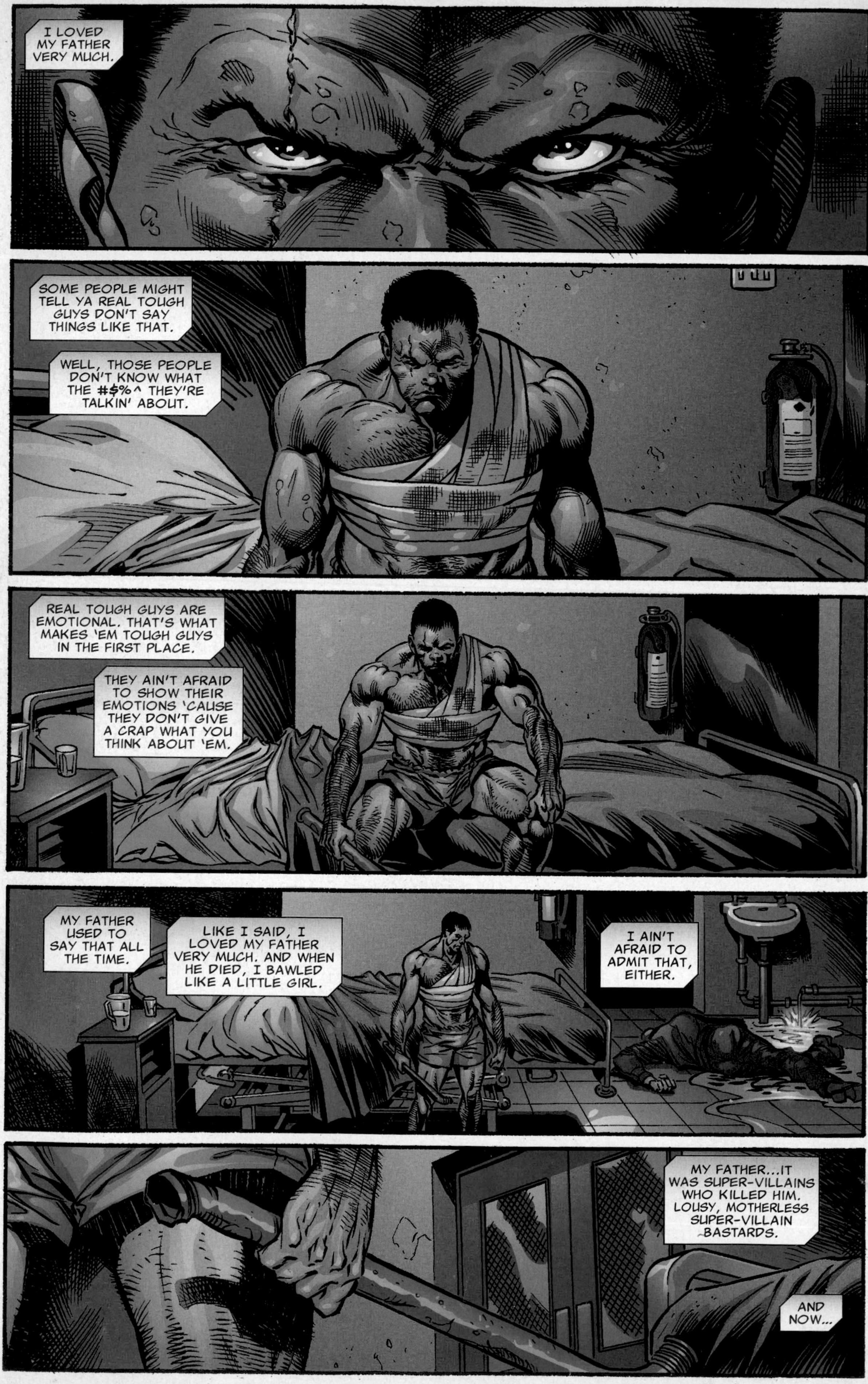

I LOVED MY FATHER VERY MUCH.
SOME PEOPLE MIGHT TELL YA REAL TOUGH GUYS DON'T SAY THINGS LIKE THAT.
WELL, THOSE PEOPLE DON'T KNOW WHAT THE #$%^ THEY'RE TALKIN' ABOUT.
REAL TOUGH GUYS ARE EMOTIONAL. THAT'S WHAT MAKES 'EM TOUGH GUYS IN THE FIRST PLACE.
THEY AIN'T AFRAID TO SHOW THEIR EMOTIONS 'CAUSE THEY DON'T GIVE A CRAP WHAT YOU THINK ABOUT 'EM.
MY FATHER USED TO SAY THAT ALL THE TIME.
LIKE I SAID, I LOVED MY FATHER VERY MUCH. AND WHEN HE DIED, I BAWLED LIKE A LITTLE GIRL.
I AIN'T AFRAID TO ADMIT THAT, EITHER.
MY FATHER...IT WAS SUPER-VILLAINS WHO KILLED HIM. LOUSY, MOTHERLESS SUPER-VILLAIN BASTARDS.
AND NOW...

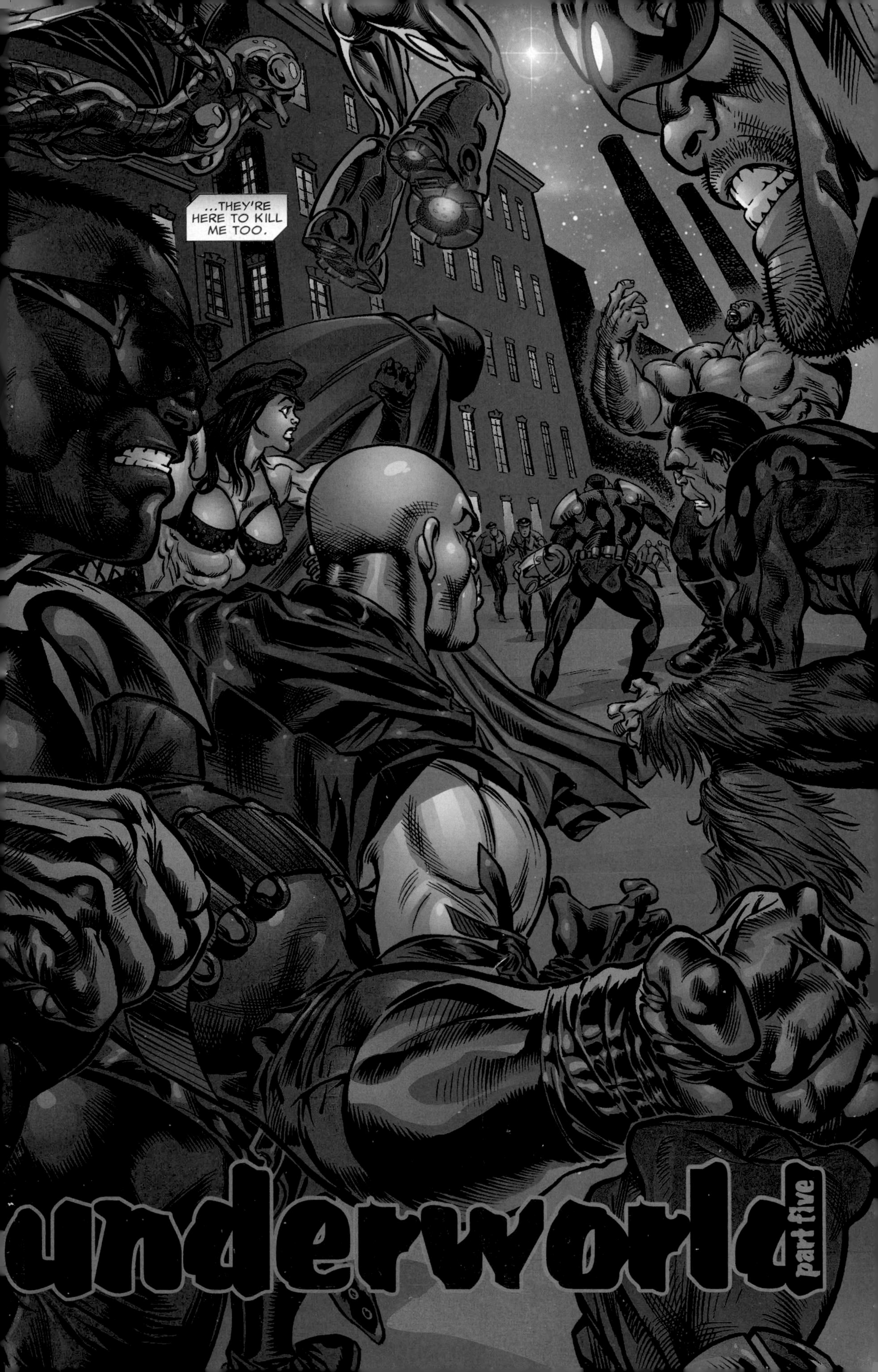
...THEY'RE HERE TO KILL ME TOO.
underworld
part five

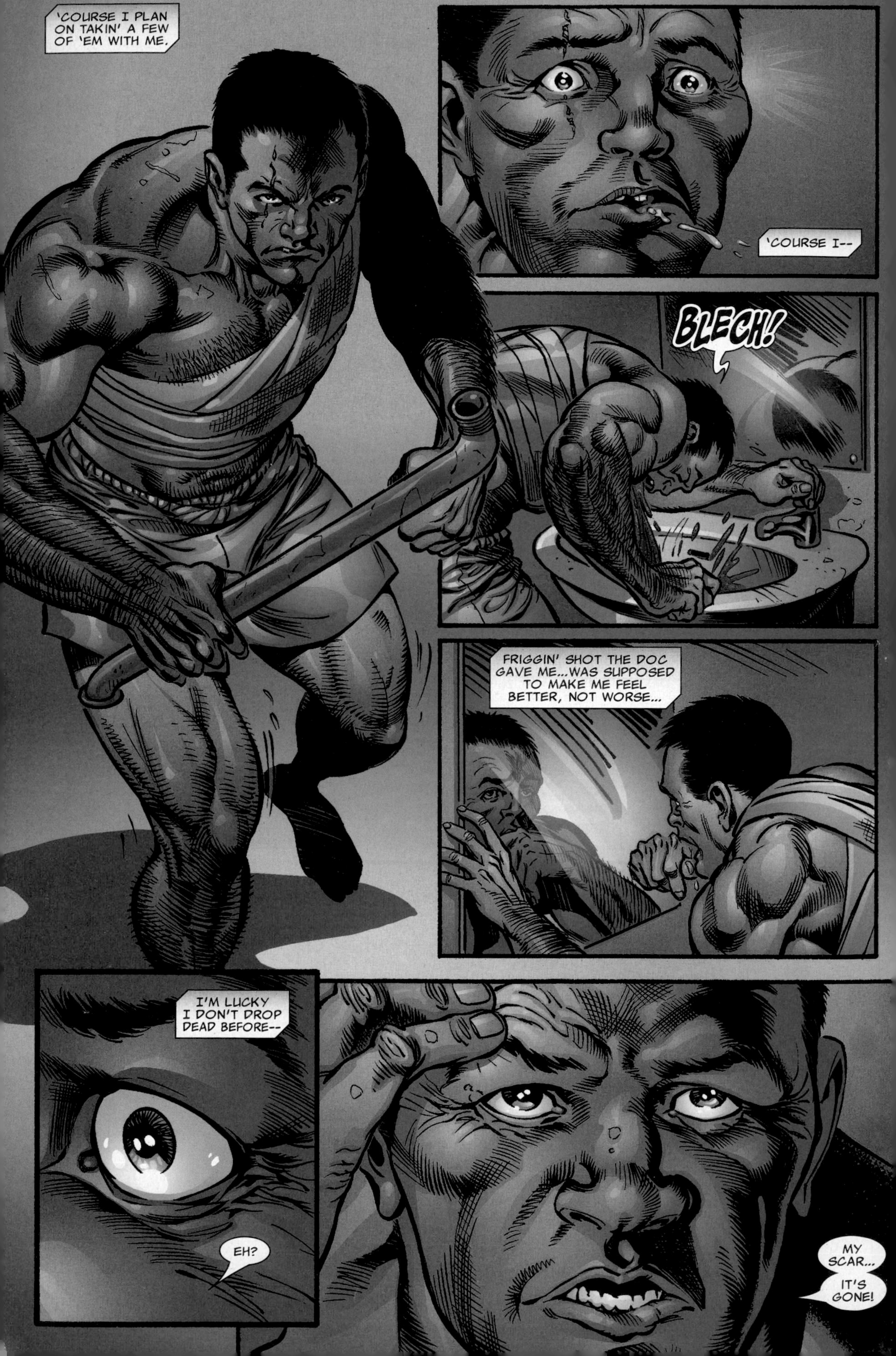
'COURSE I PLAN ON TAKIN' A FEW OF 'EM WITH ME.
'COURSE I--
BLECH!
FRIGGIN' SHOT THE DOC GAVE ME...WAS SUPPOSED TO MAKE ME FEEL BETTER, NOT WORSE...
I'M LUCKY I DON'T DROP DEAD BEFORE--
EH?
MY SCAR...
IT'S GONE!

AND NOT ONLY THAT...

I'M EVEN STARTIN' TO HEAL WHERE I GOT PLUGGED.

UN-#$%^IN'-BELIEVABLE.

WHAT THE--?!

THAT WASN'T HERE BEFORE.

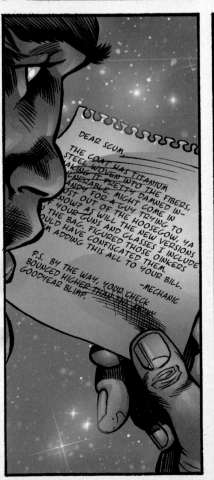

DEAR SCUM,

THE COAT HAS TITANIUM STEEL WOVEN INTO THE FIBERS, MAKING IT PRETTY DAMNED IN-VULNERABLE. MIGHT COME IN HANDY FOR A GUY TRYING TO BUST OUT OF THE HOOSEGOW, YA KNOW? AS WILL THE NEW VERSIONS OF YOUR GUNS AND GLASSES I INCLUDE IN THE BAG. FIGURED THOSE OINKERS WOULD HAVE CONFISCATED THEM.

I'M ADDING THIS ALL TO YOUR BILL.

—MECHANIC

P.S. BY THE WAY, YOUR CHECK BOUNCED HIGHER THAN THE GOODYEAR BLIMP.

WHAT DO THESE FRIGGIN' GUYS EXPECT? I AIN'T GOT TWO DIMES TO RUB TOGETHER. I JUST GOT OUTTA THE JOINT, FOR CHRISSAKES!

INVULNERABLE COAT, HUH?

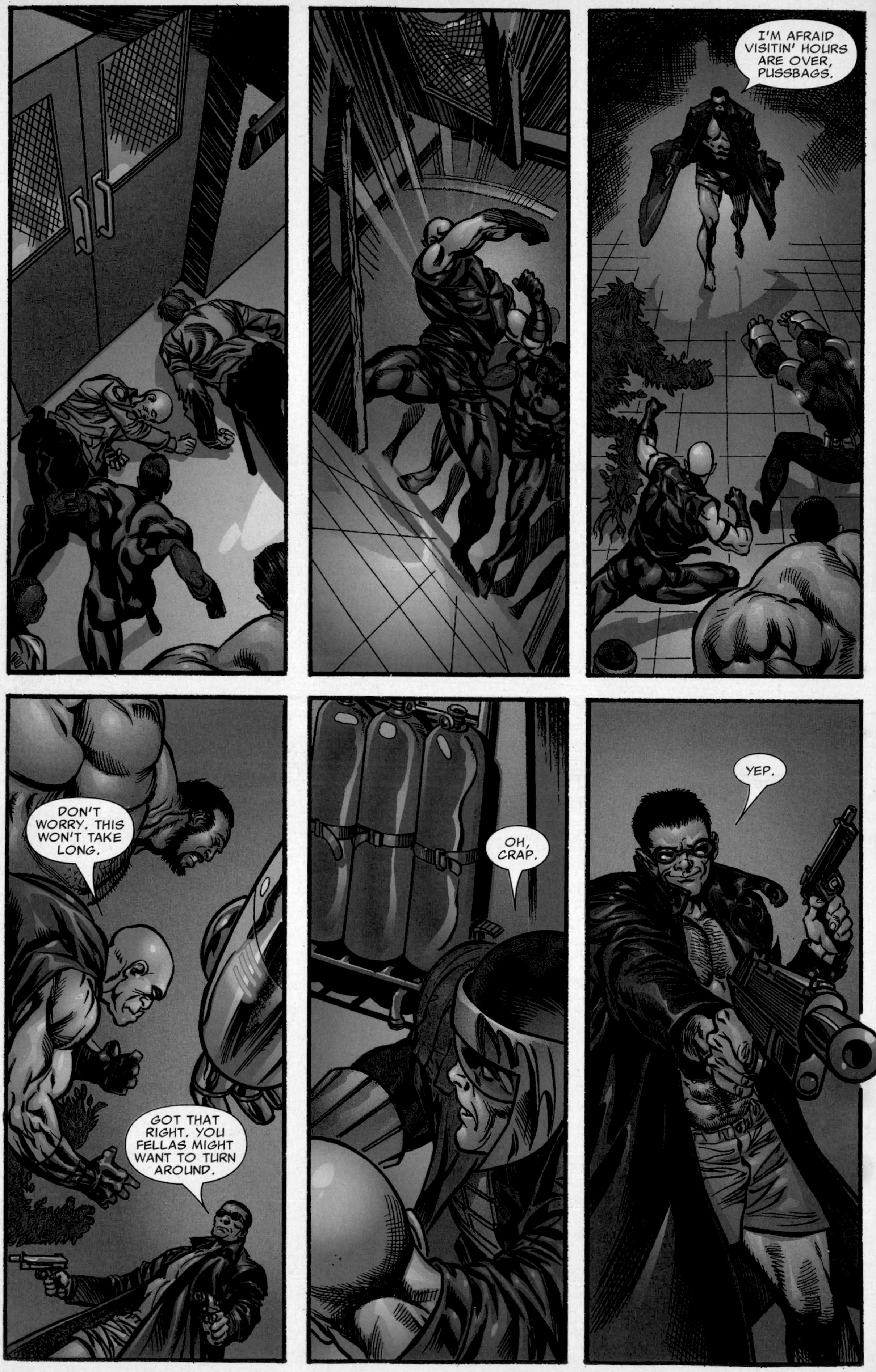
I'M AFRAID VISITIN' HOURS ARE OVER, PUSSBAGS.
DON'T WORRY. THIS WON'T TAKE LONG.
GOT THAT RIGHT. YOU FELLAS MIGHT WANT TO TURN AROUND.
OH, CRAP.
YEP.

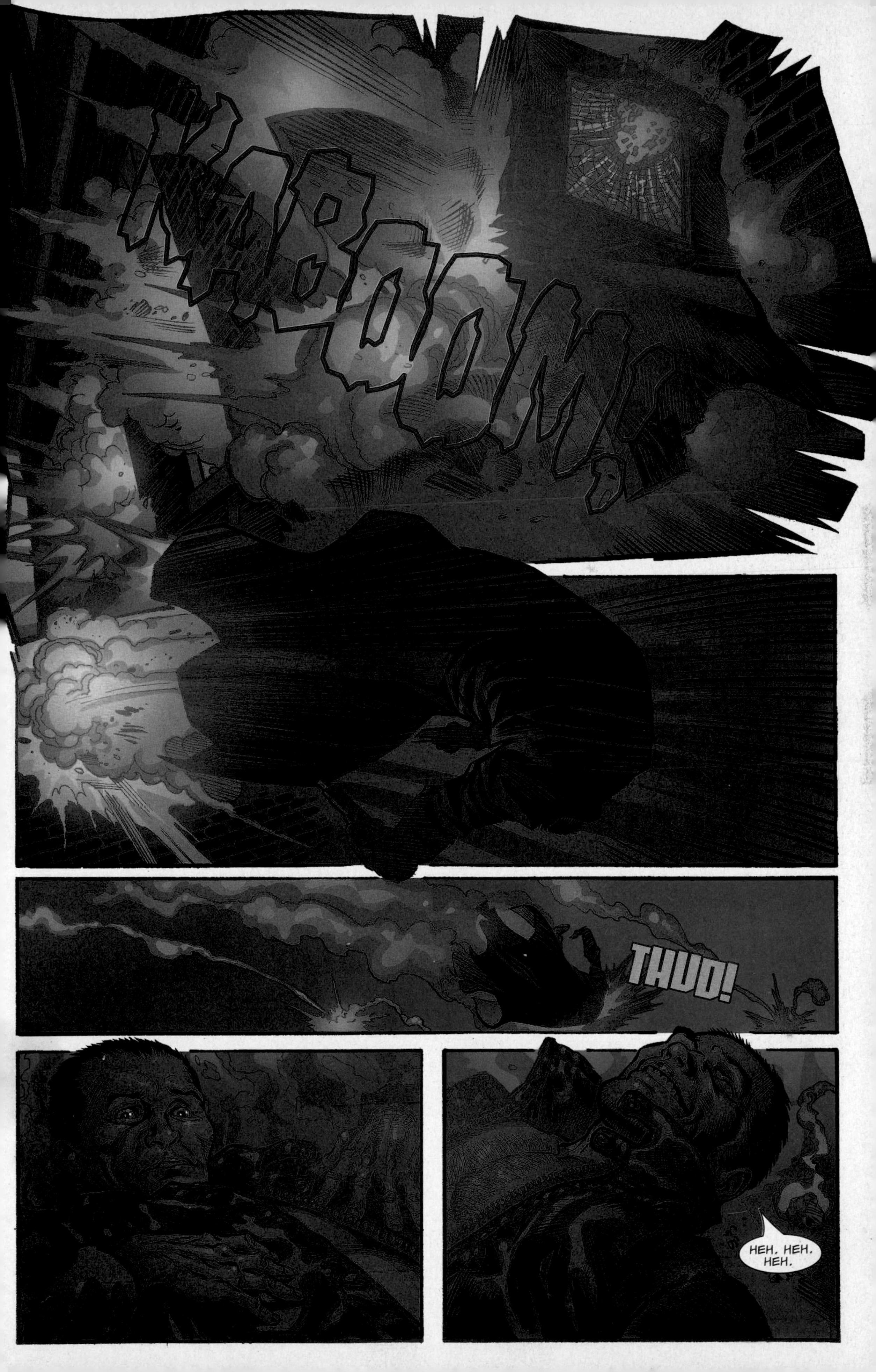
KA-BOOOM!
THUD!
HEH. HEH. HEH.

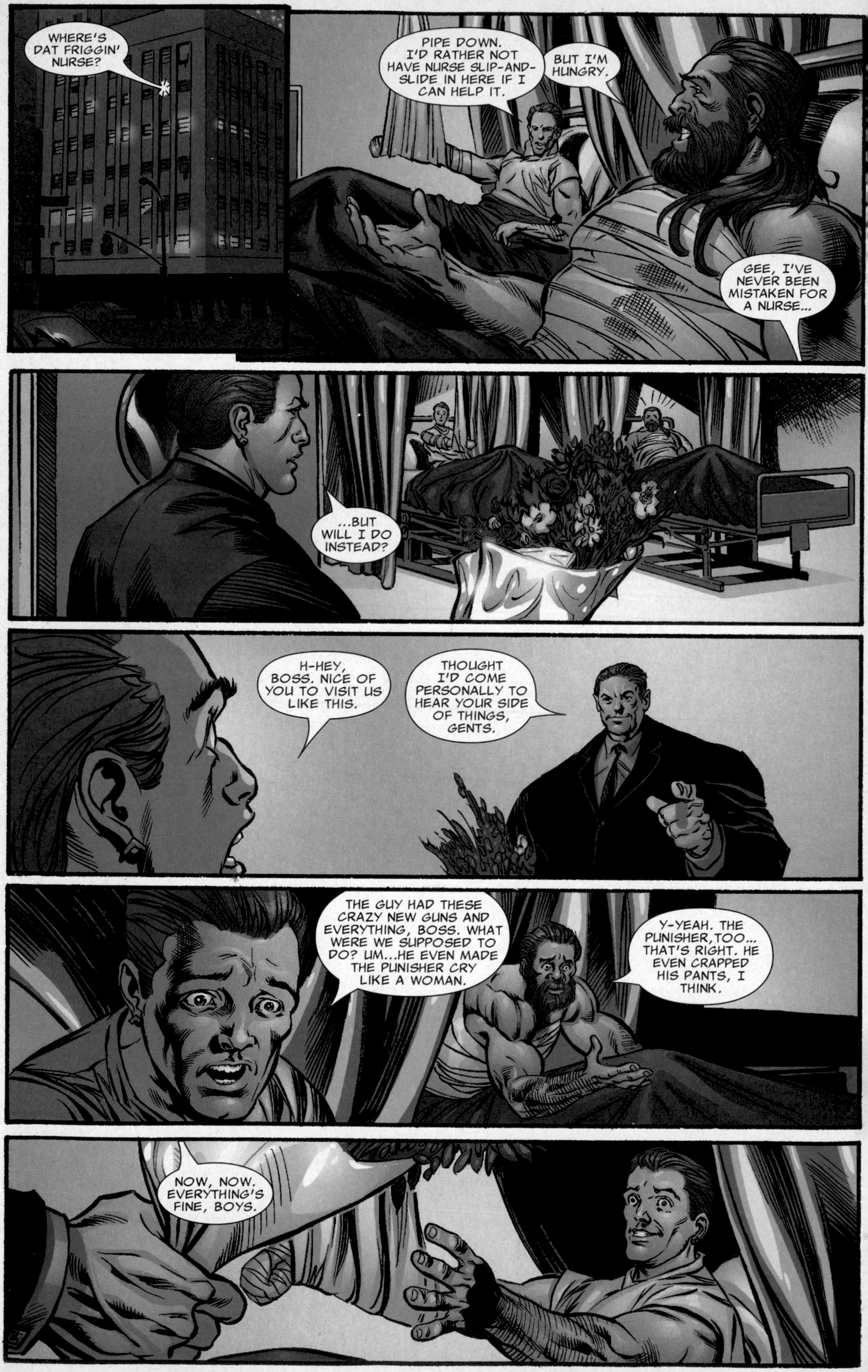

WHERE'S DAT FRIGGIN' NURSE?
PIPE DOWN. I'D RATHER NOT HAVE NURSE SLIP-AND-SLIDE IN HERE IF I CAN HELP IT.
BUT I'M HUNGRY.
GEE, I'VE NEVER BEEN MISTAKEN FOR A NURSE...
...BUT WILL I DO INSTEAD?
H-HEY, BOSS. NICE OF YOU TO VISIT US LIKE THIS.
THOUGHT I'D COME PERSONALLY TO HEAR YOUR SIDE OF THINGS, GENTS.
THE GUY HAD THESE CRAZY NEW GUNS AND EVERYTHING, BOSS. WHAT WERE WE SUPPOSED TO DO? UM...HE EVEN MADE THE PUNISHER CRY LIKE A WOMAN.
Y-YEAH. THE PUNISHER,TOO... THAT'S RIGHT. HE EVEN CRAPPED HIS PANTS, I THINK.
NOW, NOW. EVERYTHING'S FINE, BOYS.

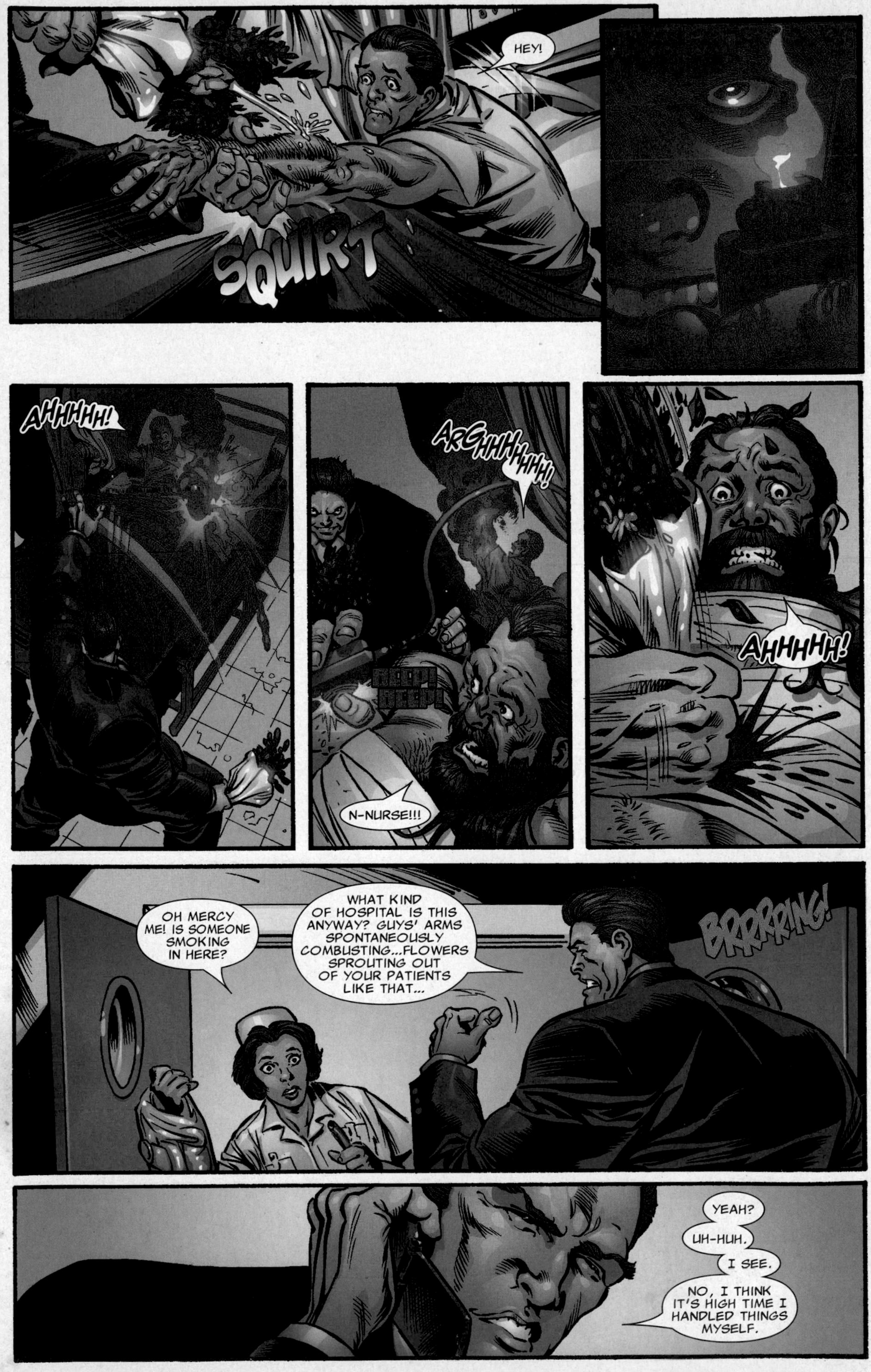
HEY!
SQUIRT
AHHHHH!
ARGHHHHHHH!
N-NURSE!!!
AHHHHH!
OH MERCY ME! IS SOMEONE SMOKING IN HERE?
WHAT KIND OF HOSPITAL IS THIS ANYWAY? GUYS' ARMS SPONTANEOUSLY COMBUSTING...FLOWERS SPROUTING OUT OF YOUR PATIENTS LIKE THAT...
BRRRRING!
YEAH?
UH-HUH.
I SEE.
NO, I THINK IT'S HIGH TIME I HANDLED THINGS MYSELF.

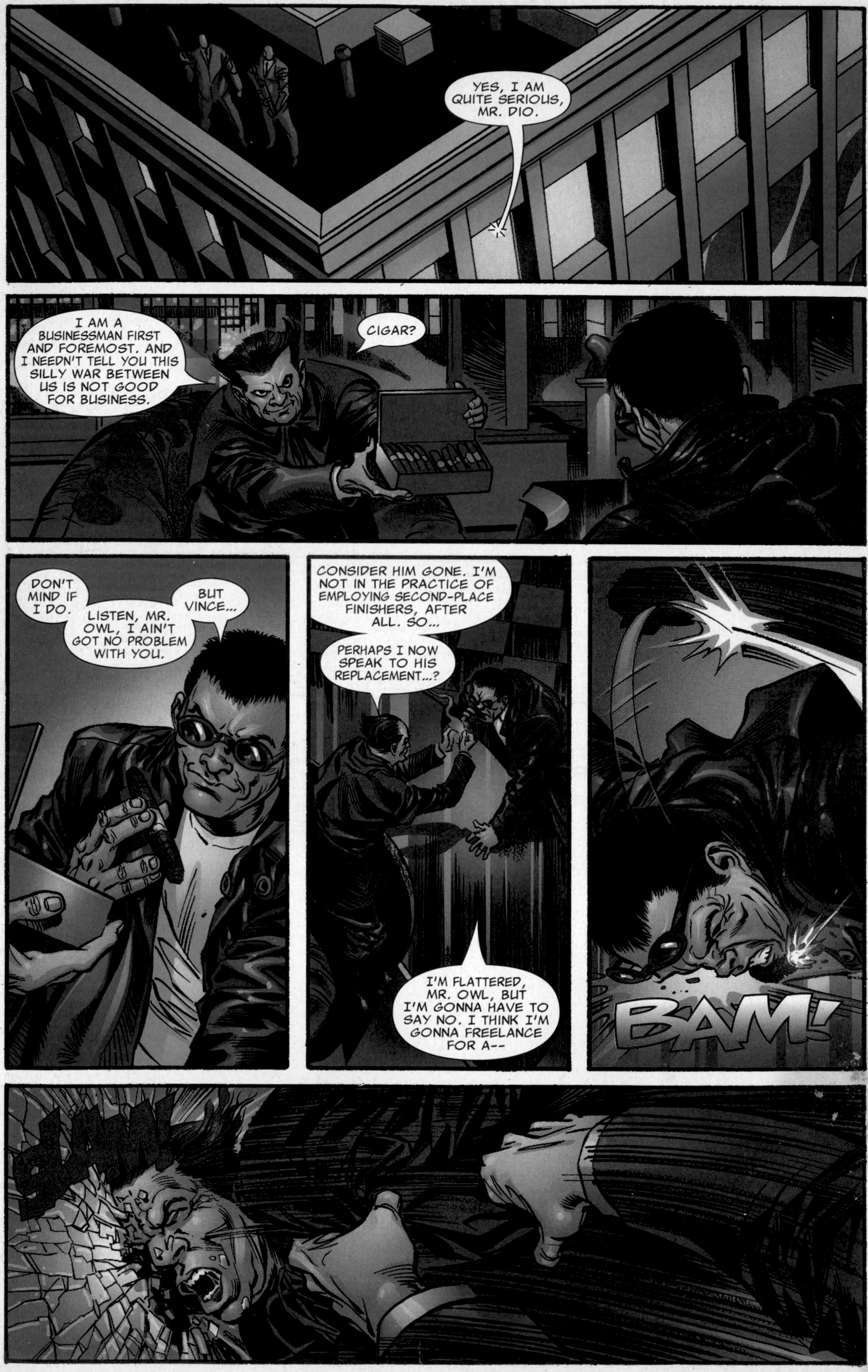
YES, I AM QUITE SERIOUS, MR. DIO.
I AM A BUSINESSMAN FIRST AND FOREMOST. AND I NEEDN'T TELL YOU THIS SILLY WAR BETWEEN US IS NOT GOOD FOR BUSINESS.
CIGAR?
DON'T MIND IF I DO.
LISTEN, MR. OWL, I AIN'T GOT NO PROBLEM WITH YOU.
BUT VINCE...
CONSIDER HIM GONE. I'M NOT IN THE PRACTICE OF EMPLOYING SECOND-PLACE FINISHERS, AFTER ALL. SO...
PERHAPS I NOW SPEAK TO HIS REPLACEMENT...?
I'M FLATTERED, MR. OWL, BUT I'M GONNA HAVE TO SAY NO. I THINK I'M GONNA FREELANCE FOR A--
BAM!

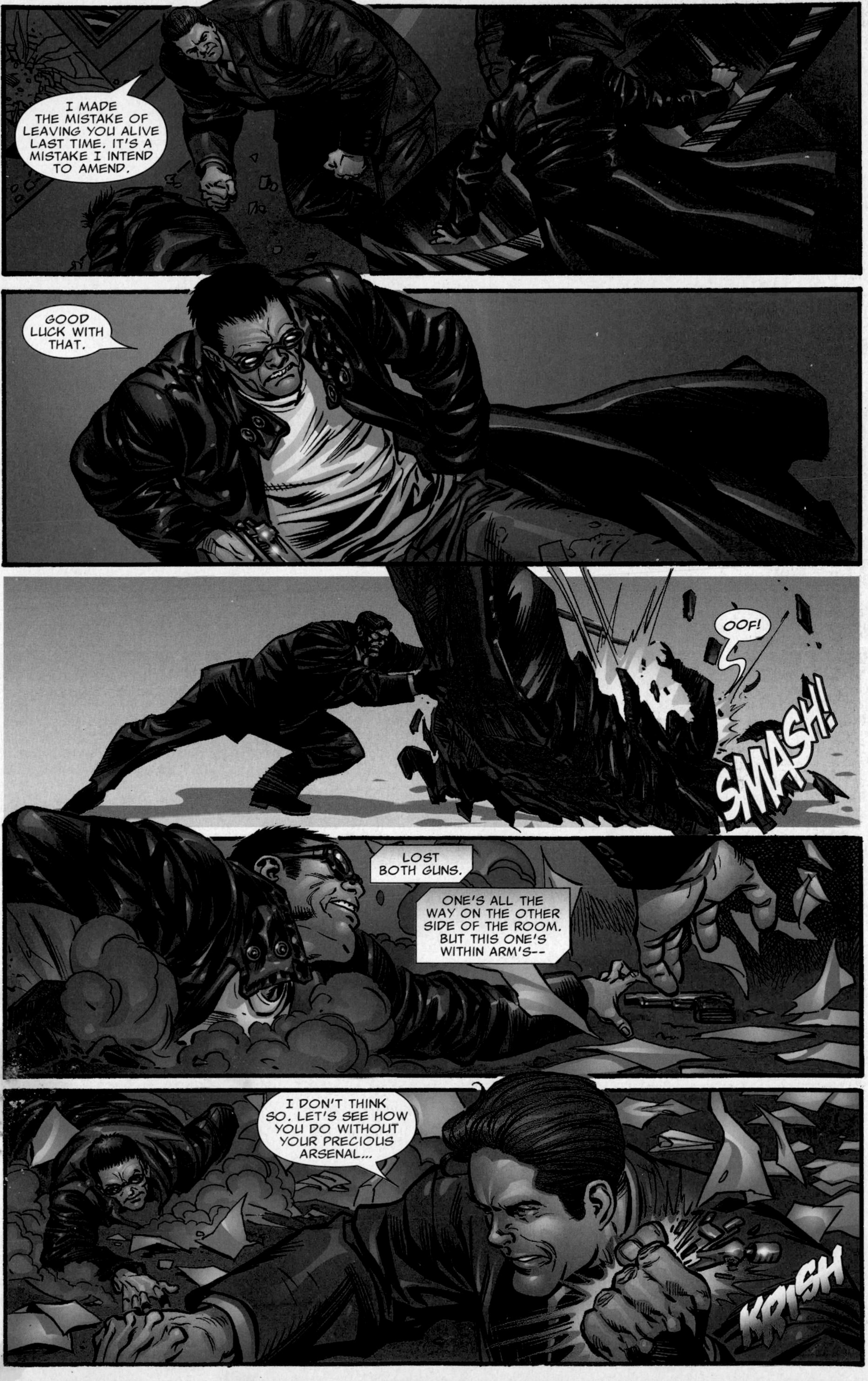
I MADE THE MISTAKE OF LEAVING YOU ALIVE LAST TIME. IT'S A MISTAKE I INTEND TO AMEND.
GOOD LUCK WITH THAT.
OOF!
SMASH!
LOST BOTH GUNS.
ONE'S ALL THE WAY ON THE OTHER SIDE OF THE ROOM. BUT THIS ONE'S WITHIN ARM'S--
I DON'T THINK SO. LET'S SEE HOW YOU DO WITHOUT YOUR PRECIOUS ARSENAL...
KRISH

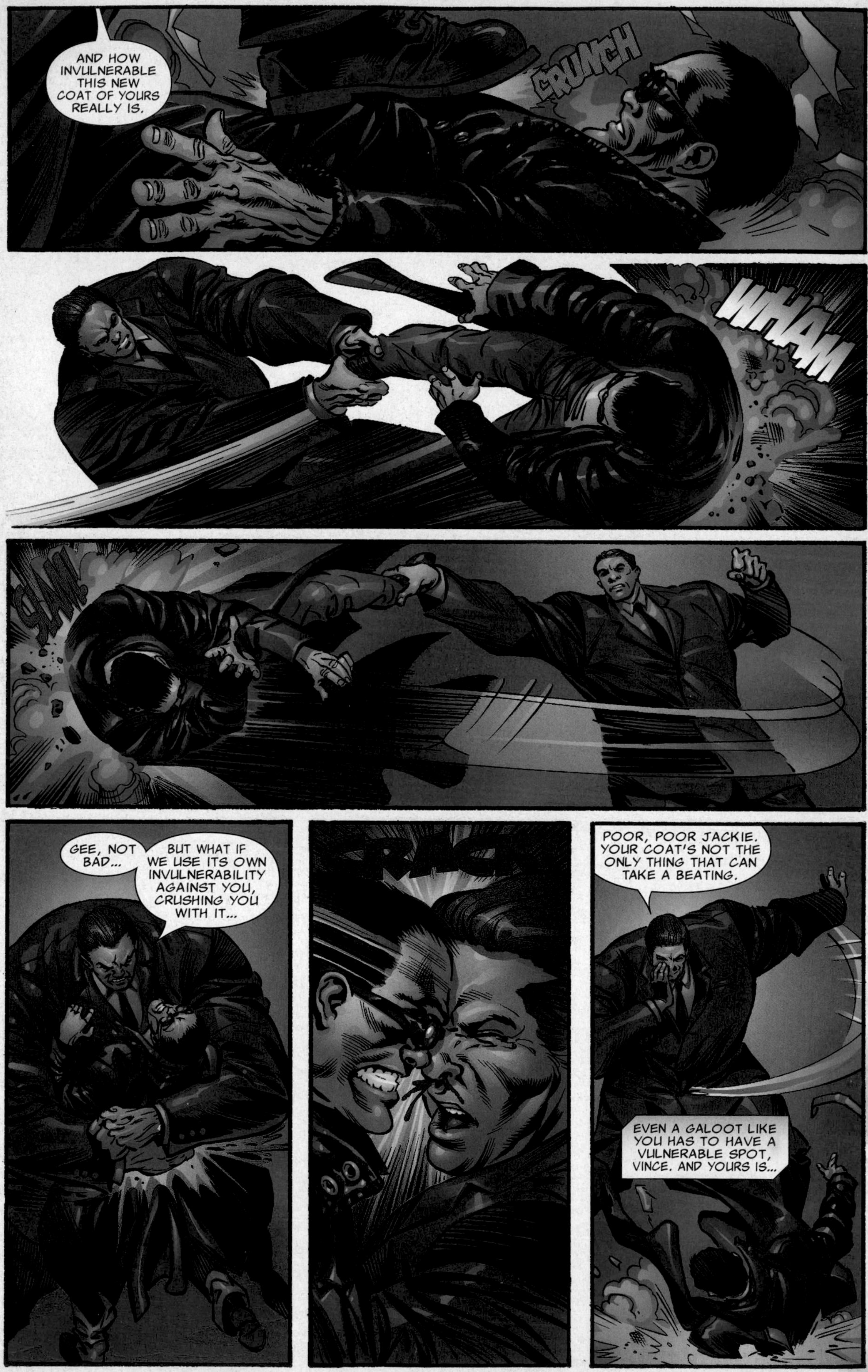
AND HOW INVULNERABLE THIS NEW COAT OF YOURS REALLY IS.
CRUNCH
WHAM
SLAM!
GEE, NOT BAD...
BUT WHAT IF WE USE ITS OWN INVULNERABILITY AGAINST YOU, CRUSHING YOU WITH IT...
POOR, POOR JACKIE. YOUR COAT'S NOT THE ONLY THING THAT CAN TAKE A BEATING.
EVEN A GALOOT LIKE YOU HAS TO HAVE A VULNERABLE SPOT, VINCE. AND YOURS IS...

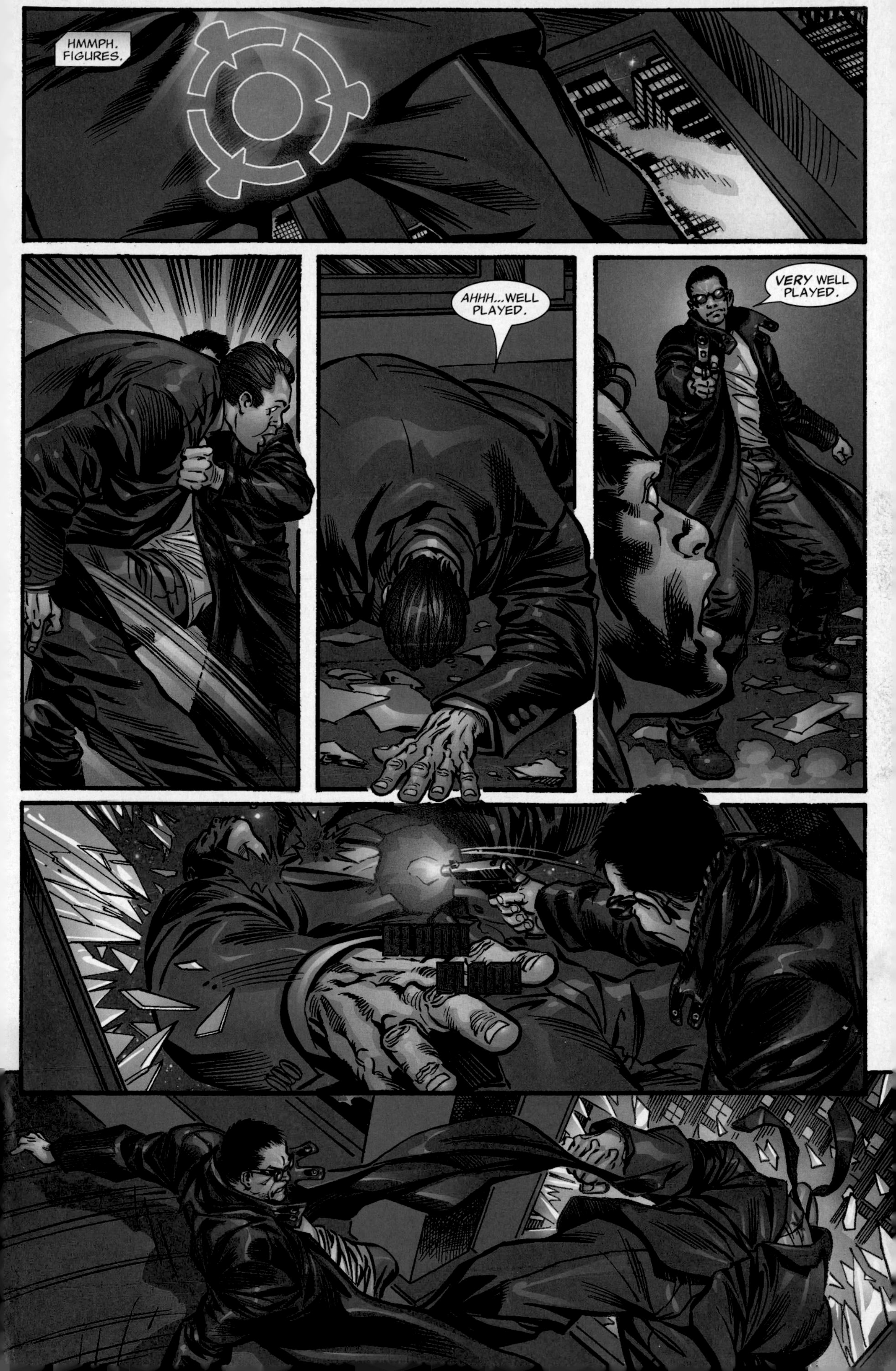
HMMPH. FIGURES.
AHHH...WELL PLAYED.
VERY WELL PLAYED.

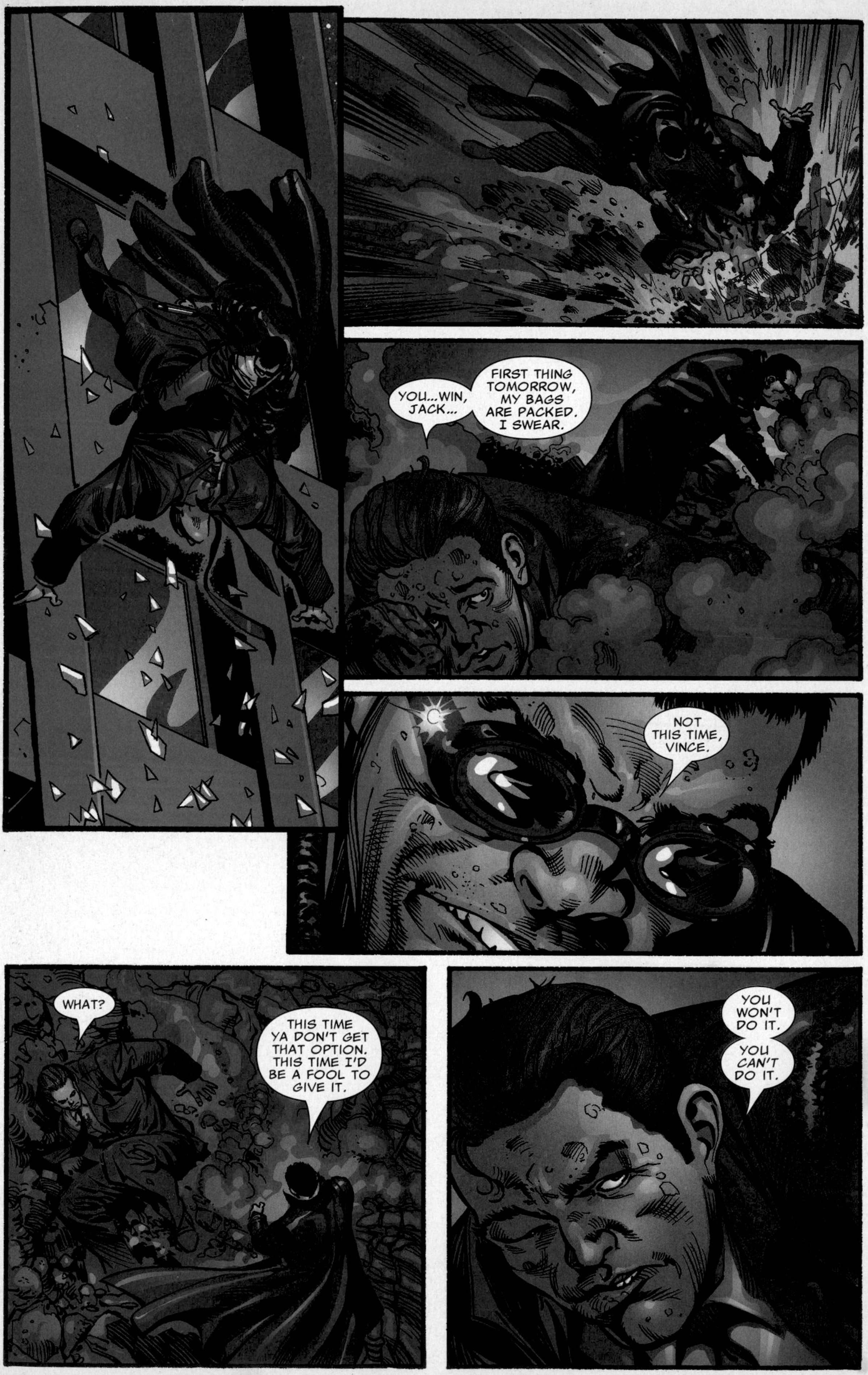
YOU...WIN, JACK...
FIRST THING TOMORROW, MY BAGS ARE PACKED. I SWEAR.
NOT THIS TIME, VINCE.
WHAT?
THIS TIME YA DON'T GET THAT OPTION. THIS TIME I'D BE A FOOL TO GIVE IT.
YOU WON'T DO IT.
YOU CAN'T DO IT.

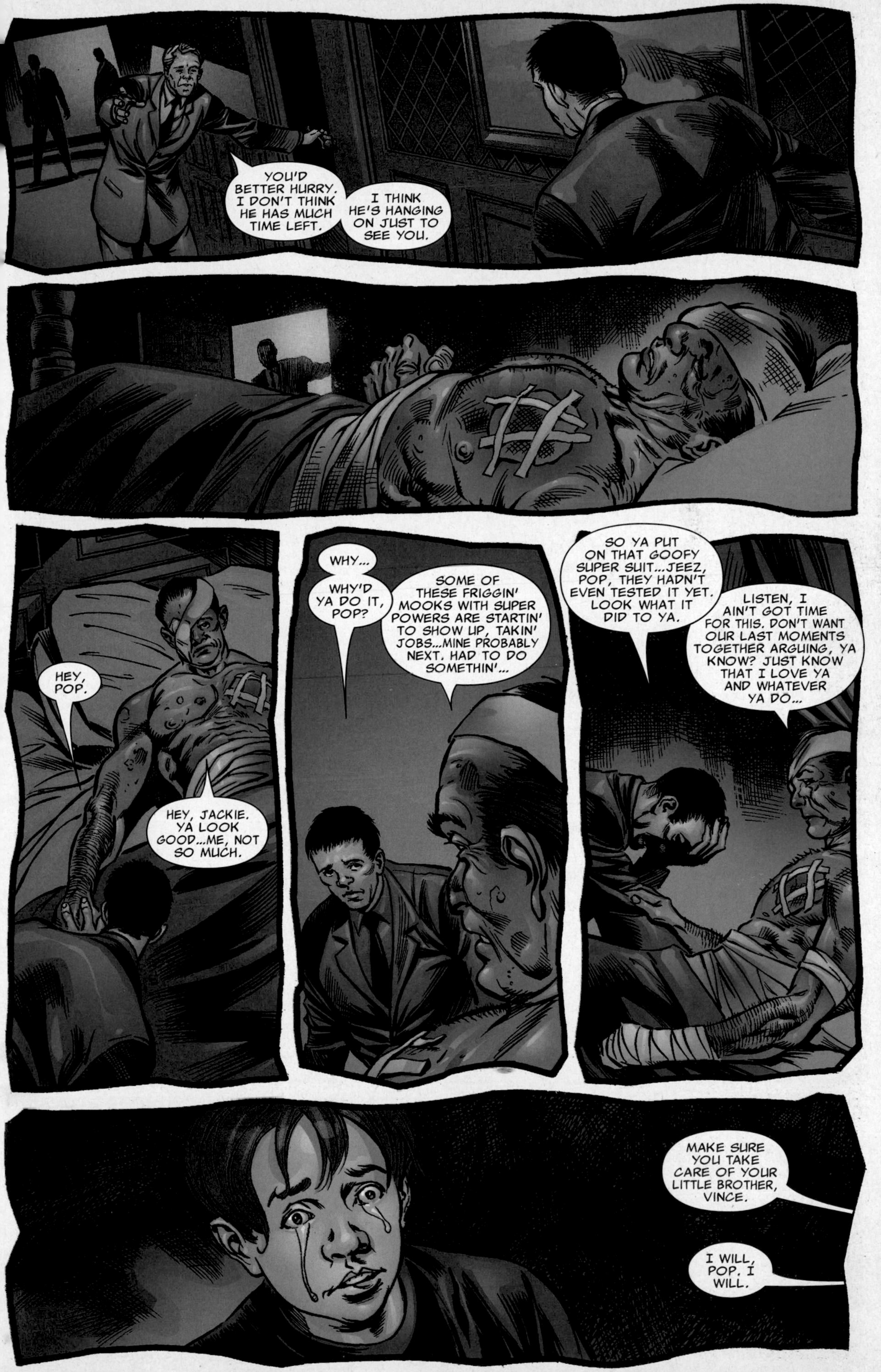
YOU'D BETTER HURRY. I DON'T THINK HE HAS MUCH TIME LEFT.
I THINK HE'S HANGING ON JUST TO SEE YOU.
HEY, POP.
HEY, JACKIE. YA LOOK GOOD...ME, NOT SO MUCH.
WHY...
WHY'D YA DO IT, POP?
SOME OF THESE FRIGGIN' MOOKS WITH SUPER POWERS ARE STARTIN' TO SHOW UP, TAKIN' JOBS...MINE PROBABLY NEXT. HAD TO DO SOMETHIN'...
SO YA PUT ON THAT GOOFY SUPER SUIT...JEEZ, POP, THEY HADN'T EVEN TESTED IT YET. LOOK WHAT IT DID TO YA.
LISTEN, I AIN'T GOT TIME FOR THIS. DON'T WANT OUR LAST MOMENTS TOGETHER ARGUING, YA KNOW? JUST KNOW THAT I LOVE YA AND WHATEVER YA DO...
MAKE SURE YOU TAKE CARE OF YOUR LITTLE BROTHER, VINCE.
I WILL, POP. I WILL.

YOU COULDN'T DO IT THAT DAY IN THE ALLEY, AND YOU CAN'T DO IT NOW.

CLICK!

I'M YOUR BROTHER! YOU JUST CAN'T KILL YOUR OWN BROTHER!

YOU JUST CAN'T!

PLEASE FORGIVE ME, DAD.

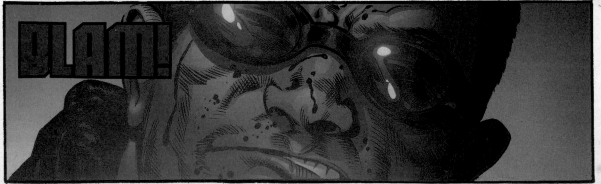

BLAM!

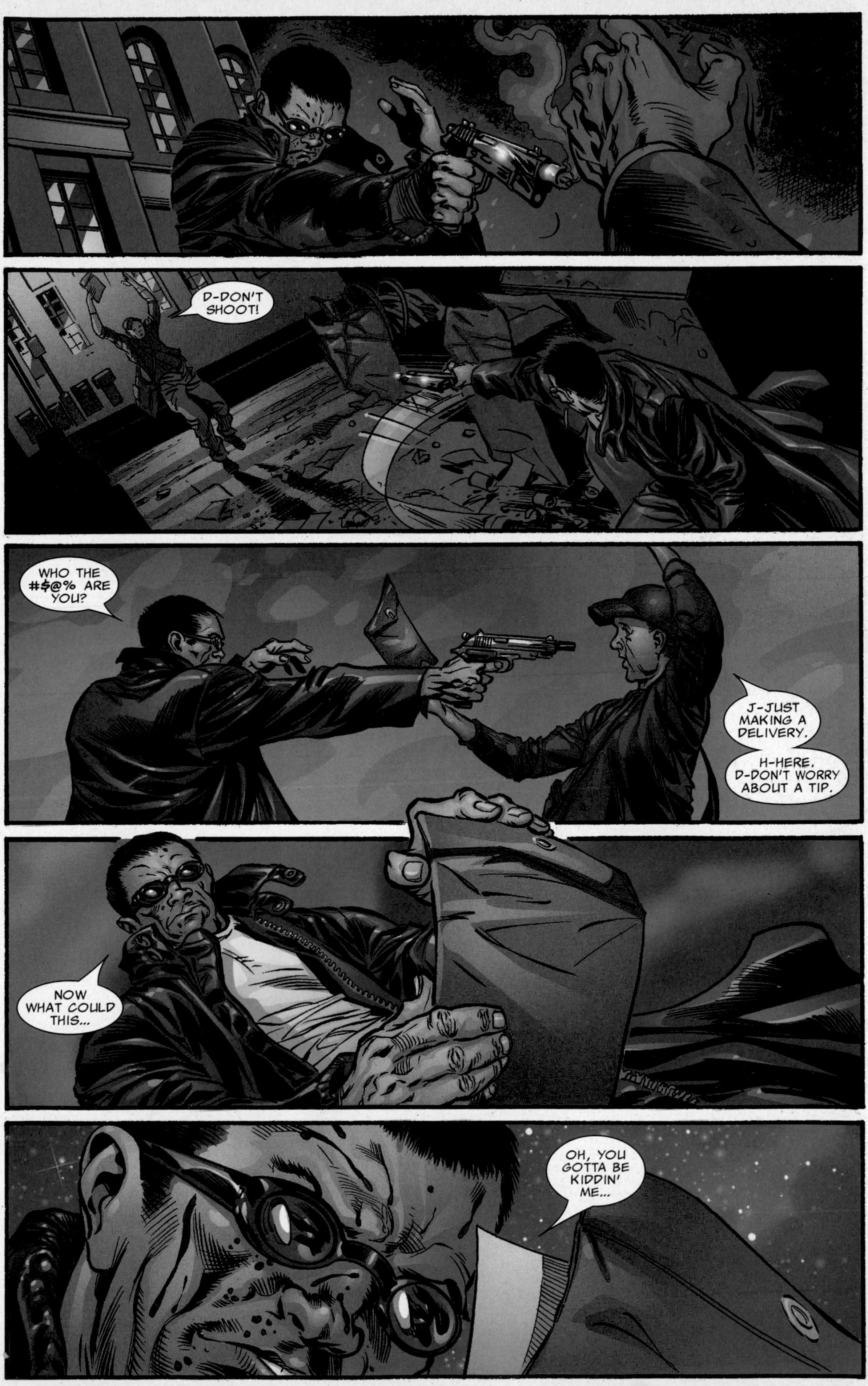
D-DON'T SHOOT!
WHO THE #$@% ARE YOU?
J-JUST MAKING A DELIVERY.
H-HERE. D-DON'T WORRY ABOUT A TIP.
NOW WHAT COULD THIS...
OH, YOU GOTTA BE KIDDIN' ME...

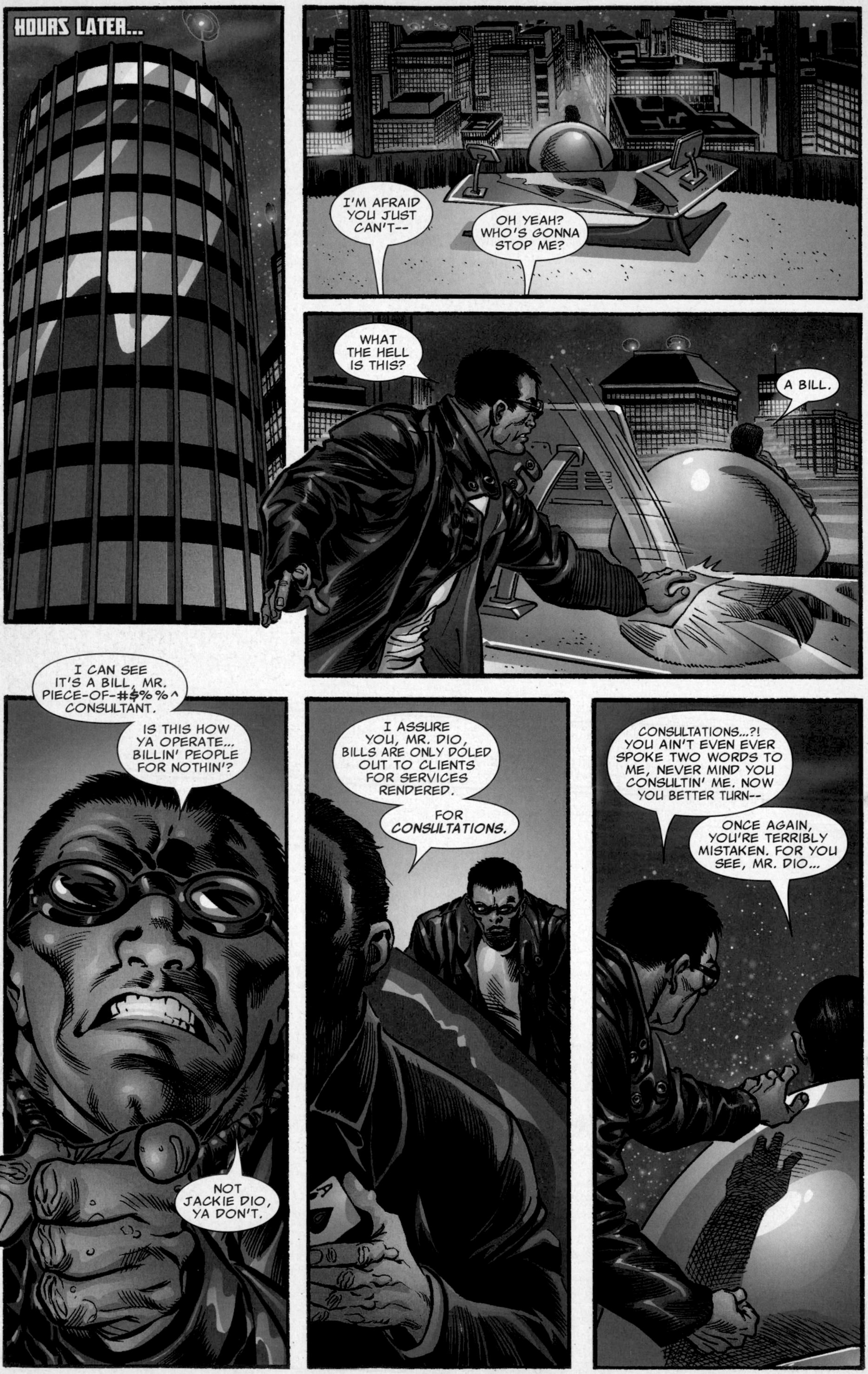
HOURS LATER...
I'M AFRAID YOU JUST CAN'T--
OH YEAH? WHO'S GONNA STOP ME?
WHAT THE HELL IS THIS?
A BILL.
I CAN SEE IT'S A BILL, MR. PIECE-OF-#$%%^ CONSULTANT.
IS THIS HOW YA OPERATE... BILLIN' PEOPLE FOR NOTHIN'?
NOT JACKIE DIO, YA DON'T.
I ASSURE YOU, MR. DIO, BILLS ARE ONLY DOLED OUT TO CLIENTS FOR SERVICES RENDERED.
FOR CONSULTATIONS.
CONSULTATIONS...?! YOU AIN'T EVEN EVER SPOKE TWO WORDS TO ME, NEVER MIND YOU CONSULTIN' ME. NOW YOU BETTER TURN--
ONCE AGAIN, YOU'RE TERRIBLY MISTAKEN. FOR YOU SEE, MR. DIO...

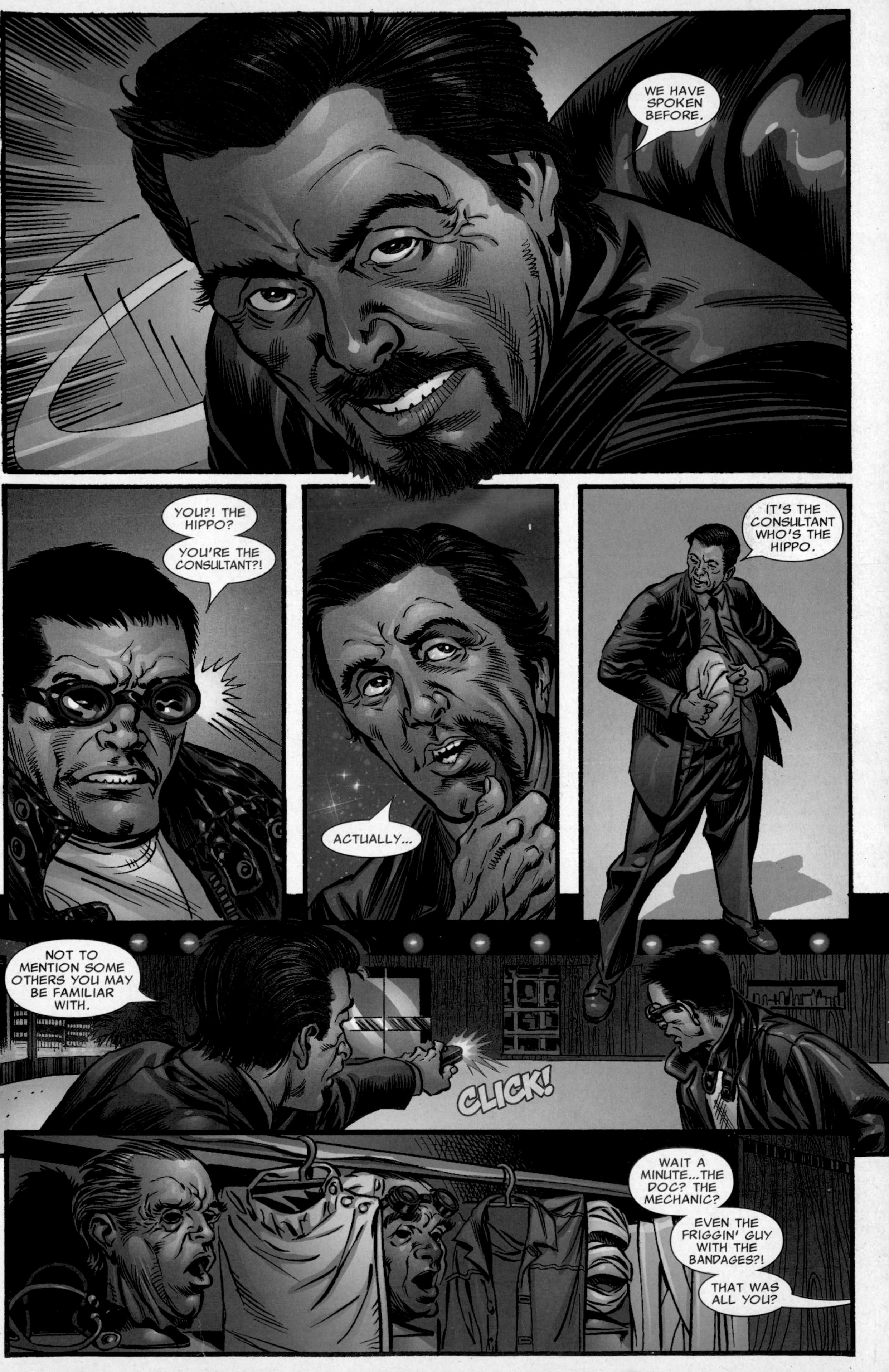
WE HAVE SPOKEN BEFORE.
YOU?! THE HIPPO?
YOU'RE THE CONSULTANT?!
ACTUALLY...
IT'S THE CONSULTANT WHO'S THE HIPPO.
NOT TO MENTION SOME OTHERS YOU MAY BE FAMILIAR WITH.
CLICK!
WAIT A MINUTE...THE DOC? THE MECHANIC?
EVEN THE FRIGGIN' GUY WITH THE BANDAGES?!
THAT WAS ALL YOU?

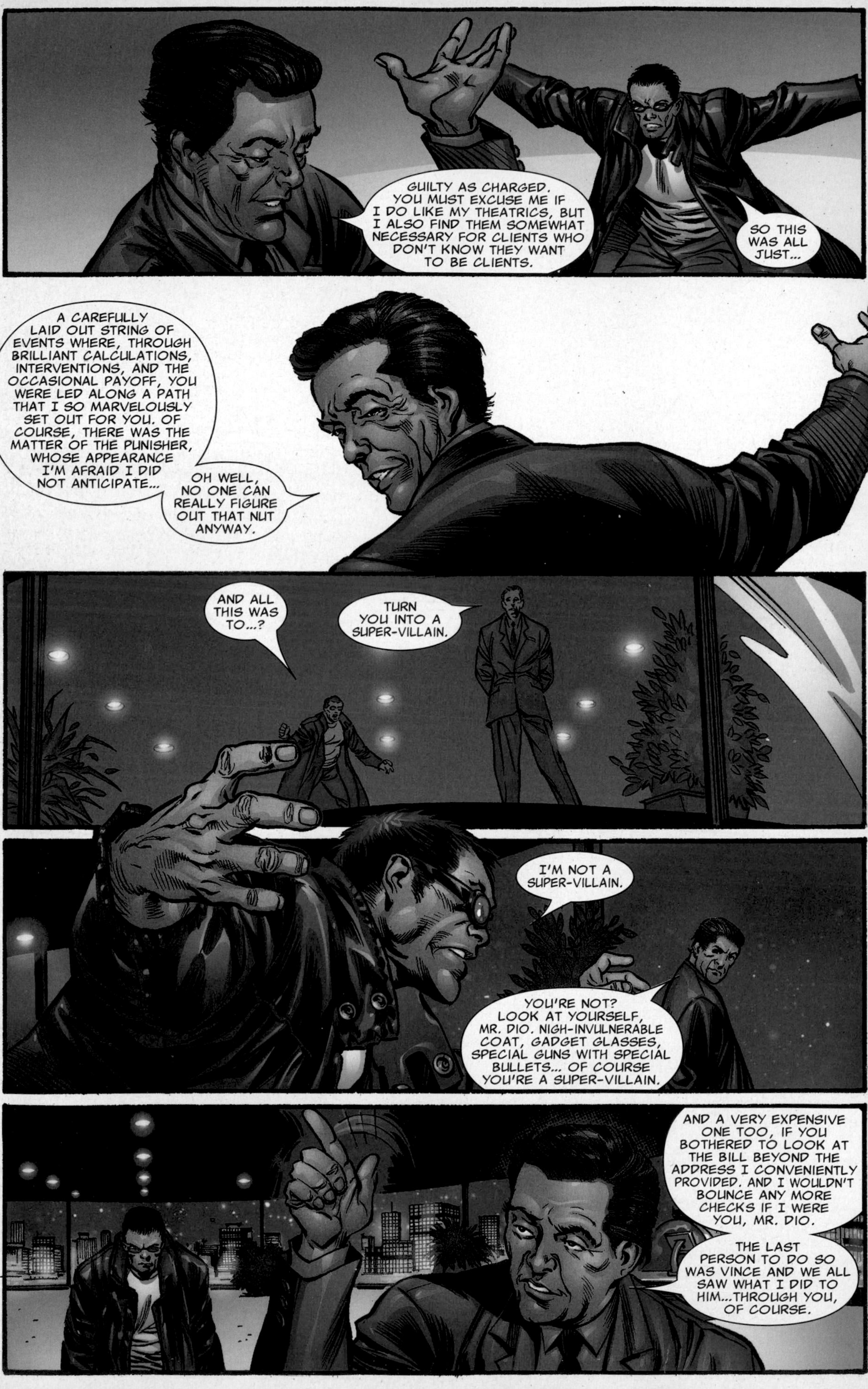
GUILTY AS CHARGED. YOU MUST EXCUSE ME IF I DO LIKE MY THEATRICS, BUT I ALSO FIND THEM SOMEWHAT NECESSARY FOR CLIENTS WHO DON'T KNOW THEY WANT TO BE CLIENTS.
SO THIS WAS ALL JUST...
A CAREFULLY LAID OUT STRING OF EVENTS WHERE, THROUGH BRILLIANT CALCULATIONS, INTERVENTIONS, AND THE OCCASIONAL PAYOFF, YOU WERE LED ALONG A PATH THAT I SO MARVELOUSLY SET OUT FOR YOU. OF COURSE, THERE WAS THE MATTER OF THE PUNISHER, WHOSE APPEARANCE I'M AFRAID I DID NOT ANTICIPATE...
OH WELL, NO ONE CAN REALLY FIGURE OUT THAT NUT ANYWAY.
AND ALL THIS WAS TO...?
TURN YOU INTO A SUPER-VILLAIN.
I'M NOT A SUPER-VILLAIN.
YOU'RE NOT? LOOK AT YOURSELF, MR. DIO. NIGH-INVULNERABLE COAT, GADGET GLASSES, SPECIAL GUNS WITH SPECIAL BULLETS... OF COURSE YOU'RE A SUPER-VILLAIN.
AND A VERY EXPENSIVE ONE TOO, IF YOU BOTHERED TO LOOK AT THE BILL BEYOND THE ADDRESS I CONVENIENTLY PROVIDED. AND I WOULDN'T BOUNCE ANY MORE CHECKS IF I WERE YOU, MR. DIO.
THE LAST PERSON TO DO SO WAS VINCE AND WE ALL SAW WHAT I DID TO HIM...THROUGH YOU, OF COURSE.

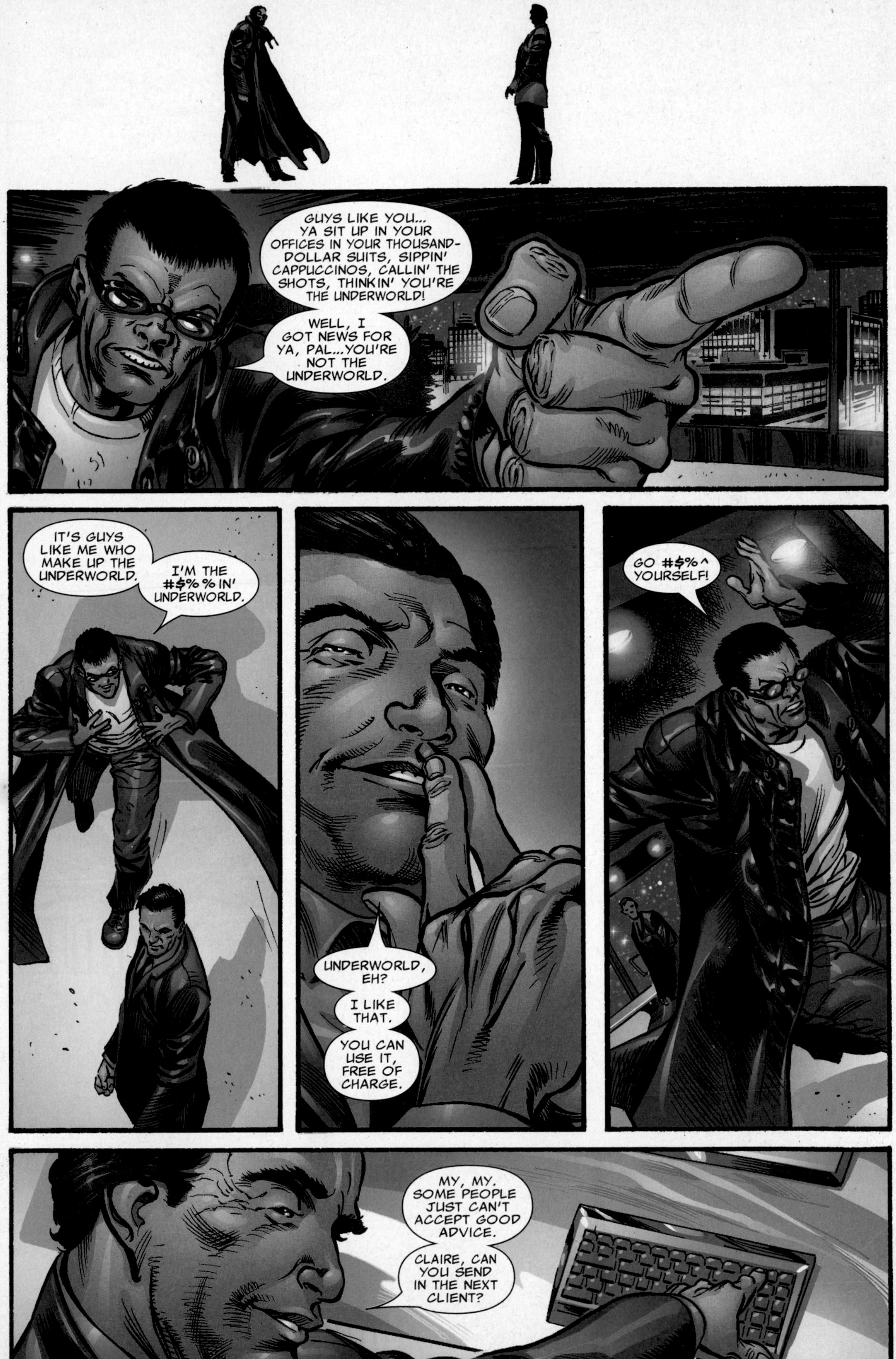
GUYS LIKE YOU... YA SIT UP IN YOUR OFFICES IN YOUR THOUSAND-DOLLAR SUITS, SIPPIN' CAPPUCCINOS, CALLIN' THE SHOTS, THINKIN' YOU'RE THE UNDERWORLD!
WELL, I GOT NEWS FOR YA, PAL...YOU'RE NOT THE UNDERWORLD.
IT'S GUYS LIKE ME WHO MAKE UP THE UNDERWORLD.
I'M THE #$%%IN' UNDERWORLD.
UNDERWORLD, EH?
I LIKE THAT.
YOU CAN USE IT, FREE OF CHARGE.
GO #$%^ YOURSELF!
MY, MY. SOME PEOPLE JUST CAN'T ACCEPT GOOD ADVICE.
CLAIRE, CAN YOU SEND IN THE NEXT CLIENT?

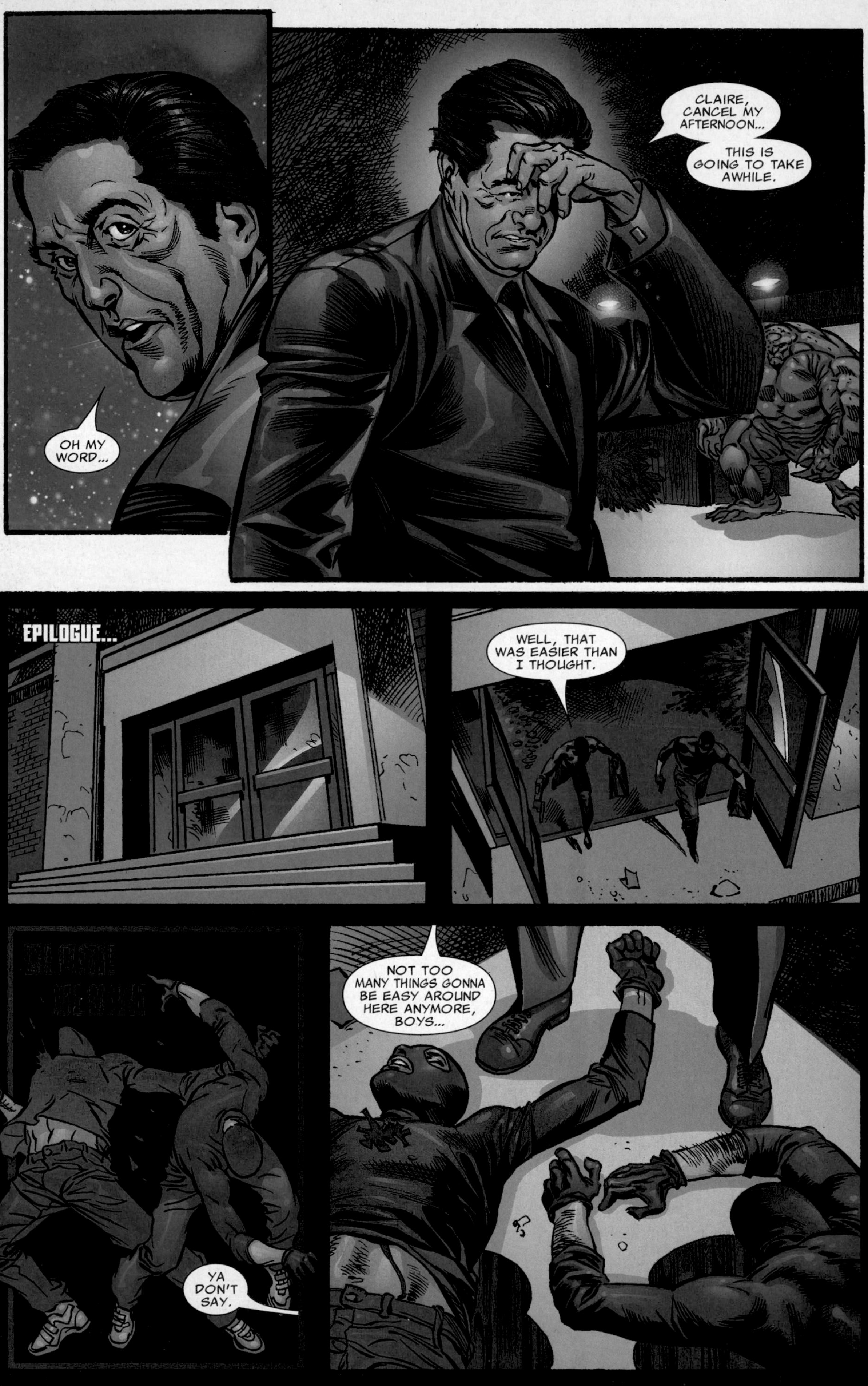
OH MY WORD...
CLAIRE, CANCEL MY AFTERNOON...
THIS IS GOING TO TAKE AWHILE.
EPILOGUE...
WELL, THAT WAS EASIER THAN I THOUGHT.
NOT TOO MANY THINGS GONNA BE EASY AROUND HERE ANYMORE, BOYS...
YA DON'T SAY.

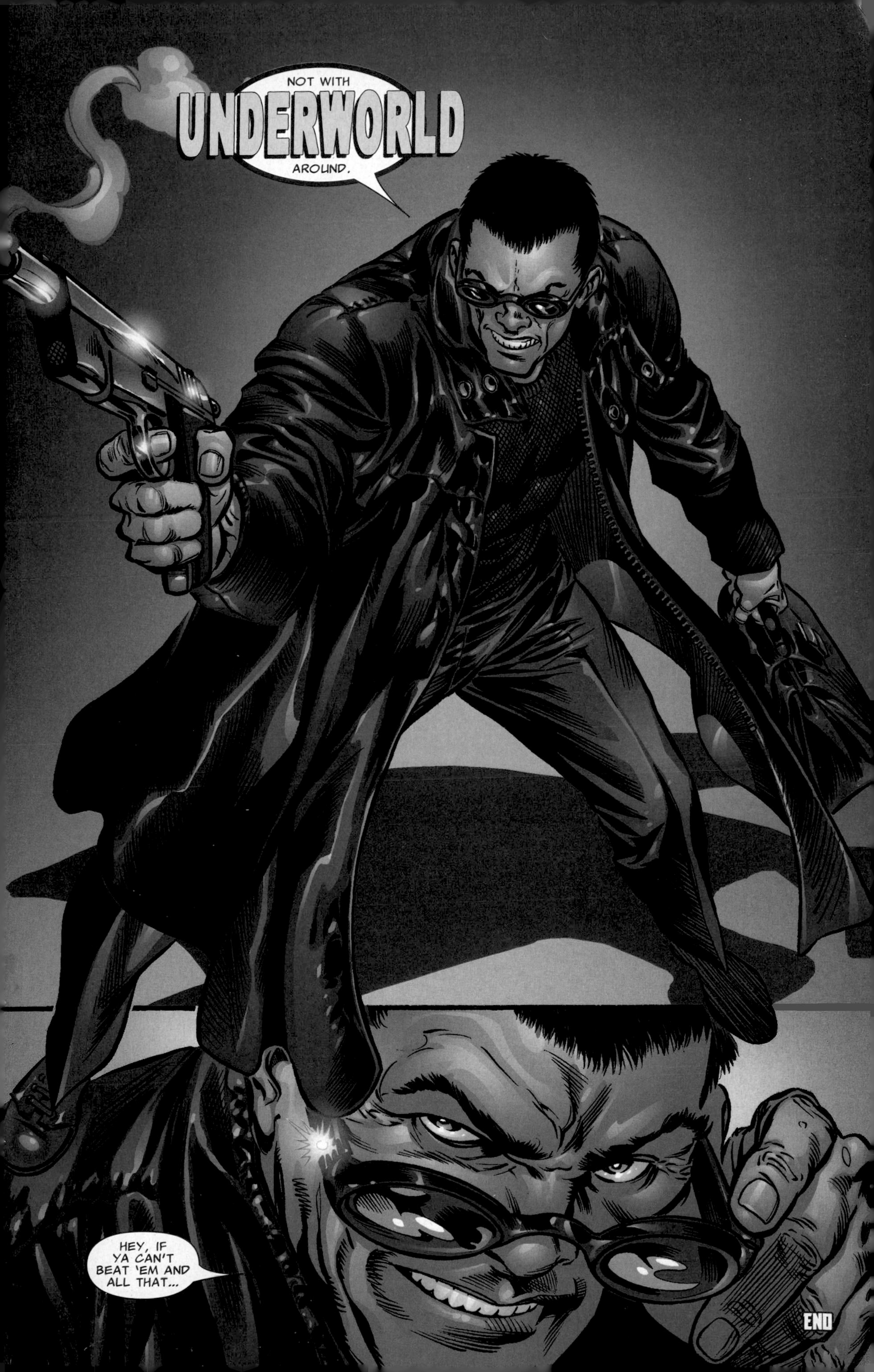
NOT WITH UNDERWORLD AROUND.
HEY, IF YA CAN'T BEAT 'EM AND ALL THAT...
END

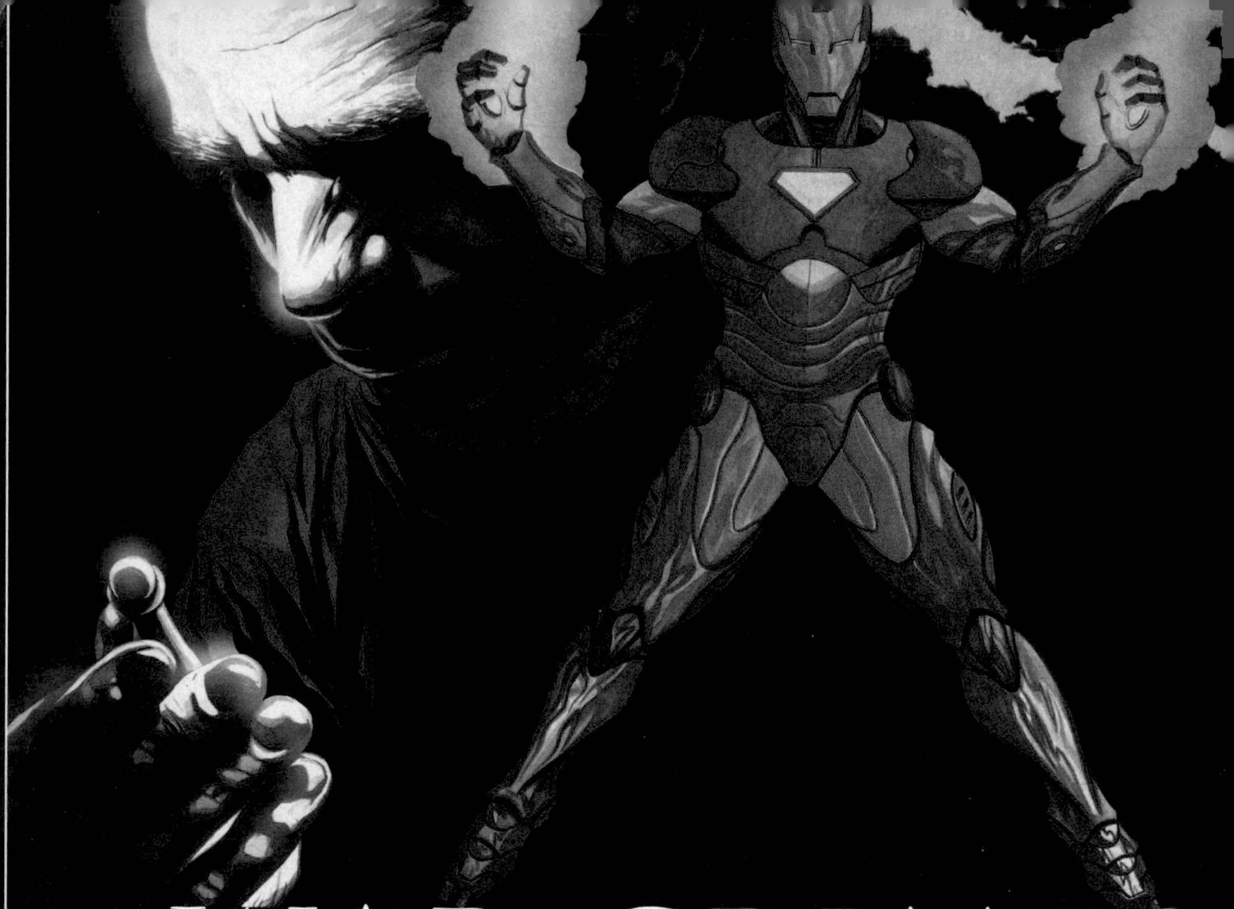

WAR CRIMES

A MARVEL COMICS EVENT

CIVIL WAR

CIVIL WAR: WAR CRIMES #1

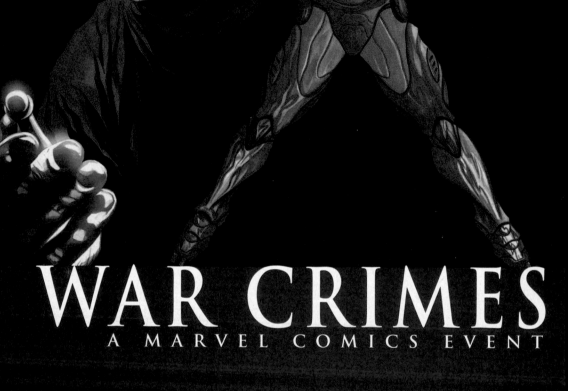

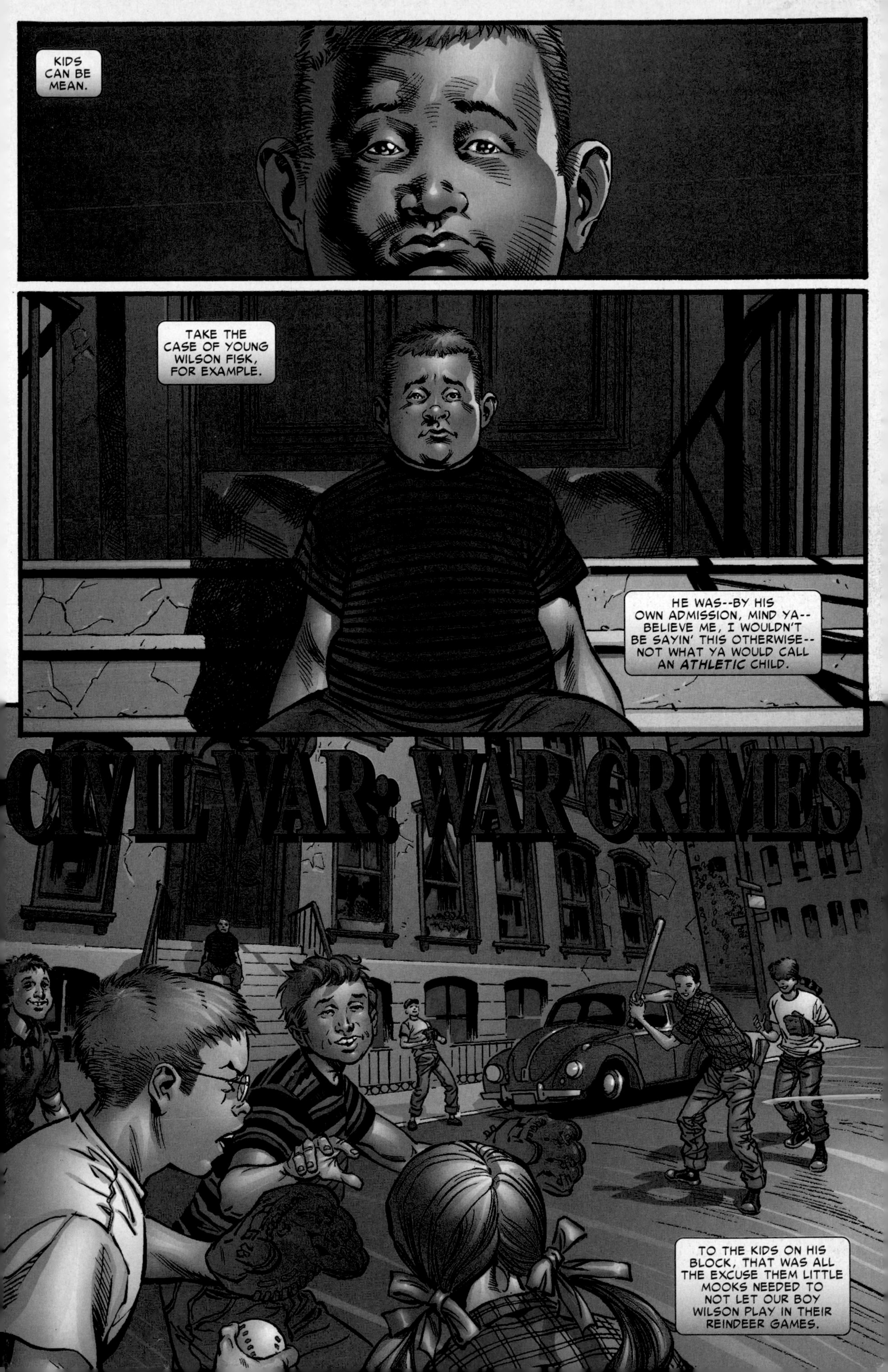
KIDS CAN BE MEAN.
TAKE THE CASE OF YOUNG WILSON FISK, FOR EXAMPLE.
HE WAS--BY HIS OWN ADMISSION, MIND YA--BELIEVE ME, I WOULDN'T BE SAYIN' THIS OTHERWISE--NOT WHAT YA WOULD CALL AN *ATHLETIC* CHILD.
CIVIL WAR: WAR CRIMES
TO THE KIDS ON HIS BLOCK, THAT WAS ALL THE EXCUSE THEM LITTLE MOOKS NEEDED TO NOT LET OUR BOY WILSON PLAY IN THEIR REINDEER GAMES.

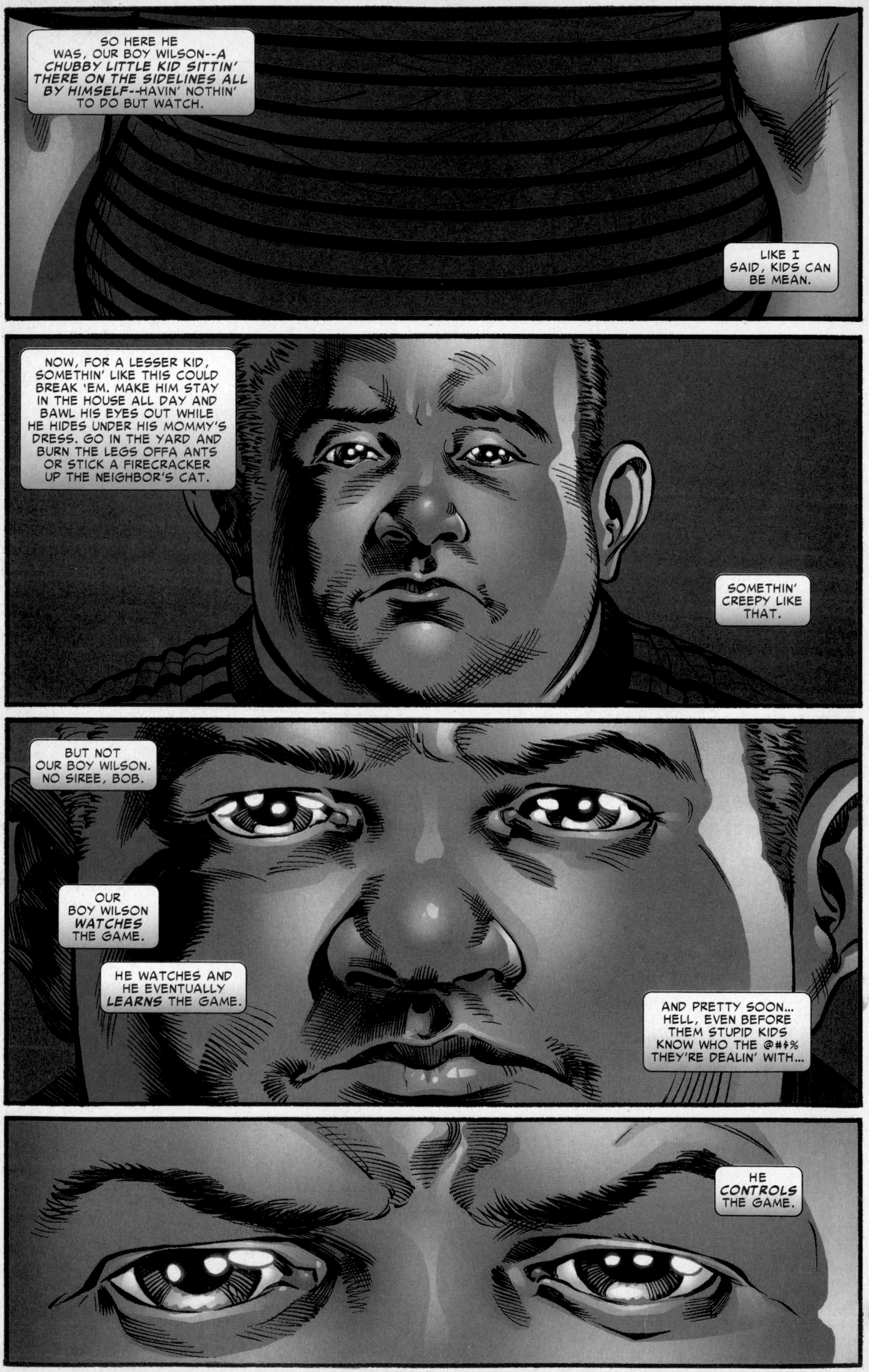
SO HERE HE WAS, OUR BOY WILSON--A *CHUBBY LITTLE KID SITTIN' THERE ON THE SIDELINES ALL BY HIMSELF*--HAVIN' NOTHIN' TO DO BUT WATCH.
LIKE I SAID, KIDS CAN BE MEAN.
NOW, FOR A LESSER KID, SOMETHIN' LIKE THIS COULD BREAK 'EM. MAKE HIM STAY IN THE HOUSE ALL DAY AND BAWL HIS EYES OUT WHILE HE HIDES UNDER HIS MOMMY'S DRESS. GO IN THE YARD AND BURN THE LEGS OFFA ANTS OR STICK A FIRECRACKER UP THE NEIGHBOR'S CAT.
SOMETHIN' CREEPY LIKE THAT.
BUT NOT OUR BOY WILSON. NO SIREE, BOB.
OUR BOY WILSON *WATCHES* THE GAME.
HE WATCHES AND HE EVENTUALLY *LEARNS* THE GAME.
AND PRETTY SOON... HELL, EVEN BEFORE THEM STUPID KIDS KNOW WHO THE @#$% THEY'RE DEALIN' WITH...
HE *CONTROLS* THE GAME.

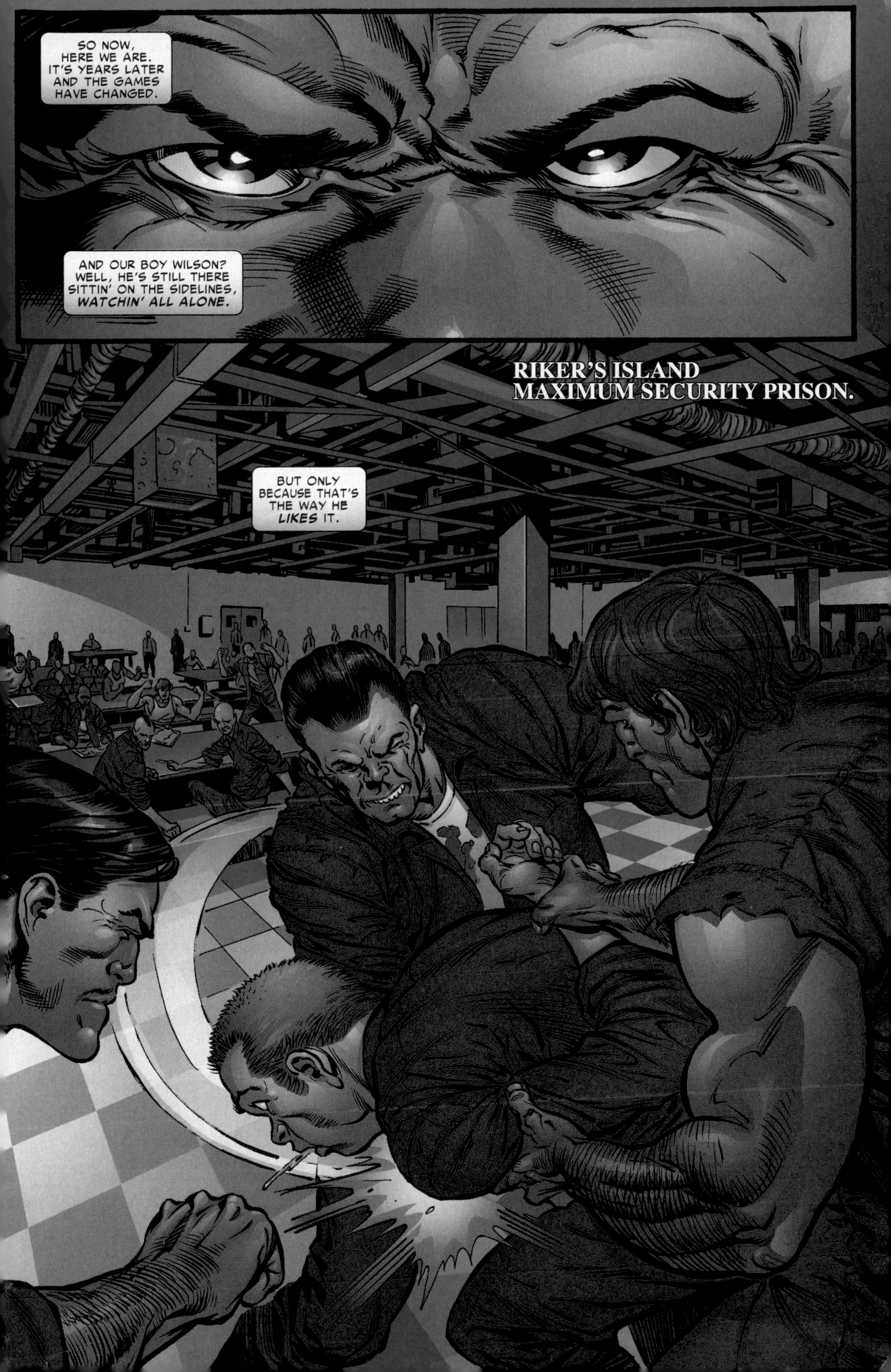
SO NOW, HERE WE ARE. IT'S YEARS LATER AND THE GAMES HAVE CHANGED.
AND OUR BOY WILSON? WELL, HE'S STILL THERE SITTIN' ON THE SIDELINES, WATCHIN' ALL ALONE.
RIKER'S ISLAND MAXIMUM SECURITY PRISON.
BUT ONLY BECAUSE THAT'S THE WAY HE LIKES IT.

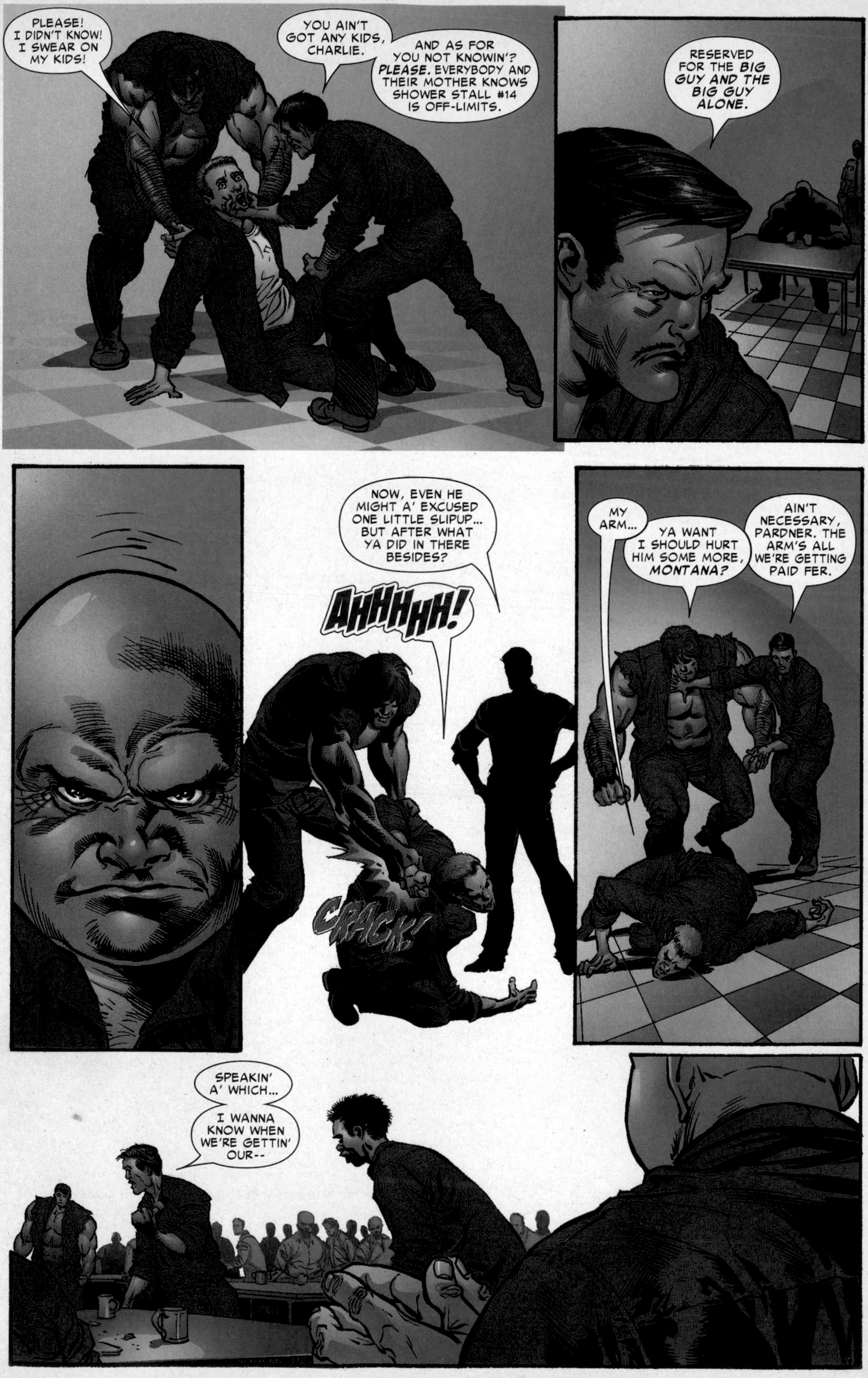
PLEASE! I DIDN'T KNOW! I SWEAR ON MY KIDS!
YOU AIN'T GOT ANY KIDS, CHARLIE.
AND AS FOR YOU NOT KNOWIN'? PLEASE. EVERYBODY AND THEIR MOTHER KNOWS SHOWER STALL #14 IS OFF-LIMITS.
RESERVED FOR THE BIG GUY AND THE BIG GUY ALONE.
NOW, EVEN HE MIGHT A' EXCUSED ONE LITTLE SLIPUP... BUT AFTER WHAT YA DID IN THERE BESIDES?
AHHHHH!
CRACK!
MY ARM...
YA WANT I SHOULD HURT HIM SOME MORE, MONTANA?
AIN'T NECESSARY, PARDNER. THE ARM'S ALL WE'RE GETTING PAID FER.
SPEAKIN' A' WHICH...
I WANNA KNOW WHEN WE'RE GETTIN' OUR--

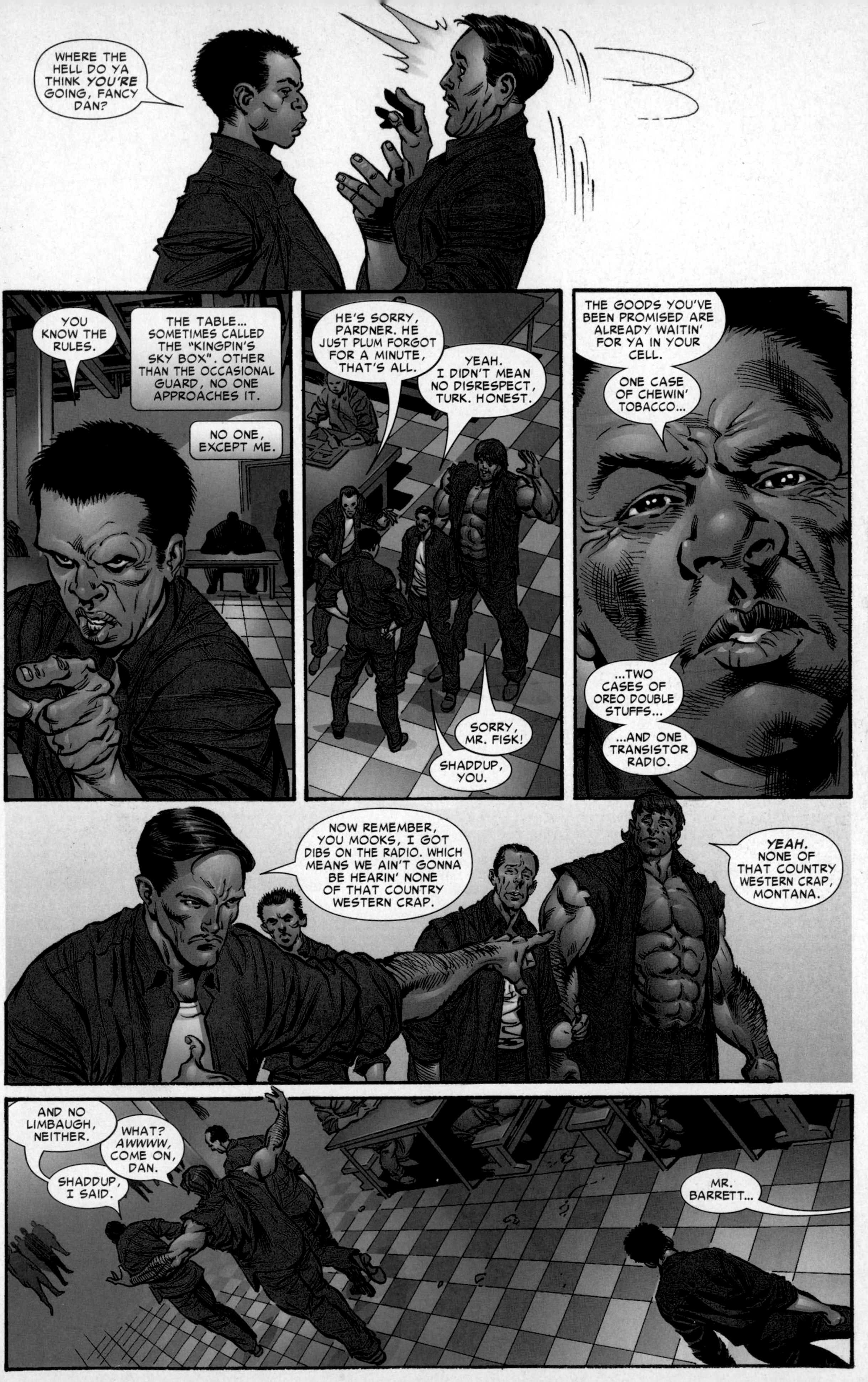
WHERE THE HELL DO YA THINK *YOU'RE* GOING, FANCY DAN?
YOU KNOW THE RULES.
THE TABLE... SOMETIMES CALLED THE "KINGPIN'S SKY BOX". OTHER THAN THE OCCASIONAL GUARD, NO ONE APPROACHES IT.
NO ONE, EXCEPT ME.
HE'S SORRY, PARDNER. HE JUST PLUM FORGOT FOR A MINUTE, THAT'S ALL.
YEAH. I DIDN'T MEAN NO DISRESPECT, TURK. HONEST.
SORRY, MR. FISK!
SHADDUP, YOU.
THE GOODS YOU'VE BEEN PROMISED ARE ALREADY WAITIN' FOR YA IN YOUR CELL.
ONE CASE OF CHEWIN' TOBACCO...
...TWO CASES OF OREO DOUBLE STUFFS...
...AND ONE TRANSISTOR RADIO.
NOW REMEMBER, YOU MOOKS, I GOT DIBS ON THE RADIO. WHICH MEANS WE AIN'T GONNA BE HEARIN' NONE OF THAT COUNTRY WESTERN CRAP.
YEAH. NONE OF THAT COUNTRY WESTERN CRAP, MONTANA.
AND NO LIMBAUGH, NEITHER.
WHAT? *AWWWW,* COME ON, DAN.
SHADDUP, I SAID.
MR. BARRETT...

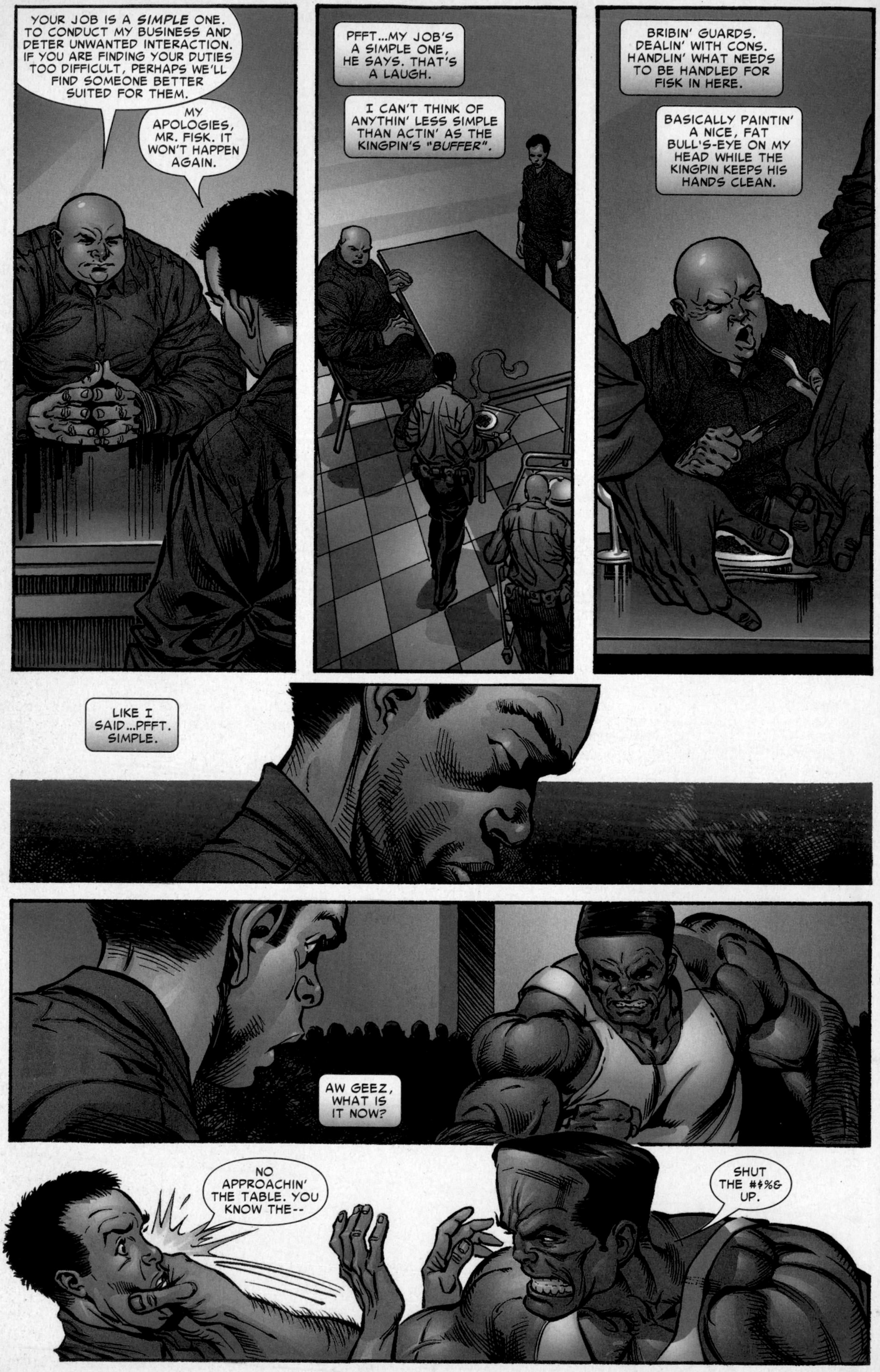
YOUR JOB IS A SIMPLE ONE. TO CONDUCT MY BUSINESS AND DETER UNWANTED INTERACTION. IF YOU ARE FINDING YOUR DUTIES TOO DIFFICULT, PERHAPS WE'LL FIND SOMEONE BETTER SUITED FOR THEM.
MY APOLOGIES, MR. FISK. IT WON'T HAPPEN AGAIN.
PFFT...MY JOB'S A SIMPLE ONE, HE SAYS. THAT'S A LAUGH.
I CAN'T THINK OF ANYTHIN' LESS SIMPLE THAN ACTIN' AS THE KINGPIN'S "BUFFER".
BRIBIN' GUARDS. DEALIN' WITH CONS. HANDLIN' WHAT NEEDS TO BE HANDLED FOR FISK IN HERE.
BASICALLY PAINTIN' A NICE, FAT BULL'S-EYE ON MY HEAD WHILE THE KINGPIN KEEPS HIS HANDS CLEAN.
LIKE I SAID...PFFT. SIMPLE.
AW GEEZ, WHAT IS IT NOW?
NO APPROACHIN' THE TABLE. YOU KNOW THE--
SHUT THE #$%& UP.

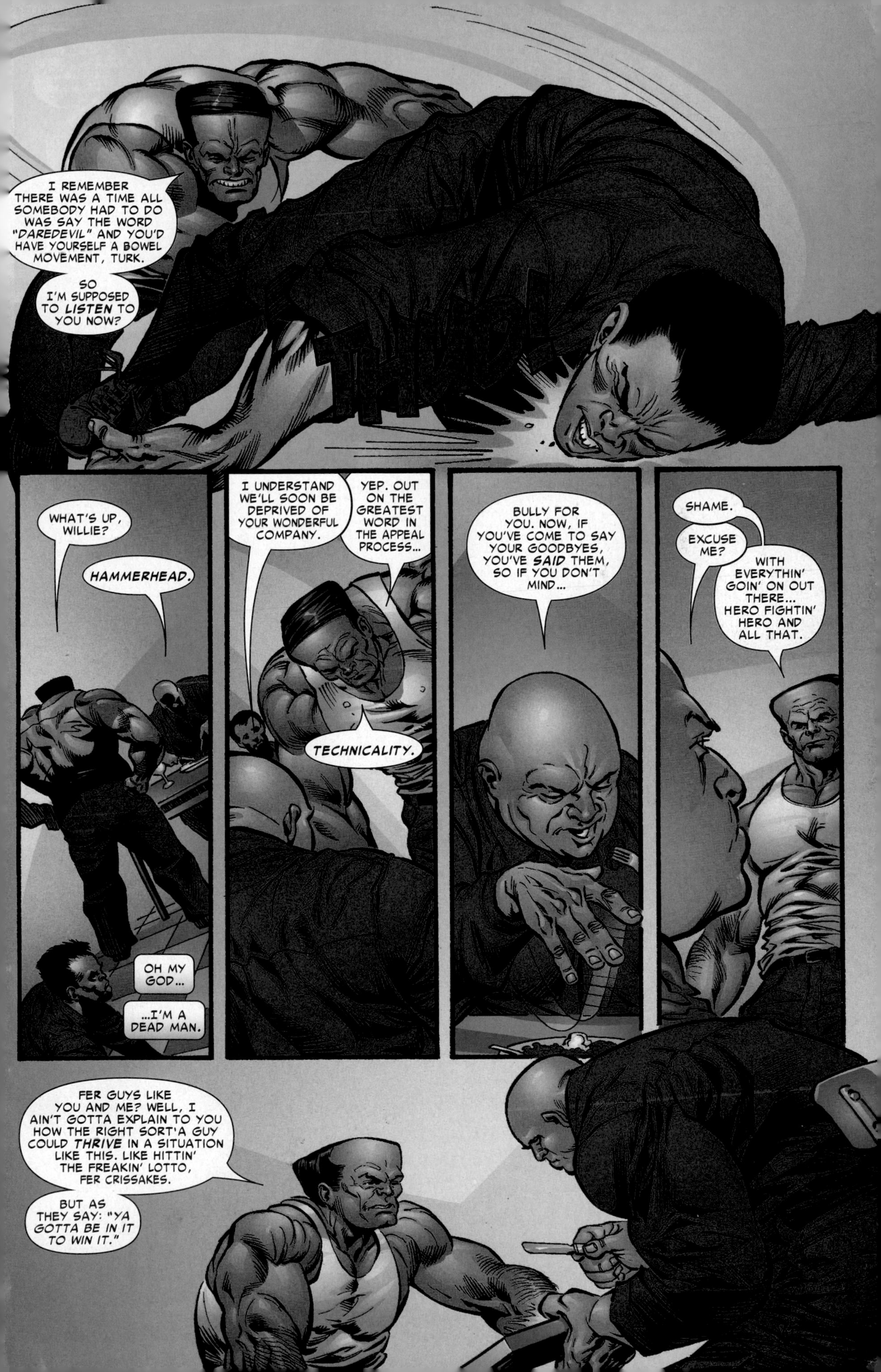
I REMEMBER THERE WAS A TIME ALL SOMEBODY HAD TO DO WAS SAY THE WORD "DAREDEVIL" AND YOU'D HAVE YOURSELF A BOWEL MOVEMENT, TURK.
SO I'M SUPPOSED TO LISTEN TO YOU NOW?
WHAT'S UP, WILLIE?
HAMMERHEAD.
OH MY GOD...
...I'M A DEAD MAN.
I UNDERSTAND WE'LL SOON BE DEPRIVED OF YOUR WONDERFUL COMPANY.
YEP. OUT ON THE GREATEST WORD IN THE APPEAL PROCESS...
TECHNICALITY.
BULLY FOR YOU. NOW, IF YOU'VE COME TO SAY YOUR GOODBYES, YOU'VE SAID THEM, SO IF YOU DON'T MIND...
SHAME.
EXCUSE ME?
WITH EVERYTHIN' GOIN' ON OUT THERE... HERO FIGHTIN' HERO AND ALL THAT.
FER GUYS LIKE YOU AND ME? WELL, I AIN'T GOTTA EXPLAIN TO YOU HOW THE RIGHT SORT'A GUY COULD THRIVE IN A SITUATION LIKE THIS. LIKE HITTIN' THE FREAKIN' LOTTO, FER CRISSAKES.
BUT AS THEY SAY: "YA GOTTA BE IN IT TO WIN IT."

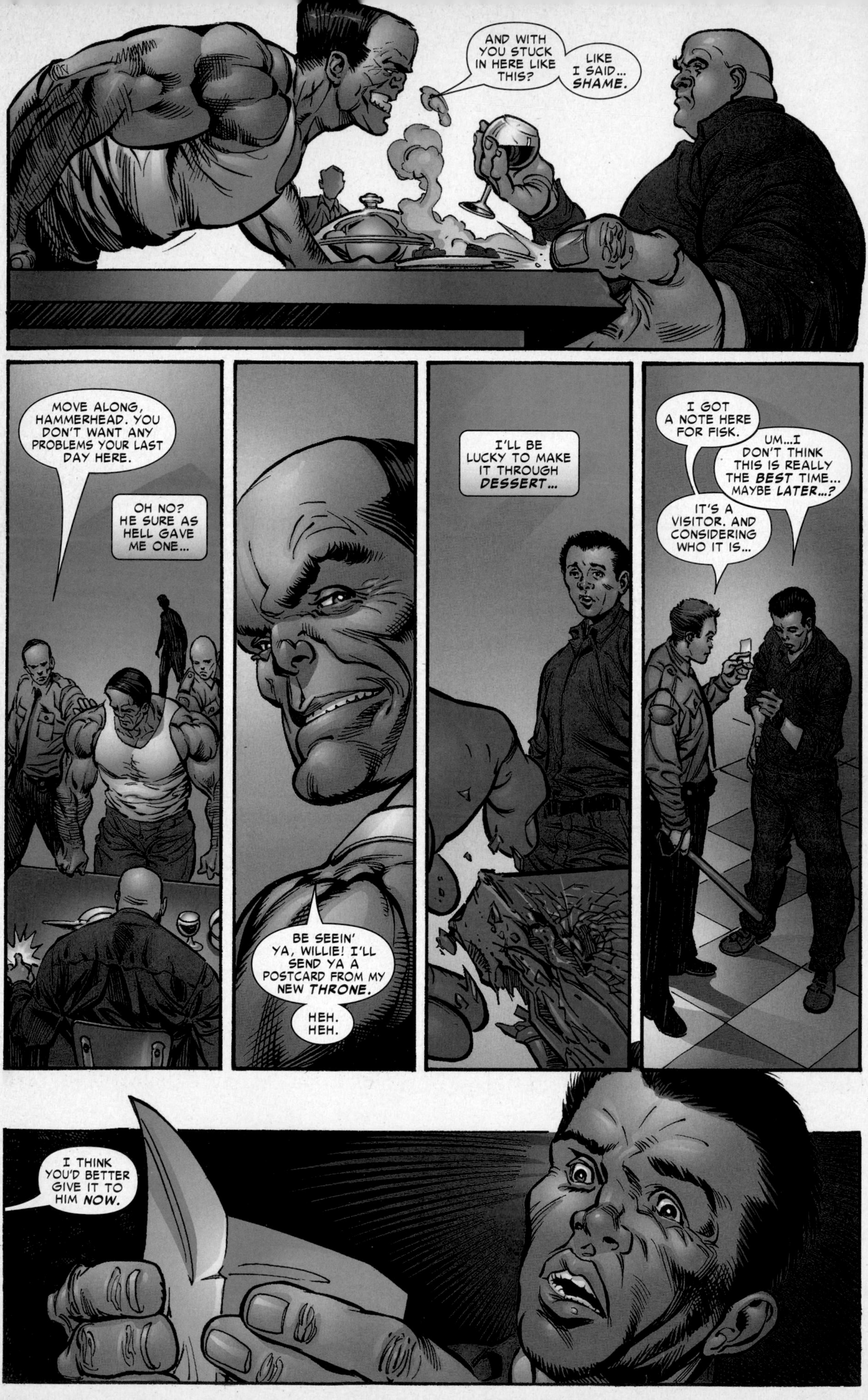
AND WITH YOU STUCK IN HERE LIKE THIS?
LIKE I SAID... SHAME.
MOVE ALONG, HAMMERHEAD. YOU DON'T WANT ANY PROBLEMS YOUR LAST DAY HERE.
OH NO? HE SURE AS HELL GAVE ME ONE...
BE SEEIN' YA, WILLIE! I'LL SEND YA A POSTCARD FROM MY NEW THRONE.
HEH. HEH.
I'LL BE LUCKY TO MAKE IT THROUGH DESSERT...
I GOT A NOTE HERE FOR FISK.
UM...I DON'T THINK THIS IS REALLY THE BEST TIME... MAYBE LATER...?
IT'S A VISITOR. AND CONSIDERING WHO IT IS...
I THINK YOU'D BETTER GIVE IT TO HIM NOW.

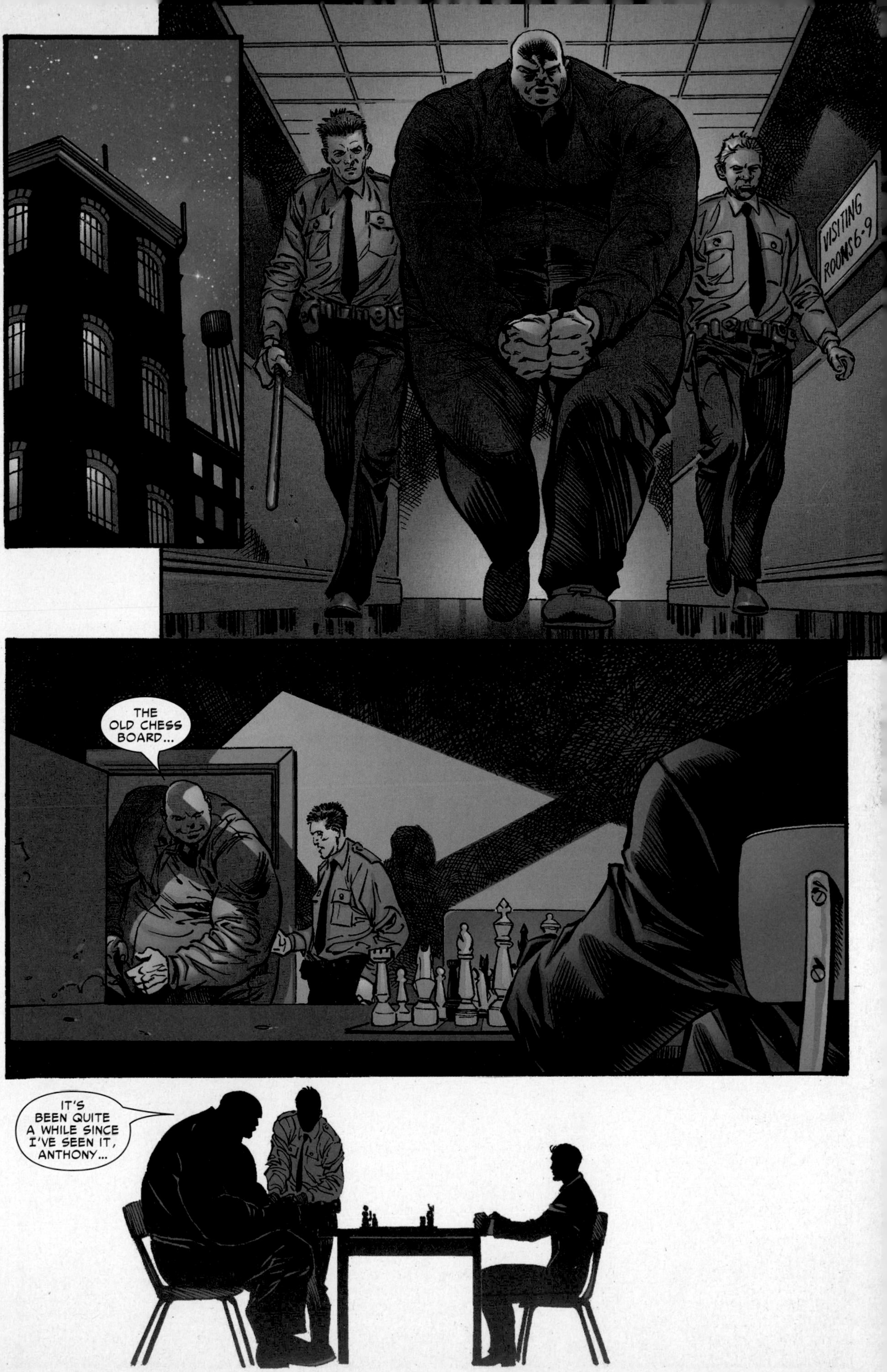
VISITING ROOMS 6-9
THE OLD CHESS BOARD...
IT'S BEEN QUITE A WHILE SINCE I'VE SEEN IT, ANTHONY...

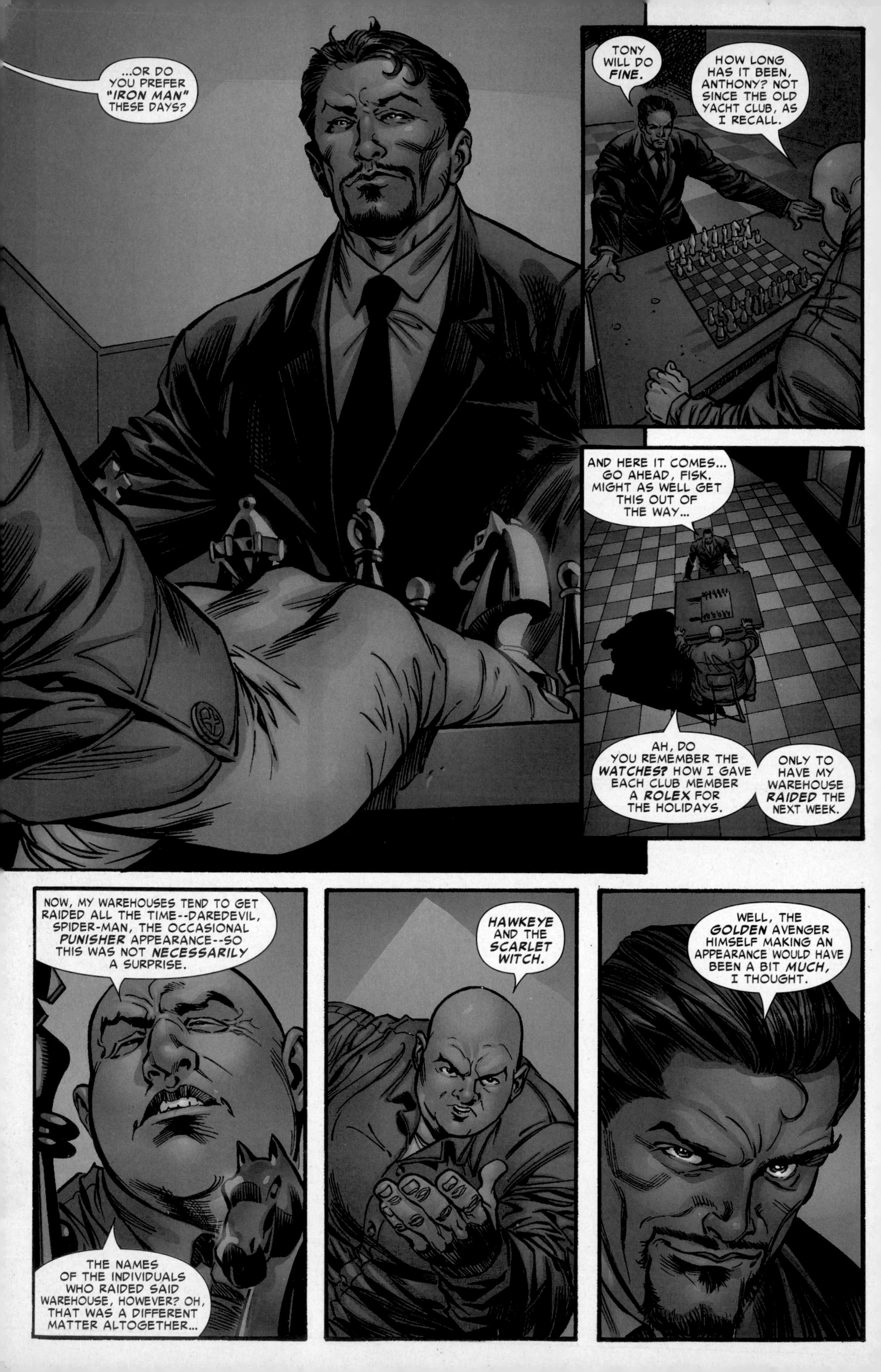
...OR DO YOU PREFER "IRON MAN" THESE DAYS?
TONY WILL DO FINE.
HOW LONG HAS IT BEEN, ANTHONY? NOT SINCE THE OLD YACHT CLUB, AS I RECALL.
AND HERE IT COMES... GO AHEAD, FISK. MIGHT AS WELL GET THIS OUT OF THE WAY...
AH, DO YOU REMEMBER THE WATCHES? HOW I GAVE EACH CLUB MEMBER A ROLEX FOR THE HOLIDAYS.
ONLY TO HAVE MY WAREHOUSE RAIDED THE NEXT WEEK.
NOW, MY WAREHOUSES TEND TO GET RAIDED ALL THE TIME--DAREDEVIL, SPIDER-MAN, THE OCCASIONAL PUNISHER APPEARANCE--SO THIS WAS NOT NECESSARILY A SURPRISE.
THE NAMES OF THE INDIVIDUALS WHO RAIDED SAID WAREHOUSE, HOWEVER? OH, THAT WAS A DIFFERENT MATTER ALTOGETHER...
HAWKEYE AND THE SCARLET WITCH.
WELL, THE GOLDEN AVENGER HIMSELF MAKING AN APPEARANCE WOULD HAVE BEEN A BIT MUCH, I THOUGHT.

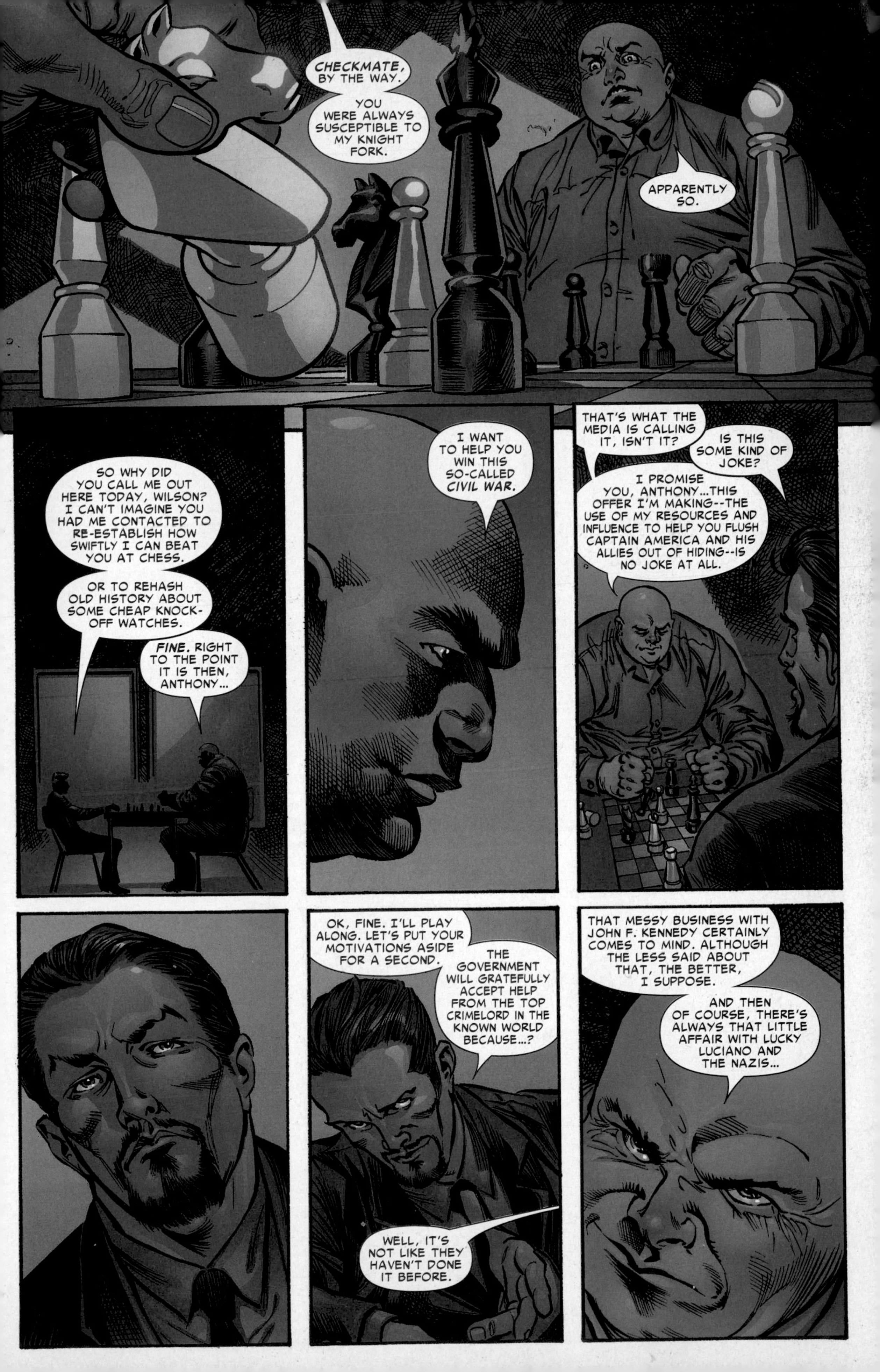
CHECKMATE, BY THE WAY.
YOU WERE ALWAYS SUSCEPTIBLE TO MY KNIGHT FORK.
APPARENTLY SO.
SO WHY DID YOU CALL ME OUT HERE TODAY, WILSON? I CAN'T IMAGINE YOU HAD ME CONTACTED TO RE-ESTABLISH HOW SWIFTLY I CAN BEAT YOU AT CHESS.
OR TO REHASH OLD HISTORY ABOUT SOME CHEAP KNOCK-OFF WATCHES.
FINE. RIGHT TO THE POINT IT IS THEN, ANTHONY...
I WANT TO HELP YOU WIN THIS SO-CALLED CIVIL WAR.
THAT'S WHAT THE MEDIA IS CALLING IT, ISN'T IT?
IS THIS SOME KIND OF JOKE?
I PROMISE YOU, ANTHONY...THIS OFFER I'M MAKING--THE USE OF MY RESOURCES AND INFLUENCE TO HELP YOU FLUSH CAPTAIN AMERICA AND HIS ALLIES OUT OF HIDING--IS NO JOKE AT ALL.
OK, FINE. I'LL PLAY ALONG. LET'S PUT YOUR MOTIVATIONS ASIDE FOR A SECOND.
THE GOVERNMENT WILL GRATEFULLY ACCEPT HELP FROM THE TOP CRIMELORD IN THE KNOWN WORLD BECAUSE...?
WELL, IT'S NOT LIKE THEY HAVEN'T DONE IT BEFORE.
THAT MESSY BUSINESS WITH JOHN F. KENNEDY CERTAINLY COMES TO MIND. ALTHOUGH THE LESS SAID ABOUT THAT, THE BETTER, I SUPPOSE.
AND THEN OF COURSE, THERE'S ALWAYS THAT LITTLE AFFAIR WITH LUCKY LUCIANO AND THE NAZIS...

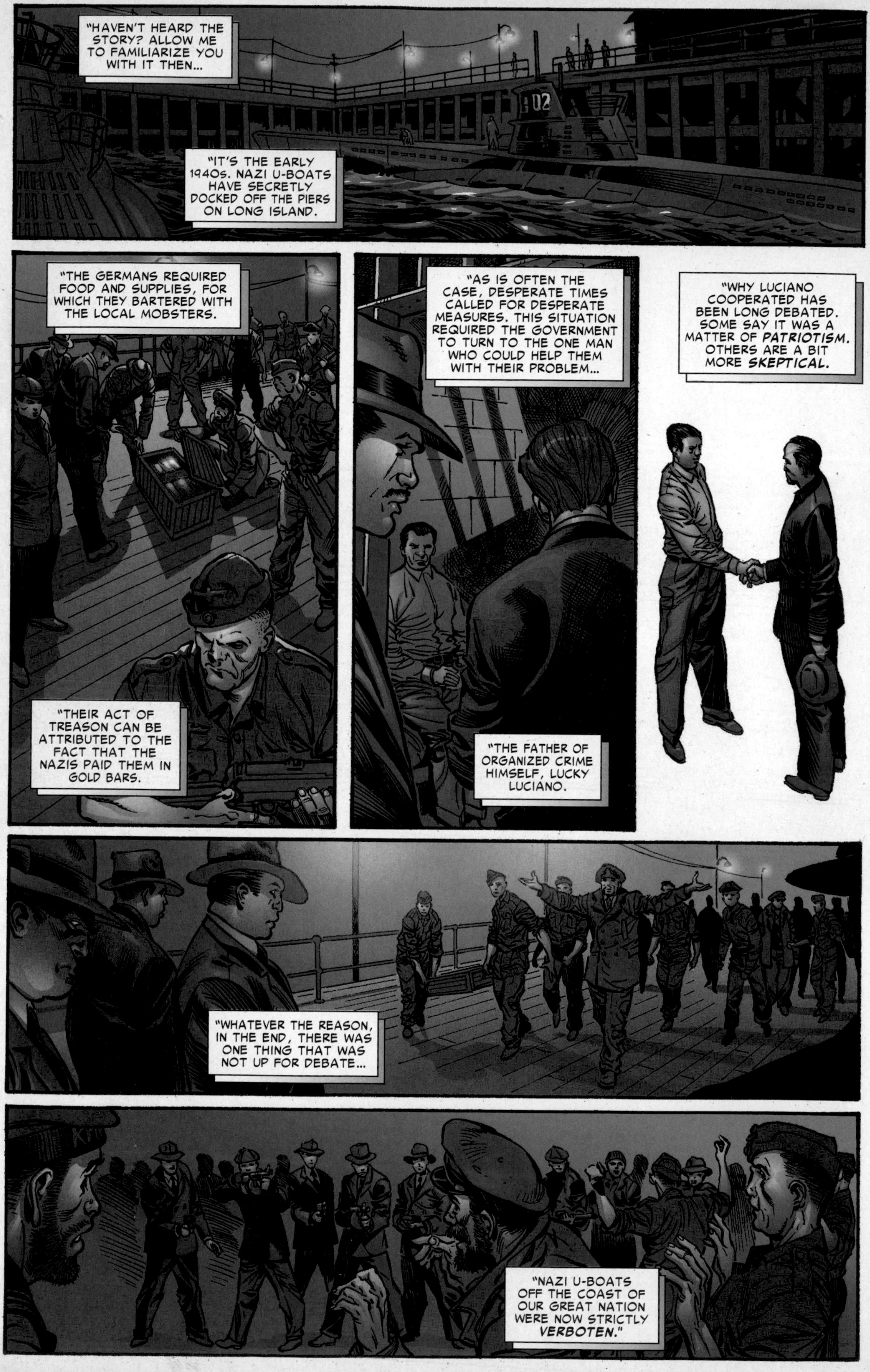
"HAVEN'T HEARD THE STORY? ALLOW ME TO FAMILIARIZE YOU WITH IT THEN...
"IT'S THE EARLY 1940s. NAZI U-BOATS HAVE SECRETLY DOCKED OFF THE PIERS ON LONG ISLAND.
"THE GERMANS REQUIRED FOOD AND SUPPLIES, FOR WHICH THEY BARTERED WITH THE LOCAL MOBSTERS.
"THEIR ACT OF TREASON CAN BE ATTRIBUTED TO THE FACT THAT THE NAZIS PAID THEM IN GOLD BARS.
"AS IS OFTEN THE CASE, DESPERATE TIMES CALLED FOR DESPERATE MEASURES. THIS SITUATION REQUIRED THE GOVERNMENT TO TURN TO THE ONE MAN WHO COULD HELP THEM WITH THEIR PROBLEM...
"THE FATHER OF ORGANIZED CRIME HIMSELF, LUCKY LUCIANO.
"WHY LUCIANO COOPERATED HAS BEEN LONG DEBATED. SOME SAY IT WAS A MATTER OF *PATRIOTISM*. OTHERS ARE A BIT MORE *SKEPTICAL*.
"WHATEVER THE REASON, IN THE END, THERE WAS ONE THING THAT WAS NOT UP FOR DEBATE...
"NAZI U-BOATS OFF THE COAST OF OUR GREAT NATION WERE NOW STRICTLY *VERBOTEN*."

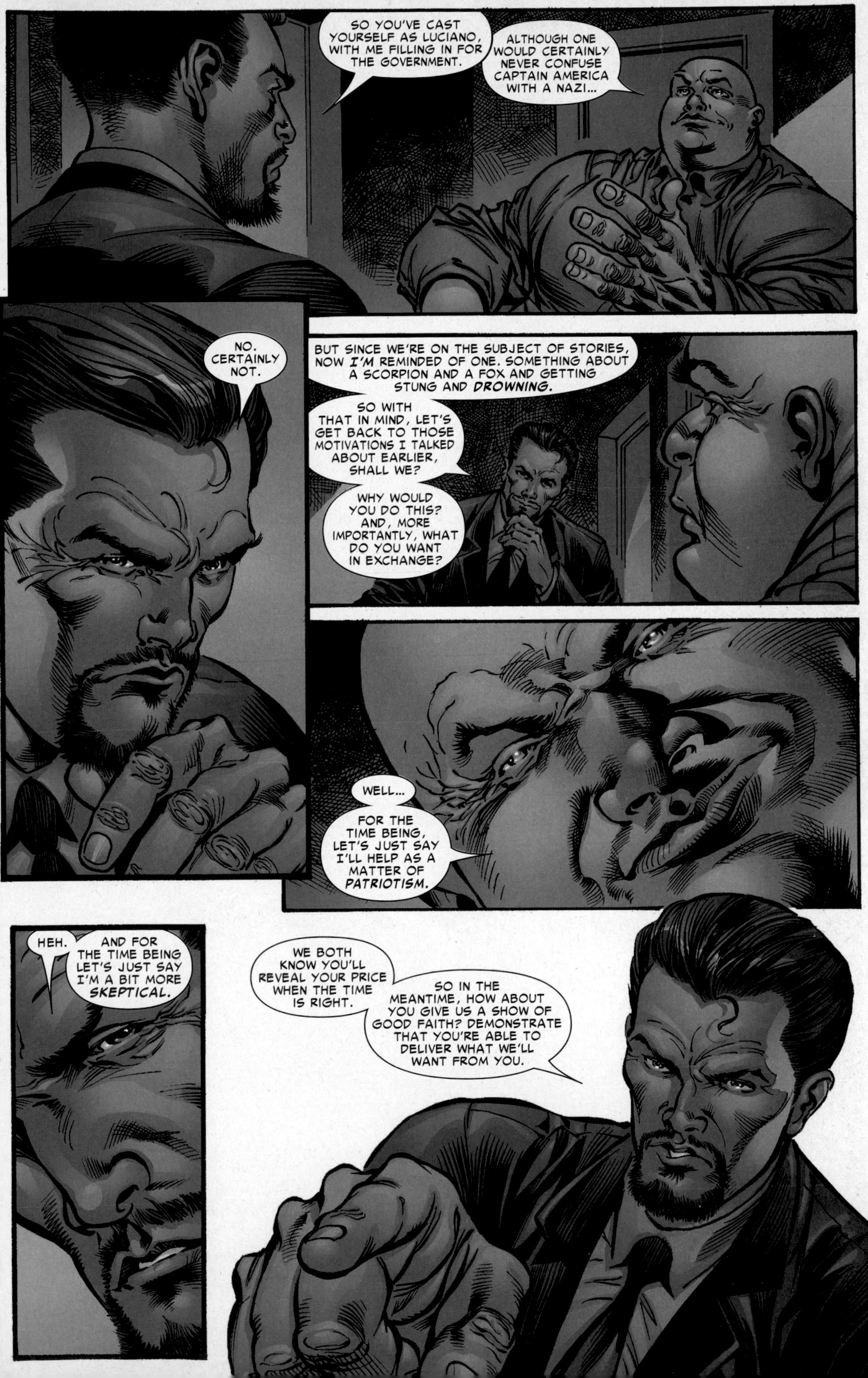

SO YOU'VE CAST YOURSELF AS LUCIANO, WITH ME FILLING IN FOR THE GOVERNMENT.
ALTHOUGH ONE WOULD CERTAINLY NEVER CONFUSE CAPTAIN AMERICA WITH A NAZI...
NO. CERTAINLY NOT.
BUT SINCE WE'RE ON THE SUBJECT OF STORIES, NOW I'M REMINDED OF ONE. SOMETHING ABOUT A SCORPION AND A FOX AND GETTING STUNG AND DROWNING.
SO WITH THAT IN MIND, LET'S GET BACK TO THOSE MOTIVATIONS I TALKED ABOUT EARLIER, SHALL WE?
WHY WOULD YOU DO THIS? AND, MORE IMPORTANTLY, WHAT DO YOU WANT IN EXCHANGE?
WELL...
FOR THE TIME BEING, LET'S JUST SAY I'LL HELP AS A MATTER OF PATRIOTISM.
HEH.
AND FOR THE TIME BEING LET'S JUST SAY I'M A BIT MORE SKEPTICAL.
WE BOTH KNOW YOU'LL REVEAL YOUR PRICE WHEN THE TIME IS RIGHT.
SO IN THE MEANTIME, HOW ABOUT YOU GIVE US A SHOW OF GOOD FAITH? DEMONSTRATE THAT YOU'RE ABLE TO DELIVER WHAT WE'LL WANT FROM YOU.

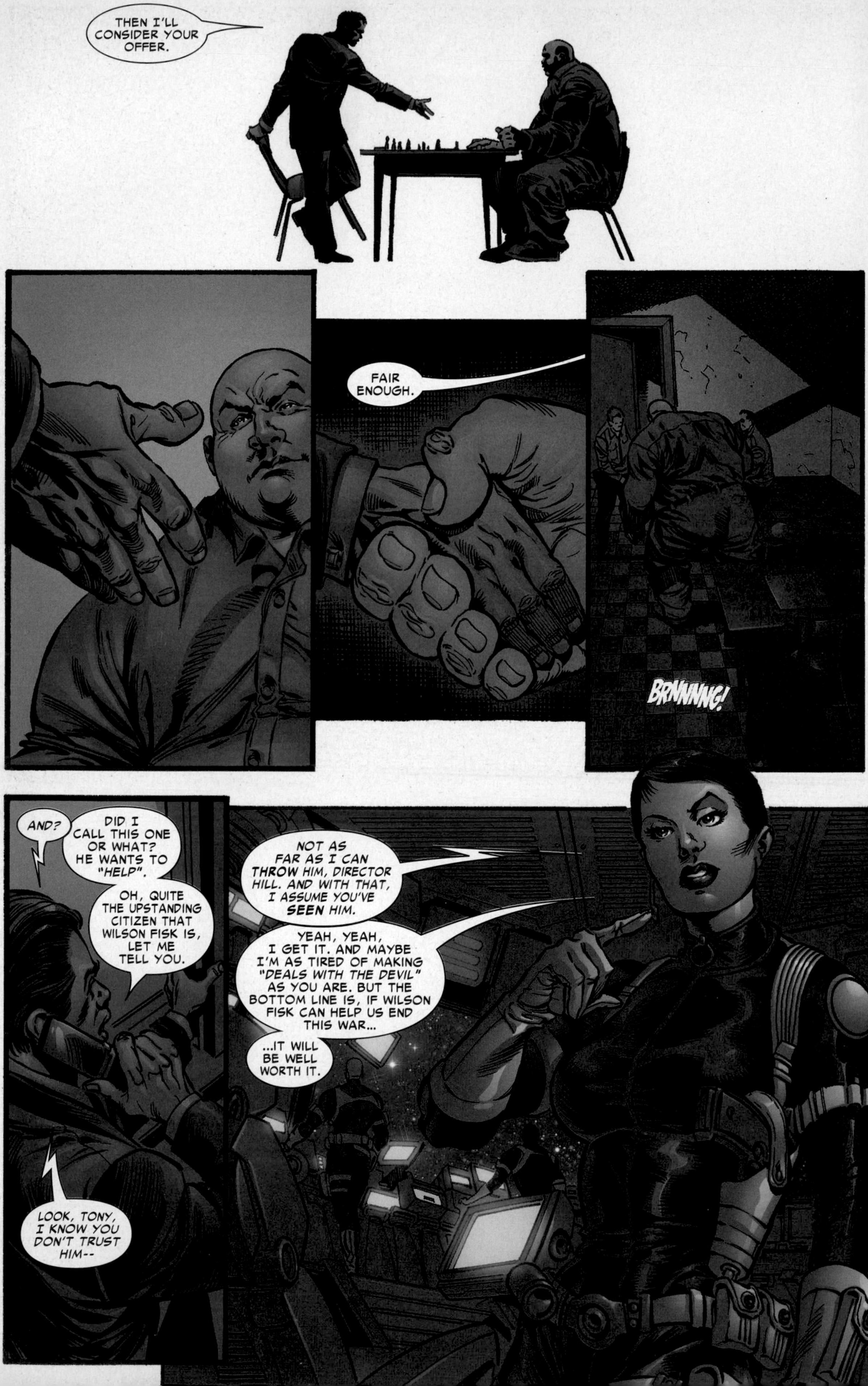
THEN I'LL CONSIDER YOUR OFFER.
FAIR ENOUGH.
BRNNNNG!
AND?
DID I CALL THIS ONE OR WHAT? HE WANTS TO "HELP".
OH, QUITE THE UPSTANDING CITIZEN THAT WILSON FISK IS, LET ME TELL YOU.
NOT AS FAR AS I CAN THROW HIM, DIRECTOR HILL. AND WITH THAT, I ASSUME YOU'VE SEEN HIM.
YEAH, YEAH, I GET IT. AND MAYBE I'M AS TIRED OF MAKING "DEALS WITH THE DEVIL" AS YOU ARE. BUT THE BOTTOM LINE IS, IF WILSON FISK CAN HELP US END THIS WAR...
...IT WILL BE WELL WORTH IT.
LOOK, TONY, I KNOW YOU DON'T TRUST HIM--

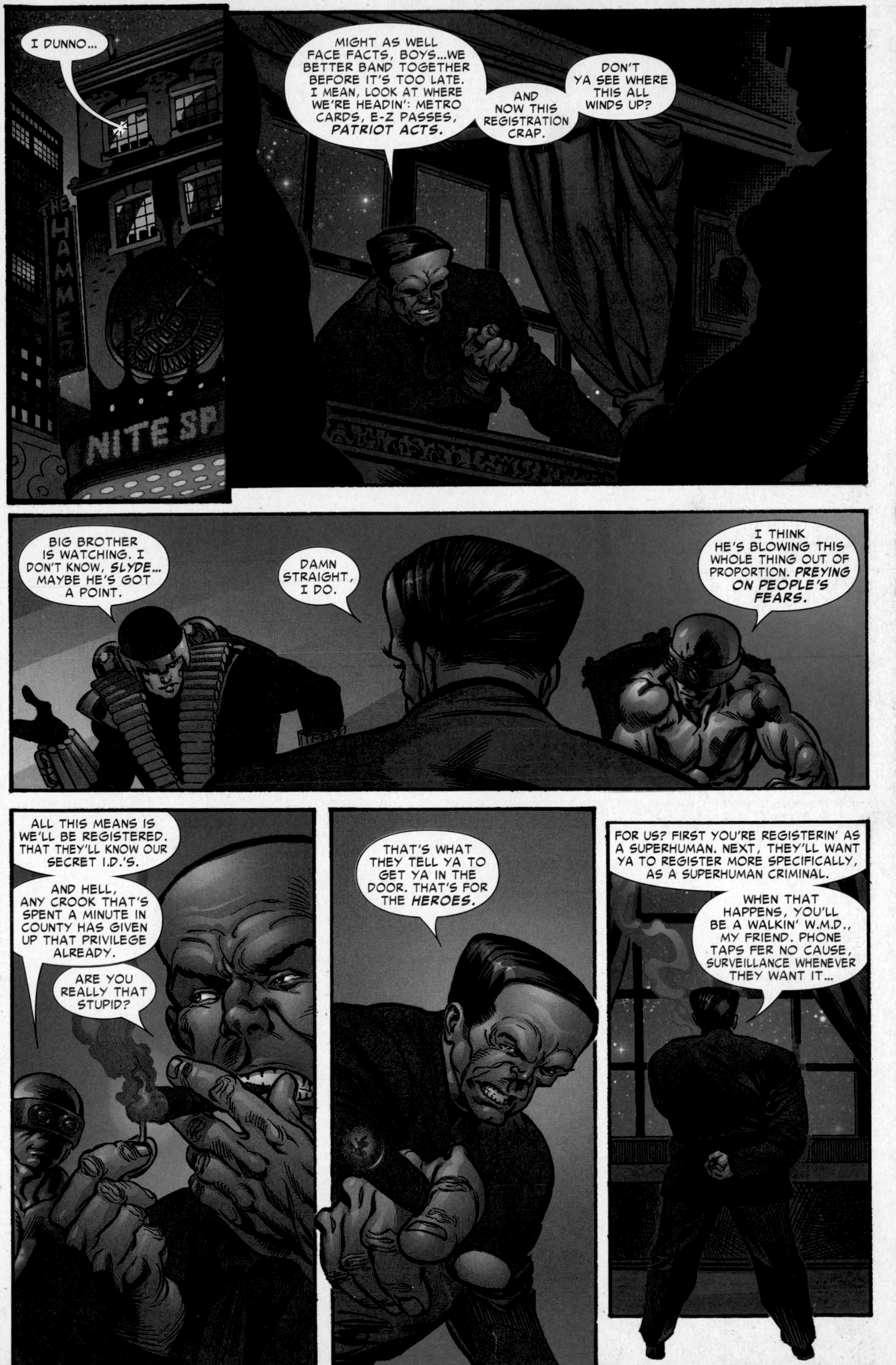
I DUNNO...
THE HAMMER
NITE SP
MIGHT AS WELL FACE FACTS, BOYS...WE BETTER BAND TOGETHER BEFORE IT'S TOO LATE. I MEAN, LOOK AT WHERE WE'RE HEADIN': METRO CARDS, E-Z PASSES, PATRIOT ACTS.
AND NOW THIS REGISTRATION CRAP.
DON'T YA SEE WHERE THIS ALL WINDS UP?
BIG BROTHER IS WATCHING. I DON'T KNOW, SLYDE... MAYBE HE'S GOT A POINT.
DAMN STRAIGHT, I DO.
I THINK HE'S BLOWING THIS WHOLE THING OUT OF PROPORTION. PREYING ON PEOPLE'S FEARS.
ALL THIS MEANS IS WE'LL BE REGISTERED. THAT THEY'LL KNOW OUR SECRET I.D.'S.
AND HELL, ANY CROOK THAT'S SPENT A MINUTE IN COUNTY HAS GIVEN UP THAT PRIVILEGE ALREADY.
ARE YOU REALLY THAT STUPID?
THAT'S WHAT THEY TELL YA TO GET YA IN THE DOOR. THAT'S FOR THE HEROES.
FOR US? FIRST YOU'RE REGISTERIN' AS A SUPERHUMAN. NEXT, THEY'LL WANT YA TO REGISTER MORE SPECIFICALLY, AS A SUPERHUMAN CRIMINAL.
WHEN THAT HAPPENS, YOU'LL BE A WALKIN' W.M.D., MY FRIEND. PHONE TAPS FER NO CAUSE, SURVEILLANCE WHENEVER THEY WANT IT...

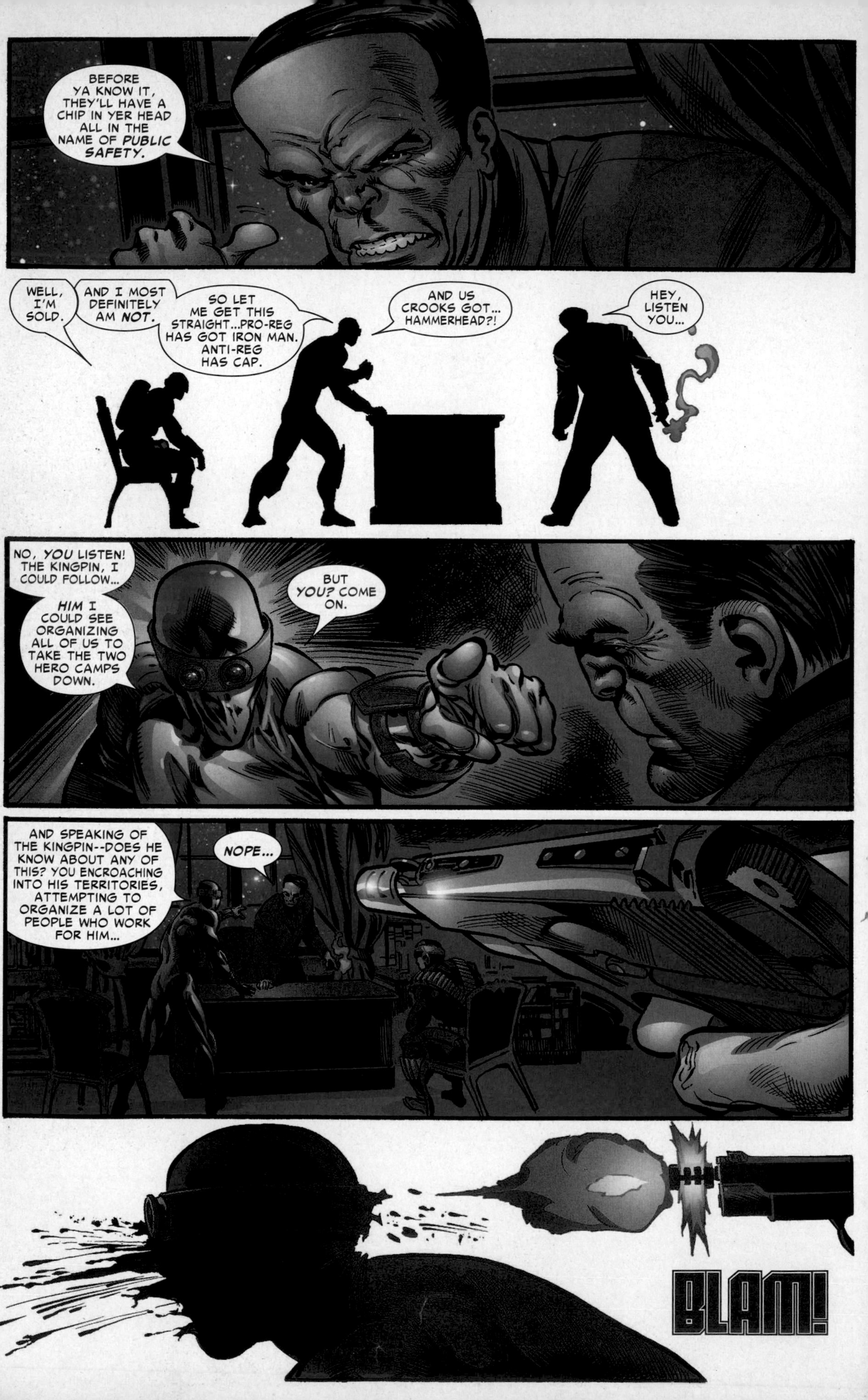
BEFORE YA KNOW IT, THEY'LL HAVE A CHIP IN YER HEAD ALL IN THE NAME OF *PUBLIC SAFETY*.
WELL, I'M SOLD.
AND I MOST DEFINITELY AM ***NOT***.
SO LET ME GET THIS STRAIGHT...PRO-REG HAS GOT IRON MAN. ANTI-REG HAS CAP.
AND US CROOKS GOT... HAMMERHEAD?!
HEY, LISTEN YOU...
NO, *YOU* LISTEN! THE KINGPIN, I COULD FOLLOW...
HIM I COULD SEE ORGANIZING ALL OF US TO TAKE THE TWO HERO CAMPS DOWN.
BUT *YOU?* COME ON.
AND SPEAKING OF THE KINGPIN--DOES HE KNOW ABOUT ANY OF THIS? YOU ENCROACHING INTO HIS TERRITORIES, ATTEMPTING TO ORGANIZE A LOT OF PEOPLE WHO WORK FOR HIM...
NOPE...
BLAM!

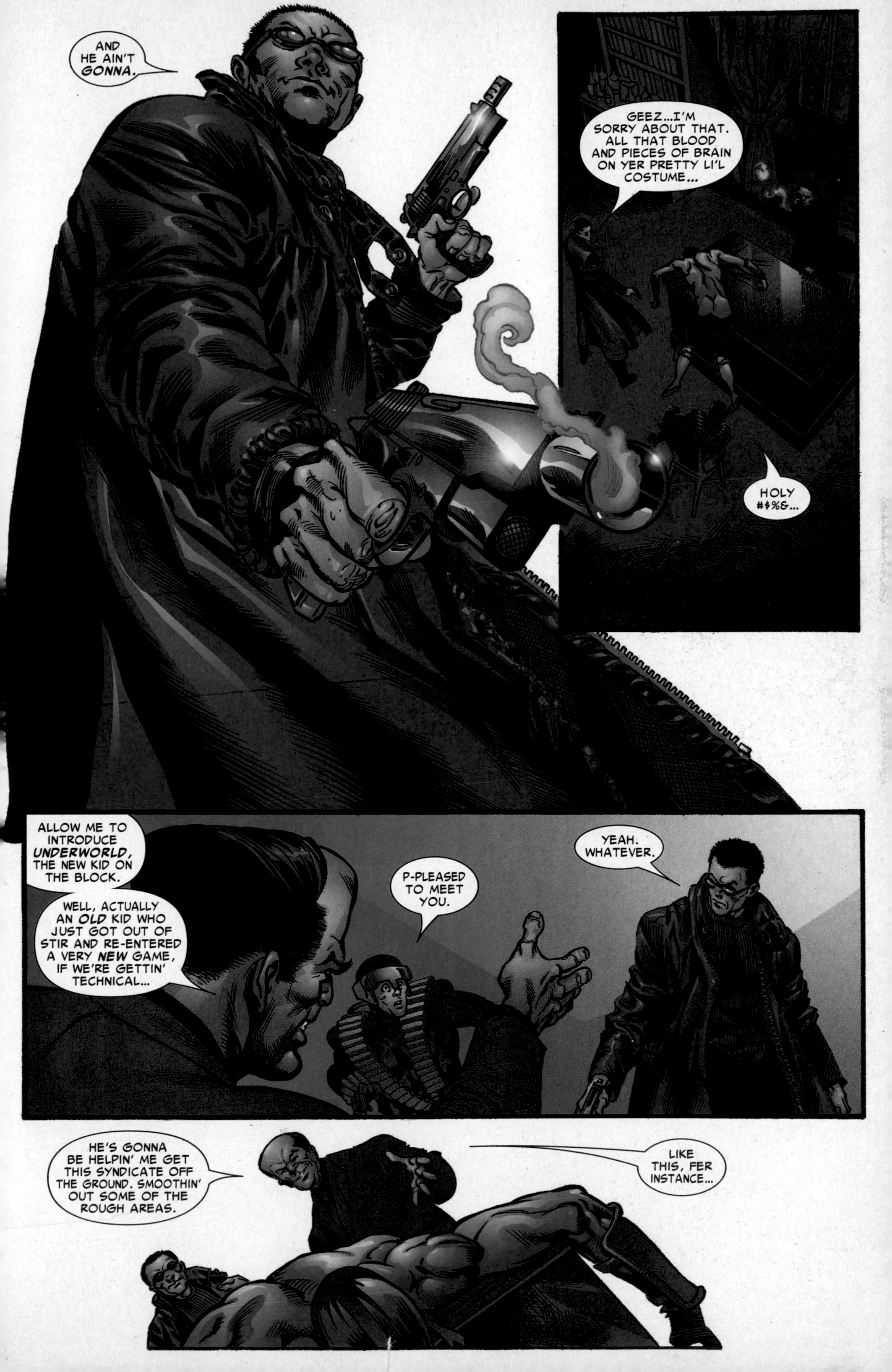
AND HE AIN'T *GONNA.*
GEEZ...I'M SORRY ABOUT THAT. ALL THAT BLOOD AND PIECES OF BRAIN ON YER PRETTY LI'L COSTUME...
HOLY #$%&...
ALLOW ME TO INTRODUCE *UNDERWORLD,* THE NEW KID ON THE BLOCK.
WELL, ACTUALLY AN *OLD* KID WHO JUST GOT OUT OF STIR AND RE-ENTERED A VERY *NEW* GAME, IF WE'RE GETTIN' TECHNICAL...
P-PLEASED TO MEET YOU.
YEAH. WHATEVER.
HE'S GONNA BE HELPIN' ME GET THIS SYNDICATE OFF THE GROUND. SMOOTHIN' OUT SOME OF THE ROUGH AREAS.
LIKE THIS, FER INSTANCE...

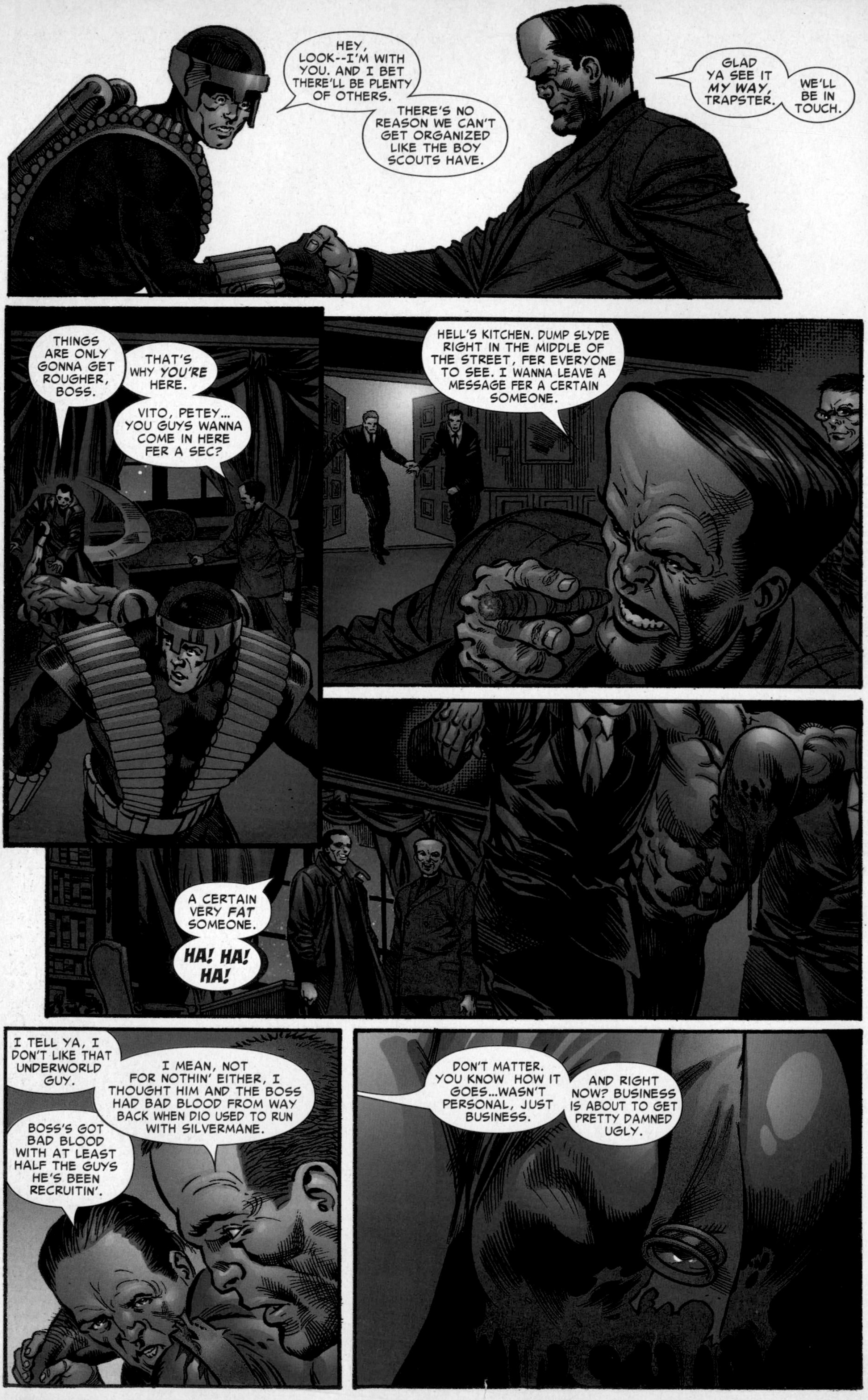
HEY, LOOK--I'M WITH YOU. AND I BET THERE'LL BE PLENTY OF OTHERS.
THERE'S NO REASON WE CAN'T GET ORGANIZED LIKE THE BOY SCOUTS HAVE.
GLAD YA SEE IT MY WAY, TRAPSTER.
WE'LL BE IN TOUCH.
THINGS ARE ONLY GONNA GET ROUGHER, BOSS.
THAT'S WHY YOU'RE HERE.
VITO, PETEY... YOU GUYS WANNA COME IN HERE FER A SEC?
HELL'S KITCHEN. DUMP SLYDE RIGHT IN THE MIDDLE OF THE STREET, FER EVERYONE TO SEE. I WANNA LEAVE A MESSAGE FER A CERTAIN SOMEONE.
A CERTAIN VERY FAT SOMEONE.
HA! HA! HA!
I TELL YA, I DON'T LIKE THAT UNDERWORLD GUY.
I MEAN, NOT FOR NOTHIN' EITHER, I THOUGHT HIM AND THE BOSS HAD BAD BLOOD FROM WAY BACK WHEN DIO USED TO RUN WITH SILVERMANE.
BOSS'S GOT BAD BLOOD WITH AT LEAST HALF THE GUYS HE'S BEEN RECRUITIN'.
DON'T MATTER. YOU KNOW HOW IT GOES...WASN'T PERSONAL, JUST BUSINESS.
AND RIGHT NOW? BUSINESS IS ABOUT TO GET PRETTY DAMNED UGLY.

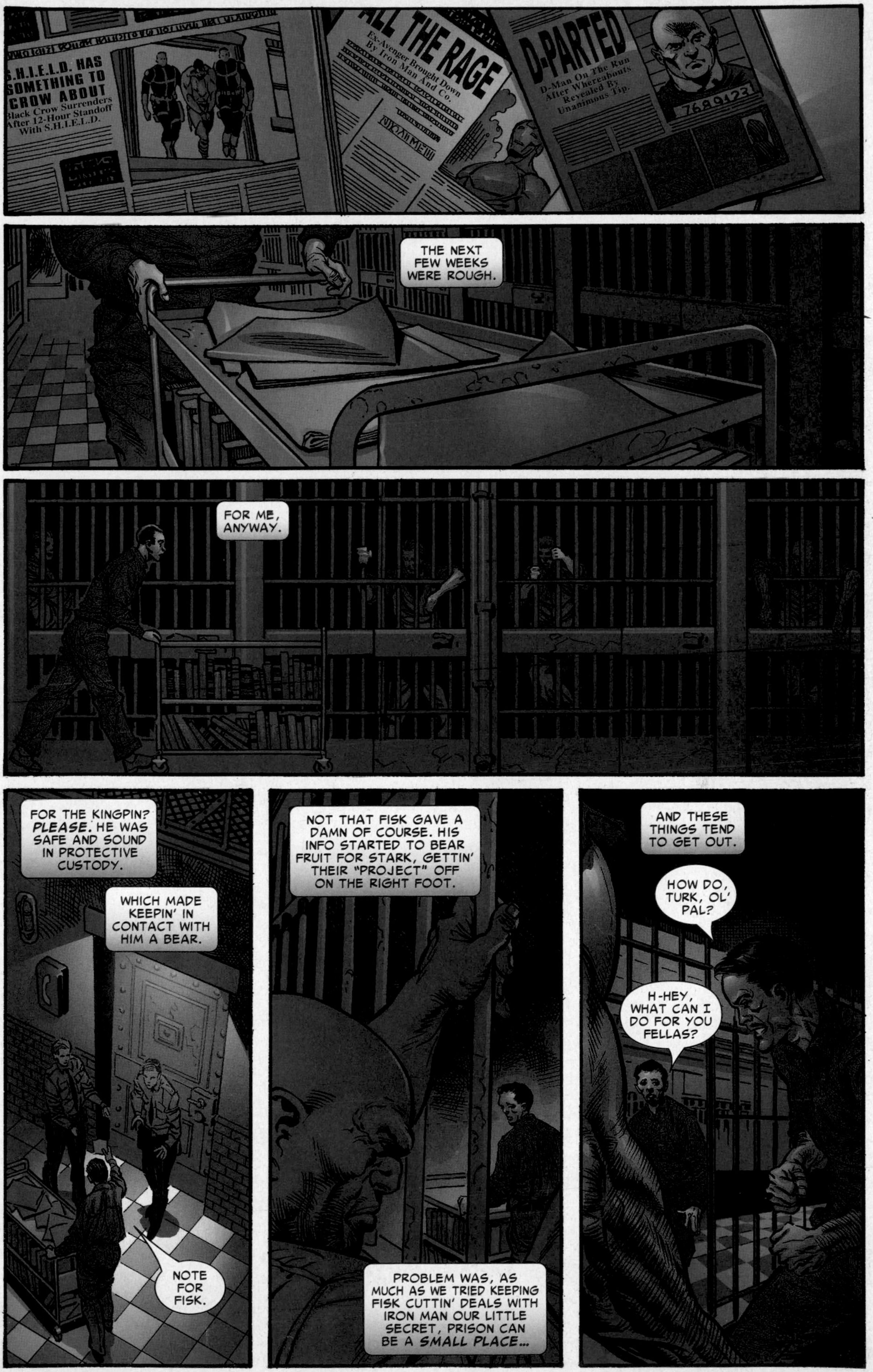
S.H.I.E.L.D. HAS SOMETHING TO CROW ABOUT
Black Crow Surrenders After 12-Hour Standoff With S.H.I.E.L.D.
ALL THE RAGE
Ex-Avenger Brought Down By Iron Man And Co.
D-PARTED
D-Man On The Run After Whereabouts Revealed By Unanimous Tip.
7689123
THE NEXT FEW WEEKS WERE ROUGH.
FOR ME, ANYWAY.
FOR THE KINGPIN? PLEASE. HE WAS SAFE AND SOUND IN PROTECTIVE CUSTODY.
WHICH MADE KEEPIN' IN CONTACT WITH HIM A BEAR.
NOTE FOR FISK.
NOT THAT FISK GAVE A DAMN OF COURSE. HIS INFO STARTED TO BEAR FRUIT FOR STARK, GETTIN' THEIR "PROJECT" OFF ON THE RIGHT FOOT.
PROBLEM WAS, AS MUCH AS WE TRIED KEEPING FISK CUTTIN' DEALS WITH IRON MAN OUR LITTLE SECRET, PRISON CAN BE A SMALL PLACE...
AND THESE THINGS TEND TO GET OUT.
HOW DO, TURK, OL' PAL?
H-HEY, WHAT CAN I DO FOR YOU FELLAS?

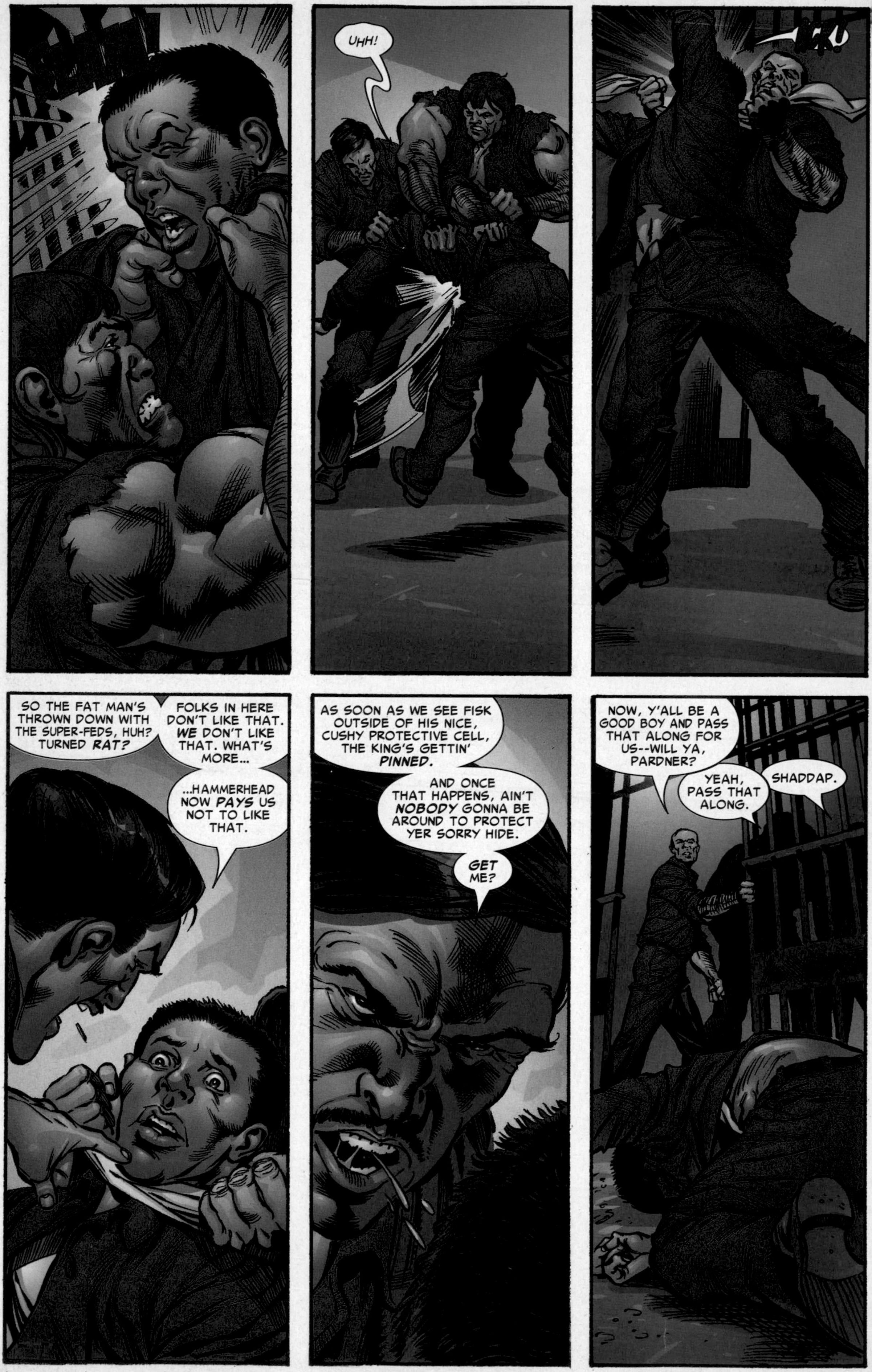
UHH!
SO THE FAT MAN'S THROWN DOWN WITH THE SUPER-FEDS, HUH? TURNED RAT?
FOLKS IN HERE DON'T LIKE THAT. WE DON'T LIKE THAT. WHAT'S MORE...
...HAMMERHEAD NOW PAYS US NOT TO LIKE THAT.
AS SOON AS WE SEE FISK OUTSIDE OF HIS NICE, CUSHY PROTECTIVE CELL, THE KING'S GETTIN' PINNED.
AND ONCE THAT HAPPENS, AIN'T NOBODY GONNA BE AROUND TO PROTECT YER SORRY HIDE.
GET ME?
NOW, Y'ALL BE A GOOD BOY AND PASS THAT ALONG FOR US--WILL YA, PARDNER?
YEAH, PASS THAT ALONG.
SHADDAP.

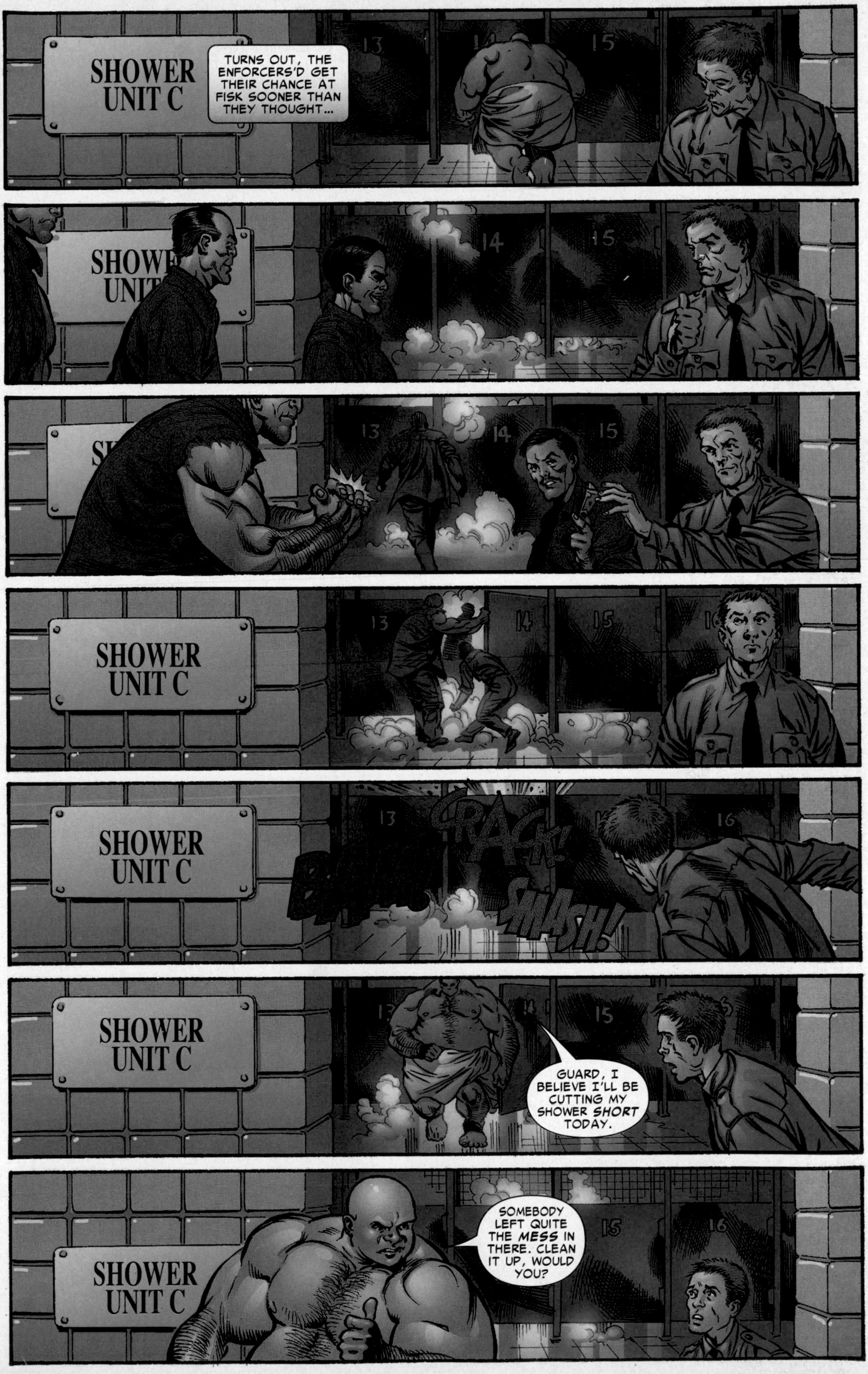
SHOWER UNIT C
TURNS OUT, THE ENFORCERS'D GET THEIR CHANCE AT FISK SOONER THAN THEY THOUGHT...
13
14
15
13
14
15
SHOWER UNIT C
13
14
15
SHOWER UNIT C
13
16
CRACK!
SMASH!
SHOWER UNIT C
15
GUARD, I BELIEVE I'LL BE CUTTING MY SHOWER **SHORT** TODAY.
SHOWER UNIT C
15
16
SOMEBODY LEFT QUITE THE **MESS** IN THERE. CLEAN IT UP, WOULD YOU?

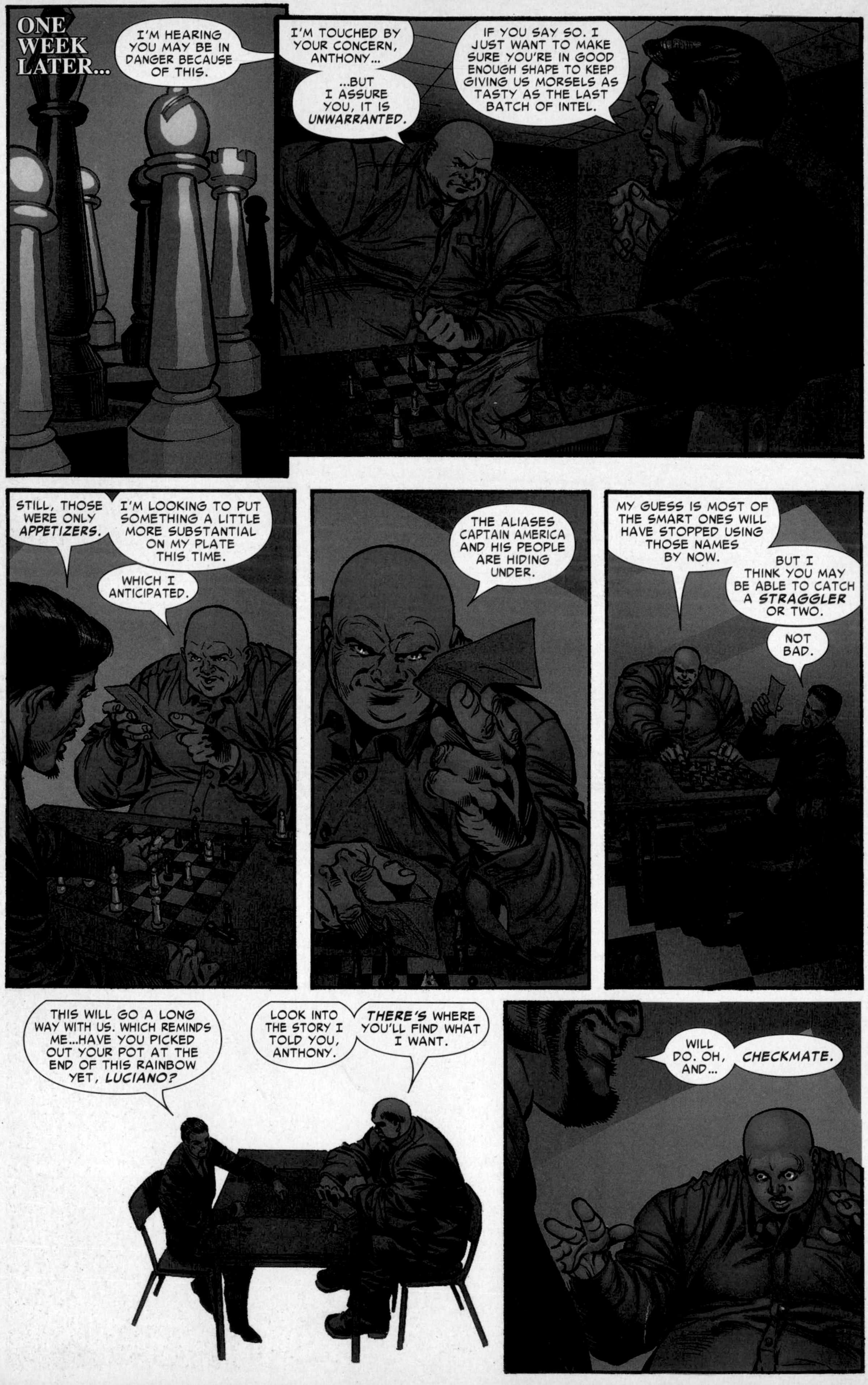
ONE WEEK LATER...
I'M HEARING YOU MAY BE IN DANGER BECAUSE OF THIS.
I'M TOUCHED BY YOUR CONCERN, ANTHONY...
...BUT I ASSURE YOU, IT IS UNWARRANTED.
IF YOU SAY SO. I JUST WANT TO MAKE SURE YOU'RE IN GOOD ENOUGH SHAPE TO KEEP GIVING US MORSELS AS TASTY AS THE LAST BATCH OF INTEL.
STILL, THOSE WERE ONLY APPETIZERS.
I'M LOOKING TO PUT SOMETHING A LITTLE MORE SUBSTANTIAL ON MY PLATE THIS TIME.
WHICH I ANTICIPATED.
THE ALIASES CAPTAIN AMERICA AND HIS PEOPLE ARE HIDING UNDER.
MY GUESS IS MOST OF THE SMART ONES WILL HAVE STOPPED USING THOSE NAMES BY NOW.
BUT I THINK YOU MAY BE ABLE TO CATCH A STRAGGLER OR TWO.
NOT BAD.
THIS WILL GO A LONG WAY WITH US. WHICH REMINDS ME...HAVE YOU PICKED OUT YOUR POT AT THE END OF THIS RAINBOW YET, LUCIANO?
LOOK INTO THE STORY I TOLD YOU, ANTHONY.
THERE'S WHERE YOU'LL FIND WHAT I WANT.
WILL DO. OH, AND...
CHECKMATE.

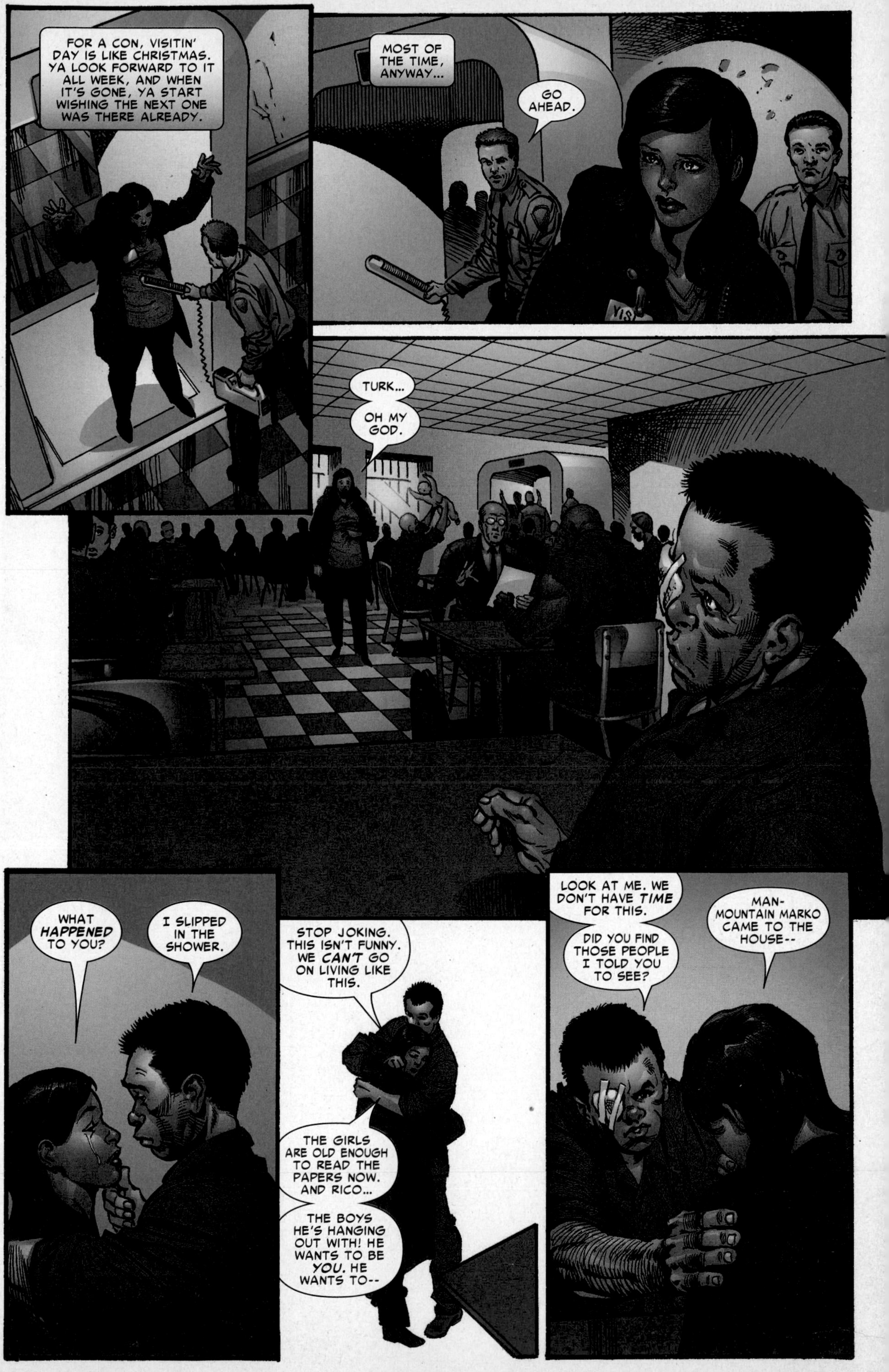
FOR A CON, VISITIN' DAY IS LIKE CHRISTMAS. YA LOOK FORWARD TO IT ALL WEEK, AND WHEN IT'S GONE, YA START WISHING THE NEXT ONE WAS THERE ALREADY.
MOST OF THE TIME, ANYWAY...
GO AHEAD.
TURK...
OH MY GOD.
WHAT *HAPPENED* TO YOU?
I SLIPPED IN THE SHOWER.
STOP JOKING. THIS ISN'T FUNNY. WE *CAN'T* GO ON LIVING LIKE THIS.
THE GIRLS ARE OLD ENOUGH TO READ THE PAPERS NOW. AND RICO...
THE BOYS HE'S HANGING OUT WITH! HE WANTS TO BE *YOU*. HE WANTS TO--
LOOK AT ME. WE DON'T HAVE *TIME* FOR THIS.
DID YOU FIND THOSE PEOPLE I TOLD YOU TO SEE?
MAN-MOUNTAIN MARKO CAME TO THE HOUSE--

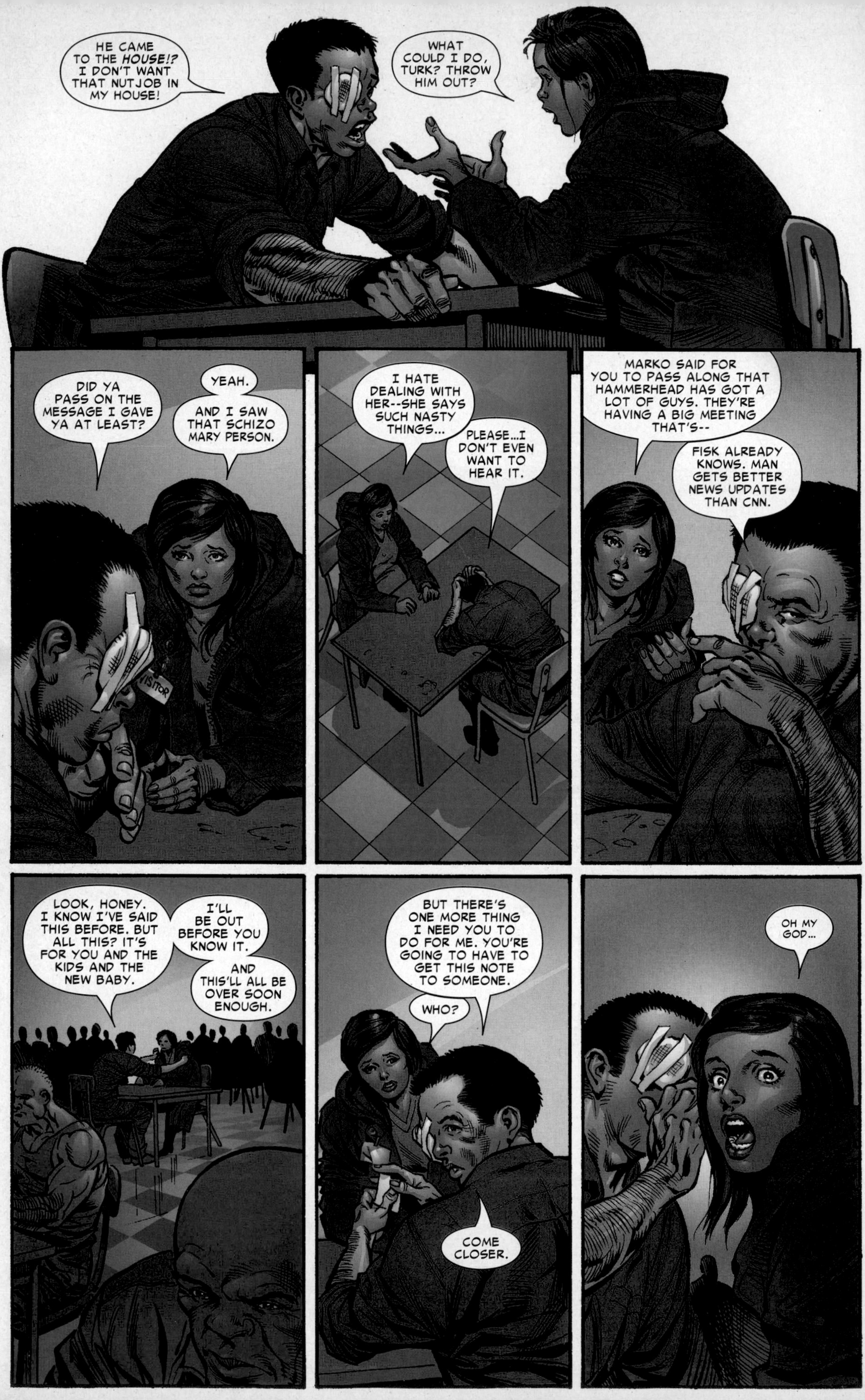
HE CAME TO THE *HOUSE!?* I DON'T WANT THAT NUTJOB IN MY HOUSE!
WHAT COULD I DO, TURK? THROW HIM OUT?
DID YA PASS ON THE MESSAGE I GAVE YA AT LEAST?
YEAH.
AND I SAW THAT SCHIZO MARY PERSON.
VISITOR
I HATE DEALING WITH HER--SHE SAYS SUCH NASTY THINGS...
PLEASE...I DON'T EVEN WANT TO HEAR IT.
MARKO SAID FOR YOU TO PASS ALONG THAT HAMMERHEAD HAS GOT A LOT OF GUYS. THEY'RE HAVING A BIG MEETING THAT'S--
FISK ALREADY KNOWS. MAN GETS BETTER NEWS UPDATES THAN CNN.
LOOK, HONEY. I KNOW I'VE SAID THIS BEFORE. BUT ALL THIS? IT'S FOR YOU AND THE KIDS AND THE NEW BABY.
I'LL BE OUT BEFORE YOU KNOW IT.
AND THIS'LL ALL BE OVER SOON ENOUGH.
BUT THERE'S ONE MORE THING I NEED YOU TO DO FOR ME. YOU'RE GOING TO HAVE TO GET THIS NOTE TO SOMEONE.
WHO?
COME CLOSER.
OH MY GOD...

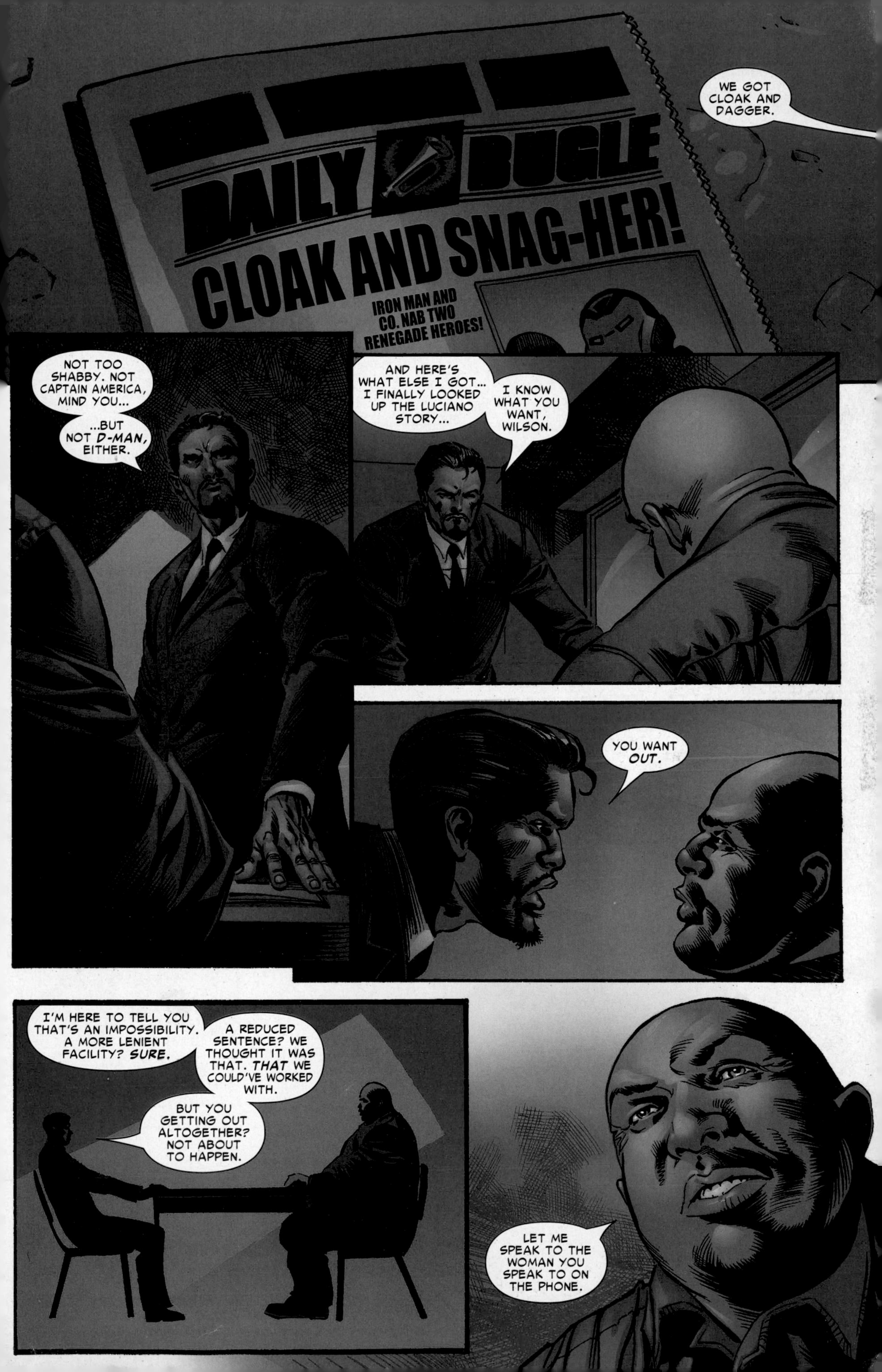

DAILY BUGLE
CLOAK AND SNAG-HER!
IRON MAN AND CO. NAB TWO RENEGADE HEROES!
WE GOT CLOAK AND DAGGER.
NOT TOO SHABBY. NOT CAPTAIN AMERICA, MIND YOU...
...BUT NOT D-MAN, EITHER.
AND HERE'S WHAT ELSE I GOT... I FINALLY LOOKED UP THE LUCIANO STORY...
I KNOW WHAT YOU WANT, WILSON.
YOU WANT OUT.
I'M HERE TO TELL YOU THAT'S AN IMPOSSIBILITY. A MORE LENIENT FACILITY? SURE.
A REDUCED SENTENCE? WE THOUGHT IT WAS THAT. THAT WE COULD'VE WORKED WITH.
BUT YOU GETTING OUT ALTOGETHER? NOT ABOUT TO HAPPEN.
LET ME SPEAK TO THE WOMAN YOU SPEAK TO ON THE PHONE.

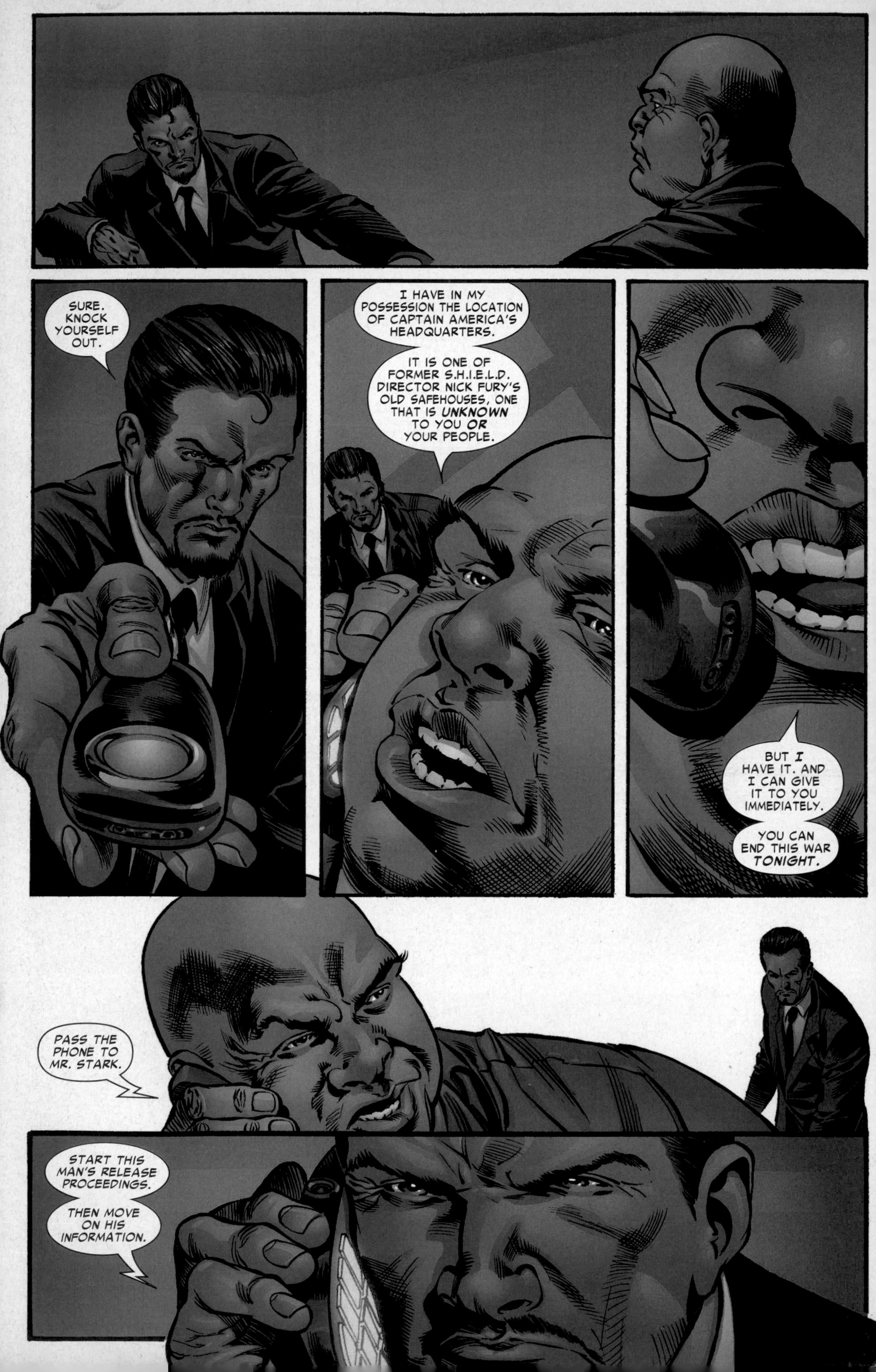
SURE. KNOCK YOURSELF OUT.
I HAVE IN MY POSSESSION THE LOCATION OF CAPTAIN AMERICA'S HEADQUARTERS.
IT IS ONE OF FORMER S.H.I.E.L.D. DIRECTOR NICK FURY'S OLD SAFEHOUSES, ONE THAT IS *UNKNOWN* TO YOU *OR* YOUR PEOPLE.
BUT *I* HAVE IT. AND I CAN GIVE IT TO YOU IMMEDIATELY.
YOU CAN END THIS WAR *TONIGHT*.
PASS THE PHONE TO MR. STARK.
START THIS MAN'S RELEASE PROCEEDINGS.
THEN MOVE ON HIS INFORMATION.

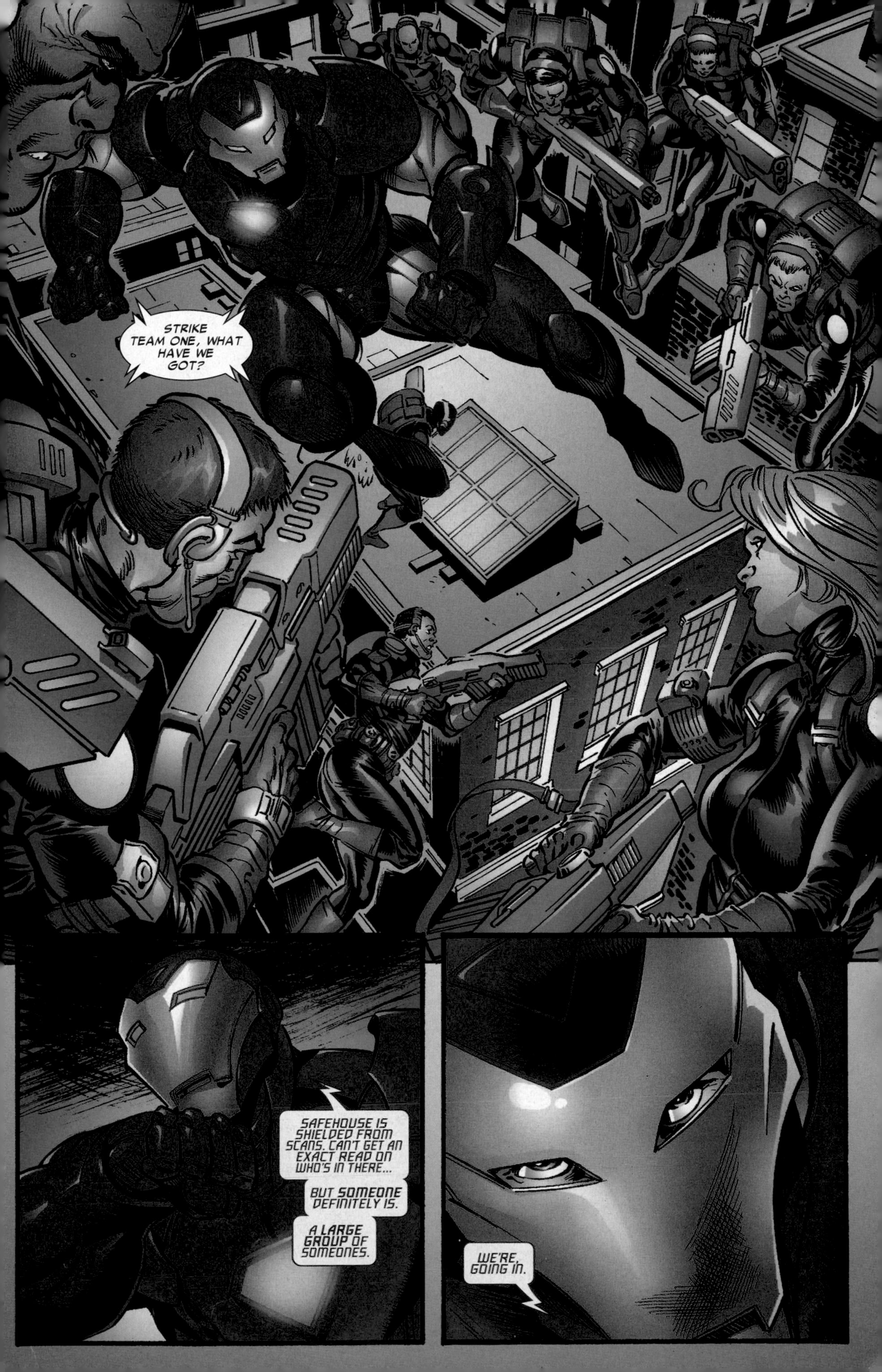
STRIKE TEAM ONE, WHAT HAVE WE GOT?
SAFEHOUSE IS SHIELDED FROM SCANS. CAN'T GET AN EXACT READ ON WHO'S IN THERE...
BUT SOMEONE DEFINITELY IS.
A LARGE GROUP OF SOMEONES.
WE'RE GOING IN.

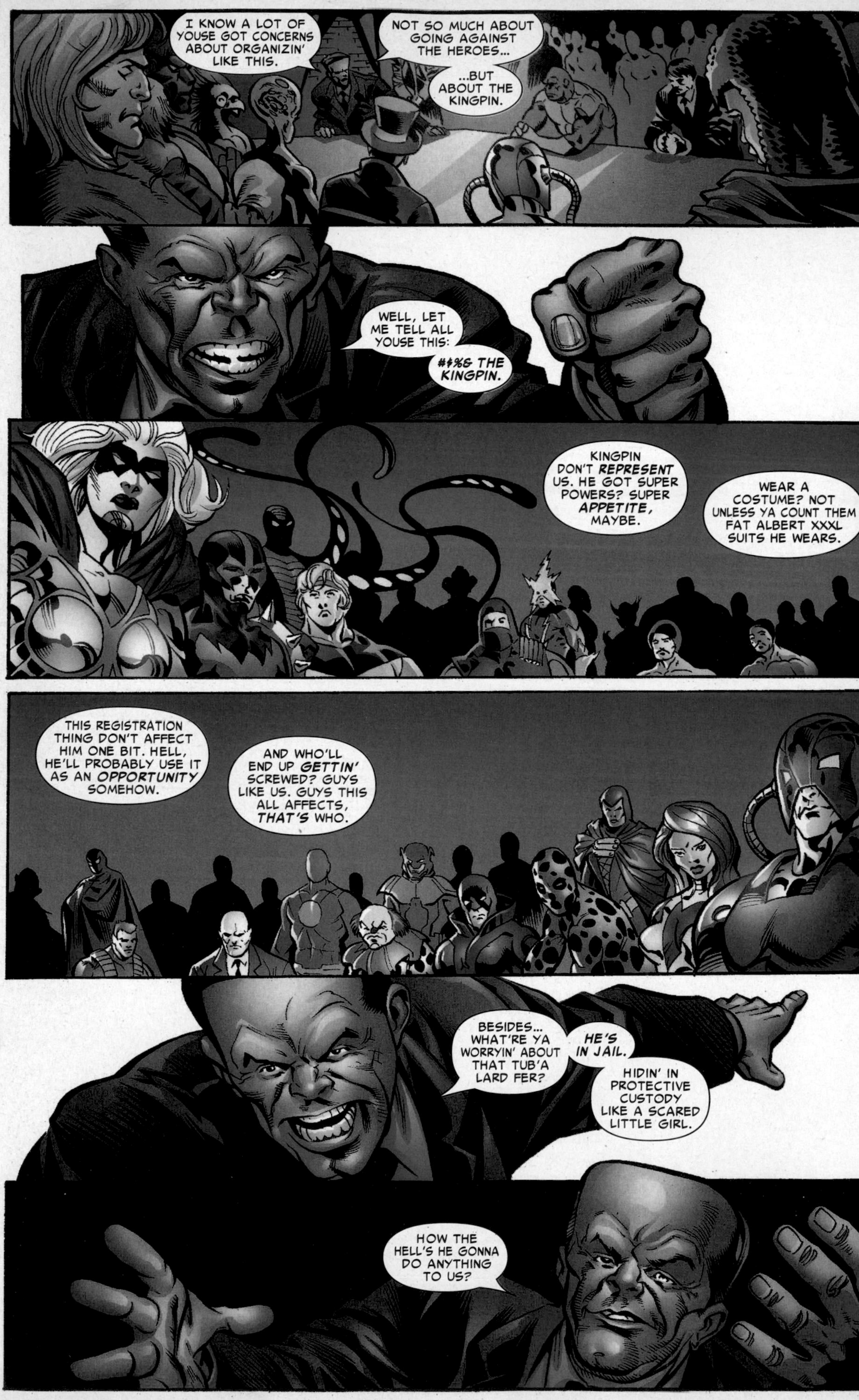
I KNOW A LOT OF YOUSE GOT CONCERNS ABOUT ORGANIZIN' LIKE THIS.
NOT SO MUCH ABOUT GOING AGAINST THE HEROES...
...BUT ABOUT THE KINGPIN.
WELL, LET ME TELL ALL YOUSE THIS:
#$%& THE KINGPIN.
KINGPIN DON'T REPRESENT US. HE GOT SUPER POWERS? SUPER APPETITE, MAYBE.
WEAR A COSTUME? NOT UNLESS YA COUNT THEM FAT ALBERT XXXL SUITS HE WEARS.
THIS REGISTRATION THING DON'T AFFECT HIM ONE BIT. HELL, HE'LL PROBABLY USE IT AS AN OPPORTUNITY SOMEHOW.
AND WHO'LL END UP GETTIN' SCREWED? GUYS LIKE US. GUYS THIS ALL AFFECTS, THAT'S WHO.
BESIDES... WHAT'RE YA WORRYIN' ABOUT THAT TUB'A LARD FER?
HE'S IN JAIL.
HIDIN' IN PROTECTIVE CUSTODY LIKE A SCARED LITTLE GIRL.
HOW THE HELL'S HE GONNA DO ANYTHING TO US?

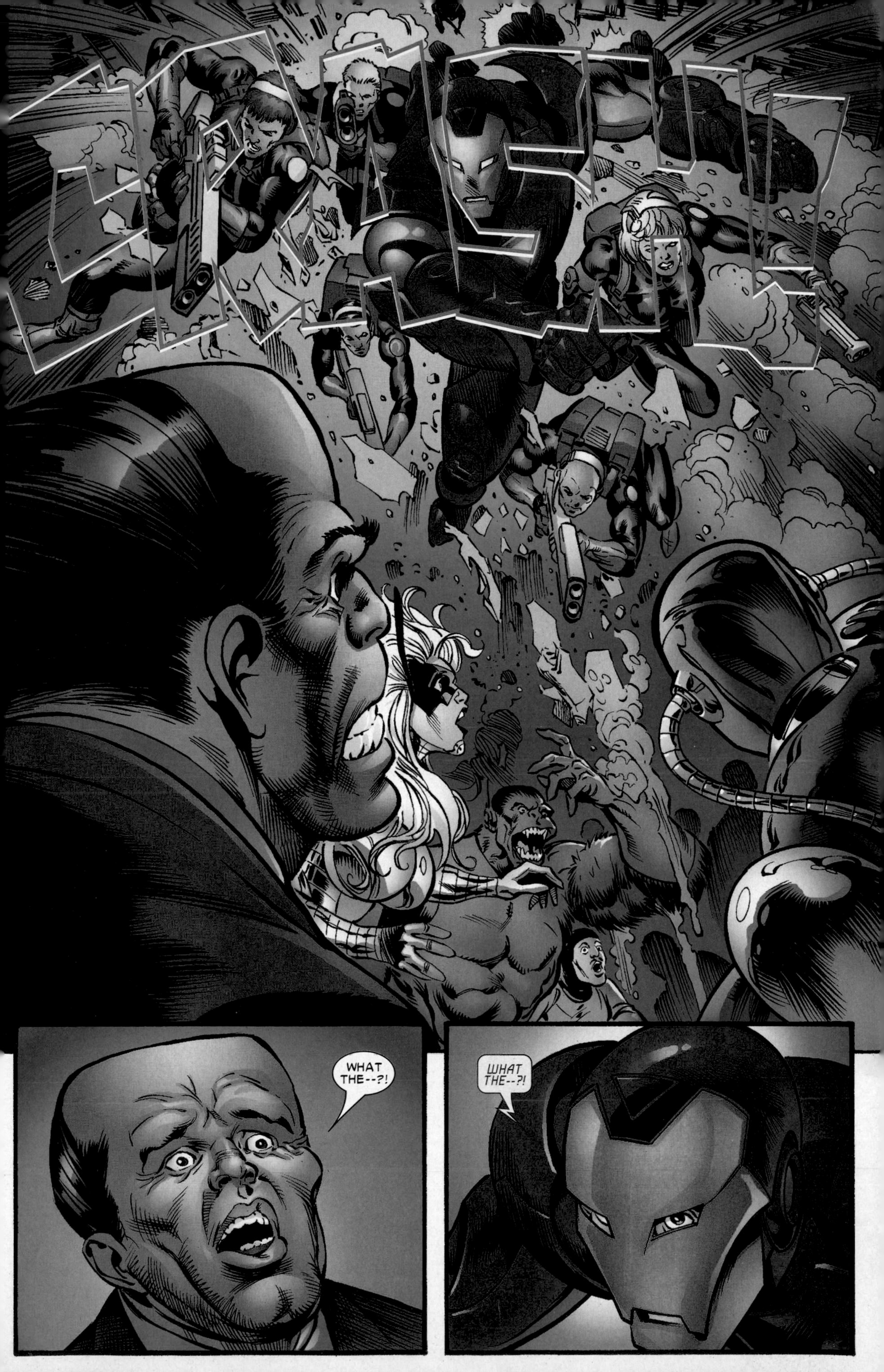
WHAT THE--?!
WHAT THE--?!

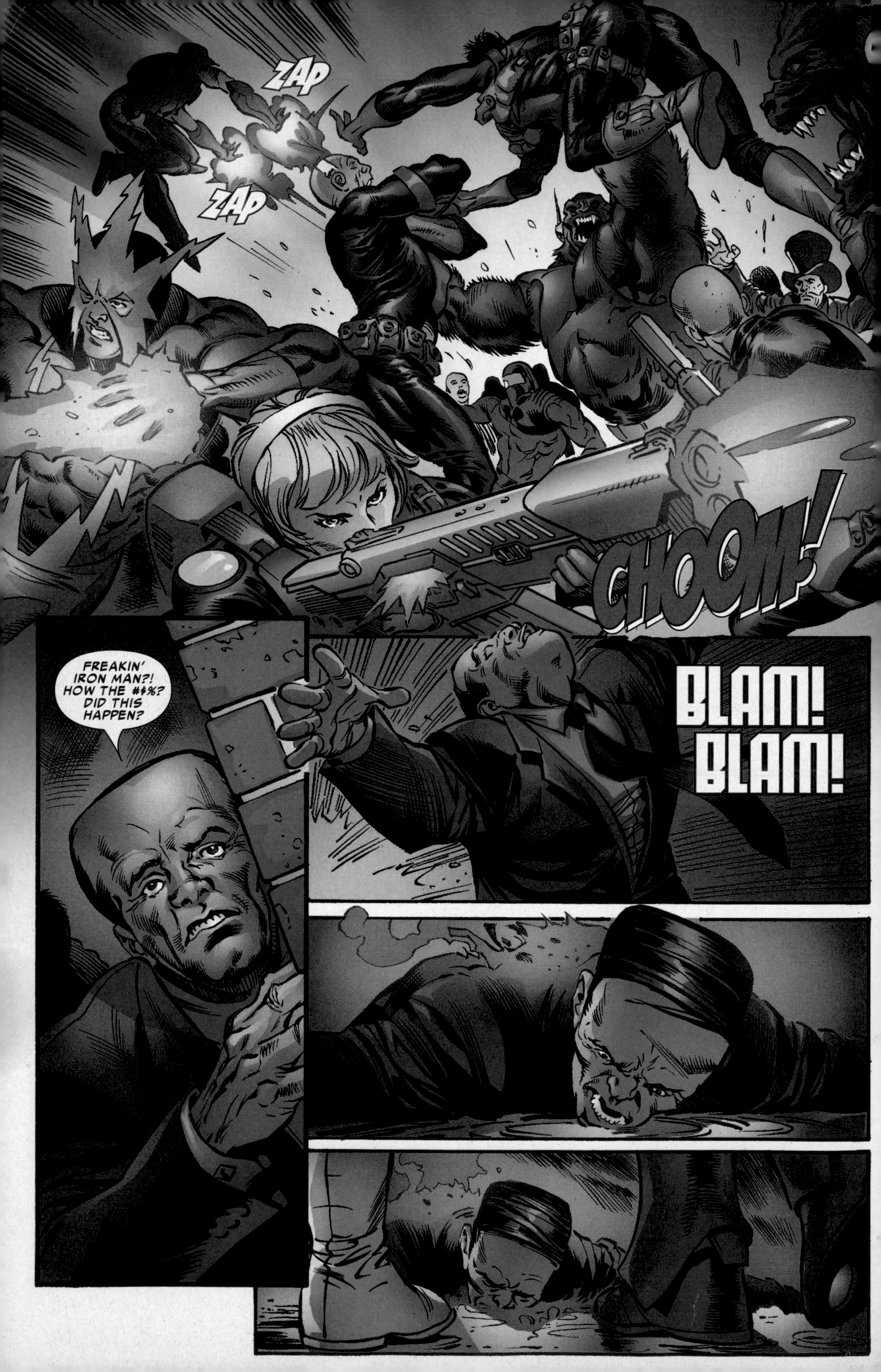
ZAP
ZAP
CHOOM!
FREAKIN' IRON MAN?! HOW THE #$%? DID THIS HAPPEN?
BLAM! BLAM!

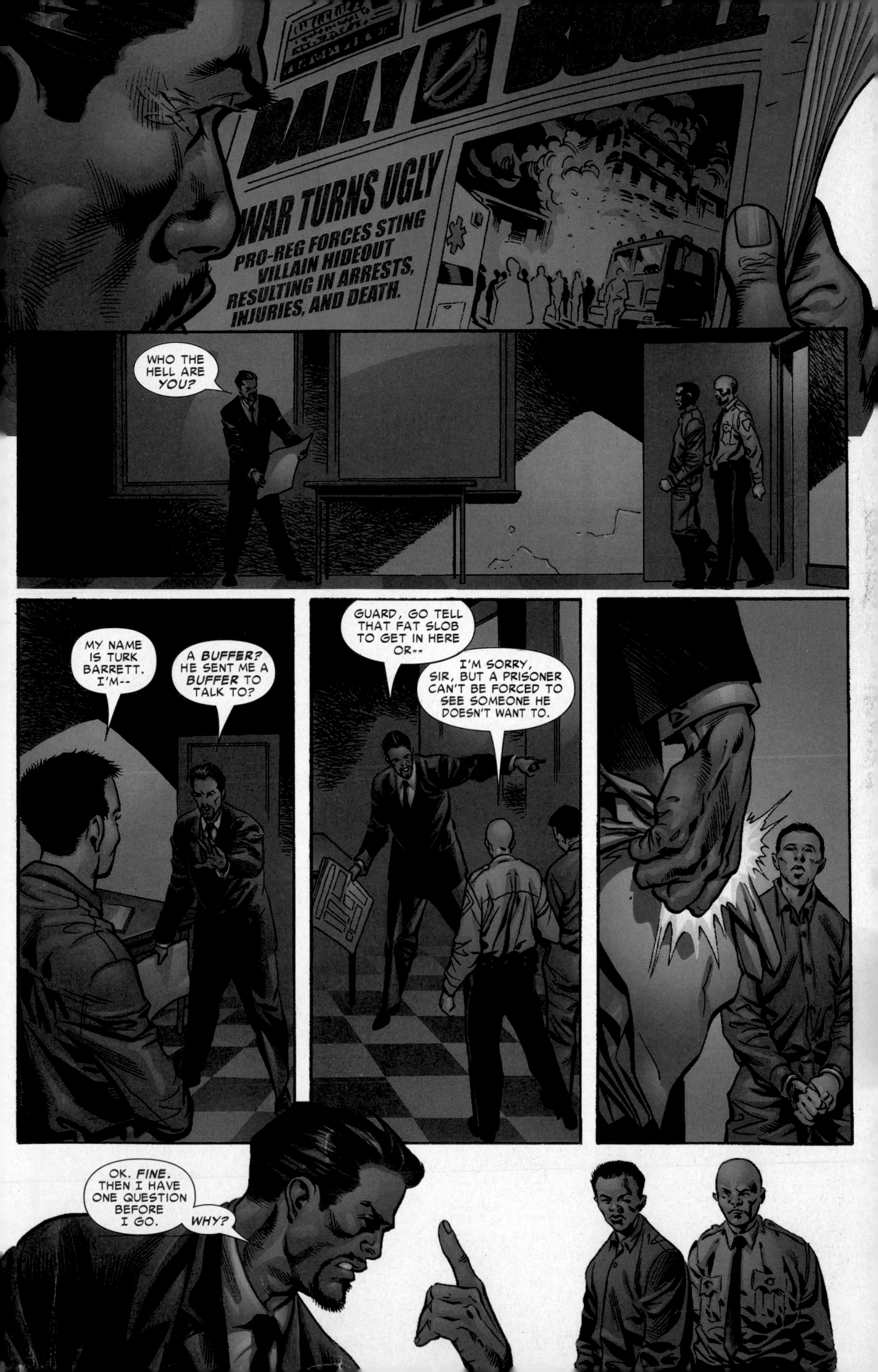
DAILY BUGLE
WAR TURNS UGLY
PRO-REG FORCES STING VILLAIN HIDEOUT RESULTING IN ARRESTS, INJURIES, AND DEATH.
WHO THE HELL ARE *YOU?*
MY NAME IS TURK BARRETT. I'M--
A *BUFFER?* HE SENT ME A *BUFFER* TO TALK TO?
GUARD, GO TELL THAT FAT SLOB TO GET IN HERE OR--
I'M SORRY, SIR, BUT A PRISONER CAN'T BE FORCED TO SEE SOMEONE HE DOESN'T WANT TO.
OK. *FINE.* THEN I HAVE ONE QUESTION BEFORE I GO.
WHY?

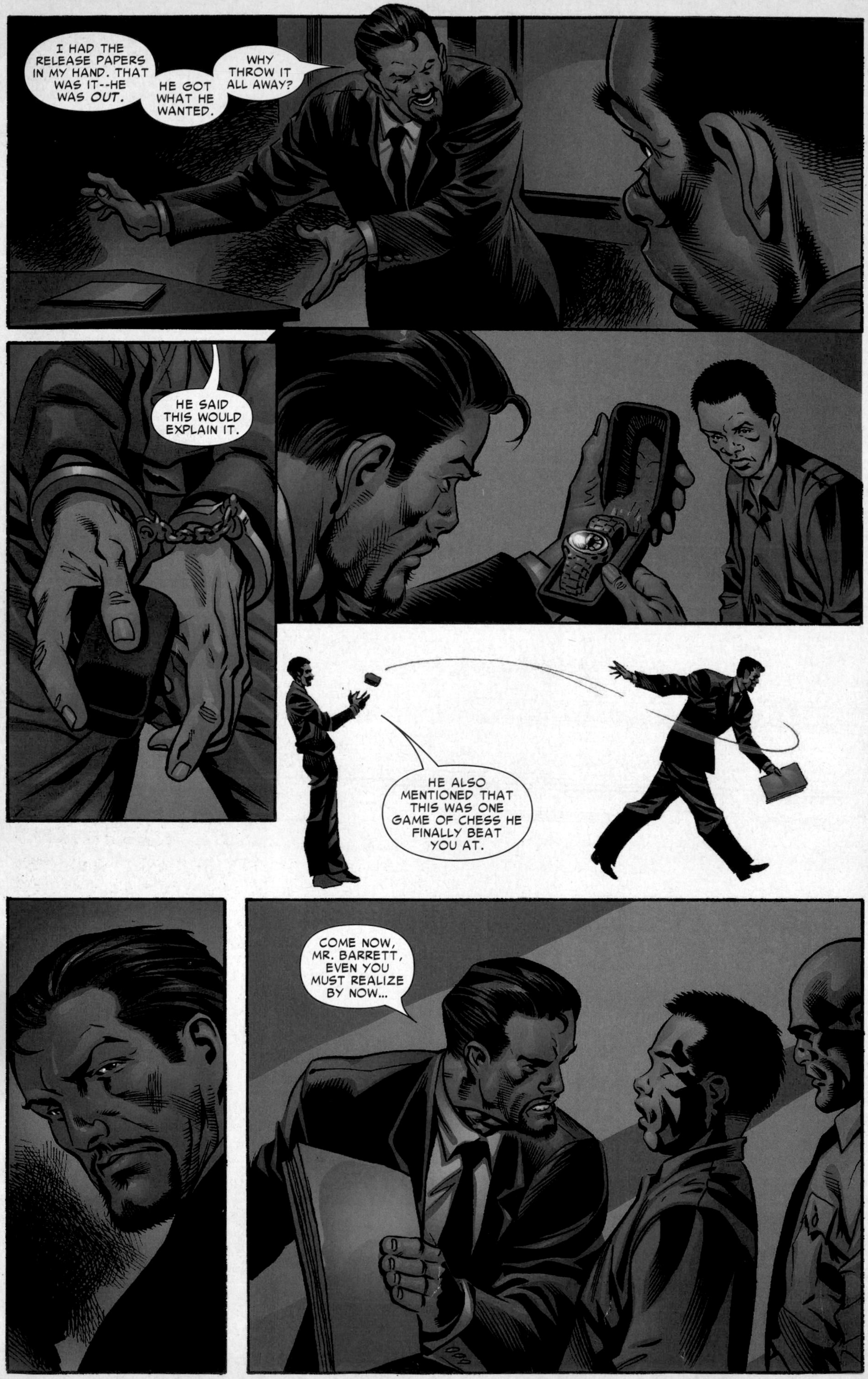
I HAD THE RELEASE PAPERS IN MY HAND. THAT WAS IT--HE WAS OUT.
HE GOT WHAT HE WANTED.
WHY THROW IT ALL AWAY?
HE SAID THIS WOULD EXPLAIN IT.
HE ALSO MENTIONED THAT THIS WAS ONE GAME OF CHESS HE FINALLY BEAT YOU AT.
COME NOW, MR. BARRETT, EVEN YOU MUST REALIZE BY NOW...

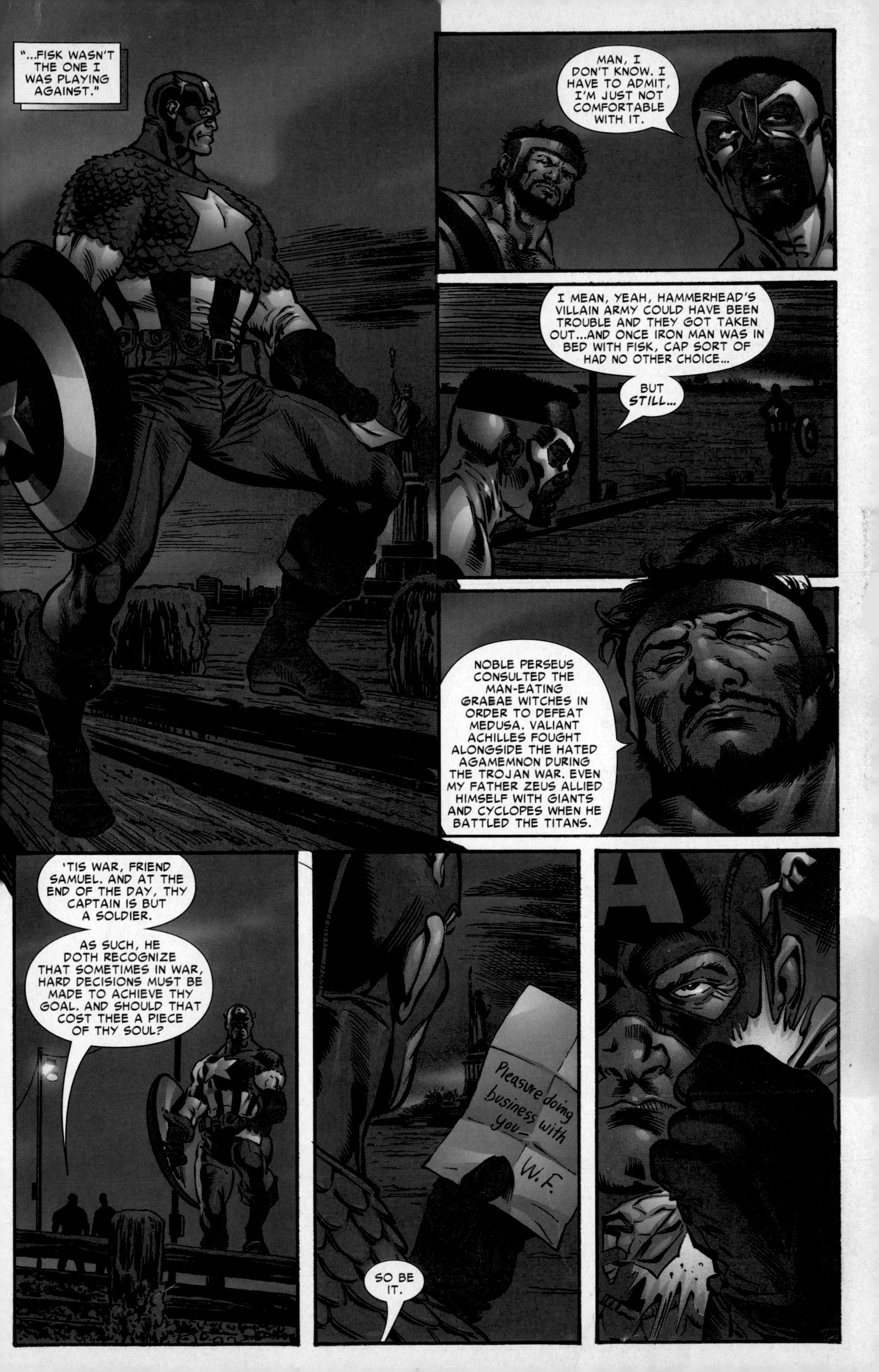
"...FISK WASN'T THE ONE I WAS PLAYING AGAINST."
MAN, I DON'T KNOW. I HAVE TO ADMIT, I'M JUST NOT COMFORTABLE WITH IT.
I MEAN, YEAH, HAMMERHEAD'S VILLAIN ARMY COULD HAVE BEEN TROUBLE AND THEY GOT TAKEN OUT...AND ONCE IRON MAN WAS IN BED WITH FISK, CAP SORT OF HAD NO OTHER CHOICE...
BUT STILL...
NOBLE PERSEUS CONSULTED THE MAN-EATING GRAEAE WITCHES IN ORDER TO DEFEAT MEDUSA. VALIANT ACHILLES FOUGHT ALONGSIDE THE HATED AGAMEMNON DURING THE TROJAN WAR. EVEN MY FATHER ZEUS ALLIED HIMSELF WITH GIANTS AND CYCLOPES WHEN HE BATTLED THE TITANS.
'TIS WAR, FRIEND SAMUEL. AND AT THE END OF THE DAY, THY CAPTAIN IS BUT A SOLDIER.
AS SUCH, HE DOTH RECOGNIZE THAT SOMETIMES IN WAR, HARD DECISIONS MUST BE MADE TO ACHIEVE THY GOAL. AND SHOULD THAT COST THEE A PIECE OF THY SOUL?
Pleasure doing business with you— W.F.
SO BE IT.

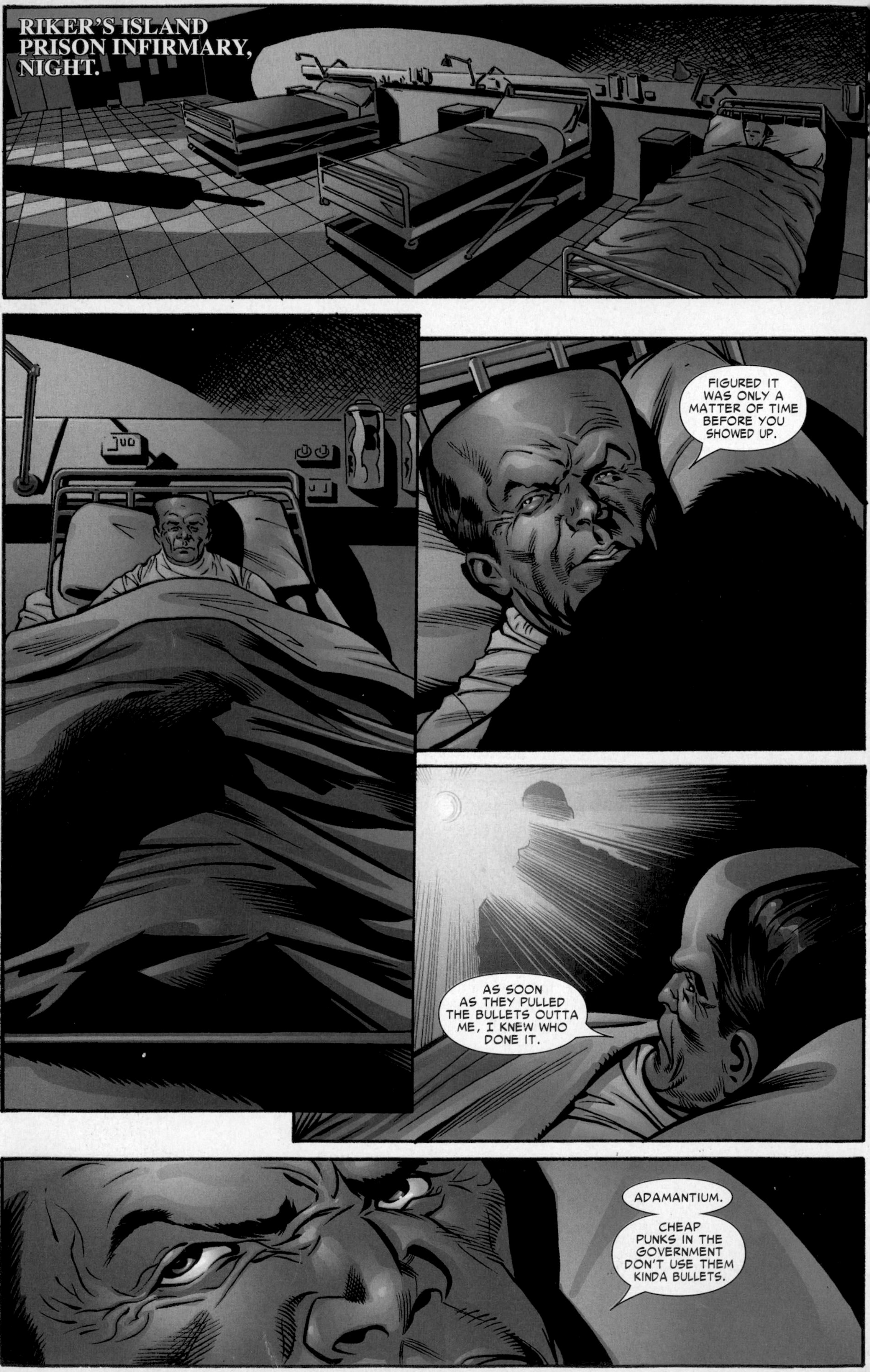
RIKER'S ISLAND PRISON INFIRMARY, NIGHT.
FIGURED IT WAS ONLY A MATTER OF TIME BEFORE YOU SHOWED UP.
AS SOON AS THEY PULLED THE BULLETS OUTTA ME, I KNEW WHO DONE IT.
ADAMANTIUM.
CHEAP PUNKS IN THE GOVERNMENT DON'T USE THEM KINDA BULLETS.

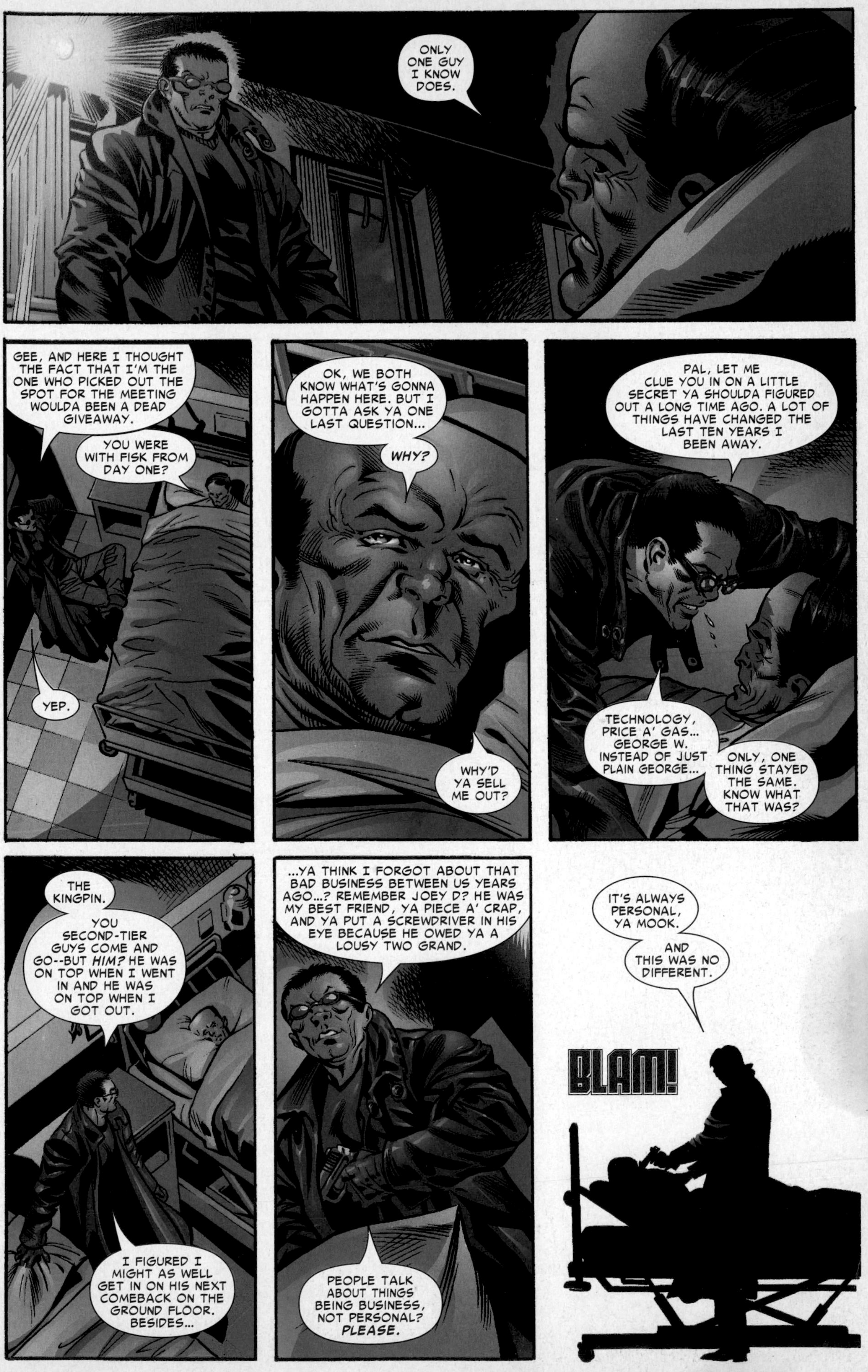
ONLY ONE GUY I KNOW DOES.
GEE, AND HERE I THOUGHT THE FACT THAT I'M THE ONE WHO PICKED OUT THE SPOT FOR THE MEETING WOULDA BEEN A DEAD GIVEAWAY.
YOU WERE WITH FISK FROM DAY ONE?
YEP.
OK, WE BOTH KNOW WHAT'S GONNA HAPPEN HERE. BUT I GOTTA ASK YA ONE LAST QUESTION...
WHY?
WHY'D YA SELL ME OUT?
PAL, LET ME CLUE YOU IN ON A LITTLE SECRET YA SHOULDA FIGURED OUT A LONG TIME AGO. A LOT OF THINGS HAVE CHANGED THE LAST TEN YEARS I BEEN AWAY.
TECHNOLOGY, PRICE A' GAS... GEORGE W. INSTEAD OF JUST PLAIN GEORGE...
ONLY, ONE THING STAYED THE SAME. KNOW WHAT THAT WAS?
THE KINGPIN.
YOU SECOND-TIER GUYS COME AND GO--BUT *HIM?* HE WAS ON TOP WHEN I WENT IN AND HE WAS ON TOP WHEN I GOT OUT.
I FIGURED I MIGHT AS WELL GET IN ON HIS NEXT COMEBACK ON THE GROUND FLOOR. BESIDES...
...YA THINK I FORGOT ABOUT THAT BAD BUSINESS BETWEEN US YEARS AGO...? REMEMBER JOEY D? HE WAS MY BEST FRIEND, YA PIECE A' CRAP, AND YA PUT A SCREWDRIVER IN HIS EYE BECAUSE HE OWED YA A LOUSY TWO GRAND.
PEOPLE TALK ABOUT THINGS BEING BUSINESS, NOT PERSONAL? *PLEASE.*
IT'S ALWAYS PERSONAL, YA MOOK.
AND THIS WAS NO DIFFERENT.
BLAM!

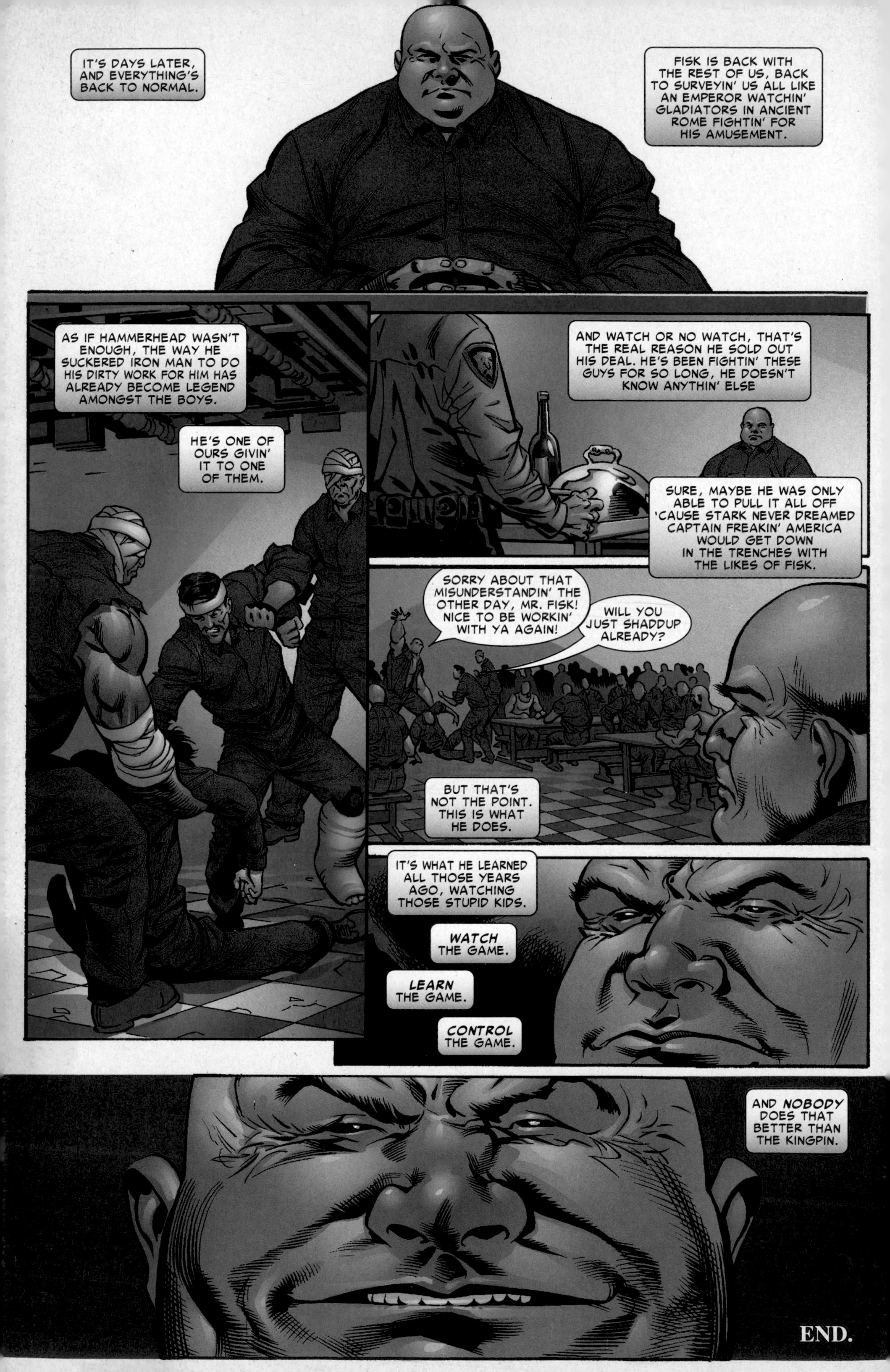
IT'S DAYS LATER, AND EVERYTHING'S BACK TO NORMAL.
FISK IS BACK WITH THE REST OF US, BACK TO SURVEYIN' US ALL LIKE AN EMPEROR WATCHIN' GLADIATORS IN ANCIENT ROME FIGHTIN' FOR HIS AMUSEMENT.
AS IF HAMMERHEAD WASN'T ENOUGH, THE WAY HE SUCKERED IRON MAN TO DO HIS DIRTY WORK FOR HIM HAS ALREADY BECOME LEGEND AMONGST THE BOYS.
HE'S ONE OF OURS GIVIN' IT TO ONE OF THEM.
AND WATCH OR NO WATCH, THAT'S THE REAL REASON HE SOLD OUT HIS DEAL. HE'S BEEN FIGHTIN' THESE GUYS FOR SO LONG, HE DOESN'T KNOW ANYTHIN' ELSE
SURE, MAYBE HE WAS ONLY ABLE TO PULL IT ALL OFF 'CAUSE STARK NEVER DREAMED CAPTAIN FREAKIN' AMERICA WOULD GET DOWN IN THE TRENCHES WITH THE LIKES OF FISK.
SORRY ABOUT THAT MISUNDERSTANDIN' THE OTHER DAY, MR. FISK! NICE TO BE WORKIN' WITH YA AGAIN!
WILL YOU JUST SHADDUP ALREADY?
BUT THAT'S NOT THE POINT. THIS IS WHAT HE DOES.
IT'S WHAT HE LEARNED ALL THOSE YEARS AGO, WATCHING THOSE STUPID KIDS.
WATCH THE GAME.
LEARN THE GAME.
CONTROL THE GAME.
AND NOBODY DOES THAT BETTER THAN THE KINGPIN.
END.

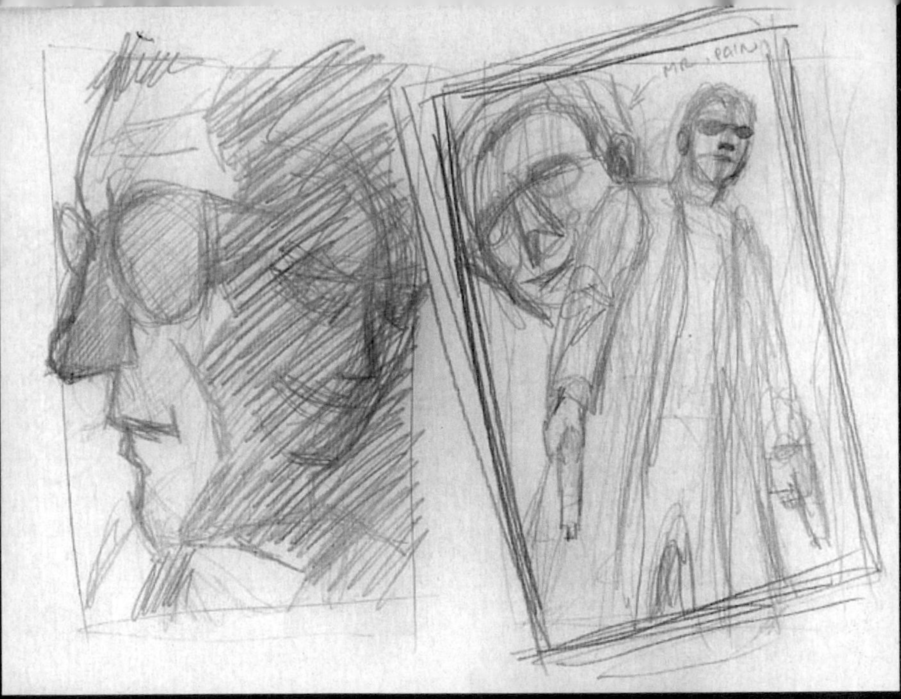

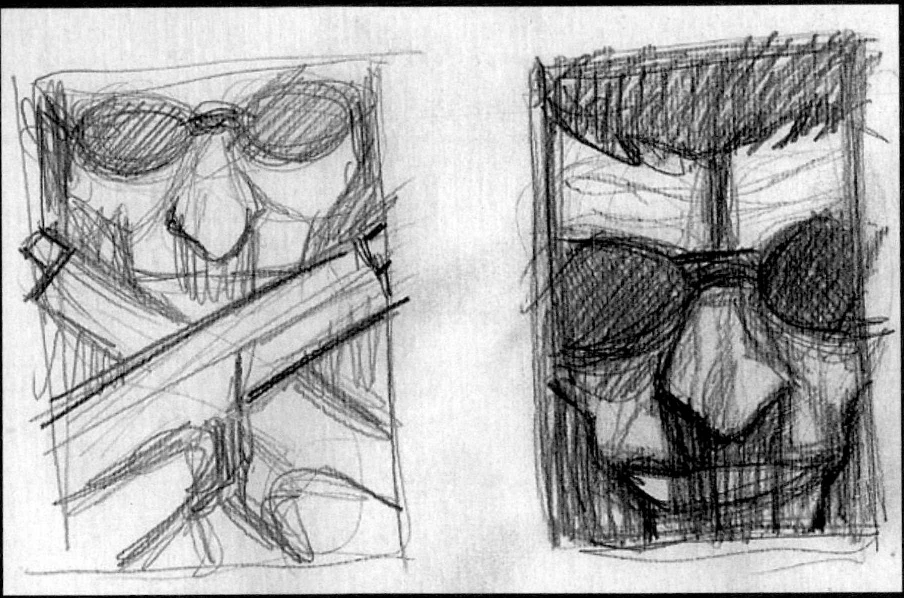

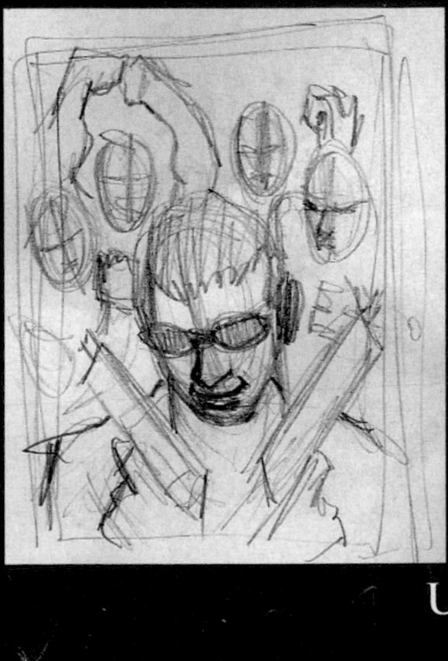

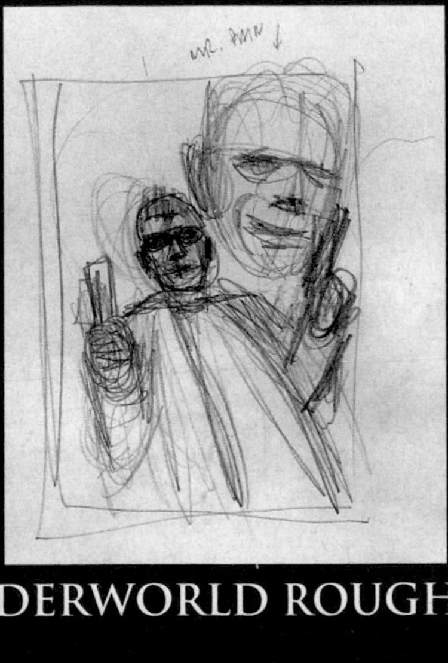

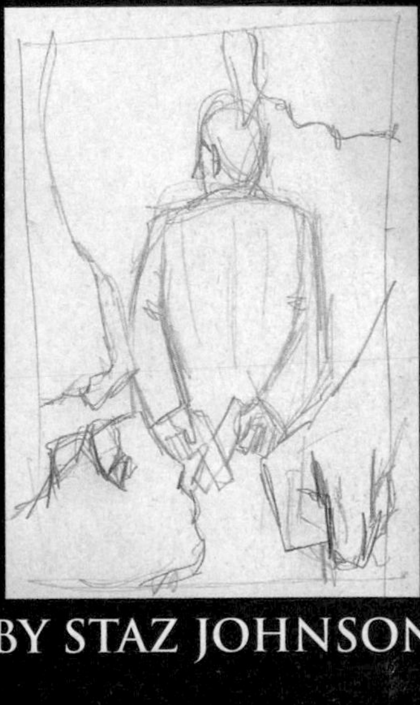

UNDERWORLD ROUGHS BY STAZ JOHNSON

GRIZZLY

REAL NAME: Maxwell Markham
ALIASES: Crazy Max
IDENTITY: Publicly known
OCCUPATION: Criminal; former wrestler
CITIZENSHIP: U.S.A. with a criminal record; formerly Canada
PLACE OF BIRTH: McKigney, Saskatchewan, Canada
KNOWN RELATIVES: Unidentified son
GROUP AFFILIATION: Formerly partner of Gibbon, Spider-Man Revenge Squad
EDUCATION: High school graduate
FIRST APPEARANCE: Amazing Spider-Man #139 (1974)

HISTORY: Maxwell Markham was a professional wrestler known as Crazy Max or the Grizzly for his ferocity in the ring, until actions such as throwing his opponent the Steel Curtain into the crowds drew negative attention from J. Jonah Jameson of the Daily Bugle, who wrote a series of scathing articles demanding the Wrestling Federation investigate Maxwell's excesses. Finally caving to public opinion, the Federation revoked Markham's license because of the bad publicity rather than actual rules infringements; Markham confronted Jameson over his career's destruction, but the reporter was unrepentant, and Markham nursed his anger for eleven years. He eventually met the Jackal (Miles Warren), a mad genius who outfitted him with a strength-enhancing exo-skeleton. Taking inspiration from his stage name, Markham wore a bear costume over the exo-skeleton and attacked the Daily Bugle offices as the Grizzly, throwing Jameson from a window. Spider-Man saved Jameson and after a couple of skirmishes, faced down Grizzly at Halberstam's Gym. Ripping apart Grizzly's costume to expose and break the exo-skeleton beneath, Spider-Man handed the depowered Markham over to the police.

Years later, the Tinkerer repaired Grizzly's exo-skeleton and Markham returned for a rematch; realizing the Grizzly just wanted to reclaim some self-respect, Spider-Man feigned defeat, and the Grizzly departed happy. He soon deduced Spider-Man had thrown the fight, and while he was fine with this at first, the ridicule of others eventually drove Markham to recruit fellow minor Spider-Man foes the Kangaroo, Gibbon and Spot, forming the Spider-Man Revenge Squad; however, Kangaroo and Spot proved more interested in robberies than revenge, and after actually catching Spider-Man, Grizzly and Gibbon began to have second thoughts when Spot suggested killing the hero. Grizzly and Gibbon defeated their erstwhile partners, and decided to become crime-fighters. Trying to stop the White Rabbit Gang from robbing a bank, they were taken hostage and ransomed on live television, but broke free and captured the villainess; this high-profile victory garnered them an action figure deal with Toy Biz, and the pair announced their intention to produce a theatrical play.

Finding it difficult to stay on the straight and narrow, Grizzly frequented underworld bars and served a brief prison term for unspecified offences; paroled, he found it nigh impossible not to associate with other criminals such as the Rhino, and considered returning to crime. His old reputation was difficult to shake; after stopping the White Rabbit from robbing another bank, he was mistakenly arrested for her crime and taken into S.H.I.E.L.D. custody until video footage cleared him. Later he fought Power Pack in New Jersey, only to be accused of a robbery in Madison Square Garden at the same time; Markham sought legal council at the offices of Goodman, Lieber, Kurtzberg and Holliway, where he suffered an unprovoked assault from Avengers member Starfox. Giving in, Grizzly took the advice of the Consultant and revamped his image, ditching his trademark bear suit and replacing it with enhanced strength, invulnerability and claw and fang implants, paying for the upgrade by plundering his son's college fund. He went to work for the Owl's head enforcer Mr. Pain and teamed with Boomerang to eliminate Jackie Dio, who had been hitting the Owl's operations. Escaping their first encounter, Jackie returned armed with Adamantium bullets, shooting Grizzly several times in the chest. Hospitalized, he and Boomerang were visited by Mr. Pain, who punished them for their failure, setting fire to Boomerang and ramming a flower bouquet into Grizzly's chest wounds. Recovering, Grizzly attended Stilt-Man's funeral, only to be poisoned and seemingly blown up by the Punisher.

6'9" | 290 lbs.
Blue | Blond, dyed red

Superhumanly strong and durable, Grizzly can lift up to 15 tons optimally; initially enhanced by an exo-skeleton, his strength is now innate following his recent power upgrade. His fingertip claws and fangs can rend steel. He is also a skilled wrestler. Grizzly was slightly asthmatic before his power upgrade.

POWER GRID	1 2 3 4 5 6 7
INTELLIGENCE	2
STRENGTH	[illegible]
SPEED	2
DURABILITY	[illegible]
ENERGY PROJECTION	1
FIGHTING SKILLS	[illegible]

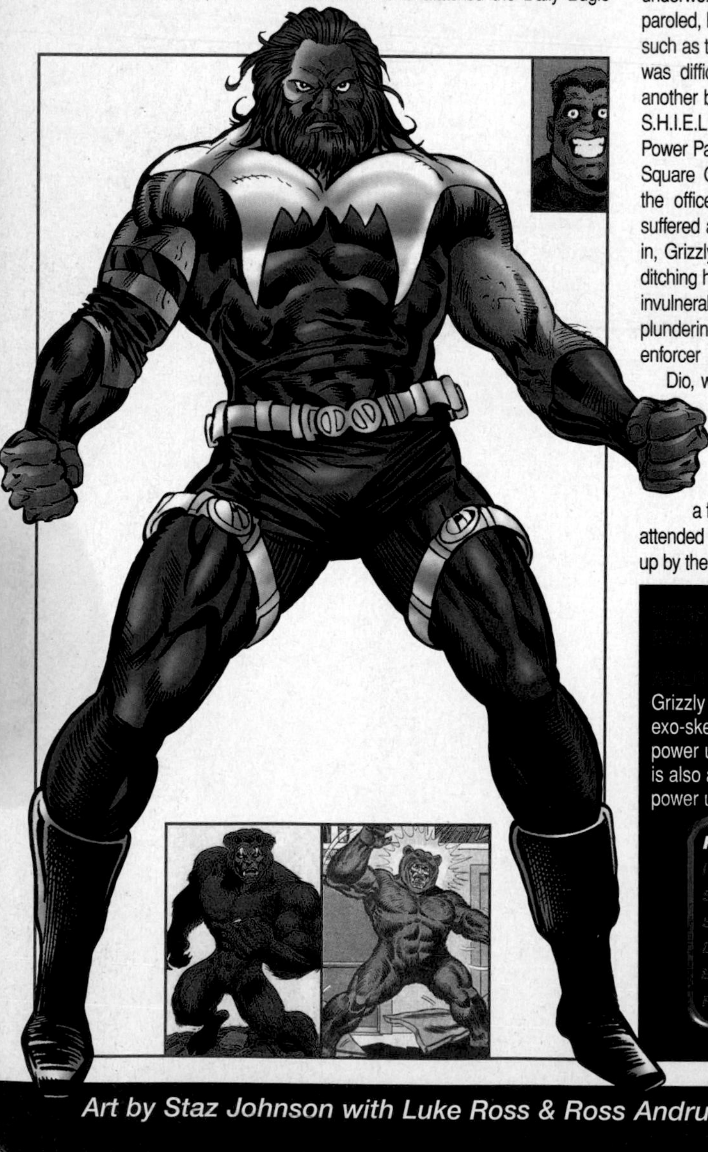

Art by Staz Johnson with Luke Ross & Ross Andru (insets)

SILVERMANE

HISTORY: Born almost ninety years ago, Silvio Manfredi was still a child when his family immigrated to the U.S., but within a decade he was a force to be reckoned with in the growing crime families of New York's Maggia. Through a combination of strategic brilliance and sheer brute force, he became the head of his own organization, strengthening the Maggia's grip on the underworld and his own grip on the Maggia. Dubbed "Silvermane" when his hair prematurely whitened in his forties, he survived countless challenges from within and outside his ranks, rivaled only by the likes of Alexander Bont and Vincent Coll of Hell's Kitchen. Not even his influence could last forever, though, and at the height of his power he was imprisoned for tax evasion.

Released from prison some thirty years ago, Silvermane returned to a Maggia fragmented by his rivals. Taking the young gangster Dominic Tyrone as a protégé and partner, he returned to the trenches to reclaim his organization. His victory complete after years of work, Silvermane, troubled by Tyrone's dreams of overthrowing the power structures Silvermane hoped to dominate and stabilize, ordered his underlings to beat and drown his idealistic ally, leaving Dominic for dead. Unburdened by Tyrone's principles, Silvermane built much of his empire on the international drug trade disdained by the powerful Don Rigoletto; Rigoletto was soon supplanted by his lieutenant Wilson Fisk, later dubbed the Kingpin of Crime.

In recent years, as superhuman criminals grew bolder and more numerous, Silvermane and his lieutenant Jackie Dio were among the few mobsters who declined to hire super-powered underlings; however, the octogenarian Silvermane was not above pursuing exotic means of lengthening his life. To this end he had Man-Mountain Marko (not yet a superhuman himself) steal the record of arcane knowledge called the Lifeline Tablet, inspired by the tales he had heard as a boy in Italy. His acquisition made all the sweeter by the knowledge that the Kingpin too sought the tablet, Silvermane had Dr. Curt Connors abducted to decipher the ancient text, neither knowing nor caring about Connors' double nature as the Lizard. Forcing Connors to concoct a formula based on his findings, Silvermane downed it and exulted over his restored youth; however, he found himself losing too many years, vanishing into non-existence. When Spider-Man arrived to rescue Connors, only Silvermane's empty clothes remained.

Following Spider-Man's departure, the tablet's power proved itself unspent, as Silvermane surged back into existence, once more in his forties and eager for new challenges. He found one in the form of Hydra agents, who sought his leadership for their Corporation-run branch of the terrorist organization. Adding the mantle of Supreme Hydra to his position as Maggia head, he used his new underlings to ferret out and crush the upstarts among his old ones, raising both organizations to new heights. No longer reluctant to surround himself with super-powered allies, he appointed Man-Killer, Commander Kraken, a sentient Dreadnought robot and others as Hydra division chiefs, and inducted his son Joseph into the ranks as the bat-controlling Blackwing. Hoping to cap his victories with the destruction of S.H.I.E.L.D., he lured S.H.I.E.L.D. director Nick Fury and his most trusted lieutenants into a trap, but even Silvermane's decades of experience proved no match for those of Fury, who sprang the trap via Life Model Decoys (LMDs), then swept in to help Daredevil and the Black Widow defeat Silvermane's division chiefs. Deposed by Hydra following this debacle, Silvermane escaped assassination via his Maggia influence, but his experiences had softened his reluctance to allow superhumans into his ranks, much to the frustration of Dio, who was captured by Spider-Man shortly thereafter.

Hoping to expand his reign again, Silvermane summoned several minor underworld leaders to a summit in hopes of forging a conglomerate to rival even the Kingpin's, but he faced a new rival in would-be crime boss Bart Hamilton, who had stolen Harry Osborn's Green Goblin identity. Besieged by both Hamilton and Spider-Man, Silvermane was

REAL NAME: Silvio Manfredi
ALIASES: "Sil," Supreme Hydra, Supreme One
IDENTITY: Publicly known
OCCUPATION: Professional criminal; former Maggia crimelord, Supreme Hydra, racketeer
CITIZENSHIP: Italy; U.S.A. (naturalized)
PLACE OF BIRTH: Palermo, Sicily
KNOWN RELATIVES: Caterina Manfredi (wife, deceased), Joseph Manfredi (Blackwing, son)
GROUP AFFILIATION: Silvermane Family of Maggia; formerly Hydra
EDUCATION: High school graduate
FIRST APPEARANCE: Amazing Spider-Man #73 (1969)

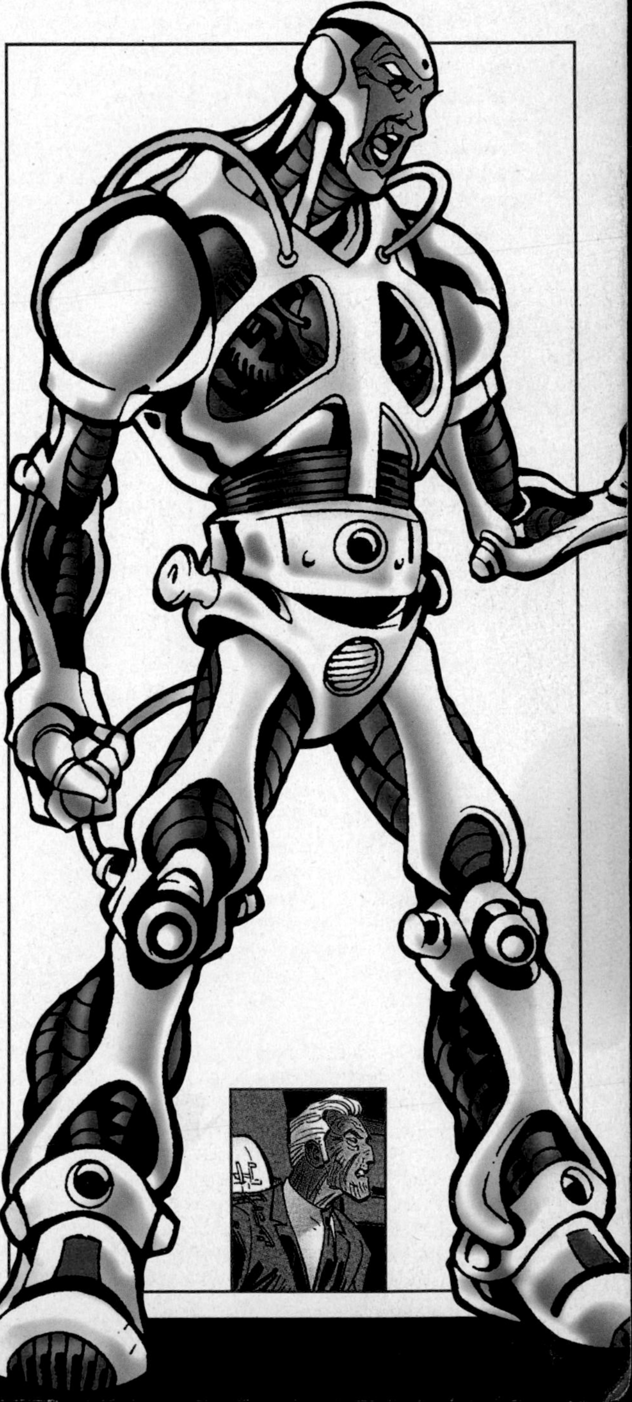

Art by Karl Kesel with John Romita Jr. (inset)

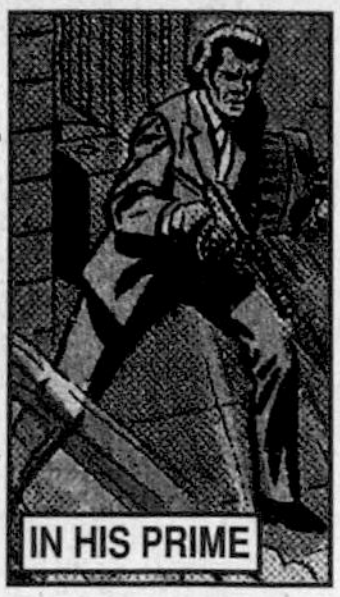
IN HIS PRIME
Art by Jim Mooney

swept into the air by Hamilton's goblin-glider, then sent plummeting to near-death. Perhaps proving the Lifeline formula was still effective, Silvermane recovered from these wounds and flexed his muscles by terrorizing the Daily Bugle for its anti-crime stance. Dominic Tyrone, having finally regained his health after Silvermane's betrayal years before, besieged the Maggia as the vigilante Rapier. Again struck down by a rival despite Spider-Man's best efforts, Silvermane's health collapsed beneath Rapier's electric sword. He spent months on life support before the fledgling vigilantes Cloak and Dagger tried to finish Rapier's job, but Silvermane's string of injuries had led him to establish a remarkable contingency, the transfer of his living head and organs into a powerful cyborg body, which he gladly accepted instead of waiting to steal a human one. Unfortunately, his eager exertions against his would-be assassins taxed his aging organs, and though Spider-Man yet again sought to keep him alive to face justice for his crimes, Dagger struck Silvermane down with her light-knives.

Ironically, Silvermane's cyborg body retained a spark of life thanks to a bond Dagger's power had created between them. The Kingpin animated his rival's body, but not his mind, in hopes of using him as an unquestioning assassin, but Spider-Man interrupted Silvermane's first endeavor. While he, the Black Cat, Cloak and Dagger were drawn into the Kingpin's machinations, Silvermane was sparked back into sentience and fled the proceedings. Stranded in cyborg form, Silvermane was bedridden once more by the time Jack O'Lantern attacked him as part of a growing gang war, but Silvermane's spirit was stronger than his cybernetics could ever be, and he clung to life while retreating to an abandoned Hydra base, seeking a means to reclaim his future. Learning through stolen data that he could be revitalized by the radioactive blood of none other than Spider-Man, Silvermane sent the Tinkerer's android Silver Squad to capture his enemy. When the Black Cat sprang to the rescue, Silvermane used a remote-controlled android duplicate to fight her by proxy, but he was left in the rubble when the battle decimated his base.

Having by now lost his Maggia preeminence, Silvermane, revitalized by synthetic blood, reclaimed another Hydra base and set about building a new drug empire, but his efforts were disrupted by the Punisher and cyborg Deathlok (Michael Collins), the pair eerily echoing his past and present circumstances. When the Kingpin went underground after his own losses, a summit of gangsters, terrorists and more assembled to divide the holdings; receiving no invitation, Silvermane crashed the party with an android army but was barely noticed by either his rivals or the vigilantes who had gathered to oppose them. Deciding a new body would command new respect, he organized a platoon of superhuman operatives and terrorized New York in an effort to extort Deathlok (Michael Collins) into surrendering his far superior cybernetic form. Once his intellect was electronically transferred into Deathlok, Silvermane betrayed his new allies, only to be overwhelmed by Spider-Man, Daredevil and the Punisher before being evicted by Deathlok's resident persona.

Ultimately transferred back to his aged human body, kept safe throughout his years as a cyborg, Silvermane indeed won back some of his underworld prestige, his scheme's failure compensated for by its sheer boldness. He regained his Maggia throne just in time for another aged gangster, Don Fortunato, to challenge the New York underworld with the support of none other than Hydra. Silvermane was among the many who gathered when foreign crimelord General Coy rallied Fortunato's rivals; facing the power of his former organization, surrounded by one-time rivals and underlings who were now his equals, Silvermane was surely as humbled as ever he had been in his long career, not even managing to contribute to Fortunato's fall before Spider-Man (Ben Reilly) and Daredevil.

Again supported by Blackwing, who tried his own hand at leadership with the group Heavy Mettle, Silvermane continued his campaign to win back the world he had carved for himself; as old age hurried to catch up with him, he occasionally transferred his consciousness back to his cyborg form just long enough for his human body to be stabilized. Most recently, a failed assassination attempt sent him back to the cyborg body, but his health was so poor that even as a cyborg he could not rally his strength; once again bedridden, Silvermane is doubtless dreaming of another climb to power.

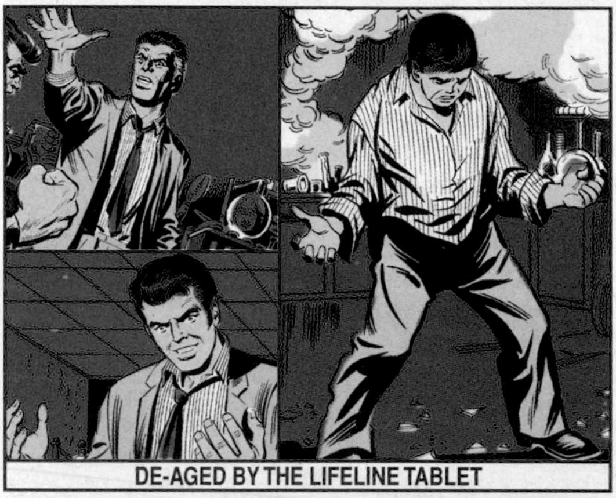
DE-AGED BY THE LIFELINE TABLET
Art by John Romita Sr.

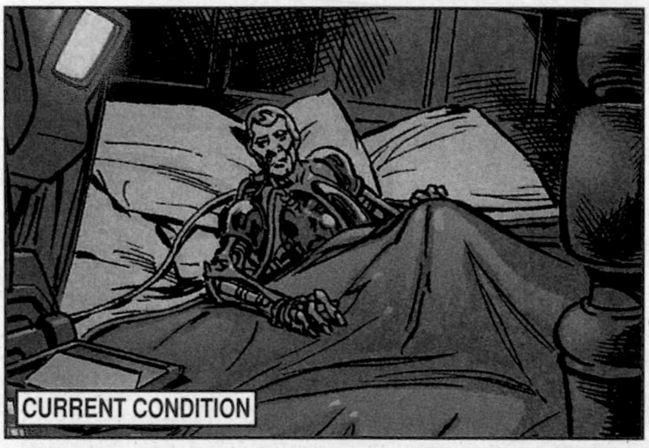
CURRENT CONDITION
Art by Staz Johnson

HEIGHT: 7' (in human body, 6'2")
WEIGHT: 440 lbs. (in human body, 195 lbs.)
EYES: Blue
HAIR: Silver (formerly brown)

ABILITIES/ACCESSORIES: When his cyborg body is fully functional, Silvermane possesses superhuman strength (lifting 15 tons), speed, senses and durability, so long as his human organs are adequately protected and augmented. He is an accomplished criminal organizer and strategist; in his prime he was an exceptional marksman and an extraordinary hand-to-hand combatant, capable of defeating opponents twice his size.

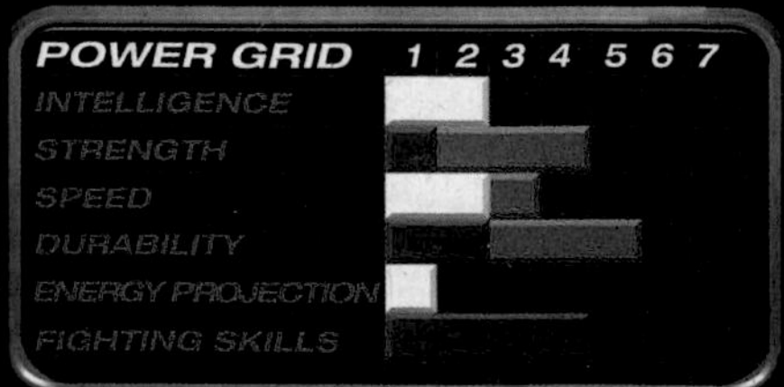
POWER GRID 1 2 3 4 5 6 7
INTELLIGENCE
STRENGTH
SPEED
DURABILITY
ENERGY PROJECTION
FIGHTING SKILLS

YELLOW BARS INDICATE RATINGS AS CYBORG

HISTORY: Jackie Dio was the son of a Silvermane crime family enforcer. Fearing one of the rising wave of new superhumans would take his job, Jackie's father donned an untested super-suit, but suffered fatal wounds battling another super-villain. He hung on long enough to make the teenage Jackie promise to take care of his younger brother, Vince. Silvermane took the boys in, with Jackie viewing him as a surrogate father, becoming the mobster's most feared soldier; Vince, however, lacked both Jackie's iron nerve and fighting talent, and was relegated to the role of ambitious lackey. Jackie counseled against hiring superpowered operatives and for years Silvermane agreed, understanding Jackie's hatred of superhumans; however, with emerging threats such as rival mobster Hammerhead and the vigilante Punisher, Silvermane finally accepted the inevitable.

Tired of living in Jackie's shadow and his verbal abuse, Vince arranged for Hydra agents to hit Jackie; they failed, and Jackie learned of Vince's treachery from the last agent before killing him. Jackie beat Vince, but spared his life because of his vow to their father, instead ordering Vince to leave town. Vince's response was to turn informant, enabling police to lure Jackie into an ambush; though surrounded by cops, Jackie disabled them all and was about to kill Vince when Spider-Man intervened. Arrested, Jackie spent most of the next decade in the top-security Cage, swiftly establishing himself as top dog and taking particular pleasure in administering beatings to super-villains depowered by the prison's dampening field. In Jackie's absence Vince sought out the Consultant, an underworld advisor who specialized in empowering criminals or assisting established super-villains in turning their ailing careers around. Gaining superhuman strength, Vince became Mr. Pain and rose to second-in-command of the Owl's mob; however, after Vince reneged on his payments, the Consultant decided to make an example of Vince.

Shortly before Jackie finished his sentence, the Consultant began a carefully orchestrated campaign of manipulation designed to reinvent the unwilling Jackie. As "the Hippo," a low-level super-villain, he shared an adjoining cell and informed Jackie about the Consultant's services. Upon release, Jackie visited Silvermane, now a bed-ridden cyborg; advised by his former mentor to seek the Owl's employ, Jackie encountered the vengeful Vince, receiving a brutal beating. Disguised variously as another victim of Mr. Pain, an underworld doctor, and underworld armorer "the Mechanic," the Consultant gradually arranged for Jackie to be exposed to SSS.2, a gaseous form of the Super-Soldier Serum, and gave him vision-enhancing sunglasses, guns with target-seeking Adamantium bullets, a titanium steel-weave coat and a healing factor. After taking down a small army of Mr. Pain's super-powered underlings,

REAL NAME: Jack "Jackie" Dio
ALIASES: None
IDENTITY: Known to authorities
OCCUPATION: Professional criminal
CITIZENSHIP: U.S.A. with criminal record
PLACE OF BIRTH: New York City, New York
KNOWN RELATIVES: Unidentified parents (deceased), Vince Dio (Mr. Pain, brother, deceased)
GROUP AFFILIATION: Kingpin's mob; formerly Hammerhead's Maggia family, Silvermane's Maggia family
EDUCATION: High school (unfinished)
FIRST APPEARANCE: (Dio) Underworld #1 (2006); (Underworld) Underworld #5 (2006)

including the Grizzly and Boomerang, and a stand-off with the Punisher, Jackie had a final rematch with Vince and killed him. Subsequently learning of the Consultant's subterfuge, Jackie was angry but finally accepted his new super-villain status, adopting the name Underworld.

Figuring the imprisoned Kingpin would soon rebuild his empire, Underworld secretly offered the crimelord his services. Kingpin had Underworld infiltrate Hammerhead's anti-Registration Act super-villain coalition, only to lure them into a S.H.I.E.L.D. ambush. Underworld later visited a hospitalized Hammerhead and put an Adamantium bullet in his head as revenge for his murder of one of Jackie's friends years before.

6'	Blue
175 lbs.	Black

Jackie possesses a healing factor able to eliminate gunshot wounds in seconds. His strength, stamina and agility have been enhanced by the Super-Soldier Serum to peak human. He wears unbreakable bulletproof glasses which also provide night vision, enable infra-red sight, pinpoint opponents' vulnerabilities and lock-on targets so that his bullets will turn in flight and continue to strike their target no matter where it moves. His guns use Adamantium bullets capable of penetrating most substances, and his coat is lined with titanium steel, rendering it virtually invulnerable.

POWER GRID 1 2 3 4 5 6 7

INTELLIGENCE	
STRENGTH	
SPEED	
DURABILITY	
ENERGY PROJECTION	
FIGHTING SKILLS	

Art by Staz Johnson